English Language Teaching Textbooks

English Language Teaching Textbooks

Content, Consumption, Production

Edited by

Nigel Harwood

Department of Language and Linguistics, University of Essex, UK

First published 2014 by
PALGRAVE MACMILLAN

Palgrave Macmillan in the UK is an imprint of Macmillan Publishers Limited,
registered in England, company number 785998, of Houndmills, Basingstoke,
Hampshire RG21 6XS.

Palgrave Macmillan in the US is a division of St Martin's Press LLC,
175 Fifth Avenue, New York, NY 10010.

Palgrave Macmillan is the global academic imprint of the above companies
and has companies and representatives throughout the world.

Palgrave® and Macmillan® are registered trademarks in the United States,
the United Kingdom, Europe and other countries.

ISBN 978–1–137–27627–8 hardback

ISBN 978–1–137–27630–8 paperback

This book is printed on paper suitable for recycling and made from fully
managed and sustained forest sources. Logging, pulping and manufacturing
processes are expected to conform to the environmental regulations of the
country of origin.

A catalogue record for this book is available from the British Library.

A catalog record for this book is available from the Library of Congress.

Contents

Tables and Figures

Tables

Figures

Acknowledgements

The authors and publishers acknowledge the following sources of copyright material and are grateful for the permissions granted.

Chapter 9:

Table 9.1. Components of genre analysis addressed in *Write like a Chemist*[a]

[a]p.7: Tabl.1.1 from *Write like a Chemist: A Guide and Resource*, by Robinson, Stoller, Costanza-Robinson, and Jones (2008), by permission of Oxford University Press, US.

Table 9.2. Common functions of different tense–voice combinations in journal-article discussion sections[a]

[a]p.189: Tabl.5.1 from *Write like a Chemist: A Guide and Resource*, by Robinson, Stoller, Costanza-Robinson, and Jones (2008), by permission of Oxford University Press, US.

Figure 9.4. The documents using *we* at least once (relative to the number using *the*) over three time periods, determined using the ACS Journals Search. (Note: *Journal of Physical Chemistry* includes *Journal of Physical Chemistry A* and *B* after 1996)

p.149: Fig. 4.2 from *Write like a Chemist: A Guide and Resource*, by Robinson, Stoller, Costanza-Robinson, and Jones (2008), by permission of Oxford University Press, US.

Table 9.4. Common examples of the x of y by z pattern found in journal article titles

Adaptation of pp.246–247: Table 7.1 from *Write like a Chemist: A Guide and Resource*, by Robinson, Stoller, Costanza-Robinson, and Jones (2008), by permission of Oxford University Press, US.

Figure 9.5. A move structure depicting the organization of a typical experimental approach section in the project description part of a research proposal.

p.437, Fig. 13.1 from *Write like a Chemist: A Guide and Resource*, by Robinson, Stoller, Costanza-Robinson, and Jones (2008), by permission of Oxford University Press, US.

Chapter 11:

Appendix A, Distraction Reduction, from *Motivating Learning*, Hadfield, J. and Dörnyei, Z. (2013), Pearson Education, ©2013.

Appendix B, Reality Check, from *Motivating Learning*, Hadfield, J. and Dörnyei, Z. (2013), Pearson Education, ©2013.

Contributors

Emily Binks-Cantrell is Clinical Assistant Professor in the Department of Teaching, Learning, and Culture at Texas A&M University and teaches reading education courses at the undergraduate and graduate levels. She is also Co-Director of the Texas A&M University Reading Clinic and adviser to the Houston Branch International Dyslexia Association Brazos Valley Regional Group. Her research interests include teacher preparation and knowledge in research-based reading instruction. She has published in various journals, including *Scientific Studies of Reading, Annals of Dyslexia*, and *Journal of Learning Disabilities*.

David Block is Research Professor in Sociolinguistics for the Institució Catalana de Recerca i Estudis Avançats, working at the Universitat de Lleida (Spain). Over the past 25 years he has published articles and chapters on a variety of applied linguistics topics, including second language acquisition, globalization, multilingualism, and identity. His books include *The Social Turn in Second Language Acquisition* (2003), *Second Language Identities* (2007), and *Social Class in Applied Linguistics* (2014).

Renata Burgess-Brigham is a doctoral student and a graduate assistant in the College of Education and Human Development, Texas A&M University. Her research interests focus on the language and literacy development of Spanish speakers, dual language education, second language acquisition (SLA), and pre-service English language learner (ELL) teacher training. She has co-authored a systematic review on SLA, which has been published in the *Review of Educational Research*.

L. Quentin Dixon is Assistant Professor of English as a Second Language and Reading at Texas A&M University. Her research interests include the literacy development of ELLs in the US and internationally and the preparation of pre-service general education teachers to teach ELLs effectively. She has published in many journals, including *Review of Educational Research, Journal of Applied Developmental Psychology, Applied Psycholinguistics*, and *System*.

Christine Feak is a lecturer at the English Language Institute, University of Michigan, where she is the lead lecturer for academic writing courses. She is a co-author of *Academic Writing for Graduate Students* and of the newly revised *English in Today's Research World* book series.

Diana Freeman is currently studying for a PhD at the University of Essex. Her doctoral thesis discusses the questions and tasks accompanying reading texts in global English as a Foreign Language (EFL) textbooks. Although her research work is chiefly in the area of language teaching materials, her broader research interests include the teaching and learning of vocabulary and grammar. She has taught BA and MA modules on Teaching English to Speakers of Other Languages (TESOL), reading, and vocabulary; is interested in teacher training; and is an experienced teacher of English as a foreign or second language, having taught in the UK, Italy, and Egypt.

Fotini Grammatosi is an English language teacher and a PhD candidate at the University of Essex. She has taught general English and English for Academic Purposes and English for Specific Purposes (EAP/ESP) for several years in different contexts in Europe and Central Asia. Her research interests focus on the role of materials in teaching and learning, on teachers' evaluation criteria, and on the impact of various factors on teachers' approach to, and evaluation/use of, materials.

John Gray is Senior Lecturer in TESOL Education at the Institute of Education, University of London. He is the author of *The Construction of English: Culture, Consumerism and Promotion in the ELT Global Coursebook* (2010) and the co-author with David Block and Marnie Holborow of *Neoliberalism and Applied Linguistics* (2012).

Jill Hadfield has worked as a teacher trainer in Britain, France, China, Tibet, Madagascar, and New Zealand and conducted short courses, seminars, and workshops for teachers in many other countries. She is currently Associate Professor in the Department of Language Studies at Unitec, New Zealand. She has written 30 books, including the *Communication Games* series, the *Oxford Basics* series, *Classroom Dynamics* and *An Introduction to Teaching English*. Her latest book, *Motivating Learning*, co-authored with Zoltan Dörnyei, was published this year.

Gregory Hadley received his PhD from the University of Birmingham (UK), with a focus in the Sociology of English Language Teaching (ELT)

Management. He has taught in Japanese higher education for over 20 years. Currently he is a visiting fellow at the University of Oxford.

Nigel Harwood is a senior lecturer in the Department of Language and Linguistics at the University of Essex, where he teaches modules relating to materials and textbook design, English for specific and academic purposes, genre analysis, and teaching/researching second language writing. He edited an earlier volume on materials, *English Language Teaching Materials: Theory and Practice*, and has published articles in various journals, including *Journal of Second Language Writing*, *Written Communication*, *Journal of Pragmatics*, and *Journal of English for Academic Purposes*. He is the co-editor of *English for Specific Purposes*.

R. Malatesha (Malt) Joshi is Professor of Reading/Language Arts Education, ESL and Educational Psychology at Texas A&M University, where he teaches and conducts research in literacy development and literacy problems among monolinguals and bilinguals. Dr Joshi is the founding editor of *Reading and Writing: An Interdisciplinary Journal* as well as the monograph series titled *Literacy Studies: Perspectives from Cognitive Neurosciences, Linguistics, Psychology and Education*.

Ahlam Menkabu is a PhD student in the Department of Language and Linguistics at the University of Essex. Her research is about how first and second language (L1 and L2) student writers use language to present themselves, express their opinions, and engage with readers in their writing. She is also a lecturer at Taif University, Saudi Arabia. She previously taught ESP for five years at the Health College in Taif.

Marin S. Robinson is Professor and Chair of Chemistry and Biochemistry at Northern Arizona University in Flagstaff, Arizona. She teaches organic chemistry and a junior-level scientific writing course. Her research interests include chemistry-specific writing and atmospheric chemistry. She has published in various journals, including *English for Specific Purposes*, *Atmospheric Environment*, and the *Journal of Chemical Education*.

Fredricka L. Stoller is Professor of English at Northern Arizona University, where she teaches in the MA in Teaching English as a Second Language (TESL) and PhD in Applied Linguistics programmes. She is a co-author of *Write like a Chemist* (2008). Other publications on disciplinary writing include those appearing in *English for Specific Purposes*,

Journal of English for Academic Purposes, Journal of Chemical Education, and *English Teaching Forum.* Her professional interests include disciplinary writing, second language reading, project-based learning, and teacher training.

John M. Swales is Professor Emeritus of Linguistics at the University of Michigan, where he was also Director of the English Language Institute from 1985 to 2001. He is on several editorial boards and he was faculty adviser for the MICASE and MICUSP Corpus projects. His latest book-length publication is the third edition of *Academic Writing for Graduate Students* (2012), co-authored with Christine B. Feak.

Ivor Timmis is Reader in English Language Teaching at Leeds Metropolitan University. He has been involved in materials writing projects for Singapore, Ethiopia, and China and is an active member of the Materials Development Association (MATSDA). His other research interests include spoken corpus analysis and the relationship between corpus linguistics and ELT. He has published on these topics in *Applied Linguistics* and *ELT Journal.*

Erin Washburn teaches courses in literacy education at Binghamton University. She has conducted research on the effectiveness of reading and writing interventions and literacy teacher knowledge and preparation. Her research has been published in *Annals of Dyslexia, Scientific Study of Reading, Dyslexia,* and *The Reading Teacher.*

Shuang Wu is a PhD student in the Department of Teaching, Learning, and Culture at Texas A&M University, specializing in English as a Second Language. Her research interests lie in bi-literacy and ESL/EFL writing. She has co-authored works that have been published in the *Review of Educational Research* and *Early Childhood Education Journal.*

1
Content, Consumption, and Production: Three Levels of Textbook Research

Nigel Harwood

Introduction: The importance of textbook research

Like my previous edited volume (Harwood, 2010a), this book is intended for teachers, teacher trainers, researchers, publishers, and materials writers who work with English Language Teaching (ELT) textbooks. The remit of the earlier book was wider, focusing on teaching materials in general rather than textbooks in particular, and so many of the chapters in the previous volume described unpublished teaching activities produced by the authors themselves. For the present purposes, in contrast, the focus is squarely on published ELT textbooks (also known as coursebooks) and, where relevant, the aids that accompany them (such as teachers' guides, workbooks, listening exercises, etc.). More specifically, much of the focus is on 'global' textbooks, normally published in the West and marketed worldwide, such as well-known series like *Headway*, *Interchange*, and *Cutting Edge*. While it is important to analyse unpublished, teacher-/researcher-produced materials, since no textbook can ever completely meet the needs of a class and, institutional and other factors permitting, teachers will wish to supplement their textbook with other materials to cater to their learners' needs, it is also essential to focus on the published textbook, because most teachers are required to use them to some degree. An oft-cited statistic is Tyson and Woodward's (1989) claim that textbooks structure up to 90 per cent of what goes on in school classrooms in the US. Whatever the figure in English as a Foreign Language/English as a Second Language (EFL/ESL) contexts, textbooks are similarly important: indeed, in many contexts, textbooks constitute the syllabus, teachers being expected to follow them more or less faithfully, with end-of-course exams being based exclusively on textbook content. Furthermore, existing textbook research has been criticized by various researchers for its lack of theoretical and methodological rigour (e.g., Harwood, 2010b; Tomlinson, 2012), and there is thus a need to extend and strengthen the research base in this area.

I argue it is important to study textbooks at three different levels – the levels of *content, consumption,* and *production* – drawing on du Gay, Hall, Janes, Mackay, and Negus (1997), and Gray (2010b) in differentiating thus. At the level of *content,* we can investigate what textbooks include and exclude in terms of topic, linguistic information, pedagogy, and culture. Unlike studies of content, which analyse textbooks outside the classroom context, at the level of *consumption* we can examine how teachers and learners use textbooks. Finally, at the level of *production,* we can investigate the processes by which textbooks are shaped, authored, and distributed, looking at textbook writers' design processes, the affordances and constraints placed upon them by publishers, and the norms and values of the textbook industry as a whole.

Each of these dimensions is covered in a survey of the field below. I draw on research in ELT, but, as in my previous survey (Harwood, 2010b), I argue that textbook research is more developed, rigorous, and sophisticated in mainstream education (i.e., non-ELT fields, such as mathematics), particularly regarding textbook consumption, and that we have much to learn from the work in this area. I therefore include in the discussion below work from mainstream education with which readers may be less familiar. The present survey is intended to complement my earlier piece, and so I focus for the most part here on literature I did not discuss previously.

Textbook content

The obvious way for teachers and researchers to begin an investigation into a textbook is to determine and evaluate the subject matter which is included – and omitted. Researchers may prefer to focus on one particular content-related aspect of the textbook (such as treatment of a specific grammar point) or attempt an overall analysis and evaluation using a framework such as Littlejohn's (2011). Below I have organized my review of content analyses around the headings of language, culture, and pragmatics.

Content analyses of language

Numerous studies evaluate the linguistic syllabus of textbooks by assessing the closeness of fit (or more commonly, lack of fit) between textbook language and the language of real life, as attested by corpora (e.g., Biber and Reppen, 2002; Conrad, 2004; Holmes, 1988; Lee, 2006; Miller, 2011; Mukundan and Khojasteh, 2011; Römer, 2005). One such study by Rühlemann (2009) analysed the treatment of reported speech in seven intermediate-level textbooks compared with British National Corpus (BNC) data, finding that a number of the most frequently used reporting verbs in real-life data were omitted from some of the textbooks, and that those verbs which were included differed widely between the books, suggesting that corpus information on frequency was not used by the writers when deciding what to include in their syllabus.

The textbook vocabulary syllabus has also been found wanting. Koprowski (2005) compared three textbooks' treatment of lexical bundles in terms of frequency and range with data in the COBUILD Corpus, finding that more than 14 per cent (118) of the 822 bundles in the textbooks were absent from the corpus. Furthermore, not one bundle featured in all three textbooks. Gouverneur's (2008) results were similar: analysing the phraseological treatment of the high-frequency verbs *make* and *take* in three intermediate and advanced textbooks, she found the books covered a varied selection of lexical phrases, with only 7 per cent and 15 per cent of *make* patterns appearing in all three advanced and intermediate textbooks respectively, and with not a single *take* collocation appearing in all advanced books. Findings such as these cause Gouverneur and Koprowski to question the criteria the textbook writers used to compile their vocabulary syllabuses. Koprowski argues that, although it may be an onerous task for the textbook writer to *begin* the development of lexical phrase textbook materials by consulting corpora, it should not be too much to expect textbook writers to *check* the frequency and range of the lexical phrases they are teaching when the materials are in draft form, refining their choice based on corpus evidence.

Other studies finding patchy treatment of vocabulary include Brown (2011). Whereas Nation (2001) describes nine different aspects of word knowledge, Brown found that 'only three aspects consistently receive attention' (p.88) in the textbook sample examined. Similarly, the textbook in focus in Criado (2009) was judged unsatisfactory in terms of the items included, with many of the most frequent words in English being absent, in terms of the frequency with which words are recycled, being too low to suggest acquisition would be likely, and in terms of the amount of words it is assumed students will learn as they progress through the book, which is far higher than research predicts. For their part, Matsuoka and Hirsh (2010) found 'few opportunities' to acquire vocabulary knowledge beyond the 2,000-word range in a best-selling textbook because of a lack of recycling (p.67); and Miller's (2011) recent study of advanced-level, academically focused ESL reading textbooks concluded that the books' vocabulary content was wanting.

An example of a content analysis focusing on a specific linguistic item is Lam's (2009) comparison of 15 textbooks' treatment of the discourse marker *well* with the use of *well* in a spoken corpus. Quantitative comparison revealed 'major discrepancies' (p.275) between textbook and corpus frequencies. And while *well* commonly occurs in either utterance-initial or medial position in the corpus, the textbooks give the impression that it occurs almost exclusively in utterance-initial position. Information is lacking in the textbooks about the various discourse functions of *well*, as are substantial, context-embedded examples.

An under-researched aspect of textbook content is pronunciation (but see Jones, 1997; Levis, 1999). Kopperoinen (2011) is a recent analysis of English as a Lingua Franca (ELF) pronunciation in two best-selling Finnish ELT textbook series. Kopperoinen studied all recordings and listening exercises, finding that outer/expanding circle accents accounted for between only 1–3 per cent of accents. In commenting on these results, Kopperoinen quotes Seidlhofer (2003:13), arguing that the outer/expanding circle speakers currently play a role of 'exotic optional extras' in the materials (p.84), despite the fact that most communication in English now takes place between second language (L2) speakers.

Content analyses of culture[1]

There have been calls for textbook evaluation checklists to make cultural concerns more prominent (Cortazzi and Jin, 1999; Feng and Byram, 2002; Kullman, 2003): as the number of culturally focused content analyses has grown, so these analyses have criticized global textbooks for cultural inappropriacy, or at least inappropriacy when the materials are used in certain contexts (e.g., Canagarajah, 1993a, 1993b; Sokolik, 2007; Suaysuwan and Kapitzke, 2005; Yuen, 2011). For instance, 'buying by credit card, ordering meals for delivery, and finding out snow conditions for skiing' are seen by Auerbach and Burgess (1985: 479) as inappropriate lifestyle-related content in textbooks used by immigrants to the US and Canada. Auerbach and Burgess also point to what is absent, with no mention of typical issues likely to be experienced by immigrants, such as communication problems and difficulties finding employment, tying in with Gulliver's (2010) analysis of textbook accounts of Canadian immigrants' lives, which found the risk of failure is underplayed.

Focusing specifically on grammar textbooks, Sokolik (2007) concludes that these are helping to transmit, and tacitly approve, a culture of consumerism, as evidenced by example sentences from the books such as the following:

They go to Florida every summer.
My watch is new.
Maria wears a lot of jewelry.
I shelled out a lot of money on the diamond engagement ring that I bought for her.
I bought a new car last month.
She's thinking about buying a new house.

And Boriboon (2004) points out that the provincial Thai learners he works with have very different social and cultural lifeworlds from those contemporary textbook characters cited by Sokolik, arguing that this may adversely affect the learners' motivation and willingness to communicate. Boriboon illustrates his argument by taking a sample communicative activity from *New Headway Intermediate* (Soars and Soars, 1996: 45) which focuses on shopping and has the learners buy petrol, pay an electricity bill, and collect plane tickets, none of which his learners are likely to have experienced.

Two particularly detailed studies of global textbook cultural content are a PhD thesis by Kullman (2003) and a book by Gray (2010b). Focusing on 12 UK-published global textbooks written in the 1970s, 1980s, and 1990s and featuring interviews with eight British textbook writers (although not the authors of the textbooks analysed), Kullman found textbooks have become more 'international' in flavour, featuring characters and settings outside the UK. Rather than focus on other people's lives, more recent books ask learners to talk about themselves, the tenor having shifted from the more 'educational' and 'serious' towards the more consumerist, emotional, and aspirational. Kullman also argues that some contemporary textbook topics will likely prove culturally inappropriate in certain contexts, singling out the treatment of 'assertiveness' in one book, which seemingly gives a straightforward message to learners that assertiveness is a useful attribute.

Examining four recent and not so recent best-selling intermediate-level textbooks, Gray (2010b) studies how textbooks have evolved in the cultural messages they transmit. He shows how the range of accents learners are exposed to moves away from mainly received pronunciation (RP) or modified RP in the older material to a more diverse range in the newer textbooks to include non-UK inner and outer/expanding circle speakers, but how all four textbooks tend to associate regional accents with characters in lower-status employment. With regards to the depiction of race and ethnicity, Gray finds a gradual progression towards multiculturalism and cosmopolitanism. He also notes the spectacular success of the fictional characters that learners encounter in the newer materials – characters who supposedly juggle jobs such as UN ambassador, film star, and best-selling author. Gray claims the discourse is consumerist and aspirational: characters are defined by freely available choices, and succeed in their choices apparently unproblematically. In subsequent research, Gray (2010a) analysed representations of the world of work, again finding that discourses of aspiration, success, and individual choice pervade the materials. Finally, Gray (2012) showed that the theme of celebrity was absent from materials until the late 1970s, since when it has become more and more apparent. The focus has shifted from an emphasis on celebrities' achievements to their wealth, and the textbook activities in Gray's dataset apparently hold up these celebrities for learners' approval.

Gender and sexist bias have been studied extensively in ELT textbooks (e.g., Carroll and Kowitz, 1994; Jones, Kitetu, and Sunderland, 1997; Matsuno, 2002; McGrath, 2004; Ndura, 2004; Sherman, 2010; Sunderland, 2000). Sunderland (2000) and Matsuno (2002) specify how and where sexist content may occur, Matsuno's classification being as follows: (i) in the omission or under-representation of females; (ii) in the depiction of females' occupations; (iii) in stereotypical gender identities; and (iv) in sexist language items (*chairman, houseman,* etc.) (pp.84–85). Sunderland suggests that there are fewer content analyses of gender nowadays, perhaps because bias is less evident in contemporary materials, and Gray's (2010b) study of textbooks' treatment of gender supports Sunderland's claims: in the older materials, men have a greater presence in the artwork and the listening tapescripts as well as in the textbook readings and practice dialogues. Women occupy subordinate positions, and are sometimes depicted as dependent on men and incapable of making decisions alone. In contrast, Gray finds the recent textbooks portray men and women more equally. Nonetheless, in their analysis of six textbooks, Carroll and Kowitz (1994) found that 'the most important adjectives used to describe women are *busy, beautiful, pretty* and *tall*' and that women are associated with 'passivity, physical characteristics, menial roles, irrational worries, [and] constant undemanding activities' (pp.79, 82). Other accounts of locally produced textbooks which have identified gender bias include Matsuno (2002), Sherman (2010), and McGrath (2004), who reports on a large study of 289 textbooks conducted in Hong Kong, where 71 per cent of some 32,000 gender-specific references were to males, and where women were sometimes stereotyped as weak and emotional.

When it comes to cultural representations in textbooks, however, McGrath (2004) raises the difficult issue of how 'real' textbook writers' portrayals should be: 'Is it the role of textbooks simply to reflect reality or to change it for (what we think of as) the better?' (p.357). And, as we shall see below, when we focus on studies of textbook production, these choices are not always in the writers' hands: publishers avoid including materials which may provoke controversy since this can impact upon sales figures or even result in a textbook being excluded from a state-approved list. In the end, though, however well intentioned or politically correct the message of the textbook content, there is no guarantee this message will be taken up: as Gray (2010b) puts it, teachers and students may 'read against' or resist the intended meaning or message of the textbook (p.26).

Content analyses of pragmatics

Attention to the pragmatics of English should not be regarded as an optional extra in a textbook syllabus, since pragmatic norms in one language or culture do not always transfer straightforwardly to the target language:

> What is considered in one culture to be a normal amount of complimenting may seem excessive in another. What may be viewed as accepted topics of phatic communion (i.e., small talk) in one culture may be perceived negatively in another.
>
> (Meier, 1997: 24)

The potential dangers of miscommunication because of pragmatic failure (see Thomas, 1983) are very real, then. However, some studies of textbooks' handling of pragmatics conclude that treatment is 'arbitrary' and 'oversimplistic' (Meier, 1997: 24; see also Bardovi-Harlig, Hartford, Mahan-Taylor, Morgan, and Reynolds, 1991; Boxer and Pickering, 1995; Lee and Park, 2008; Millard, 2000; Nguyen, 2011; Wong, 2002), and that acquisition of pragmatic competence is 'highly unlikely' (Vellenga, 2004: 1) on the basis of the inadequate information textbooks provide.

One of the problems researchers find with textbooks' treatment of pragmatics is that learners are often presented with insufficient context when the target language is introduced; hence it is difficult to appreciate how factors such as the relationship between speakers in a dialogue would influence what interlocutors say. Another problem concerns the choice of speech acts focused on: these can appear idiosyncratic, with two of the textbooks in Vellenga's (2004) study teaching learners how to threaten, for instance, but not how to apologize. And a highly restricted set of linguistic items may be associated with a given speech act: in the same study by Vellenga, the only means of expressing making suggestions and giving advice is *should*. Vellenga's study is particularly noteworthy in that it includes an examination of both teachers' and students' versions of the materials, with the teachers' material also found wanting, containing 'no metapragmatic information or extensions beyond what was provided in the textbook' (p.14).

Nguyen's (2011) study of the presentation of speech acts in EFL textbooks produced in Vietnam identifies problems with the type of language presented and how it is taught. The books teach bald on record language of disagreement (*I completely disagree; That's wrong*, etc.: see Brown and Levinson 1987), which corpora suggest speakers largely avoid. It is therefore possible that

> textbooks might mislead learners to falsely believe that English NSs [native speakers] tend to disagree more frequently and more directly than is the case, and that it is appropriate to use these unmitigated forms to express oppositional ideas, which might consequently cause learners to be perceived as impolite. (p.24)

Furthermore, while learners are taught constructions giving and receiving compliments, Nguyen points out that in Vietnamese speakers may be less likely to accept compliments than in Western contexts, and that therefore a useful textbook activity would have been to have the learners compare and contrast speech acts and responses across cultures. However, such activities are lacking.

Content analyses of pragmatic information in business English textbooks find similar deficiencies to those identified above. For instance, Handford (2010) notes that the best-selling business textbooks he analysed featured expressions such as *I disagree with you*, but that this expression was entirely absent from his 900,000-word corpus of business meetings (see also Angouri, 2010, for similar findings with regard to business meetings). It is not that disagreement is absent from the meetings; rather, disagreements are prefaced or hedged in the authentic data. As Handford notes, this mismatch is no trivial matter, as *I disagree with you* and some of the other expressions taught by the textbooks are 'potentially highly face-threatening in many situations', and 'learners are in danger of acquiring linguistic behaviour that may be highly detrimental to their professional career' (pp.251–252). Similar corpus–textbook mismatches are described in a series of studies by Cheng and co-researchers, focusing on: opinion language (Cheng and Warren, 2006); language to disagree or check understanding (Cheng and Warren, 2005, 2007); language to interrupt a speaker (Cheng, 2007); and language to repair an utterance (Cheng and Cheng, 2010). Despite these gloomy findings, it is noteworthy that Handford and colleagues have now authored business English textbooks which are informed by corpus data and feature authentic readings and listenings (see Handford, 2012).

Other content analyses

Teachers' guides

Very little research has been done on ELT teachers' guides, and Coleman (1986) describes a teacher guide evaluation instrument, as well as providing analysis of extracts from a selection of guides. Coleman asks whether the pedagogical approach the guide claims to follow is ever properly explained. The framework also evaluates the extent to which teachers are assisted with what may be unfamiliar cultural elements in the materials, the demands the guide places on the teacher to supplement the textbook and to test learners' progress, and its overall clarity and organization. Coleman concludes that, on the basis of the samples evaluated, 'many [guides] appear to be little more than incidental afterthoughts [...], that far less care seems to have gone into their creation than into the materials for learners' (p.31), and that there is a danger that poorly written guides will lead to poor textbook use. The few more recent pieces focusing on teachers' guides are equally critical. Mol and Tin (2008), for instance, complain that one of the weaknesses of English for Academic Purposes (EAP) textbooks is they 'focus on *what* to teach rather than *how* to teach' (p.88), and they suggest that information about research findings on second language acquisition, motivation, and other aspects of language learning could be usefully added to the guides to empower teachers. Interestingly, evaluations of teachers' guides in mainstream education are no more favourable (e.g., Manouchehri and Goodman, 1998; Nicol and Crespo, 2006): for instance, Nicol and Crespo (2006) found that guides need to provide better support for inexperienced teachers as far as both subject knowledge and pedagogical knowledge are concerned, with textbook writers explaining how the materials could be used in various situations and with different learners.

Limitations of content analysis

I end this section by describing some problems associated with textbook content studies. Some of these problems reveal the need for more rigorous research designs, and others the need for complementary research approaches.

In my earlier survey chapter (Harwood, 2010b) I criticized the sketchiness of the methodological procedures included in many content analyses; accounts such as those by Canagarajah (1993a, 1993b) contain few or no details of coding procedures or reliability checks, leaving open the possibility that they fail to represent fairly the overall content and messages of the textbooks. An example of content analysis which reports its methodological procedures carefully is Matsuda (2002), but such accounts, in the field of ELT at least, are currently the exception rather than the rule. (In mainstream education the standards appear to be higher, at least in the leading journals.)

Content analyses also lack data from (i) textbook creators (writers and publishers) and (ii) users (teachers and learners). Although content analysis is excellent at determining *what* is present or absent in textbooks, it is much less good at determining *why* this content looks the way it does: it is to publishers and writers that we must turn for answers to this question. And content analysis does not tell us what the teacher *intended* by their textbook use and what the teacher *enacted*: that is, *how* the textbook is used and the anticipated and actual effects in the classroom on teacher and learners – information we can gather only by extending our analysis to include textbook users.

To clarify my arguments, I briefly return to the content analyses of gender reviewed above. Sunderland (2000) rightly points out that simply examining a textbook page cannot accurately predict its effects:

> Even an agreed case of gender bias in a text [...] cannot be said in any deterministic way to *make* people think in a gender-biased way [...] A text is arguably as good or as bad as the treatment it receives from the teacher who is using it; in particular, a text riddled with gender bias can be rescued and that bias put to good effect, pedagogic and otherwise.
>
> (pp.153, 155)

However misleading or inappropriate the content of a textbook may be, there is no guarantee that the teacher will exploit it as specified by the teacher's guide: textbooks are interactive artefacts and can be exploited in any number of ways. Neither can we predict how the materials will be received by learners. Thus Littlejohn (2011) usefully distinguishes between *materials as they are* and *materials-in-action*, the former being the materials at the level of the textbook page, 'with the content and ways of working that they propose', and the latter being '[p]recisely what happens in classrooms and what outcomes occur when materials are brought into use' (p.181; see also Tomlinson, 2003, for a similar distinction). Hence the need to consider users' attitudes and how the textbook is used *in situ*, addressed when we turn to studies of textbook consumption.

Textbook consumption

There are relatively few studies exploring how ELT teachers and students use textbooks inside and outside the classroom, a gap which has been recognized by well-known figures in the field (e.g., Tomlinson and Masuhara, 2010; Tomlinson, 2011, 2012). I therefore draw on high-quality work in mainstream education to complement the discussion of ELT-related research.

Mainstream education researchers have long acknowledged the importance of studying textbook consumption, recognizing that varying patterns of textbook usage are possible. Hence in their seminal article Ball and Cohen (1996) speak of 'a gap between [textbook] developers' intentions for students and what actually happens in lessons. Developers' designs [...] turn out to be ingredients in – not determinants of – the actual curriculum' (p.6). So, although many understand a curriculum to mean the contents of a policy document or textbook (the *intended* curriculum), it is the study of the *enacted* curriculum, 'jointly constructed by teachers, students, and materials in particular contexts' (p.7), which can enable a deeper understanding and evaluation of textbooks.

Another mainstream education researcher who theorizes about textbook use is Brown (2009), drawing parallels between teaching and music: like jazz musicians improvising from a musical score, two teachers may shape the same set of materials differently, and no two renditions (of the music or the materials) will be the same. For Brown, then, teachers are designers who craft textbook content to best meet their needs – like musicians, 'practitioners practice and plan according to instructions [...], but they also adapt and improvise in response to local factors and creative ability' (p.22). It is therefore important to understand 'how teachers' skills, knowledge, and beliefs' influence their textbook use (p.22). There are various theoretical frameworks in mainstream education that attempt this, some of which will be described later, but at this point I turn to ELT contributions in the area.

Eunice Hutchinson's study (1996) is an important ELT textbook consumption study, although, because it is in the form of an unpublished doctoral thesis, it is not especially well known. Hutchinson explores textbook use on an EAP course in a Philippines fisheries college, particularly that of two teachers, Nancy and Marcia, who were observed repeatedly over a semester, interviewed, and an analysis conducted of the materials they used. Although Nancy had seven years' teaching experience, most of this was teaching undergraduate psychology; she had never taught English for Fisheries Technology before, and her ELT training was 'very meagre' (p.186). Unsurprisingly then, Nancy stuck closely to the textbook – nearly all textbook activities in the units Hutchinson observed were used, and Nancy never reordered them. Nancy did not supplement her textbook with any other materials, and appeared to choose modules from the book to teach which contained 'relatively easy subject matter that she felt she could manage' in terms of content (p.192). Hence a lack of content knowledge emerged as a factor in accounting for Nancy's patterns of textbook use. In contrast, Marcia had 17 years' experience and was much better qualified, holding a master's in ESL. She also had some background knowledge of fisheries technology. This greater content and pedagogical knowledge led to a more assured handling of the textbook: Marcia used the textbook more flexibly than Nancy, adapting the textbook to meet the learners' needs.

Hutchinson (1996: 47–48, 99–100) shows that variation in textbook use is likely down to a number of factors: (i) the textbook (its content); (ii) the teacher (e.g., beliefs, training, pedagogical and content knowledge, experience, preferred teaching style, perception and evaluation of the textbook, attitude towards top-down mandates (e.g., school/state syllabus, directives from school principal)); (iii) the learners (e.g., level, aptitude, previous learning experiences, preferred learning styles); (iv) the classroom (e.g., physical layout); and (v) the school (e.g., timetable constraints, principal's attitudes towards textbook use and to EFL as a subject). There are more complex frameworks in the mainstream education literature accounting for teacher–textbook interaction (e.g., Remillard, 1999, 2005), but Hutchinson's succeeds in capturing the context-bound, mediated nature of textbook use.

Shawer (2010a, 2010b; Shawer, Gilmore, and Banks-Joseph, 2009) studied the textbook use of ten EFL teachers, using repeating observation and pre-/post-lesson interview cycles, categorizing participants into three groups:

(i) *curriculum-makers* rarely if ever used a textbook, creating their own materials in response to an initial needs analysis. Although much of the subject matter taught did not appear in the textbook, sometimes the book and its table of contents were used as inspiration for creating these materials. The teachers' guide was never consulted.

(ii) *curriculum-developers* freely adapted their textbook to best suit their learners, creating materials if they felt the textbook fell short, albeit not on the scale of the curriculum-makers. The teachers' guide was seldom or never used.

(iii) *curriculum-transmitters* strictly adhered to their textbook, proceeding exercise by exercise, page by page, rarely if ever changing the task order. The teachers' guide was consulted regularly.

Interestingly, Shawer found the freedom or otherwise that the teachers' schools afforded teachers regarding (non-)textbook use did not predict which category teachers belonged to: in other words, teachers who were curriculum-transmitters worked at the same schools as makers or developers. Similarly, all of Shawer's teachers were experienced, and so neither was an experienced/inexperienced descriptor predictive. Hence Shawer's work indicated that the impact of context and teaching experience on textbook use is not straightforward.

Shawer (2010a) also studied the link between textbook use and professional development. Teachers who adapted or created their own materials reportedly acquired a range of new pedagogical skills. For instance, because they sought to improve their textbook's treatment of grammar, the curriculum-makers and developers claimed they expanded their content knowledge:

> Where I don't like what's in the textbook, [say] a grammatical point, I go and look elsewhere [...] and that's developing my own understanding. (p.607)

These teachers were also said to have improved their adaptation, content-sequencing, and materials evaluation skills, together with the ability to conduct needs analyses, as they strove to tailor materials for their learners. In sum, then, Shawer (2010a) claims that curriculum-makers and developers enhanced their subject knowledge, pedagogical knowledge, and curricular content knowledge, but that curriculum-transmitters made little if any progress.

Wette (2009, 2010, 2011) investigates how highly qualified, experienced ESL teachers shape their curriculum in general and textbook materials in particular, focusing on planning and organizing behaviours. Teachers' contextual conditions varied from high-constraint environments, such as intensive exam preparation classes, to low-constraint environments, in which no external syllabus or testing impinged on teachers' choice and use of materials. Wette found that teachers only planned at a 'modest, informal and tentative' level (2009: 348), since they also assessed how materials were received by the learners and responded accordingly. Hence plans were often changed during the lesson – various types of adaptations, additions, and deletions were made to the materials – and longer-term plans were modified in the light of learners' responses as the course progressed. However, in the high-constraint contexts this was problematic because of time pressures: exams loomed, and the syllabus needed covering. In sum, then, like Brown (2009), Wette finds teaching to be an essentially improvised activity, with context, syllabus, and learners exercising a profound effect on how materials are used.

Surveying 100 EFL teachers in Indonesia, Zacharias (2005) canvassed views of global and locally produced textbooks, the vast majority of teachers being L2 speakers. Global rather than local textbooks were favoured for teaching grammar and the skills, particularly with regard to listening and pronunciation: global textbooks were felt to consist of 'natural', 'authentic', and error-free language, to provide accurate cultural information, and to be of superior quality in terms of content and production to local equivalents, which were viewed with 'a general attitude of distrust' (pp.29–30). However, not all teachers found global textbooks easy to work with: some complained the material was too advanced for learners and difficult to understand in terms of cultural content (for both teachers and learners). Nonetheless, despite these difficulties, the overall preference was for global textbooks, despite the fact that for certain parts of the syllabus (e.g., reading) teachers felt local materials would be more likely to focus on content relevant to learners' lives.

Gray (2010b) interviewed experienced EFL teachers working in Barcelona about textbook cultural content. Overtly British subject matter in the textbooks was viewed 'with considerable reservation' (p.146), perceived as irrelevant for students learning English as a lingua franca rather than in order to move to the UK. Textbook content which stereotyped attracted censure: for instance, one teacher objected to a listening about women being bad drivers because she felt by doing the activity she was giving these views her tacit seal of approval. However, other data revealed how culturally focused material may vary in relevance depending on the teaching context: one teacher explained how a listening about a group of women car mechanics made for a 'fantastically successful lesson in Cairo' but had 'died a thousand deaths' in Barcelona because Catalans found the idea of female mechanics unremarkable (p.152). And while the teachers were generally critical of the consumerist, aspirational tenor of contemporary materials, some of them conceded it was often successful in the classroom, inasmuch as it generated discussion. It would thus seem a formidable task to produce textbooks that satisfy most of the teachers – and learners – most of the time.

I now turn briefly to selected textbook consumption studies in mainstream education which feature rigorous, triangulated research designs and sizeable datasets. For instance, Drake and Sherin's (2009) study of textbook use was conducted over two years, with each teacher observed and then interviewed 15–30 times. Other projects, such as Collopy (2003), also feature large datasets, inter-rater reliability tests, and member-checking. Studies such as these are on a scale and of a quality not seen in ELT, and we have much to learn from them.

Mainstream educators have compared textbook use among beginning and trainee teachers (e.g., Behm and Lloyd, 2009), novice and experts' planned/actual use of textbooks (Borko and Livingston, 1989), and the development over time of trainee/inexperienced teachers' use of/beliefs about the textbook (e.g., Grossman and Thompson, 2008; Nicol and Crespo, 2006). An interesting line of research is the effect of innovative or 'educative' teaching materials – those materials designed to support and develop teacher learning at the content and the pedagogical level (e.g., Collopy, 2003; Grossman and Thompson, 2008; Manouchehri and Goodman, 1998; Remillard, 2000; Remillard and Bryans, 2004; and see Davis and Krajcik, 2005, for more on educative materials). For instance, Collopy (2003) shows that innovative textbooks do not necessarily help develop teachers: only one of her two highly experienced teachers changed their pedagogical approach as a result of using an educative textbook. The other teacher initially attempted to bend the textbook to her will (and make it suit her traditional pedagogy), before abandoning it altogether. Manouchehri and Goodman (1998) demonstrate the influence of context when assessing the impact of innovative textbooks: they show how teachers were more likely to persevere with the books in schools where there was mentoring and a supportive attitude towards innovation among colleagues. And Smagorinsky and colleagues (e.g., Smagorinsky, Lakly, and Johnson, 2002; Smagorinsky, Cook, Moore, Jackson, and Fry, 2004) chart teacher *accommodation, acquiescence,* and *resistance* towards mandated materials and curricula.

I close this brief review of mainstream education consumption studies with work featuring imaginative data collection methods. Chval, Chávez, Reys, and Tarr (2009) point out that one of the most common methods associated with studies of textbook use – classroom observations – is expensive and difficult to implement on a large scale. Thus for their study of 70 teachers and 4,000 students in 11 schools, teachers used diaries to record what resources were used and how, while Davis, Beyer, Forbes, and Stevens (2011) had teachers write reflective narratives to explain textbook adaptations. Finally, Ziebarth, Hart, Marcus, Ritsema, Schoen, and Walker's (2009) fascinating five-year study examined how textbook writers and teachers using the writers' pilot materials interacted and how and why the materials changed as a result. Sometimes, in the light of teachers' uses and evaluations of the activities, the textbook writers revised the materials in line with teachers' wishes (e.g., to include more coverage of topics which featured in state examinations), but at other times writers' revisions were slight or nonexistent, as the teachers' proposals did not align with the writers' aims and pedagogy. The study illustrates how textbook writers must satisfy as best they can the needs and wishes of their readership without abandoning their principles, a theme continued in the studies of textbook production below.

Consumption of teachers' guides

Bonkowski (1995, cited in Hutchinson, 1996) is a rare study of the use of ESL teachers' guides. Focusing on three experienced teachers, Bonkowski found teachers' use of textbooks and guides varied, with several factors apparently accounting for this variation: teacher-related factors, such as the differences in teaching styles and pedagogical beliefs; textbook-related factors, such as the nature of the materials being used; and context-related factors, such as teachers' beliefs about the learners and their interests, and the time of day the class took place. The most experienced teacher in the study used the textbook the least, and all three teachers adapted and reinterpreted the teaching suggestions in the textbook guides. Again we see teachers shaping textbooks in response to their own beliefs, and to the micro- and macro-environment.

Bonkowski apart, we must once more look to mainstream education for consumption research on teachers' guides, particularly to Remillard's studies (Remillard, 1999; Remillard and Bryans, 2004), where we find some teachers following the guide closely to enhance their content and pedagogical knowledge, while others skip over or ignore the guide completely (see also Behm and Lloyd, 2009). The latter behaviour is sometimes associated with inexperienced teachers who adhere closely to the materials in the students' version of the textbook, believing it is enough simply to cover the material without considering how it would be most effectively exploited with their learners, or is associated with experienced teachers who already possess pedagogical routines and repertoires and apparently feel no need to question or add to them (see Collopy, 2003). These teachers' pedagogies and philosophies therefore remain intact and unchallenged however innovative the guides may be, since the advice therein is resisted or ignored (Remillard and Bryans, 2004).

Learners' textbook consumption

It is striking that most textbook consumption studies focus on teachers, with little or no attention paid to the use of materials by learners. This is regrettable because students are the largest group of textbook users, and their views on and use of the textbook will play a major part in determining its success or otherwise.

Peacock has published several studies on how learners consume materials. For instance, Peacock (1997) investigated learners' views on authentic and inauthentic materials, pointing out that it is sometimes assumed that the former better motivate learners, despite a lack of proper testing of this assumption. Peacock's study involved Korean EFL beginners over seven weeks and 20 lessons, using authentic materials one day and inauthentic materials the next to supplement learners' routine textbook-based work. As the study progressed, learners' motivation and time on-task increased when using authentic materials, suggesting that learners unaccustomed to using authentic materials take time to adjust. Surprisingly, learners also judged the authentic materials to be less interesting than their artificial counterparts. So while Peacock's findings support the untested claims regarding the motivating qualities of authentic tasks, the finding that learners judged authentic materials significantly less interesting is worthy of further investigation.

Peacock (1998) also compared teacher/learner perspectives on the usefulness of different activity types. Building on previous studies (e.g., Kern, 1995; Nunan, 1988; Willing, 1988), Peacock canvassed the views of Hong Kong learners and their teachers, using self-report questionnaires and short interviews. Like earlier studies, Peacock found significant mismatches between learner and teacher beliefs regarding different types of materials and their usefulness: learners rated error correction and grammar exercises more highly than teachers, and group/pair work was evaluated more favourably by teachers than learners. In sum, teachers rated 'communicative' activities most useful, while learners preferred 'traditional' activities, and Peacock's work suggests it is important for textbook writers to thoroughly research and cater for both parties' preferences.

Another type of learner consumption research examines the relative effectiveness of different task/activity types. Folse (2006) compared two vocabulary practice activities: (i) cloze exercises; and (ii) sentence-writing using target words, via a pre-/post-test design. The difference between the post-test scores for the two exercises was not significant, and so it could not be demonstrated that one activity led to superior acquisition. However, Folse, like Keating (2008), was able to show that asking learners to retrieve target words multiple times led to increased post-test scores, having implications for the amount of recycling textbooks should contain. And Gilmore (2011) measured the gains in communicative competence of two groups of Japanese learners over ten months, one group using predominantly authentic materials and the other working with predominantly inauthentic texts found in ELT textbooks. Post-tests indicated learners working with the authentic materials made greater gains.

To close this section, I add a brief word about other types of learner-focused consumption studies. Shak and Gardner (2008) studied Bruneian young learners' reactions to four different focus on form grammar tasks. Sakai and Kikuchi's (2009) survey of 656 Japanese high school students asked learners to identify demotivating factors associated with learning English, with several findings directly or indirectly referencing textbooks and teaching materials. And some learner consumption studies focus on culture, such as the study by Wu and Coady (2010), which solicited ESL immigrant students' reactions to a programme of reading materials they were studying in the US. Learners reported that, although they were able to relate to some of the cultural content of the materials (e.g., immigrants' difficulties in adjusting to life in the US), other parts created identity conflict, with one of the learners feeling that the materials were 'trying to force him to assimilate into the "American" way of life' (p.159).

Textbook production

Production studies tell us why textbooks are the way they are (cf. Littlejohn, 1992), providing insights into the 'culture and commerce' of textbook creators and distributors (cf. Apple, 1985). We can divide textbook production accounts into narratives by writers and those by publishers/developers. These accounts underline the formidable nature of producing a textbook, reminding us of the inevitable and often unenviable constraints placed upon writers and publishers, and may therefore help explain why content and consumption studies continue to identify weaknesses and shortcomings in textbooks. Nonetheless, the narratives also highlight some industry practices which seem highly questionable.

Textbook writers' perspectives

A key textbook writers' account is by Jan Bell and Roger Gower, writers of the successful *Matters* series. Bell and Gower (2011) describe the compromises global textbook writers make: rather than designing materials that they themselves would be comfortable using, writers 'need to cater for a wide range of students, teachers and classroom contexts with which they have no personal acquaintance', anticipating as best they can what materials will be successful across cultures, in classes of various sizes, fronted by teachers with contrasting pedagogies (p.135). These difficulties are apparent from Bell and Gower's publisher design brief for the *Matters* textbooks. The textbook series was to be used for UK intensive courses (15–21 hours/week) and less intensive courses overseas (2–3 hours/week), from Europe to the Middle East. Supposedly working on a course for adults, Bell and Gower realized some schools would nevertheless use their textbooks with younger learners. Hence they were writing for a diverse audience of both teachers and learners, inevitably leading to some dissatisfaction: for instance, some teachers complained that the book's authentic listenings were too difficult. And because they were limited to a set number of pages, Bell and Gower were obliged to omit many practice activities.

Bell and Gower also write briefly about the piloting of the textbook. Although pilots were conducted, teacher feedback was 'often contradictory' and 'not [...] as helpful as we had hoped' (p.149). Crucially, there was little piloting of the final version of the materials because of publishers' budgets and production scheduling, with the writers obliged to rely instead on their 'own experience and the experience of advisors' (p.149).

Like Bell and Gower, Mares' (2003) account shows that global textbook writing is no easy task, and that compromise is key. Mares admits his early writing attempts were naïve and impractical, aimed at producing textbooks 'free of graded grammatical syllabuses' and indeed 'free of virtually any conventional constraints with respect to unit length or template' (p.136). These efforts were problematic because they were (subconsciously) authored for a specialized audience – 'clones of myself':

> I was not writing for non-native teachers with low confidence in their command of the English language, but in the world of 'the market' these teachers make up a sizeable slice. (p.131)

Mares eventually accepted that 'the art of compromise is a vital one to learn for any writer' (pp.136–137), and designed more conventional materials, featuring graded grammar syllabuses. This is not to say Mares agreed with all the compromises he had to make: he describes the requirement that the grammar syllabus be graded not in line with SLA research, but 'apparently to precedent',

> which as far as we could tell meant that the simple past could not be addressed until around Unit 7. This seemed odd to us, but apparently it was a market constraint. (p.137)

Mares closes by predicting that more innovative textbooks will eventually find their way into print, but portrays the industry as conservative and wary of change.

The difficulty of writing for diverse audiences is also apparent in McCullagh (2010). McCullagh co-authored a textbook on medical communication skills, and she describes its evaluation by a set of users from diverse locations and cultures. Although some topics were intentionally omitted because of cultural sensitivities, users nevertheless objected to some content: the textbook contains material on 'dealing with sensitive issues' (sexual health, alcohol consumption) and 'breaking bad news' (including a listening on a patient with HIV), but 'The fact that the materials were aimed at doctors intending to work in an English speaking context meant that the cultural specificity of the materials could not be avoided' (p.392). Her account also reveals how textbooks can be used in ways writers never intended: although the textbook was intended as a supplementary communication skills resource, some users expected it to serve as a core medical English textbook, believing it should contain more practice of medical terminology and summary reading activities.

Prowse (2011) is an account of 16 textbook writers' practices elicited via questionnaires and correspondence which emphasizes the creativity of the design process. Writers also describe their experiences of working with designers and illustrators, reporting that relationships can become fraught because of the different perspectives of the different parties ('[The designer] wants the design to be aesthetically pleasing and you want it to be pedagogically effective', p.161). Textbook illustrations may differ from the designs writers requested and thus reduce the pedagogical effectiveness of the accompanying activities, and budget restrictions may result in poor artwork. There is little detail throughout the chapter, however, about whether and to what extent the writers take account of SLA/applied linguistics research in their materials. Accounts of piloting are also mostly absent. Although we are not provided with copies of the instruments used to collect the data, it appears that this missing information is explained by the focus of Prowse's instruments on 'syllabus, ideas and procedures' rather than on 'learning principles and objectives' (pp.165–166).

At this point I briefly review a textbook writer's account from mainstream education, Biemer (1992), which echoes many of the ELT writers' difficulties described above. Writing US history and social studies textbooks, Biemer was constrained in her writing by (i) the state syllabus; (ii) the publisher; and (iii) external reviewers of the draft manuscript. Biemer wished to go beyond the syllabus, which her publisher initially agreed to. However, the draft manuscript as a result was 150 pages longer than the publisher would entertain, because a book of this length was judged to be too expensive for the market. And while Biemer wanted to cover a narrower range of history topics in more depth, the reviewers, the publishers, and the teachers piloting the materials all wanted more breadth, to help prepare students for exams. Biemer also found through talking to teachers that her materials were sometimes used in ways she had not intended – including ways that the teachers' guide signalled were inappropriate. Biemer concludes that while textbook writing is seen in university departments as a low-status activity, criticizing textbooks is easier than producing one of high quality.

In sum, then, we get a sense from these accounts of the difficulties writers face, and of the trickiness of writing for such a diverse set of needs. However, there are question marks over some of the writers' practices and of those practices imposed on writers by publishers.

Textbook writers and corpora

There are several pieces describing textbook authors' accounts of engaging (or refusing to engage) with corpora. Jeanne McCarten and Michael McCarthy describe how corpora have informed their *Touchstone* textbooks, providing examples of how spoken corpus data contradict conventional textbook linguistic information. However, McCarthy and

McCarten also focus on 'the challenges of producing spoken corpus-based materials that are usable, useful and non-threatening to teachers and learners alike' (McCarthy and McCarten, 2012: 226). Some of the most frequently occurring words may be tricky for low-level learners in terms of meaning and grammatical structure; and word frequencies differ across spoken and written registers, meaning frequency information shared with the learner may be more complex and nuanced than the writer would wish. McCarten and McCarthy (2010) also describe the difficulties of incorporating authentic conversation data into textbook materials: such data can make much use of obscure, taboo, and 'incorrect' language, such as uses of *less* + plural countable noun (p.21). In addition:

> real conversations rarely contain the number and variety of examples of a target language item [a textbook writer may wish for....] [M]ost conversations are not particularly interesting in themselves [...] and teaching material needs more than anything to capture students' interest in some way... (p.22)

There are also certain publishing constraints placed upon writers: while 'real' conversations can be lengthy, textbook writers of lower-level materials are 'sometimes restricted by publishers to as few as fifty-sixty words' (p.22). So textbook writers need to strike a balance between the real and the pedagogically effective.

EAP textbook authors have also drawn on corpora to good effect: *Write like a Chemist* (Robinson, Stoller, Costanza-Robinson, and Jones, 2008) is corpus-informed, and in Robinson, Stoller, and Jones (2008) the writers describe how they resisted basing their book on mere assumptions about chemistry-writing norms, arguing that these could be outdated, biased towards one particular chemistry subdiscipline – or just plain inaccurate. Hence the writing team built a corpus of chemistry journal articles as well as consulting other, larger, ready-made corpora in the same field. And a more recent account, Stoller and Robinson (2013), provides an in-depth account of how the corpus analysis which informed the content of *Write like a Chemist* was validated by disciplinary specialists (i.e., chemists rather than applied linguists). To take another example, John Swales and Christine Feak are also well known for their corpus-informed materials. In Swales and Feak (2010), for instance, they describe how their textbook *Abstracts and the Writing of Abstracts* (Swales and Feak, 2009), draws on corpus data, and another account can be found in Swales (2002).

It is unsurprising that textbooks co-authored by McCarthy, Stoller, Swales, and Feak are corpus-informed, given their work as corpus linguists as well as textbook writers. In contrast, Burton (2012) surveys the uses of and attitudes towards corpora by the wider community of ELT textbook writers. Five of Burton's 13 writers who did not consult corpora spoke of not knowing how to use a corpus well enough, not having access to a corpus, not having time to use one, not believing a corpus was relevant to their textbook writing, and of corpora not yet being good enough to use. In contrast, nearly all writers reported accessing corpus data indirectly, using corpus-based dictionaries and/or grammars – although we are not told how extensively or otherwise these resources are consulted and inform the materials, and the sense is that corpora are perceived as time-consuming and difficult to use, neither of which mixes well with the demands of the job ('Ease of availability is crucial. We are working under tremendous time constraints and need to have the information at our fingertips', p.103). Hence some textbook writers remain to be persuaded that accessing corpora directly is worthwhile. Burton also reminds us that applied linguists and publishers approach textbooks from fundamentally different perspectives: an applied linguist's lens is that of *academic* research and a publisher's is of *market* research, and no matter how unsatisfactory an applied linguist may find a textbook to be, a publisher's 'only incentive for real change [in his/her company's product] is demand from the market' (p.97). Burton finds no evidence that teachers, school administrators, or policy makers currently demand a greater use of corpora in textbooks, meaning publishers have no incentive to move in this direction.

Methodological limitations associated with textbook writers' accounts

The writers' accounts reviewed above are useful, although, as Atkinson (2008) points out, they do not offer us in-depth accounts of writers' actual behaviour. Atkinson adds that, while there are some studies of expert task designers at work (e.g., Johnson, 2003; Ormerod and Ridgway, 1999), task design is not the same as textbook design; textbooks require multiple tasks to dovetail and for the product as a whole to be balanced and coherent. We could add that Johnson's and Ormerod and Ridgway's studies may inaccurately represent what textbook writers do, because in both studies participants were given a task and an imaginary situation around which to design their work, rather than the writing process being studied in a naturalistic environment, as in Atkinson's case study of an experienced writer, where stimulated recall video sessions enabled the writer to view and comment upon his design behaviour retrospectively. This naturalistic approach has the potential to enable us to more fully understand the textbook writing process.

Publishers' and developers' perspectives

Valuable insights into ELT publishers' perspectives, particularly concerning piloting, are provided by Amrani (2011), updating an earlier insider account by Donovan (1998). Amrani explains that changing industry practices make extensive testing and trialling of textbooks difficult:

> Whereas in the early 1990s a development time of seven years for a course from concept to launch was not unheard of, most publishers are now working to development cycles of only two or three years. This leaves little [or] no time for full piloting, which [...] requires almost a year to test sequencing and a full range of units across the same school year in order to ensure standardised results. (p.268)

So while a whole textbook may have been piloted in the 1980s, such thorough trialling is rare nowadays. The expense of producing pilot editions is considerable, it can be difficult to secure the cooperation of pilotee teachers, and when cooperation *is* secured, the motivated, experienced pilotees who often come forward may be unrepresentative of the teachers the textbook was designed for. Other problems include receiving overly brief, vague, and unhelpful comments by pilotees (e.g., expressing dissatisfaction with the materials but failing to explain why) and the fact that pilot materials could be seen by publishing rivals.

These difficulties mean that publishers may rely instead on other techniques to evaluate draft materials. For instance, experienced teachers may evaluate sample units via questionnaire, without classroom testing, although Amrani does not talk about the drawbacks of the questionnaire as an evaluation instrument – that respondents are often unwilling to provide extensive responses to open questions, or may not believe the closed questions identify the most salient features which need to be commented on, etc. (see Masuhara, 2011, for further criticisms). Alternatively, teacher focus groups may be used, and focus group coordinators may ask participants to quickly plan a lesson for a class using some of the materials in order to better evaluate them. Again, however, the textbook is not piloted with actual learners.

Amrani also makes clear how difficult it is to publish global textbooks that please most of the people most of the time. He points out that it is particularly difficult for publishers to ascertain learners' wants and needs across diverse settings, lamenting that 'There is no real opportunity to gradually review and refine materials already in use' (p.271). Clearly the difficulties Amrani describes are formidable; yet surely a way to reduce this knowledge gap would be to reintroduce more extensive piloting and trialling before and after publication.

Another informative piece is by Singapore Wala (2003), who was part of a Singaporean textbook development team, and whose narrative opens with a description of a change in government textbook policy. In 1998, parliament announced that as of 2000 the Ministry of Education would no longer produce textbooks, publishers being free to issue their own materials. However, the Ministry would continue to draw up syllabuses, and to ensure textbooks adequately covered these there would be an official authorization process, the Ministry reviewing each textbook and releasing an approved list. The Ministry expected materials to be submitted for their approval just over a year after the syllabuses appeared, with no requirements for publishers to trial or pilot.

Singapore Wala's team used a teachers' questionnaire and two teacher focus group meetings to determine the kind of textbook teachers wanted, but no piloting was conducted because of time constraints: given the time needed for proofing and printing, only six months were available to write the students' book and workbook. The team were therefore limited to informal feedback, obtained by 'showing the proofs of the units [...] to different teachers' (p.150). The draft materials were duly submitted to the Ministry on schedule. While waiting for the Ministry's evaluation, the team piloted a sample of the materials. However, this proved far from straightforward: some school authorities were reluctant to grant permission, 'thinking of the disruption and extra work piloting would cause' (p.152), while others saw no benefit to taking part and simply refused. Five schools eventually agreed to piloting, but publishers were not permitted to observe the classes, relying instead on teacher questionnaires for feedback. And teachers from only three schools returned the questionnaires – the fourth provided oral feedback, and the fifth provided nothing. But due once more to tight deadlines, there was insufficient time to use the feedback to revise the materials. Like the accounts by Amrani (2011) and Donovan (1998), Singapore Wala highlights the difficulties of piloting. It seems reasonable to conclude that at least some of the shortcomings in the textbooks produced were attributable to the excessively tight deadlines imposed by government, which made proper piloting impossible. And it is noteworthy that there are similar accounts of ministries failing to provide publishers with adequate time for trialling in textbook production accounts in other contexts (see Lee and Park, 2008).

Publishers' guidelines to textbook writers

Gray (2010b) analyses British ELT publishers' guidelines to textbook writers regarding acceptable content, providing insights into the constraints and affordances of textbook production. Gray finds there is a requirement to portray both sexes equally in terms of the number of male/female appearances and in terms of the characters' status. With regard to 'inappropriate topics', authors are granted freer rein in 'UK and northern European markets' but must exercise caution when writing materials for 'more conservative and religious markets' (p.119). References to religion, drugs, alcohol, sex/sexuality, and political controversies may be ruled off-limits. Further examples of publishers' constraints emerge from Gray's (2010b) interviews with editors and publishing managers. What Gray calls the 'extreme market-sensitivity' (p.175) of ELT publishing brings to mind constraints imposed on writers producing textbooks for other educational settings (see Ravitch, 2003; Skoog, 1992).

Conclusions and implications

The foregoing discussion has shown that textbooks, writers, and publishers are often subject to criticism (see also McBeath, 2006, for a humorous example of a catalogue of criticisms, and Viney, 2006, for a reply). However, in the current chapter and previously (Harwood, 2005, 2010b), I have stressed that the difficulty of writing and producing successful textbooks should not be understated: as Mares (2003) puts it, textbooks 'are far easier to criticize than they are to write' (p.136). When a teacher and/or learners negatively evaluate a textbook, we need to ask whether the book was an apt choice given the profile of the micro-/ macro-context; if not, it is difficult to see why the textbook and the textbook writers are to blame. And if the textbook *does* appear suitable, was it being used appropriately? If not, it may be that teachers are inadequately trained to exploit textbooks. Alternatively, teachers' lack of access to or failure to consult the teachers' guide could partly explain unsuccessful textbook use, since no account is taken of the writers' intentions. Nonetheless, there is plenty of evidence above to suggest legitimate concerns regarding textbook quality, and, where criticisms of textbooks, writers, and publishers are valid, we need to specify ways in which things could be improved.

Implications for textbook writers

We saw how many analyses judge textbooks to be falling short in terms of content, and how textbooks may be consumed in markedly different ways, for various reasons. Writers should draw on this research to assess the soundness of their materials and to consider the purposes for which their books are used.

Particularly significant for writers are consumption studies of teachers' guides. Although the area is under-researched, it is clear that innovative guides can develop teachers, expanding their content and pedagogical knowledge through exposure to the latest research findings and ideas for activities they never previously considered (Remillard and Bryans, 2004; Valencia, Place, Martin, and Grossman, 2006; see also Remillard, 1999). However, there is also evidence that guides which provide teachers with insufficient information can frustrate users and result in less teacher development than would have otherwise occurred; and that some teachers simply ignore these parts of the textbook as a result of these frustrations (Remillard, 2000). All of this suggests that writers should accord a higher priority to teachers' guides than is sometimes the case, as can be seen in the fact that guides may not even be authored by the writers responsible for the students' material. Rather than seeing teachers' guides as 'little more than student editions with [...] answer keys' (Sheldon, 1988: 239), textbook writers should see them as potentially powerful tools for teacher development and learning.

Davis and Krajcik (2005) and Remillard (2000) specify how to produce truly 'educative' guides. Guides should stress the rationale behind activities, present alternative tasks and pedagogical approaches, and include transcripts of student and student/teacher classroom interactions resulting from using the materials. These transcripts could then include commentary by the writers to show readers how and why the materials were used (in)effectively. Guides could also feature reflections by real or fictional teachers about adaptations and their rationale behind these adaptations, with the aim of enhancing readers' content/pedagogical knowledge and their ability to adapt the book to best meet their needs. In sum, Remillard (2000) contends that too often guides simply focus on telling teachers how to implement activities without explaining the pedagogical/content rationale behind them. Proposals such as these would necessitate extensive classroom trialling to help textbook writers determine how students are likely to react to the activities and the kind of output which could result (Ball and Cohen, 1996), but have rich potential.

Implications for textbook publishers

Like textbook writers, publishers need to pay careful heed to the research surveyed here: if the findings are ignored or dismissed by industry insiders, very little will change. Indeed, the lines of communication between writers, teachers, learners, publishers, and textbook researchers need enhancing (cf. Harwood, 2010b; Masuhara, 2011; Tomlinson, 2011). Masuhara (2011) focuses on teacher–publisher communication, arguing that teachers' needs and wants should be more carefully analysed and addressed in materials. She proposes various approaches publishers could use to enhance their dialogue with teachers, including fora in which teachers critique samples of materials which are at an early stage in the production process so the textbook writer could revise accordingly.

Another cause for concern for textbook publishers is the contrast between the mainstream education and ELT literature regarding textbook piloting (e.g., see Ziebarth et al., 2009, and Amrani, 2011, respectively; see also Viney's (2006) disturbing accounts of ELT piloting). Ziebarth et al. drafted multiple versions of mathematics textbook units, re-shaping each draft in response to teacher–writer focus groups, multiple classroom observations of the materials in use, and individual teacher and learner interviews. The contrast with Amrani's account, which explains why systematic piloting is rare in ELT, is sobering. Certainly one would be more confident that a textbook which was the product of careful and rigorous trialling would be more likely to do its job than another book which was not; and so, logistics and costs notwithstanding, it is difficult to see a pedagogical downside to more systematic piloting during ELT textbook writing.

Implications for teacher education

Pre-service textbook education

Some pre-service teacher education programmes apparently encourage a sceptical attitude towards textbooks, viewing their use as 'uncreative' (see Ball and Feiman-Nemser, 1988; Nicol and Crespo, 2006). And in Grossman and Thompson's (2008) study, trainees focused on creating materials from scratch rather than learning how best to exploit textbooks. This is profoundly unhelpful, given that the textbook occupies a central position in most classrooms.

The research shows us that textbooks can be exploited in many ways, and we can agree with Shawer (2010b) that trainees should be made aware of these possibilities. However, some pre-service manuals emphasize exhaustive planning and faithful adherence to these plans, behaviour markedly at odds with how expert teachers exploit textbooks (Wette, 2009, 2010). Pre-service teachers must be made aware that teaching in general and textbook use in particular are 'fundamentally organic, relational and contextualized [...] it is vital for [teachers] to monitor how the curriculum is being received by learners, and [...] respond to the implicit and explicit feedback they receive' (Wette, 2010: 570).

In-service textbook education

If there is evidence of inadequate textbook training on pre-service teacher education programmes, it would seem sensible to bolster in-service instruction. There is also a case for highly experienced teachers to take in-service textbook refresher courses: in Remillard and Bryans (2004) we see that it is the most experienced teachers who fail to develop when using an innovative textbook because they are unwilling to depart from their familiar classroom routines and repertoires. Remillard's work (Remillard, 1999, 2000; Remillard and Bryans, 2004) shows that innovative, carefully written textbooks are capable of developing teachers; but to achieve their full potential teachers should have the opportunity to reflect on and reconsider their textbook use.

Future directions for textbook research

We can point to research gaps in all areas – at the levels of content, consumption, and production. At the level of content, there is less analysis of local as opposed to global textbooks, including the under-researched area of teachers' guides, where Qu and Tin's (2010) comparison and contrast of local and global teachers' guides suggests a potentially interesting avenue of exploration for future researchers. Finally, as Kullman (2003) points out, little research has been conducted on the visual aspect of ELT textbooks.

Ideas for textbook consumption research include studies of the effects of different kinds of teachers' guides on teacher behaviour. Another interesting question posed by Remillard (2005) is how the teacher–textbook relationship changes when the textbook is used over an extended period. Gray (2010b) calls for more research into learners' views of textbooks, and we would also benefit from studies of how and to what extent learners use textbooks outside of class. And Maley (2011) calls for materials which provide 'greater flexibility in decisions about content, order, pace and procedures' (p.380), proposing several possible forms such resources could take, and their efficacy needs to be studied from both teachers' and learners' perspectives.

Production studies of textbook writers at work featuring think-alouds or stimulated recall interviews, as in Atkinson (2008), Johnson (2003), and Ormerod and Ridgway (1999), would give us a better understanding of the design process. Indeed, the latter authors used their findings on the processes of experienced and inexperienced task designers to create an online task design guide which provides designers with video clips and transcripts of both efficient and inefficient examples of materials writing practices, with the aim of enhancing users' design procedures. This is an innovative proposal for the training and development of textbook writers, and its effectiveness could be investigated. There are currently a few studies of textbook development projects in non-centre contexts (e.g., Katz, Byrkun, and Sullivan, 2008; Popovici and Bolitho, 2003), but much more fine-grained research which examined individual textbook designers' behaviour in these and other contexts, with or without the aid of design guides, would be most welcome. We also need more researchers to write textbooks – and conduct content/consumption/production research on them, reporting their findings.

Coda

ELT textbook research is on the rise; a number of books in the field were appearing or were due to appear as this volume went to press (e.g., Garton and Graves, 2013; Gray, 2013; McGrath, 2013; Tomlinson, 2013), and lively debates proliferate online (see Scott Thornbury's posts and the responses, including some from well-known textbook writers: for instance http://scottthornbury.wordpress.com/2013/04/14/r-is-for-representation/#comments and http://scottthornbury.wordpress.com/tag/critical-pedagogy/). Indeed, Rixon and Smith (2012) recently spoke of 'the coming of age in ELT textbook research' (p.383). A note of caution is in order, however; while textbook research may have come of age in mainstream education, we have seen how ELT-related studies, particularly studies of consumption, are relatively rare and do not bear comparison in terms of quality with those in education, such as Valencia et al.'s (2006) work, where teachers and their textbook use were studied for four years, with each teacher being observed on at least 17 occasions and interviewed at least 32 times. The resources needed to conduct studies on this scale are, of course, very considerable. On the issue of funding, Lloyd, Remillard, and Herbel-Eisenmann (2009) explain how in the US there is 'intense pressure' being placed on schools to raise children's test scores as a result of the No Child Left Behind Act, and how there are substantial research grants available for mainstream education researchers to investigate the impact of innovative textbooks (p.4). It is therefore not difficult to see why many US school principals would welcome textbook researchers who wish to study the effects of textbooks which publishers claim will raise test scores. In ELT the picture is very different, with funding severely restricted or non-existent in many locations, and textbook research operating within these constrained budgets. Nonetheless, while the resources and opportunities for ELT researchers may not always be equivalent to those from mainstream education, we can learn much from the latter field, and adopt and adapt relevant methods and study designs. Hence I must agree with Tomlinson's (2012) claim that 'For the field of materials development to become more credible it needs to become more empirical' (p.146), which means more, and better, consumption studies.

Overview of this volume

Following this chapter, Part I, Studies of Textbook Content, begins with John Gray and David Block's chapter on the depiction of the working class in textbooks from the 1970s to the present day. Gray and Block find that working-class characters have been largely written out of recent materials, and discuss the implications of this result. Diana Freeman presents a taxonomy for the analysis of reading comprehension questions and examines the distribution of these question types in and across four best-selling global textbook series. Interestingly, she finds some marked variations from edition to edition of the same textbook. Lastly in this section, Quentin Dixon and colleagues analyse what 39 textbooks tell pre-service general education teachers in four countries about reading instruction. As well as showing that the textbooks treat various aspects of reading instruction unevenly, Dixon and colleagues also find the books provide little advice about teaching reading to L2 speakers.

Part II, Studies of Textbook Consumption, comprises three studies of textbook use in tertiary education contexts. Ahlam Menkabu and

Nigel Harwood study teachers' views on and use of the textbook on an English for Medical Purposes course in Saudi Arabia, including the degree to which teachers departed from the materials and the problems associated with textbook implementation. Fotini Grammatosi and Harwood focus on a teacher's infrequent textbook use on an intensive preparatory EAP programme in the UK, exploring the reasons behind the teacher's behaviour, identifying factors related to the textbook, the teacher, the learners, and the school. Closing the section, Gregory Hadley describes the socio-political background to the introduction of a global textbook on a language programme in a Japanese university, a move initially resisted by the university management. Hadley was able to demonstrate students' learning gains to the managers by presenting pre- and post-test enrolment scores, and questions the validity of some of the anti-textbook arguments found in the literature.

Part III, Studies of Textbook Production, begins with Ivor Timmis' account of his first experience of writing a textbook for publication. Draft materials were produced in response to a design brief which was short on detail but which appeared to align with the writing team's approach, although it turned out that the team and the publisher had rather different products in mind. We then have two accounts of the production of well-known EAP textbooks. Fredricka Stoller and Marin Robinson describe the process of authoring *Write like a Chemist* around the following steps: (i) articulating priorities and principles; (ii) scaffolding the instructional approach; (iii) selecting target genres, then compiling and analysing corpora featuring these genres; (iv) converting analytical findings into materials; (v) piloting and assessing materials; and (vi) using feedback to improve materials. They conclude with suggestions for writers wishing to embark on similar textbook projects. Christine Feak and John Swales describe the revision of two of their textbooks, *English in Today's Research World* and *Academic Writing for Graduate Students*, and the sometimes conflicting expectations of the parties involved: the authors, various members of the publishing team, and the teachers reviewing and using the materials. Like Timmis, Feak and Swales chart not only conflicts and compromises but also lessons learned. Finally, Jill Hadfield focuses on her writing process when designing a teacher resource book by drawing on data from a reflective log. Hadfield concludes that the design process can veer between the linear and the recursive, but that throughout, textbook writers draw on a tacit set of principles.

Note

1. 'Culture' is defined broadly for the present purposes, to include a range of issues such as lifestyle, ideology, and values.

References

Amrani, F. (2011). The process of evaluation: A publisher's view. In B. Tomlinson (Ed.), *Materials development in language teaching* (2nd ed., pp.267–295). Cambridge: Cambridge University Press.

Angouri, J. (2010). Using textbook and real-life data to teach turn taking in business meetings. In N. Harwood (Ed.), *English language teaching materials: Theory and practice* (pp.373–394). New York: Cambridge University Press.

Apple, M.W. (1985). The culture and commerce of the textbook. *Journal of Curriculum Studies*, 17, 147–162.

Atkinson, D. (2008). Investigating expertise in textbook writing: Insights from a case study of an experienced materials writer at work. In M. KhosraviNik and A. Polyzou (Eds.), *Papers from the Lancaster University postgraduate conference in linguistics and language teaching*, vol.2 (pp.1–20). Lancaster: Dept of Linguistics and English Language, Lancaster University. Retrieved from http://www.ling.lancs.ac.uk/pgconference/v02/01-Atkinson.pdf.

Auerbach, E.R. and Burgess, D. (1985). The hidden curriculum of survival ESL. *TESOL Quarterly*, 19, 475–495.

Ball, D.L. and Cohen, D.K. (1996). Reform by the book: What is – or might be – the role of curriculum materials in teacher learning and instructional reform? *Educational Researcher*, 25, 6–8, 14.

Ball, D.L. and Feiman-Nemser, S. (1988). Using textbooks and teachers' guides: A dilemma for beginning teachers and teacher educators. *Curriculum Inquiry*, 18, 401–423.

Bardovi-Harlig, K., Hartford, B.A.S., Mahan-Taylor, R., Morgan, M.J., and Reynolds, D.W. (1991). Developing pragmatic awareness: Closing the conversation. *ELT Journal*, 45, 4–15.

Behm, S.L. and Lloyd, G.M. (2009). Factors influencing student teachers' use of mathematics curriculum materials. In J.T. Remillard, B.A. Herbel-Eisenmann, and G.M. Lloyd (Eds.), *Mathematics teachers at work: Connecting curriculum materials and classroom instruction* (pp.205–222). New York: Routledge.

Bell, J. and Gower, R. (2011). Writing course materials for the world: A great compromise. In B. Tomlinson (Ed.), *Materials development in language teaching* (2nd ed., pp.135–150). Cambridge: Cambridge University Press.

Biber, D. and Reppen, R. (2002). What does frequency have to do with grammar teaching? *Studies in Second Language Acquisition*, 24, 199–208.

Biemer, L.B. (1992). The textbook controversy: The role of content. In J.G. Herlihy (Ed.), *The textbook controversy: Issues, aspects and perspectives* (pp.17–25). Norwood: Ablex.

Bonkowski, F. (1995). *Teacher use and interpretation of textbook materials in the secondary ESL classroom in Quebec*. Unpublished PhD thesis, Lancaster University.

Boriboon, P. (2004). 'We would rather talk about *plaa raa* than hamburgers': Voices from low-proficient EFL learners in a rural Thai context. Retrieved from http://teacher.snru.ac.th/phaisit/admin/about/spaw2/uploads/files/boriboon2004.pdf.

Borko, H. and Livingston, C. (1989). Cognition and improvisation: Differences in mathematics instruction by expert and novice teachers. *American Educational Research Journal*, 26, 473–498.

Boxer, D. and Pickering, L. (1995). Problems in the presentation of speech acts in ELT materials: The case of complaints. *ELT Journal*, 49, 44–58.

Brown, D. (2011). What aspects of vocabulary knowledge to textbooks give attention to? *Language Teaching Research*, 15, 83–97.

Brown, M.W. (2009). The teacher-tool relationship: Theorizing the design and use of curriculum materials. In J.T. Remillard, B.A. Herbel-Eisenmann, and G.M. Lloyd (Eds.), *Mathematics teachers at work: Connecting curriculum materials and classroom instruction* (pp.17–36). New York: Routledge.

Brown, P. and Levinson, S.C. (1987). *Politeness: Some universals in language usage*. Cambridge: Cambridge University Press.

Burton, G. (2012). Corpora and coursebooks: Destined to be strangers forever? *Corpora*, 7, 91–108.

Canagarajah, A.S. (1993a). American textbooks and Tamil students: Discussing ideological tensions in the ESL classroom. *Language, Culture and Curriculum*, 6, 143–156.

Canagarajah, A.S. (1993b). Critical ethnography of a Sri Lankan classroom: Ambiguities in student opposition to reproduction through ESOL. *TESOL Quarterly*, 27, 601–626.

Carroll, D. and Kowitz, J. (1994). Using concordancing techniques to study gender stereotyping in ELT textbooks. In J. Sunderland (Ed.), *Exploring gender: Questions and implications for English language education* (pp.73–82). New York: Prentice Hall.

Cheng, W. (2007). 'Sorry to interrupt, but...': Pedagogical implications of a spoken corpus. In M.C. Campoy and M.J. Luzón (Eds.), *Spoken corpora in applied linguistics* (pp.199–215). Bern: Peter Lang.

Cheng, W. and Cheng, P. (2010). Correcting others and self-correcting in business and professional discourse and textbooks. In A. Trosborg (Ed.), *Pragmatics across languages and cultures* (pp.443–466). Berlin: de Gruyter.

Cheng, W. and Warren, M. (2005). Well I have a different thinking you know: A corpus-driven study of disagreement in Hong Kong business discourse. In F.B. Chiappini and M. Gotti (Eds.), *Asian business discourse(s)* (pp.241–270). Bern: Peter Lang.

Cheng, W. and Warren, M. (2006). 'I would say be very careful of...': Opine markers in an intercultural business corpus of spoken English. In J. Bamford and M. Bondi (Eds.), *Managing interaction in professional discourse: Intercultural and interdiscoursal perspectives* (pp.46–57). Rome: Officina Edizioni.

Cheng, W. and Warren, M. (2007). Checking understandings: Comparing textbooks and a corpus of spoken English in Hong Kong. *Language Awareness*, 16, 190–207.

Chval, K.B., Chávez, Ó, Reys, B.J., and Tarr, J. (2009). Considerations and limitations related to conceptualizing and measuring textbook integrity. In J.T. Remillard, B.A. Herbel-Eisenmann, and G.M. Lloyd (Eds.), *Mathematics teachers at work: Connecting curriculum materials and classroom instruction* (pp.70–84). New York: Routledge.

Coleman, H. (1986). Evaluating teachers' guides: Do teachers' guides guide teachers? *JALT Journal*, 8, 17–36.

Collopy, R. (2003). Curriculum materials as a professional development tool: How a mathematics textbook affected two teachers' learning. *The Elementary School Journal*, 103, 287–311.

Conrad, S. (2004). Corpus linguistics, language variation, and language teaching. In J.McH. Sinclair (Ed.), *How to use corpora in language teaching* (pp.67–85). Amsterdam: John Benjamins.

Cortazzi, M. and Jin, L. (1999). Cultural mirrors: Materials and methods in the EFL classroom. In E. Hinkel (Ed.), *Culture in second language teaching and learning* (pp.196–219). Cambridge: Cambridge University Press.

Criado, R. (2009). The distribution of the lexical component in ELT coursebooks and its suitability for vocabulary acquisition from a cognitive perspective. A case study. *International Journal of English Studies*, 9, 39–60.

Davis, E.A., Beyer, C., Forbes, C.T., and Stevens, S. (2011). Understanding pedagogical design capacity through teachers' narratives. *Teaching and Teacher Education*, 27, 797–810.

Davis, E.A. and Krajcik, J.S. (2005). Designing educative curriculum materials to promote teacher learning. *Educational Researcher*, 34, 3–14.

Donovan, P. (1998). Piloting – a publisher's view. In B. Tomlinson (Ed.), *Materials development in language teaching* (pp.149–189). Cambridge: Cambridge University Press.

Drake, C. and Sherin, M.G. (2009). Developing curriculum vision and trust: Changes in teachers' curriculum strategies. In J.T. Remillard, B.A. Herbel-Eisenmann, and G.M. Lloyd (Eds.), *Mathematics teachers at work: Connecting curriculum materials and classroom instruction* (pp.321–337). New York: Routledge.

du Gay, P., Hall, S., Janes, L., Mackay, H., and Negus, K. (1997). *Doing cultural studies/the story of the Sony Walkman*. Milton Keynes: The Open University/Sage.

Feng, A. and Byram, M. (2002). Authenticity in college English textbooks – an intercultural perspective. *RELC Journal*, 33, 58–84.

Folse, K.S. (2006). The effect of type of written exercise on L2 vocabulary retention. *TESOL Quarterly*, 40, 273–293.

Garton, S. and Graves, K. (2013). *International perspectives on materials*. Basingstoke: Palgrave Macmillan.

Gilmore, A. (2011). 'I prefer not text': Developing Japanese learners' communicative competence with authentic materials. *Language Learning*, 61, 786–819.

Gouverneur, C. (2008). The phraseological patterns of high-frequency verbs in advanced English for general purposes: A corpus-driven approach to EFL textbook analysis. In F. Meunier and S. Granger (Eds.), *Phraseology in foreign language teaching and learning* (pp.223–243). Amsterdam: John Benjamins.

Gray, J. (2010a). The branding of English and the culture of the new capitalism: Representations of the world of work in English language textbooks. *Applied Linguistics*, 31, 714–733.

Gray, J. (2010b). *The construction of English: Culture, consumerism and promotion in the ELT global coursebook*. Basingstoke: Palgrave Macmillan.

Gray, J. (2012). Neoliberalism, celebrity and 'aspirational content' in English language teaching textbooks for the global market. In D. Block, J. Gray, and M. Holborow (Eds.), *Neoliberalism and applied linguistics* (pp.86–113). Abingdon: Routledge.

Gray, J. (2013). *Critical perspectives on language teaching materials.* Basingstoke: Palgrave Macmillan.

Grossman, P. and Thompson, C. (2008). Learning from curriculum materials: Scaffolds for new teachers? *Teaching and Teacher Education*, 24, 2014–2026.

Gulliver, T. (2010). Immigrant success stories in ESL textbooks. *TESOL Quarterly*, 44, 725–745.

Handford, M. (2010). *The language of business meetings.* Cambridge: Cambridge University Press.

Handford, M. (2012). Professional communication and corpus linguistics. In K. Hyland, C.M. Huat, and M. Handford (Eds.), *Corpus applications in applied linguistics* (pp.13–29). London: Continuum.

Harwood, N. (2005). What do we want EAP teaching materials for? *Journal of English for Academic Purposes*, 4, 149–161.

Harwood, N. (2010a). *English language teaching materials: Theory and practice.* New York: Cambridge University Press.

Harwood, N. (2010b). Issues in materials development and design. In N. Harwood (Ed.), *English language teaching materials: Theory and practice* (pp.3–30). New York: Cambridge University Press.

Holmes, J. (1988). Doubt and certainty in ESL textbooks. *Applied Linguistics*, 9, 21–44.

Hutchinson, E.G. (1996). What do teachers and learners actually do with textbooks? Teacher and learner use of a fisheries-based ELT textbook in the Philippines. Unpublished PhD thesis, Lancaster University.

Johnson, K. (2003). *Designing language teaching tasks.* Basingstoke: Palgrave Macmillan.

Jones, M.A., Kitetu, C., and Sunderland, J. (1997). Discourse roles, gender and language textbook dialogues: Who learns what from John and Sally? *Gender and Education*, 9, 469–490.

Jones, R.H. (1997). Beyond 'listen and repeat': Pronunciation teaching materials and theories of second language acquisition. *System*, 25, 103–112.

Katz, A., Byrkun, L., and Sullivan, P. (2008). Challenges in translating change into practice: Textbook development in Ukraine. In D.E. Murray (Ed.), *Planning change, changing plans* (pp.43–61). Ann Arbor: University of Michigan Press.

Keating, G.D. (2008). Task effectiveness and word learning in a second language: The involvement load hypothesis on trial. *Language Teaching Research*, 12, 365–386.

Kern, R.G. (1995). Students' and teachers' beliefs about language learning. *Foreign Language Annals*, 28, 71–92.

Kopperoinen, A. (2011). Accents of English as a lingua franca: A study of Finnish textbooks. *International Journal of Applied Linguistics*, 21, 71–93.

Koprowski, M. (2005). Investigating the usefulness of lexical phrases in contemporary coursebooks. *ELT Journal*, 59, 322–332.

Kullman, J.P. (2003). *The social construction of learner identity in the UK-published ELT coursebook.* Unpublished PhD thesis, Canterbury Christ Church University College/University of Kent.

Lam, P.W.Y. (2009). Discourse particles in corpus data and textbooks: The case of Well. *Applied Linguistics*, 31, 260–281.

Lee, H. and Park, K.-C. (2008). Sociocultural appropriateness in Korean middle school English textbooks. *English Language and Linguistics*, 26, 215–240.

Lee, J. (2006). Subjective were and indicative was: A corpus analysis of English language teachers and textbook writers. *Language Teaching Research*, 10, 80–93.

Levis, J.M. (1999). Intonation in theory and practice, revisited. *TESOL Quarterly*, 33, 37–63.

Littlejohn, A. (1992). *Why are English language teaching materials the way they are?* Unpublished PhD thesis, Lancaster University.

Littlejohn, A. (2011). The analysis of language teaching materials: Inside the Trojan Horse. In B. Tomlinson (Ed.), *Materials development in language teaching* (2nd ed., pp.179–211). Cambridge: Cambridge University Press.

Lloyd, G.M., Remillard, J.T., and Herbel-Eisenmann, B.A. (2009). Teachers' use of curriculum materials: An emerging field. In J.T. Remillard, B.A. Herbel-Eisenmann, and G.M. Lloyd (Eds.), *Mathematics teachers at work: Connecting curriculum materials and classroom instruction* (pp.3–14). New York: Routledge.

Maley, A. (2011). Squaring the circle – reconciling materials as constraint with materials as empowerment. In B. Tomlinson (Ed.), *Materials development in language teaching* (2nd ed., pp.379–402). Cambridge: Cambridge University Press.

Manouchehri, A. and Goodman, T. (1998). Mathematics curriculum reform and teachers: Understanding the connections. *Journal of Educational Research*, 92, 27–41.

Mares, C. (2003). Writing a coursebook. In B. Tomlinson (Ed.), *Developing materials for language teaching* (pp.130–140). London: Continuum.

Masuhara, H. (2011). What do teachers really want from coursebooks? In B. Tomlinson (Ed.), *Materials development in language teaching* (2nd ed., pp.236–266). Cambridge: Cambridge University Press.

Matsuda, A. (2002). Representation of users and uses of English in beginning Japanese EFL textbooks. *JALT Journal*, 24, 182–200.

Matsuno, S. (2002). Sexism in Japanese radio business English program textbooks. *JALT Journal*, 24, 83–97.

Matsuoka, W. and Hirsh, D. (2010). Vocabulary learning through reading: Does an ELT course book provide good opportunities? *Reading in a Foreign Language*, 22, 56–70.

McBeath, N. (2006). How to write really rotten materials: The best way to get it wrong. *Modern English Teacher*, 15, 53–56.

McCarten, J. and McCarthy, M. (2010) Bridging the gap between corpus and course book: The case of conversation strategies. In F. Mishan and A. Chambers (Eds.), *Perspectives on language learning materials development* (pp.11–32). Bern: Peter Lang.

McCarthy, M. and McCarten, J. (2012). Corpora and materials design. In K. Hyland, C.M. Huat and M. Handford (Eds.), *Corpus applications in applied linguistics* (pp.225–241). London: Continuum.

McCullagh, M. (2010). An initial evaluation of the effectiveness of a set of published materials for Medical English. In B. Tomlinson and H. Masuhara (Eds.), *Research for materials development in language learning: Evidence for best practice* (pp.381–393). London: Continuum.

McGrath, I. (2004). The representation of people in educational materials. *RELC Journal*, 35, 351–358.

McGrath, I. (2013). *Teaching materials and the roles of EFL/ESL teachers: Practice and theory*. London: Bloomsbury.

Meier, A.J. (1997). Teaching the universals of politeness. *ELT Journal*, 51, 21–28.

Millard, D.J. (2000). Form-focused instruction in communicative language teaching: Implications for grammar textbooks. *TESL Canada Journal*, 18, 47–57.

Miller, D. (2011). ESL reading textbooks vs. university textbooks: Are we giving our students the input they may need? *Journal of English for Academic Purposes*, 10, 32–46.

Mol, H. and Tin, T.B. (2008). EAP materials in New Zealand and Australia. In B. Tomlinson (Ed.), *English language learning materials: A critical review* (pp.74–99). London: Continuum.

Mukundan, J. and Khojasteh, L. (2011). Modal auxiliary verbs in prescribed Malaysian English textbooks. *English Language Teaching*, 4, 79–89.

Nation, I.S.P. (2001). *Learning vocabulary in another language*. Cambridge: Cambridge University Press.

Ndura, E. (2004). ESL and cultural bias: An analysis of elementary through high school textbooks in the western United States of America. *Language, Culture and Curriculum*, 17, 143–153.

Nguyen, M.T.T. (2011). Learning to communicate in a globalized world: To what extent do school textbooks facilitate the development of intercultural pragmatic competence? *RELC Journal*, 42, 17–30.

Nicol, C.C. and Crespo, S.M. (2006). Learning to teach with mathematics textbooks: How preservice teachers interpret and use curriculum materials. *Educational Studies in Mathematics*, 62, 331–355.

Nunan, D. (1988). *The learner-centred curriculum*. Cambridge: Cambridge University Press.

Ormerod, T.C. and Ridgway, J. (1999). Developing task design guides through cognitive studies of expertise. In S. Bagnara (Ed.), *Proceedings of the third European conference on cognitive science, ECCS '99* (pp.401–410). Siena: Consiglio Nazionale Della Richerche.

Peacock, M. (1997). The effect of authentic materials on the motivation of EFL learners. *ELT Journal*, 51, 144–156.

Peacock, M. (1998). Exploring the gap between teachers' and learners' beliefs about 'useful' activities for EFL. *International Journal of Applied Linguistics*, 8, 233–250.

Popovici, R. and Bolitho, R. (2003). Personal and professional development through writing: The Romanian Textbook Project. In B. Tomlinson (Ed.), *Developing materials for language teaching* (pp. 505–517). London: Continuum.

Prowse, P. (2011). How writers write: Testimony from authors. In B. Tomlinson (Ed.), *Materials development in language teaching* (2nd ed., pp.151–173). Cambridge: Cambridge University Press.

Qu, J. and Tin, T.B. (2010). Cultures of learning in three language coursebooks in China: 'Read with your heart', 'listen and check' and 'fill in the blank and use the language'. In B. Tomlinson and H. Masuhara (Eds.), *Research for materials development in language learning: Evidence for best practice* (pp.273–290). London: Continuum.

Ravitch, D. (2003). *The language police: How pressure groups restrict what students learn*. New York: Alfred Knopf.

Remillard, J.T. (1999). Curriculum materials in mathematics education reform: A framework for examining teachers' curriculum development. *Curriculum Inquiry*, 29, 315–342.

Remillard, J.T. (2000). Can curriculum materials support teachers' learning? Two fourth-grade teachers' use of a new mathematics text. *The Elementary School Journal*, 100, 331–350.

Remillard, J.T. (2005). Examining key concepts in research on teachers' use of mathematics curricula. *Review of Educational Research*, 75, 211–246.

Remillard, J.T. and Bryans, M.B. (2004). Teachers' orientations toward mathematics curriculum materials: Implications for teacher learning. *Journal for Research in Mathematics Education*, 35, 352–388.

Rixon, S. and Smith, R. (2012). Survey review: The work of Brian Abbs and Ingrid Freebairn. *ELT Journal*, 66, 383–393.

Robinson, M.S., Stoller, F.L., Costanza-Robinson, M.S., and Jones, J.K. (2008). *Write like a chemist: A guide and resource*. New York: Oxford University Press.

Robinson, M.S., Stoller, F.L., and Jones, J.K. (2008). Using the ACS Journals Search to validate assumptions about writing in chemistry and improve chemistry writing instruction. *Journal of Chemical Education*, 85, 650–654.

Römer, U. (2005). *Progressives, patterns, pedagogy: A corpus-driven approach to English progressive forms, functions, contexts and didactics*. Amsterdam: John Benjamins.

Rühlemann, C. (2009). Discourse presentation in EFL textbooks: A BNC-based study. In A. Renouf and A. Kehoe (Eds.), *Corpus linguistics: Refinements and reassessments* (pp.415–435). Amsterdam: Rodopi.

Sakai, H. and Kikuchi, K. (2009). An analysis of demotivators in the EFL classroom. *System*, 37, 57–69.

Seidlhofer, B. (2003). *A concept of International English and related issues: From 'Real English' to 'Realistic English'*. Strasbourg: Council of Europe.

Shak, J. and Gardner, S. (2008). Young learner perspectives on four focus-on-form tasks. *Language Teaching Research*, 12, 387–408.

Shawer, S. (2010a). Classroom-level teacher professional development and satisfaction: Teachers learn in the context of classroom-level curriculum development. *Professional Development in Education*, 36, 597–620.

Shawer, S.F. (2010b). Classroom-level curriculum development: EFL teachers as curriculum-developers, curriculum-makers and curriculum-transmitters. *Teaching and Teacher Education*, 26, 173–184.

Shawer, S., Gilmore, D., and Banks-Joseph, S. (2009). Learner-driven EFL curriculum development at the classroom level. *International Journal of Teaching and Learning in Higher Education*, 20, 125–143.

Sheldon, L.E. (1988). Evaluating ELT textbooks and materials. *ELT Journal*, 42, 237–246.

Sherman, J.E. (2010). Multiple levels of cultural bias in TESOL course books. *RELC Journal*, 41, 267–281.

Singapore Wala, D.A. (2003) Publishing a coursebook: Completing the materials development circle. In B. Tomlinson (Ed.), *Developing materials for language teaching* (pp.141–161). London: Continuum.

Skoog, G.D. (1992). The coverage of evolution on secondary school biology textbooks, 1900–1989. In J.G. Herlihy (Ed.), *The textbook controversy: Issues, aspects and perspectives* (pp.71–87). Norwood: Ablex.

Smagorinsky, P., Cook, L.S., Moore, C., Jackson, A.Y., and Fry, P.G. (2004). Tensions in learning to teach: Accommodation and the development of a teaching identity. *Journal of Teacher Education*, 55, 8–24.

Smagorinsky, P., Lakly, A., and Johnson, T.S. (2002). Acquiescence, accommodation, and resistance in learning to teach within a prescribed curriculum. *English Education*, 34, 187–213.

Soars, L. and Soars, J. (1996). *New Headway English course intermediate student's book*. Oxford: Oxford University Press.

Sokolik, M.E. (2007). Grammar texts and consumerist subtexts. *TESL-EJ*, 11, 1–9.

Stoller, F.L. and Robinson, M.S. (2013). Chemistry journal articles: An interdisciplinary approach to move analysis with pedagogical aims. *English for Specific Purposes*, 32, 45–57.

Suaysuwan, N. and Kapitzke, C. (2005). Thai English language textbooks, 1960–2000. In Y. Nozaki, R. Openshaw, and A. Luke (Eds.), *Struggles over difference: Curriculum, texts, and pedagogy in the Asia-Pacific* (pp.79–97). Albany: State University of New York Press.

Sunderland, J. (2000). New understandings of gender and language classroom research: Texts, teacher talk and student talk. *Language Teaching Research*, 4, 149–173.

Swales, J.M. (2002). Integrated and fragmented worlds: EAP materials and corpus linguistics. In J. Flowerdew (Ed.), *Academic discourse* (pp.150–164). Harlow: Longman.

Swales, J.M. and Feak, C.B. (2009). *Abstracts and the writing of abstracts*. Ann Arbor: University of Michigan Press.

Swales, J.M. and Feak, C.B. (2010). From text to task: Putting research on abstracts to work. In M.F. Ruiz-Garrido, J.C. Palmer-Silveira, and I. Fortanet-Gómez (Eds.), *English for professional and academic purposes* (pp.167–180). Amsterdam: Rodopi.

Thomas, J. (1983). Cross-cultural pragmatic failure. *Applied Linguistics*, 4, 91–112.

Tomlinson, B. (2003). Materials evaluation. In B. Tomlinson (Ed.), *Developing materials for language teaching* (pp.15–36). London: Continuum.

Tomlinson, B. (2011). Comments on Part C. In B. Tomlinson (Ed.), *Materials development in language teaching* (2nd ed., pp.296–300). Cambridge: Cambridge University Press.

Tomlinson, B. (2012). Materials development for language teaching and learning. *Language Teaching*, 45, 143–179.

Tomlinson, B. (2013). *Applied linguistics and materials development*. London: Bloomsbury.

Tomlinson, B. and Masuhara, H. (2010). Published research on materials development for language learning. In B. Tomlinson and H. Masuhara (Eds.), *Research for materials development in language learning: Evidence for best practice* (pp.1–18). London: Continuum.

Tyson, H. and Woodward, A. (1989). Why students aren't learning very much from textbooks. *Educational Leadership*, 47, 14–17.

Valencia, S.W., Place, N.A., Martin, S.D., and Grossman, P.L. (2006). Curriculum materials for elementary reading: Shackles and scaffolds for four beginning teachers. *The Elementary School Journal*, 107, 93–120.

Vellenga, H. (2004). Learning pragmatics from ESL and EFL textbooks: How likely? *TESL-EJ*, 8, 1–18. Retrieved from http://www.tesl-ej.org/wordpress/issues/volume8/ej30/ej30a3/

Viney, P. (2006). How not to write really rotten materials: A reply to Neil McBeath. *Modern English Teacher*, 15, 50–55.

Wette, R. (2009). Making the instructional curriculum as an interactive, contextualized process: Case studies of seven ESOL teachers. *Language Teaching Research*, 13, 337–365.

Wette, R. (2010). Professional knowledge in action: How experienced ESOL teachers respond to feedback from learners within syllabus and contextual constraints. *System*, 38, 569–579.

Wette, R. (2011). Meeting curriculum, learning and settlement needs: Teachers' use of materials in courses for adult migrants. *TESOL in Context*, 21, 59–77.

Willing, K. (1988). *Learning styles in adult migrant education*. Adelaide: National Curriculum Resource Centre.

Wong, J. (2002). 'Applying' conversation analysis in applied linguistics: Evaluating dialogue in English as a second language textbooks. *IRAL*, 40, 37–60.

Wu, C.-h. and Coady, M.R. (2010). 'The United States is America?': A cultural perspective on READ 180 materials. *Language, Culture and Curriculum*, 23, 153–165.

Yuen, K.-M. (2011). The representation of foreign cultures in English textbooks. *ELT Journal*, 65, 458–466.

Zacharias, N.T. (2005). Teachers' beliefs about internationally-published materials: A survey of tertiary English teachers in Indonesia. *RELC Journal*, 36, 23–37.

Ziebarth, S.W., Hart, E.W., Marcus, R., Ritsema, B., Schoen, H.L., and Walker, R. (2009). High school teachers as negotiators between curriculum intentions and enactment: The dynamics of mathematics curriculum development. In J.T. Remillard, B.A. Herbel-Eisenmann, and G.M. Lloyd (Eds.), *Mathematics teachers at work: Connecting curriculum materials and classroom instruction* (pp.171–189). New York: Routledge.

Part I
Studies of Textbook Content

2

All Middle Class Now? Evolving Representations of the Working Class in the Neoliberal Era: The Case of ELT Textbooks

John Gray and David Block

Summary

UK-produced English language teaching textbooks aimed at the global market are core products in a multi-million-pound Teaching English to Speakers of Other Languages (TESOL) industry that includes language teaching and testing, teacher education, academic publishing, and educational consultancy work and quality assurance for ministries of education globally. The growth of this industry coincides largely with the birth of the neoliberal era, dating more or less from the late 1970s. This is a period which has been characterized not only by the deregulation of financial markets, the abolition of trade barriers, and the imposition of structural readjustment programmes on developing world countries, but also by an ideology that promotes and celebrates individualism over class-based and other collective identity inscriptions. Elsewhere in our work (Block, 2010; Gray, 2010a, 2010b, 2012), we have argued that UK-produced textbooks frequently reproduce and legitimize neoliberal ideology, and in this chapter we turn our attention specifically to representations of the working class. The chapter begins with a short discussion of the supposed demise of the working class before moving on to a discussion of what class means in the highly complex world we live in today. This is followed by quantitative and qualitative analysis of a set of textbooks dating from the 1970s to the end of the first decade of the 21st century. The analysis reveals a largely superficial treatment of class in general and a progressive editing out of working class characters and issues relating to working class life from these textbooks. We conclude by arguing that this writing out of the working class from language learning materials can be seen as both a failure to educate students (by providing them with a very skewed view of the world) and a simultaneous betrayal of working class language learners, who are denied recognition.

Introduction

Quite apart from any methodological approach to language teaching and learning, at the heart of the English Language Teaching (ELT) textbook is a regime of representation, a way of constructing the world that suggests what it means to be a speaker of English in the world. Such regimes of representation are perforce political, in the sense that what is selected for inclusion is determined by parties with vested interests (such as publishers, authors, Ministries of Education, educational institutions, commercial language schools, etc.). They are also ideological, in the Marxist sense that the forms the representations take tend to reproduce existing power relations, particularly with regard to class, race, gender, and sexual orientation (Azimova and Johnston, 2012) – although overtly sexist representations of women are now largely a thing of the past, at least in materials produced for the global market (Gray, 2010a). In their analysis of a wide range of textbooks for a variety of subject areas in North American schools, Christine Sleeter and Carl Grant (2011: 85) argue that representational practices merit the analyst's scrutiny for the following three reasons:

  (i) symbolic representations in books and other media often are used to confer legitimacy on the dominant status of particular social groups;
 (ii) symbolic representations in the curriculum render socially constructed relations as natural; subjective interpretations of reality and value judgements are projected as fact;
(iii) the curriculum screens in and out certain ideas and realms of knowledge. Students are given selective access to ideas and information.

One of several worrying consequences of such practices is that students can be deprived of a vocabulary for talking about the world and be denied access to conceptual frameworks for thinking about their place in it (Sleeter and Grant, 2011). Jean Anyon's (1985: 51) analysis of North American history books, which revealed the almost complete writing out of the working class (as a named class formation) from US history, led her to conclude:

Without such a label, workers are not easily called to mind as a group, and the objective fact of the working class has no subjective reality. In this way the textbooks predispose workers and others against actions on behalf of the interests that working people have in common.

We do not have to see this systematic editing out in such straight-forwardly cause-and-effect terms to view it as problematic – although clearly the withholding of categorical labels and concepts may indeed militate against the framing of events in particular ways. Such a denial of recognition may also (perhaps more plausibly) be perceived by working class students as yet another of the myriad 'hidden injuries of class' (Sennett and Cobb, 1972) and as a possible reminder that education is not for them.

It is with this kind of erasure in mind that we turn our attention in this chapter to the under-researched issue of class in ELT textbooks. We take the view that the concept of class, and specifically that of the working class, remains important, not only heuristically in terms of making sense of the world, but also in terms of an objective social reality. The chapter seeks to explore this issue with regard to UK-produced ELT textbooks, given that they are likely to remain, despite all the criticisms that have been levelled against them, key artefacts in language classrooms around the world. Elsewhere in our work (Block, 2010; Gray, 2010a, 2010b, 2012) we have been particularly critical of commercially produced ELT materials, arguing that their overwhelming focus on consumerism and the lifestyles of a cosmopolitan middle class amount to little more than a celebration of neoliberal ideology. Here we look at a sample of textbooks from the 1970s to the present, with an eye to their treatment of issues related specifically to representation of the working class. We begin with an account of the supposed demise of the working class as a way into a more theoretical discussion of class itself. This is followed by an account of the methodology we adopted and the resulting analysis. The chapter concludes with a discussion of what we see as the implications for materials development in the future.

The supposed demise of the working class

To mark the birth of the world's seven-billionth person in 2011, *National Geographic* magazine produced a profile of the world's 'most typical person',[1] something which was subsequently much commented on in the media. Problematic though such averaged-out pictures are, the profile does serve to cast some light on class when seen from a global perspective. Thus we are told that the world's most typical person is male, he is 28 years old, and he earns less than $12,000 a year. He has a mobile phone, but, in common with 75 per cent of humanity, he does not have a bank account. He is also a member of the world's largest ethnic group – Han Chinese. Some of the details of his life and that of his female counterpart have been captured more concretely and in greater detail by Ching Kwan Lee (2007) in her ethnographic study of contemporary Chinese workers. The accounts of their working conditions which she reproduces are a powerful reminder of the hidden realities of many workers' lives – as this Shenzhen textile worker's testimony shows:

> There is no fixed work schedule. A twelve-hour day is minimum. With rush orders, we have to work continuously for thirty hours or more. Day and night [...] the longest shift we had worked non-stop lasted forty hours [...] It's very exhausting because we have to stand all the time, to straighten the denim cloth by pulling. Our legs are always hurting. There is no place to sit on the shop floor. The machines do not stop during our lunch breaks. Three workers in a group will just take turns eating, one at a time [...] The shop floor is filled with black dust. Our bodies become black working day and night indoors. When I get off from work and spit, it's all black.
>
> (Ching Kwan Lee, 2007: 235)

This worker, living in what is today known as 'the developing world', with no money in the bank and only his or her labour to sell, is someone Karl Marx and Friedrich Engels would have had no trouble in recognizing (Lanchester, 2012). We only have to compare this account with Engels' description of textile workers' lives in mid-19th-century Leicester for the similarities to become clear:

> The winders, like the threaders, have no specified working time, being called upon whenever the spools on a frame are empty, and are liable, since the weavers work at night, to be required at any time in the factory or workroom [...] The work is very bad for the eyes [...] inflammations of the eye, pain, tears, and momentary uncertainty of vision during the act of threading are engendered [...] The work of the weavers themselves is very difficult, as the frames have constantly been made wider, until those now in use are almost all worked by three men in turn, each working eight hours, and the frame being kept in use the whole twenty-four. Hence it is that winders and

threaders are so often called upon during the night, and the frame being kept in use the whole twenty-four.

(Engels, 1993 [1845]: 199–200)[2]

And yet the Chinese textile worker is a member of a class – the working class – whose obituary has been written and rewritten repeatedly since (at the very least) the 1970s. In fact, the very concept of class (explored below) is one that has taken a severe battering from a number of perspectives in both lay and academic settings.

In the context of British politics in the 1980s, Margaret Thatcher (1987) famously stated in an interview for the magazine *Woman's Own* that society itself did not exist, arguing that there were 'only individual men and women and [...] families'. Some ten years later, then Prime Minister Tony Blair argued the case for Britain becoming a meritocracy, which meant 'opening up economy and society to merit and talent [in order to] recognise talent in all its forms [...and] allow [...] people's innate ability to shine through' (Blair, 2001, cited in Platt, 2011: 37). Still more recently, in 2010, Prime Minister David Cameron introduced the somewhat amorphous notion of the 'Big Society', which seemed to mean that individuals should take responsibility for and carry out many of the activities for which governments had previously been responsible, such as setting up schools and running public libraries. What all of these neoliberal assertions and policy statements have in common (apart from the fact that they are all taken from British politics) is a declaration of war against collectives and a glorification of the individual as *the* historical actor in modern society.

At the same time, a number of scholars on the left also took the view that changes brought about by technological innovation in the late 20th century (e.g., the rise of the Internet, digital technology, etc.) meant that thinking about society in terms of class (or at least in terms of class alone) was perhaps outdated. Thus, for example, André Gorz's *Farewell to the Working Class: An Essay on Post-Industrial Socialism* (1982) argued that a society based on mass unemployment as a consequence of increased automation in the production process was coming into being, which (supposedly) presaged the end of the traditional working class. Gorz (1982: 67) argued that capitalist development was producing a 'non-class of non-workers' and that it was necessary to look to the feminist and ecology movements as the new collective drivers of social change. This was held to be necessary as the members of the hypothesized emerging non-class would – it was claimed – have no sense of themselves as a collective, given that they would alternate between long-term unemployment and short-term flexible contracts. Over a decade later, Manuel Castells (1996) posited the rise of the 'network society', in which technology was held to have produced a kind of structural change which in effect rendered previous class perspectives on society outdated. While Castells (2000: 18) was at pains to point out that such a reconfiguration of society 'does not preclude exploitation, social differentiation and social resistance', he argued that this view meant that 'production-based, social classes, as constituted, and enacted in the Industrial Age, cease to exist in the network society'. Alain Touraine (2007), in a discussion of globalization and its effects on the organization of post-industrial societies, has argued along similar lines.

These perspectives have been critiqued as being misguided. For example, Kevin Doogan (2009) has argued persuasively that new technologies have not significantly brought about mass unemployment; rather, they have served to create different kinds of jobs. Furthermore, he points out that the concept of the network society has little to say to nursing, road sweeping, and other forms of employment that do not revolve around the generation, processing, and dissemination of digital information. At the same time, although Doogan argues that the extent of out-sourcing of jobs to the developing world has been exaggerated, there is no doubt that one feature of contemporary capitalism is the way in which whole swathes of the developing world *are* increasingly involved in the manufacture of goods for the global market. John Lanchester (2012: 8) provides the following example, which resonates strikingly with that of Ching Kwan Lee (2007):

> Take as a case study of this process the world's most valuable company, which at the moment is Apple. Apple's last quarter was the most profitable of any company in history: it made $13 billion in profits on $46 billion in sales. Its bestselling products are made at factories owned by the Chinese company Foxconn [...] The company's starting pay is $2 an hour, the workers live in dormitories of six or eight beds for which they are charged rent of $16 a month, their factory in Chengdu, where the iPad is made, runs 24 hours a day, employs 120,000 people [...] and isn't even Foxconn's biggest plant: that's in Shenzhen and employs 230,000 people, who work 12 hours a day, six days a week.

This perspective is notably at odds with the picture of Shenzhen painted in *New Headway Pre-Intermediate* (Soars and Soars, 2000), where the emphasis is firmly on change and the exciting nature of this. In a reading entitled 'Megalopolis', students are told that:

> The town of Shenzhen, just forty kilometres north of Hong Kong, is the world's biggest building site [...] China is changing. It is no longer a country where absolutely everything is owned and controlled by the state. Developers are welcome. As Deng Xioping, the Chinese leader, said in 1992, 'To get rich is glorious'. The old China of bicycles and Little Red Books is disappearing. A world of mobile phones and capitalism is arriving.
>
> (Soars and Soars, 2000: 75)

This is followed by the assertion that the 'Chinese people seem to welcome dramatic change' and that they 'don't worry about losing traditional ways of life' (p.75). The piece ends with the assessment that this Chinese city of the future will be 'the greatest city on earth. It won't be beautiful, but its power, energy, and wealth will be felt in all corners of the world' (p.75). Despite being accompanied by two pictures of building work in which manual labourers are clearly visible, there are no references in the text to the conditions under which such workers live, nor are students invited to consider these. Instead, they are asked to answer questions which direct their attention onto the city itself ('What are some of the statistics about Shenzhen that make it a remarkable place?', p.74), and onto 'the people' as consumers, rather than as workers ('How are the people changing? Why do they want to own a car?', p.74). The issues raised by this type of representation are precisely those we explore later in this chapter.

To recap, then, on the position we are outlining: we argue that the concept of the working class remains integral to capitalism, and in line with Anthony Giddens (1973) we take the view that capitalist society is perforce a class society – however great the attempt has been at eliding the significance of class or ignoring its reality. Such an acknowledgement, however, does not imply that what class means is self-evident. For this reason, before beginning our analysis of the textbooks, we turn briefly in the next section to class itself – given that that is an inherently problematic concept to pin down.

What is class?

Marx is often looked to as the starting point for any discussion of class, although, as has been noted by numerous authors (e.g., Wright, 1985),

Marx never actually provided a clear-cut definition of class. Indeed, for more clearly articulated definitions, we must turn to Marxist scholars such as Vladimir Lenin, who in his adaptation of Marxism to Russian realities of the early 20th century wrote:

> Classes are large groups of people which differ from each other by the place they occupy in a historically determined system of social production, by their relation (in most cases fixed and formulated in law) to the means of production, by their role in the social organization of labour and, consequently, by the dimensions and method of acquiring the share of social wealth of which they dispose. Classes are groups of people one of which can appropriate the labour of another owing to the different places they occupy in a definitive system of social economy.
>
> (Lenin, 1947 [1919]: 492)

It is worth noting that in this definition, and indeed in Marxist scholarship in general, class is framed not as an attribute of people or as a static position in stratified societies, but as a social relation, as emergent in the social world of interactions with others and the collective associations that people engage with, all arising out of the economic order in societies.

A range of more recent scholars has noted that any conceptualization of the construct must be consonant with the increasing complexification of societies since Marx's death in 1883. Similarly to Marx, Max Weber wrote about an economic order in industrialized societies, and about how class and class position are relational. However, Weber's notion of what constituted this economic order differed sharply from Marx's: while Marx saw the economic order in terms of the relationships between capital and labour power, leading to the exploitation of the latter by the former, Weber viewed the economic order as a market in which stratification and inequality arose in the exchange of assets by individuals with unequal access to and possession of these assets. For Weber, ' "[c]lass situation" and "class" refer only to the same (or similar) interests which an individual shares with others', which include 'the various controls over consumer goods, means of production, assets, resources and skills which constitute a particular class situation' (Weber, 1968: 302). His view of class was therefore not just about production, but also about economic exchange occurring after production (i.e., consumption).

Writing about what class had become in the wealthy West by the end of the 20th century, Pierre Bourdieu took the following view:

class or class fraction is defined not only by its position in the relations of production, as identified through indices such as occupation,
income, or even educational level, but also by a certain sex-ratio,
a certain distribution in geographical space (which is never socially
neutral) and by a whole set of subsidiary characteristics which may
function, in the form of tacit requirements, as real principles of selection or exclusion without ever being formally stated (this is the case
with ethnic origin and sex). A number of official criteria: for example, the requiring of a given diploma can be a way of demanding a
particular social origin.

(Bourdieu, 1984: 102)

In this mix, there are capitals beyond economic capital. On the one
hand, there is cultural capital, the possession of legitimized knowledge
and know-how, which might be transformed creatively and genera-
tively into sub-capitals or derived capitals such as 'educational capital',
'linguistic capital', 'artistic capital', and so on. On the other hand,
there is social capital, seen as the use to which cultural (and economic) capital is put in the form of power derived from particular
social relations which facilitate paths to success in some individuals'
life trajectories. For Bourdieu (1984: 114), these capitals can be quan-
tified and are understood 'as the set of actually usable resources and
powers' people may draw on. Importantly, one sees how capital is distributed differentially across individuals engaging in practices across
a variety of fields, which are domains of social practices constituted
and shaped by particular ways of thinking and acting (e.g., education,
football, cinema, etc.). Here class is framed as a social relation and
as emergent in the day-to-day activities of human beings. It becomes
embodied in the individual, forming a class *habitus*, which is an ever
evolving set of internalized dispositions, formulated out of engagement in situated social practices taking place in fields, and shaped by
institutions as well as larger social structures, such as global economic
forces.

As has been noted elsewhere (Block, 2012a, 2012b, 2014), a perusal
of relatively recent publications about class (e.g., Bennett, Savage, Silva,
Warde, Gayo-Cal, and Wright, 2009; Bottero, 2005; Crompton, 2008;
Savage, 2000) reveals a strong (though by no means exclusive) tendency
to frame the construct in a Bourdieusian manner. Drawing on these
sources, David Block (2012a, 2012b, 2014) has elaborated a list of key
dimensions associated with class as an identity inscription. As the reader
will note, there is conflation here of the Weberian notions of class and
status (Table 2.1).[3]

Table 2.1   Key dimensions of class (Block, 2012b: 194)

Dimension	Gloss
Property	This refers to one's material possessions, such as land, housing, electronic goods, clothing, books, art, and so on.
Wealth	This refers to disposable income/money and patrimony (e.g., what owned property is worth in financial terms).
Occupation	This refers to the kind of work done across a range of job types, such as blue-collar manual labour vs. white-collar knowledge-based labour, or service sector jobs vs. manual jobs, and so on.
Place of residence	This can refer either to the type of neighbourhood one lives in (is it identified as poor, working class, middle class, an area in the process of gentrification, or upper class?) or the type of dwelling (individual house, flat, caravan, etc.).
Education	This refers to the level of schooling attained and the acquired cultural capital one has at any point in time. There is a close link here to Bourdieu's notion of cultural capital.
Social networking	This refers to the often unspoken reality whereby middle class people tend to socialize with middle class people, working class people with working class people, and so on. There is a close link here to Bourdieu's notion of social capital.
Consumption patterns	This might refer to behaviour patterns like buying food at a supermarket that positions itself as 'cost-cutting' vs. buying food at one that sells 'healthy', organic, and expensive products. Or it might refer to buying particular goods (e.g., food, clothing, gadgets) in terms of type and brand.
Symbolic behaviour	This includes how one moves one's body, the clothes one wears, the way one speaks, how one eats, the kinds of pastimes one engages in, etc.
Spatial relations	This refers to living conditions such as physical mobility (does the person frequently travel abroad?) or the spatial conditions in which one lives (size of bedroom, size of dwelling, proximity to other people during a range of day-to-day activities).

Several caveats are in order as regards this table. First, there is the Marxist notion, outlined above, that class must be understood not as an individual characteristic but as a social relation. In addition, class, however it is understood, is intertwined with other identity inscriptions, such as gender, ethnicity, race, nationality, and so on. Indeed, it is one of the challenges of class-based research today to work out exactly how these different identity inscriptions interact with class (e.g., see Bradley, 1996; Burkitt, 2008; Skeggs, 2004). Furthermore, no one of these dimensions ever offers an airtight means of classifying people, especially when viewed relationally, with respect to other dimensions. Thus, wealth might be associated with particular types of employment which require years of formal education leading to specific qualifications *and* with more manual professions requiring few or no educational qualifications.

Methodology

In setting out to explore the issue of working class representation in ELT textbooks we decided to look at a sample of best-selling textbooks produced over four decades, beginning in the 1970s, when the boom in English language teaching may be said to have begun. In this way we felt that we would be able to identify any changes that appeared to have taken place over the period. We chose two textbooks from each decade, both at the intermediate level – where publishers report that sales are highest (Gray, 2010a). In light of the success of the *Headway* series and the influence it has had on ELT publishing since the mid-1980s, when it first appeared (Holliday, 2005), we made the decision to include the first edition of the first *Headway* book and subsequent new editions from the 1990s and 2000s (Table 2.2).

It is also important to state that all these textbooks have their origins in commercial ELT and were designed for young adults and older

Table 2.2 Textbook sample

Textbook	Author(s)	Year of publication/publisher
English in Situations	O'Neill, R.	1970/Oxford University Press
Kernel Lessons Intermediate	O'Neill, R.	1971/Longman
Building Strategies	Abbs, B. and I. Freebairn	1984/Longman
Headway Intermediate	Soars, J and L. Soars	1986/Oxford University Press
New Headway Intermediate	Soars, L. and J. Soars	1996/Oxford University Press
Lifelines Intermediate	Hutchinson, T.	1997/Oxford University Press
New Cutting Edge Intermediate	Cunningham, S. and P. Moor	2005/Pearson Longman
New Headway intermediate	Soars, L. and J. Soars	2009/Oxford University Press

teenagers. In this sector, the aim has traditionally been to provide entertainingly packaged linguistic content, with little in the way of any broader educational remit. *English in Situations* and *Kernel Lessons Intermediate*, the two oldest textbooks being analysed here, originated in Eurocentres, a commercial language teaching organization whose website (http://www.eurocentres.com) states that it was founded on the idea that 'learning a language should be a fun, enriching and personal experience and at the same time, increase awareness and understanding between cultures'.

Our approach was similar to that adopted in other textbook analysis studies (Azimova and Johnston, 2012; Gray, 2010b; Sleeter and Grant, 2011) – namely an initial quantitatively oriented content analysis followed by a more qualitative examination of the data. Given that our earlier studies (referred to above) suggested an increasingly pervasive focus on the working lives and lifestyles of the cosmopolitan middle class, we approached the sample with an initial focus on employment, but guided by the dimensions of class listed in Table 2.1. Our analysis was conducted with the following questions in mind:

- Are there any representations of characters who are working class in terms of their employment, or references to working class employment in these textbooks?
- If so, what form do these representations/references take?
- Is there any treatment of themes that can be related to working class experience in these textbooks?
- If so, what form does this treatment take?

While making decisions about class based on employment is clearly problematic (as Table 2.1 suggests), it can be a useful starting point for analysis. A number of frameworks of varying complexity exist for the assignation of class based on occupation – for example, the UK National Readership Survey (NRS; http://www.nrs.co.uk), which is widely used in market research, makes use of six broad classes: A (upper middle class, defined on the NRS website as 'higher managerial, administrative and professional'); B (middle class, defined as 'intermediate managerial, administrative and professional'); C1 (lower middle class, defined as 'supervisory, clerical and junior managerial, administrative and professional'); C2 (skilled working class, defined as 'skilled manual workers'); D (working class, defined as 'semi-skilled and unskilled manual workers'); and E (a catch-all category, defined as 'state pensioners, casual and lowest-grade workers, unemployed with state benefits only'). In this taxonomy, groups C2 to E are considered working class. Other taxonomies, such as the UK government's National Statistics Socio-Economic Classification (NS-SEC), make use of slightly more categories. However, one of the problems with such approaches is that many forms of lower paid, highly routinized clerical occupations are categorized as falling within the broad middle class occupation grouping, despite the fact that, as Anthony Heath and Nicky Britten (1984: 481) argue, such workers (who are often women) occupy a 'fundamentally proletarian market position'. For this reason we also categorized such clerical workers as working class, unless the representation was marked in some way as indicating a middle class lifestyle.

We began by recording all instances (including artwork) in which it was made clear that a character was working class (e.g., someone being clearly identified as a factory worker, a cleaner, a clerical worker, etc.), along with any mention of employment that could be deemed working class (e.g., true/false statements related to a reading, such as 'The tractor driver earns less than the other man does' (O'Neill, 1971: 45)). We also recorded any reading or listening activity that dealt with a theme that could be said to index working class experience (e.g., accounts of fighting for better conditions at work, education and life chances, discrimination based on class, etc.). By way of example, the following reference was recorded as a clear representation of a working class character:

> Harry Evans is a young factory-worker. Every evening at 5 o'clock exactly the same thing happens. A bell rings at 5. The men stop work, turn off their machines, run out, put their overcoats on, and hurry home.
>
> (O'Neill, 1970: 28)

However, the following reference was deemed not to suggest a working class character in such a clear manner and was not counted:

> Jane Martin is very athletic. She is a good skier and tennis-player and is also good at golf. She has a job as a typist and she is at work now.
>
> [...]
>
> It is a cold winter day. Jane is in Norway and she has her skis on.
>
> (O'Neill, 1970: 2)

While the job of 'typist' could be indicative of lower-paid routine employment and while any individual typist might be deemed working class in terms of the dimensions listed in Table 2.1, when we consider the profile in the light of these, Jane Martin is arguably not working class. Rather, the sporting activities she engages in are indexical of middle class leisure activities and consumption patterns – as all three sports require considerable disposable income, in terms of kit, probable club membership fees, and the money needed for travel.[4] Following Nigora Azimova and Bill Johnston's (2012) approach, we noted the number of pages in which such references occurred and then compared that with the total number of pages in the textbook. This was followed by the qualitative analysis, in which we considered the actual nature of the representation, in terms of language used, authorial point of view, and image composition (if artwork was included).

Textbook analysis

As can be seen in Table 2.3, there is a progressive decline in the representation of working class characters, mentions of working class employment, and themes relating to working class experience in these

Table 2.3 Occurrences of working class representation

Textbook	Number of pages	Number of pages with representations of/ references to working class characters/ employment; themes relating to working class experience	Number of pages with representations as percentage of the total number of pages
English in Situations	200	83	41.5%
Kernel Lessons Intermediate	151	87	57.6%
Building Strategies	144	29	20.1%
Headway Intermediate	120	27	22.5%
New Headway Intermediate	159	29	18.2%
Lifelines Intermediate	144	18	12.5%
New Cutting Edge Intermediate	175	24	13.7%
New Headway Intermediate	159	23	14.4%

textbooks. The two textbooks from the 1970s stand out in terms of quantity of representations, with the percentage for *Kernel Lessons Intermediate* showing that over half the pages contained some form of reference to the working class.

It is perhaps no accident that this decline parallels the supposed demise of the working class in this period, as textbooks came to reflect the embourgeoisement of society proclaimed by the mainstream media and successive neoliberal governments, a process which, it must be noted, was accompanied by the concomitant stigmatization of the working class (Jones, 2011) – paradoxical though this was, given its hypothesized exit from the world stage. As has been noted elsewhere (Gray, 2010a), as textbooks moved from embedding language practice primarily in native speaker/inner circle cultures (e.g., the US, the UK) to embedding it in what might be understood to be a global culture of consumerism, the reference point – the *society* of English speakers – shifted from nation-states with their corresponding class systems to a floating global culture in which the main players represented are middle class and wealthy people.

However, the figures from the content analysis on their own serve to shed little light on the specific nature of the representational practices being deployed in these materials. If meanings are to be drawn from these figures, it is necessary to look more closely at the textbooks themselves. Marked working class characters are a recurring element in *English in Situations* and *Kernel Lessons Intermediate*. Thus, situations and events in the lives of lorry driver Bill Parks, factory workers Harry Evans, Frank Martin, and Bill Rawlings, and office worker Julia Frost feature repeatedly throughout as the contexts for the introduction of new language. Furthermore, incidental references to working class characters, employment, or activity also feature frequently in the practice drills or grammar explanations which follow these. For example, *Kernel Lessons Intermediate* introduces 'some, any, a few, a little' as follows: in the initial 'situation stage' the students focus on a number of line drawings, one of which shows four men standing outside a closed factory gate. A clock above the gate shows that it is four o'clock. One of men is carrying a placard that reads 'FEWER HOURS MORE MONEY'. Three are wearing cloth caps which (given that this is 1971) can be read as signifiers of their working class status. A poster attached to the factory wall states 'Manchester United vs. Leeds Kick Off 3.30' – so we can deduce that the match is currently in progress. In the foreground there are two policemen, one of whom appears to be looking at the clock (possibly thinking about the match he is missing). Students are asked to focus on the picture and then to form questions based on the following cues:

(a) When/strike?
(b) Where/policemen and strikers?
(c) What day?
(d) What/most of the men?
(e) Reporters there?

(O'Neill, 1971: 26)

The answers are found in a short reading on the opposite page. In the grammar summary, several pages later, students are informed: '*a few* means a small number, and we use it with Unit words – a few policemen/ a few people/ a few strikers' (O'Neill, 1971: 31). However, it should be noted that at no stage are students told what the strike is about, nor is the word 'picket' taught (although this is clearly implied in the line drawing). In addition, the police presence at the factory is not commented on in any way.[5] This approach is typical of both textbooks in the sense that, while working class characters and phenomena such as a factory workers' strike *are* represented, there is no attempt to encourage students to think or talk seriously about the issues raised – for example, why workers go on strike, why the strikers are being policed, and so on. In part this can be attributed to the fact that both textbooks pre-date the communicative revolution, and classroom talk, where it occurred, tended to be very controlled and focused on accurate reproduction of grammatical structures. It is also, we would suggest, related to the 'fun' imperative so central to commercial language teaching referred to above (Anderson, 2002), whereby engagement with serious content is held in check for fear of alienating fee-paying students whose entertainment needs have to be catered for. Elsewhere in both textbooks the lives of working people are frequently shown to be difficult, whether in terms of poor working conditions or limited life chances or constrained by regimes of time-keeping in the workplace. But again the issues raised are ignored, as the following example shows:

> Bill Rawlings thinks he was born unlucky. He works in a factory and hates it. 'It's very boring work!' he often says. The air in the factory is very dirty. 'You've never breathed such dirty air!' he told his wife yesterday. Last year he and his wife went to the seaside and it rained

every day. 'What terrible weather!' he said. 'Nobody has such terrible luck as I do!' Bill often says to himself.

(O'Neill, 1970: 134)

While the assessment of the working conditions provided by the narrative voice ('The air in the factory is very dirty') coincides with that of Bill (thereby endorsing his point of view for the reader), the accompanying questions simply ask students to retrieve information from the text (e.g., 'What is the air like and what did he tell his wife about it?', p.134). There is no invitation to students to consider what action Bill might take – such as raising the issue at a union meeting. Furthermore, the somewhat banal transition into Bill's holiday tribulations serves to undermine the very different type of problem he encounters in the workplace.

Problems associated with work also feature in the two textbooks from the 1980s. As Table 2.3 shows, the mention of working class characters, along with working class employment and experience, decreases sharply in this decade and, as we shall see, the treatment overall is also somewhat different. The globally successful *Strategies* series, as Shelagh Rixon and Richard Smith (2012) point out, was written by a team who had begun their careers producing materials for migrants to the UK, many of whom were employed as factory workers. Although *Building Strategies* was not written for migrants, something of its authors' earlier seriousness with regard to the world of work is evident throughout the textbook – in the sense that it is based on the lives (and in particular the working lives) of a group of realistically drawn (albeit middle class) characters (Gray, 2010a). In fact, none of the central characters is working class – although 50-something Peggy Cooper works as a supermarket cashier. However, when we look at her profile in terms of the dimensions listed in Table 2.1, Peggy is clearly middle class. She is married to Jack, who, while a member of the trade union, is also the production manager in an electrical components factory, Western Aeronautics. Photographs of dinner parties in the Coopers' house show a typical middle class interior of the period, with soft lighting, a candlelit table, and crystal wine glasses. We also discover from a letter written by Peggy to her friend Stella that as children they had both holidayed in the south of France – hardly a destination for working class British tourists in the immediate post-war period when Peggy would have been young.[6]

All references to the working class are in fact incidental – working class characters appear as anonymous participants in service encounters or as minor characters whose occupations are mentioned only in passing. Reference *is* made to a wage dispute at the factory where Jack and Rod (another central character) work, but this is seen in terms of its impact on Jack. Peggy's letter to Stella introduces the dispute as follows:

> Unfortunately, things aren't going too well at Western. There's a lot of trouble over wage claims and Jack thinks there's probably going to be a strike. Jack has mixed feelings about the situation, but between you and me, I think he's getting tired of it all. In fact he's thinking of putting in an application to join the project which Western are setting up on the Continent.
>
> (Abbs and Freebairn, 1984: 78)

Students are given no indication as to the nature of the wage claim or why Jack has mixed feelings. However, the implication is that it is the dispute rather than Western Aeronautics that he is tiring of, given his thoughts about relocating to France without leaving the company. In fact, Jack subsequently applies for the job, and he and Peggy relocate to France in what is presented as a good career move (the company's rent-free accommodation means an increase in real earnings). Because most of what happens in *Building Strategies* is seen though the eyes of its central characters, the world that emerges on its pages is a predominantly middle class one. For all its virtues (e.g., non-sexist representation of women), this textbook is part of a trend in which a working class point of view on the world is erased and engagement in activities such as striking are seen as a nuisance, and the possibility that action taken against management in a pay dispute might be justified is not considered.

The 1986 edition of *Headway Intermediate* might be said to continue this trend, in that working class characters tend to feature only in passing, rather than being the centre of attention – although an interview with a postman about why he likes his job is a notable exception. That said, there is an element in this textbook (the first of the series to be published) that makes it different from subsequent editions and indeed the series as a whole – namely a recurring seriousness of tone. In a unit on describing people and places, students are asked to discuss why different groups of people come together. The groups include a trade union, a football crowd, and freemasons, among others. Students are then asked: 'To how many of these groups can you attach a certain social class?' (Soars and Soars, 1986: 35). The example answer reads: 'People who belong to trade unions are traditionally working class, but many of them are also middle class' (p.35). The final stage of the speaking activity asks 'How much of a class system is there in your country? How does it show itself? Is there an aristocracy?' (p.35). Given the way in which the *Headway* series would develop into a global brand and the values of consumerism and individualism it would come to celebrate (Gray, 2010a, 2010b, 2012), it is notable how different this first textbook is (written while its authors were still classroom teachers) in explicitly raising the issue of class. In a subsequent unit the impact of computers on work is addressed and students listen to an interview with a female representative of the Low Pay Unit (http://www.lowpayunit. org.uk), which is described accurately in the rubric as 'a voluntary organization which monitors the effects of government policy and union action on the worst-paid members of the work force' (Soars and Soars, 1986: 76). The interviewee explains that developments in new technology mean that increasingly more people will be able to work from home and that, while there are positive aspects of this, there are also potential downsides in the form of lower wages, job insecurity, and poorer working conditions. The following extracts are noteworthy for several reasons – in the first place there is the interviewee's obvious distrust of employers seeking to cut corners to increase profits, and the implied value for workers of trade unions; and second, neither the interviewer nor any of the activities the students are asked to do seeks to challenge the arguments made by the speaker. The extracts are also consonant with what has been described as the 'feminization' of textbook content in the 1980s (Gray, 2010a) – namely the way in which content from this period onwards sought to represent women as active members of the workforce (rather than as housewives, as was often the case in the 1970s), and in non-sexist terms (although that is not an issue here):

[…] there are three million women in Britain whose jobs involve processing information, and many employers would like to have them out of the way at home, with none of the protection they would get if they were in an office.

These type of arrangements do suit a lot of women. But what we're concerned about is the question of […] well […] exploitation. […] it would be very easy for an employer to exploit these people further by keeping them beyond the protection of the health and safety laws, and of course beyond any possible contacts with trade unions.

(Soars and Soars, 1986: 118–9)

This kind of content is altogether different from that encountered in *English in Situations* and *Kernel Lessons Intermediate* – the Low Pay Unit is an actual body, and issues addressed in the interview are both serious *and* seriously addressed. That said, the follow-up activity leads students away from the issues raised in the interview into a more general discussion about the advantages and disadvantages of working from home, whether or not students would like to work in this way, and the possibilities of shopping and doctor consultation by computer. Given what is known about the way in which UK-produced textbooks developed over the following decades, it is no surprise that the discussion of class and the interview with the representative of the Low Pay Unit were removed from all subsequent editions of the book.

Employment continued to be a theme in the series as our analysis of *New Headway Intermediate* (1996 edition) shows, although the focus here shifts noticeably towards a view of work as a source of great personal satisfaction in the lives of highly agentive individuals who are driven by passion and for whom choice with regard to employment is unproblematically exercised. In a unit dedicated to the theme of work, three young people from privileged backgrounds, and against their parents' wishes, choose jobs more usually associated with the working class. Thus, a judge's daughter becomes a nanny, the son of a landowning family opts to become a cook, while an Oxford student disappoints his parents (one a surveyor, the other an interior designer) by becoming a gardener. These choices are presented favourably – photographs of all three characters show them at work, smiling at the viewer, and each first-person account of their decision to pursue non-traditional employment (for them) is accompanied by a parent's perspective in which belated approval is given. These individualists are far removed from those working class characters found in *English in Situations*, many of whom are presented as constrained by their class position. The following comment resonates with what many of the informants in Sennett and Cobb's (1972) *Hidden Injuries of Class* say about their lives:

> Bill Rawlings was feeling very sorry for himself. 'I'm never going to have any money. I'm going to be a factory worker for the rest of my life,' he said to himself.
>
> (O'Neill, 1970: 144)

In fact, the abovementioned *New Headway Intermediate* (1996 edition) characters can be seen as entrepreneurs, both in the original sense of 'undertaker of a project' (Holborow, 2012), in this case the project of the self (Giddens, 1991), in which they pursue their individual dreams in the face of parental disapprobation, but also in a more neoliberal, innovative, risk-taking, and wealth-generating sense – the cook, students are informed, has already opened his own restaurant, and the gardener's family entertain hopes he may become a millionaire. In the role play which follows, students are encouraged to engage with these issues by assuming the roles of parents and children. Those playing the children are tasked as follows:

> A and B are your parents. They want you to become a lawyer or doctor, but you have different ideas! You want to be one of the following (or choose one of your own):
>
> a dancer a musician a poet an explorer a model a jockey an astronaut.
>
> (Soars and Soars, 1996: 72)

Actual working class characters feature only in passing, and then almost invariably as unnamed participants in service encounters. This is also the case for *Lifelines Intermediate*, *New Cutting Edge Intermediate*, and the 2009 edition of *New Headway Intermediate*. Where a traditionally working class job is focused on, as in *New Cutting Edge Intermediate*, agency and choice are shown to be central. Thus students listen to 26-year-old Clare Davis describe how she gave up her job as a secondary-school teacher to retrain as a plumber – 'I was getting really fed up [...] It just wasn't the right job for me' (Cunningham and Moor, 2005: 165). As earlier analysis has shown (Gray, 2010b), this approach to work, in which agency and personal choice are foregrounded, is accompanied by an increasing focus on consumerism. As Zygmunt Bauman (2007: 61) has pointed out, '[t]he individual member of the society of consumers is defined, first and foremost, as *homo eligens*' – and choice extends not only to what to buy but also to which job to choose freely or to abandon unproblematically. As Clare says with regard to her decision to try plumbing: 'If I don't enjoy it, I'll try something else' (Cunningham and Moor, 2005: 53).

Overall the analysis of these textbooks shows the progressive decline in the representation of working class characters and the erasure of a very limited working class perspective on life. For all the recurrence of characters such as Harry Evans and Bill Rawlings in *English in Situations* and *Kernel Lessons Intermediate* there is little in the way of serious engagement of issues surrounding class. Paradoxically the most serious treatment of class is found in the first edition of *Headway Intermediate* – a textbook in which the actual number of working class characters is shown to be on the decline. But even here, although the listening on low-paid home workers clearly lays out the issue in terms of exploitation, the actual activities that students are asked to do fail to confront this. Overall, these findings resonate with other studies of representations of class in mainstream textbooks – namely, that class receives little in the way of serious treatment (Sleeter and Grant, 2011). In the next section we speculate on how materials might change in this respect.

Discussion

To begin to imagine an alternative approach to working class representation it is useful to look at how this has been done in different settings in the past and in the present. A series of textbooks entitled *English for You*, produced in East Germany in the late 1960s and early 1970s, provides, as might be expected, an altogether different perspective on working class experience. As with the pre-*Headway* textbooks analysed here, students are introduced to a set of characters whose lives they become increasingly familiar with. The main characters in *English for You 1* (Gräf, Hoffmann, and Klein, 1968) are Peggy Miller, a secretary and part-time journalist for the *Morning Star*, the British Communist daily newspaper, and her friend Tom Young, a factory worker. Much of what happens in the textbook is related to their lives as workers and committed Communists. For example, in one unit Tom, in his role as shop steward, threatens the boss with calling a union meeting if Peggy, who has just started working in the factory, is not paid the agreed union rate. What is interesting about this material is that students are not asked to discuss such issues or relate them to their own lives or experience of work – workplace exploitation and industrial action are represented as exclusively phenomena of the capitalist West and any problems Eastern Bloc workers might have are not addressed. The textbook simply provides an officially endorsed perspective on international politics and British working class life – although the focus is consistently on the working class.

A somewhat different approach is found in Elsa Auerbach and Nina Wallerstein's *Problem-Posing at Work: English for Action* (2004). This material is aimed at immigrants in North America and draws on the Freirean notion of 'conscientização', sometimes translated as 'critical consciousness', whereby, as the promotional material for the book explains, students 'share and analyze their experiences, to acquire the language, skills, and information necessary for greater power over their circumstances, and to strategize together for changes'. Thus students read case histories of real workers and their documented battles and successes with exploitative employers, are given information about their legal rights, and are provided with materials on how concepts such as globalization have consequences in their daily lives. Unlike the East German material, students are repeatedly asked to reflect on real world social issues, as the following extract, entitled 'Language and power', shows:

The way we communicate with people depends on our relationships with those people. In some situations, we have more power than other people. In other situations, other people have more power than we do. Most people have more power than others in some situations and less power than others in some situations.

You can often tell who has power in a situation by the way people use language. Answer these questions about your workplace:

- Who speaks loudly? Who speaks softly?
- Who gives orders or tells others what to do? Who follows orders?
- Who speaks a lot? Who is silent?
- Who asks questions? What kinds of questions? Who answers questions?
- Who calls people by their first names? Who uses titles like Mr. or Ms.?
- Who apologizes?
- Who starts conversations?
- Who interrupts?

What do your answers show about who has power?

Now discuss the same questions about your home, your class, a medical clinic, or other places. How does language use show power relations in these situations?

(Auerbach and Wallerstein, 2004: 78)

Clearly such an exclusive focus on work is not suitable for students in all situations. Auerbach and Wallerstein's book is based in two nation-states (the US and Canada) and therefore can deal more directly with the ins and outs of the North American class systems than the books analysed here, which have global pretensions. However, we take the view that producers of ELT textbooks (of whatever kind) have much to learn from this kind of material. As English has become ever more globally disseminated, one feature of contemporary UK-produced textbooks for the global market is the way in which they are increasingly peopled by spectacularly successful middle class cosmopolitans (Gray, 2010a) – something which, as we have seen, is accompanied by the near total erasure of the global working class. This editing out of class is problematic in our view and cannot be seen as simply a textbook publishing phenomenon. Rather, it needs to be understood as part of a more general and profoundly ideological attempt at reconfiguring reality in such a way that the concept of class is seen as being redundant. Earlier we referred in passing to the UK government's National Statistics Socio-Economic Classification taxonomy – Owen Jones (2011: 98) explains how this title was introduced (to the surprise of the sociologist John Goldthorpe, on whose research it was based) to replace the existing Social Class based on Occupation classification as part of 'New Labour's dogged determination to scrub class from the country's vocabulary'. Class is a problematic term because it entails thinking about society in terms of structural inequality and economic stratification – notions which sit uneasily with the neoliberal mantra that 'we're all middle class now', an assertion which allows poverty to be explained by individual fecklessness or lack of aspiration.[7] While textbooks of the kind under investigation here have been and continue to be consumed in the private sector globally where the global middle class receive language skills training, they are also used in many state education systems around the world, partly because they emanate from 'the centre' where English is spoken as a native language and partly because they carry the imprimatur of prestigious publishing houses. In such settings, where there is an educational agenda, students surely deserve better. The erasure of the working class from ELT textbooks can be seen both as representative of a failure to educate and as a betrayal of working class language learners.

Notes

1. This is available at http://ngm.nationalgeographic.com/7-billion.
2. Similar points are made by Ching Kwan Lee (2007) and Hunt (2009).
3. There is obviously a debate to be had about this conflation. However, space does not allow us to explore this here. See Block (2014).
4. And, as Bourdieu noted, the economic barriers to the practice of sports such as skiing and tennis are just part of the story. There are also social barriers, 'such as family tradition and early training, or obligatory manner (of dress and behaviour), and socializing techniques, which keep these sports closed to the working class [. . .]' (Bourdieu (1984: 217)).
5. It should be noted that textbook writers can suggest alternative approaches to the exploitation of materials in the teachers' book which generally

accompanies the students' book. However, none of the teachers' books to which we've had access suggests alternatives of the kind mentioned here.

6. It is possible that the authors were trying to convey something of the complexity of class in the UK in the wake of the significant, though by no means overwhelming, social mobility which occurred in post-World War II Britain.

7. Indeed, those who attempt to introduce class into discussions of contemporary societies are all too often accused of 'practising class warfare', usually framed as an old-fashioned and outdated way of viewing the world. This is an interesting reversal of logic when one considers how over the past 30 years we have seen the emergence of a new 'transnational capitalist class' (Carroll, 2010), composed of individuals who both think and act globally and who, in effect, have won the latest round of class warfare, Thus, these individuals have increased their income far more than ordinary middle and working class individuals while claiming that the very opposite has been going on, that the past 30 years have been a bonanza for everyone. By 2006, how many people in Ireland and the southern European countries thought that they had finally managed to lift themselves to *quasi* northern European standards of living, only for 2007 to arrive, with the effects and consequences that we have all witnessed?

References

Abbs, B. and Freebairn, I. (1984). *Building strategies*. Harlow: Longman.

Anderson, C. (2002). Deconstructing teaching English to speakers of other languages: Problematising a professional discourse. Unpublished PhD thesis, Canterbury Christ Church University College.

Anyon, J. (1985). Workers, labor and economic history, and textbook content. In M.W. Apple and L. Weis (Eds.), *Ideology and practice in schooling* (pp. 37–60). Philadelphia: Temple University Press.

Auerbach, E. and Wallerstein, N. (2004). *Problem-posing at work: English for action*. Edmonton: Grass Roots Press.

Azimova, N. and Johnston, B. (2012). Invisibility and ownership of language: Problems of representation in Russian language textbooks. *The Modern Language Journal*, 96, 337–349.

Bauman, Z. (2007). *Consuming life*. Cambridge: Polity Press.

Bennett, T., Savage, M., Silva, E., Warde, A., Gayo-Cal, M. and Wright, D. (2009). *Culture, class, distinction*. London: Routledge.

Blair, T. (2001). The government's agenda for the future. *Speech*, 8 February 2001.

Block, D. (2010). Globalisation and language teaching. In N. Coupland (Ed.), *Handbook of language and globalisation* (pp. 287–304). Oxford: Blackwell.

Block, D. (2012a). Economising globalisation and identity in applied linguistics in neoliberal times. In D. Block, J. Gray, and M. Holborow (Eds.), *Neoliberalism and applied linguistics* (pp. 56–85). London: Routledge.

Block, D. (2012b). Class and SLA: Making connections. *Language Teaching Research*, 16, 188–205.

Block, D. (2014). *Social class in applied linguistics*. London: Routledge.

Bottero, W. (2005). *Stratification: Social division and inequality*. London: Routledge.

Bourdieu, P. (1984). *Distinction*. London: Routledge.

Bradley, H. (1996). *Fractured identities: Changing patterns of inequality*. Cambridge: Polity Press.

Burkitt, I. (2008). *Social selves*. London: Sage.

Carroll, W.K. (2010). *The making of a transnational capitalist class: Corporate power in the 21st century*. London: Zed Books.

Castells, M. (1996). *The rise of the network society*. Oxford: Blackwell.

Castells, M. (2000). Materials for an exploratory theory of the network society. *British Journal of Sociology*, 51, 5–24.

Crompton, R. (2008). *Class and stratification* (3rd ed.). Cambridge: Polity Press.

Cunningham, S. and Moor, P. (2005). *New cutting edge intermediate*. Harlow: Pearson Education.

Doogan, K. (2009). *New capitalism? The transformation of work*. Cambridge: Polity Press.

Engels, F. (1993 [1845]). *The condition of the English working class*. Oxford: Oxford University Press.

Giddens, A. (1973). *The class structure of advanced societies*. London: Hutchinson.

Giddens, A. (1991). *Modernity and self-identity: Self and society in the late modern age*. Cambridge: Polity Press.

Gorz, A. (1982). *Farewell to the working class: An essay on post-industrial socialism*. London: Pluto Press.

Gräf, G., Hoffmann, S., and Klein, F. (1968). *English for you*. Berlin: Volkseigener Verlag.

Gray, J. (2010a). *The construction of English: Culture, consumerism and promotion in the ELT global coursebook*. Basingstoke: Palgrave Macmillan.

Gray, J. (2010b). The branding of English and the culture of the new capitalism: Representations of the world of work in English language textbooks. *Applied Linguistics*, 31, 714–733.

Gray, J. (2012). Neoliberalism, celebrity and 'aspirational content' in English language teaching textbooks for the global market. In D. Block, J. Gray, and M. Holborow (Eds.), *Neoliberalism and applied linguistics* (pp. 86–113). London: Routledge.

Heath, A.F. and Britten, N. (1984). Women's jobs do make a difference: A reply to Goldthorpe. *Sociology*, 18, 475–490.

Holborow, M. (2012). Neoliberal keywords and the contradictions of an ideology. In D. Block, J. Gray, and M. Holborow (Eds.), *Neoliberalism and applied linguistics* (pp. 33–55). London: Routledge.

Holliday, A. (2005). *The struggle to teach English as an international language*. Oxford: Oxford University Press.

Hunt, T. (2009). *The frock-coated communist: The life and times of the original champagne socialist*. London: Penguin.

Hutchinson, T. (1997). *Lifelines intermediate*. Oxford: Oxford University Press.

Jones, O. (2011). *Chavs: The demonization of the working class*. London: Verso.

Lanchester, J. (2012). Marx at 193. *London Review of Books*, 34, 7–10.

Lee, C.K. (2007). *Against the law: Labor protests in China's rustbelt and sunbelt*. Berkeley: University of California Press.

Lenin, V.I. (1947 [1919]). A great beginning. In V.I. Lenin (Ed.), *The essentials of Lenin in two volumes*. London: Lawrence and Wishart. Retrieved from http://www.marxists.org/archive/lenin/works/1919/jun/19.htm

O'Neill, R. (1970). *English in situations*. Oxford: Oxford University Press.

O'Neill, R. (1971). *Kernel lessons intermediate*. London: Longman.

Platt, L. (2011). *Understanding inequalities: Stratification and difference*. Cambridge: Polity Press.

Rixon, S. and Smith, R. (2012). The work of Brian Abbs and Ingrid Freebairn. *ELT Journal*, 66, 383–393.

Savage, M. (2000). *Class analysis and social transformation*. Buckingham: Open University Press.

Sennett, R. and Cobb, J. (1972). *The hidden injuries of class*. New York: Norton.

Skeggs, B. (2004). *Class, self, culture*. London: Routledge.

Sleeter, C. and Grant, C. (2011). Race, class, gender, and disability in current textbooks. In E. F. Provenzo Jr, A.N. Shaver, and M. Bello (Eds.), *The textbook as discourse: Sociocultural dimensions of American schoolbooks* (pp. 183–215). London: Routledge.

Soars, J. and Soars, L. (1986). *Headway intermediate*. Oxford: Oxford University Press.

Soars, L. and Soars, J. (1996). *New Headway intermediate*. Oxford: Oxford University Press.

Soars, J. and Soars, L. (2000). *New Headway pre-intermediate*. Oxford: Oxford University Press.

Soars, L. and Soars, J. (2009). *New Headway intermediate*. Oxford: Oxford University Press.

Thatcher, M. (1987). Interview for *Woman's Own*. Retrieved from http://www.margaretthatcher.org/document/106689

Touraine, A. (2007). *A new paradigm for understanding today's world*. Cambridge: Polity Press.

Weber, M. (1968 [1924]). *Economy and society,* volumes 1 and 2. Berkeley: University of California Press.

Wright, E.O. (1985). *Classes*. London: Verso.

3
Reading Comprehension Questions: The Distribution of Different Types in Global EFL Textbooks

Diana Freeman

Summary

This chapter presents research into the types of questions and tasks that accompany the reading texts in global EFL textbooks. In essence, the rationale for undertaking such an investigation is the crucial role that reading and questions play both in learning per se and in language learning in particular and the still dominant place that textbooks hold in many classrooms. I have identified the different types of comprehension questions and tasks in textbooks and created a taxonomy which consists of two tiers: the first tier represents pre-reading question types and is composed of five different types, and the second tier, which will be the focus of this chapter, represents post-reading comprehension and task question types (comp-qs). The latter, the comp-q types, comprises eight different question types, and these are grouped into three categories: Content, comprising three question types spanning lower to higher order thinking; Language, comprising three question types, not hierarchical; and Affect, two question types, one lower order and the other higher order. I then apply this taxonomy to the questions and tasks accompanying the readings in four series of global intermediate-level EFL textbooks, each of which has undergone at least one revised edition: Cutting Edge *(Cunningham and Moor, 1998, 2005),* English File *(Oxenden and Latham-Koenig, 1999, 2006),* Headway *(Soars and Soars, 1986, 1996, 2003, 2009), and* Inside Out *(Kay and Jones, 2000, 2009). I have considered the distribution of the question types in terms of frequency, which measures how many of each question type is asked; in terms of their occurrence, which measures which question types are present or not in a given reading, regardless of how many times they appear; and in terms of their range, which measures how many different question types there are in any given text, edition or series (that is, how many out of the eight possible comprehension question types are used, irrespective of how many of each type, or which type). The results contain a combination of the expected – the existence of very basic, lower order questions – and the perhaps less anticipated – the proportion of questions that promote higher order thinking and linguistic skills. Across all ten textbooks in the study, the most widely used comprehension question types are those that require inferential comprehension, although different series demonstrate their own preferences. In order to provide an informed discussion of these results, I held semi-structured interviews with the writers and editors of the series in this study. This has allowed me to gain an insight into the approaches and priorities these writers have when they are creating the reading skills elements of their textbooks.*

Introduction

The specific textbook feature I have chosen to examine focuses on the texts found in the reading syllabus, and in particular the types of questions and tasks that accompany these texts. There are several reasons for this: reading plays a vital role in language learning; questions contribute to that learning; all modern textbooks have reading texts and accompanying questions and tasks, which enables direct comparison; and finally, reading texts are probably one of the easiest elements for the teacher to supplement in the quest to tailor a course more closely to the specific interests, needs, and objectives of their learners. With this latter point in mind, while opportunities abound for teachers to find suitable, appropriate, and relevant texts, less emphasis has been placed on what is or can be *done* with those texts. Creating a taxonomy of different types of questions not only allows for comparison and contrast of different textbooks; it also provides a basis for teacher training and development in the field of language learning materials and illustrates the range of different options available once a text has been selected. Having decided on the feature to be examined, I then needed to decide on the textbooks to examine. Since the mid-1990s there has been a steady increase in the publication of revised editions of existing textbook series, as distinct from new series. I therefore used this as a criterion of textbook selection for my study as it would allow me to identify 'changes', since the writers remain the same and revised editions allow them the opportunity to modify, alter, or refine (or not) their earlier work.

In this chapter, I have used the term 'question' as a wide umbrella term, which encompasses not only genuine interrogatives but also instructions for any text-related tasks. The term *'question type'* is used to refer to the kind of thinking, action, or approach which is required of the learner in order for them to provide an appropriate response to a specific question or task. Question 'type' is distinguished from question *'form'*, which I take to refer to the *structure* of a question, such as the binary question, which allows only two possibilities as an answer (yes/no, true/false, either/or), the multiple-choice question (three or more possibilities), or a more open Wh-question (who, what, where, why, when, etc).

Literature review: Question types

There are relatively few taxonomies in the literature of the kind I have created, but the few that exist are based either directly or indirectly on Bloom's Taxonomy of Educational Objectives (Bloom, Engelhart, Furst, Hill, and Krathwohl, 1956). This was a study undertaken to identify and categorize desirable educational outcomes which could be applied across all scholastic disciplines and could provide a means to measure these outcomes by creating a 'framework [which] could do much to promote the exchange of test materials and ideas about testing' (Bloom et al., 1956: 4). There are six levels to Bloom's taxonomy, and they are ordered in a cumulative hierarchy, beginning with easier, less cognitively challenging tasks, moving progressively through each level to arrive at a final level of highly sophisticated thinking. In the context of reading, such 'higher order' thinking incorporates the ability to take information presented in texts and combine it with external knowledge to perform a variety of functions. These functions could be: applying information presented in a passage to a new context; examining, identifying, and distinguishing properties of a text or situation; or appraising the validity, merit, or quality of an argument. Bloom's levels are *Knowledge, Comprehension, Application, Analysis, Synthesis* and *Evaluation*.

At the *Knowledge* level the learner is required only to recognize, remember, or memorize information. The second level, *Comprehension*, places a slightly greater cognitive demand on the learner. This level demands a degree of interpretation, discovering relationships among data and the ability to reorder, rearrange, or transfer information from one medium to another (e.g., graph to words or vice versa). It includes low-level extrapolation, such as predicting a continuing trend. The

Application level, where the higher order thinking skills begin to be incorporated, relates to problem-solving tasks and the ability for the learner to carry these out 'without having to be prompted [...] or [...] shown' (Bloom et al., 1956: 120). *Analysis* is the ability to examine an issue closely and draw conclusions, 'to distinguish fact from hypothesis [...], relevant from extraneous material [...], dominant from subordinate ideas' (ibid.: 144). *Synthesis* involves creation and integration. It requires the combining of information from different sources to constitute a new 'entity'. The final level, *Evaluation*, calls for judgement. This level requires the reader to assess the calibre, attributes, and worth of an argument or procedure according to a predetermined set of criteria.

The influence of Bloom's Taxonomy has been both substantial and durable; its impact has been wide-ranging and profound, having been used in an extensive range of educational disciplines. In addition to enjoying a wide application, Bloom's Taxonomy has also inspired and formed the basis of further taxonomies with slightly narrower focuses. Sanders (1966) used Bloom as a basis to create a taxonomy of *classroom* questions and was designed to provide classroom teachers with a practical framework regarding how to write questions that address Bloom's different levels.

Both Bloom's and Sanders' taxonomies contributed to that of Barrett (cited in Clymer, 1968, and Smith and Barrett, 1974), who created his taxonomy for teaching reading comprehension to address an issue previously identified by Guszak (1967), that too great an emphasis is placed on 'retrieval of the trivial factual makeup of stories' (Guszak, 1967: 233), at the expense of promoting more sophisticated critical thinking skills such as conjecture, inference, and evaluation.

In addition, each of Barrett's levels contains between four and eight sub-categories referring to specific reading purposes, and these sub-categories are also graded in increasing levels of difficulty, as not all tasks within a single level are 'necessarily of equal difficulty' (Smith and Barrett, 1974: 53). So within the initial level, '*Literal Recognition and Recall*', retrieving ideas of cause and effect, supposedly requires greater cognitive effort than retrieving a main idea, and within the level *Inferential Comprehension*, inferring character traits is said to be more challenging than inferring supporting details. Indeed, even the same sub-category may have different grades of difficulty depending on the reading passage. For instance, inferring sequence in a narrative text could involve greater conjecture than inferring sequence in an expository text.

Pearson and Johnson's (1978) taxonomy is centred on the interaction between the reader and the text, and is based on the source the reader must access to produce an appropriate answer. It reflects Gray's (1960) three-level guide that one can 'read the lines, read between the lines and read beyond the lines'. This taxonomy comprises three levels: *Textually Explicit*, for questions whose answers can be located directly in the text both in terms of content and language – that is, there is a word match between question and answer; *Textually Implicit*, where although the answer is still given in full in the text, retrieving it is nevertheless slightly more challenging for the reader as it requires 'at least one step of logical or pragmatic inferring [...] to get from the question to the response and both question and response are derived from the text' (Pearson and Johnson, 1978: 161); and finally *Scriptally Implicit*. Pearson and Johnson have adopted Schank's (1973) term *script* to refer to schema, or prior knowledge and personal experience, and this third level covers any question requiring any element of reader contribution to answer it.

Nuttall (1982, 1996) created a taxonomy of question types, closely based on Barrett but applied to the L2 reading context. The subcategories found in Barrett were eliminated, and two new question types were created: The first, the *'Personal Response'* question type, asks for the reader's individual and personal reactions to what they have read. The second, Nuttall's final question type, raises learners' awareness regarding exactly 'what they do when they interpret text' (Nuttall, 1996: 189). This second new question type is called *'How writers say what they mean'* and promotes the conscious use of reading strategies aimed at the wider skill of 'handling texts in general, rather than simply helping them to understand one particular text' (Nuttall, 1996: 189). Questions of this type promote word-attack skills (strategies to deal with unknown vocabulary in a text) and text-attack skills (strategies to deal with syntax and cohesion in a text).

Day and Park's (2005) taxonomy closely resembles Nuttall's, but they introduce a new question type, *'Prediction'*, which covers questions requiring students to predict what will happen next in the text, to be confirmed or otherwise by further reading of the text, and they omitted the question type focusing on reading strategies.

These taxonomies span five decades and cover the broad macro features of general educational objectives and classroom questions for all disciplines, as well as the concerns of L1 and L2 reading contexts. Given the diversity of these taxonomies, I needed to establish whether one taxonomy was noticeably more suitable than any of the others, or whether a combination of taxonomies would be the most effective for my research focus: the L2 reading context.

Trialling the taxonomies

As previously stated, not all the taxonomies examined were created for the L2 reading context. Both Bloom's and Sanders' goals encompassed the wider, multi-disciplinary domain. Barrett and Pearson and Johnson targeted reading, but reading in L1. Only Nuttall and Day and Park targeted the L2 reading context.

However, I felt it useful to investigate whether there were categories in those taxonomies not specifically dedicated to L2 reading which might nevertheless prove to be applicable for my research as well as investigating the applicability of the categories in the L2 reading taxonomies. In addition, I needed to investigate whether types of questions might be present in the textbook reading activities which are not represented in any of the existing taxonomies. In order to examine these issues I applied all the taxonomies to the comprehension questions and tasks accompanying the reading texts in a single unit of the four editions of *Headway Intermediate* (Soars and Soars, 1986, 1996, 2003, 2009) to see if one proved to be better than the others. Should no single taxonomy surpass all other taxonomies, I would create my own taxonomy by judicious selection of individual elements of these taxonomies. I chose the *Headway* series for this initial trial because the series is so 'widely used and influential' (Waters, 2012: 443), and with four editions it offered the greatest range of texts. I selected the readings from Unit 8 because I specifically wanted to include a comparison of the questions and tasks accompanying a text which had been repeated from one edition to another ('Who wants to be a Millionaire?', present in both the 2nd and 3rd edition (Soars and Soars, 1996: 80–81 and 2003: 66–67)). This would allow me to see whether questions and tasks change even when texts in a revised edition remain the same.

No single taxonomy proved to be wholly suitable and superior to its counterparts. There were question types in these taxonomies which were not present in my textbook sample (Bloom's and Sanders' *Application, Analysis, Synthesis,* and *Evaluation,* Barrett's *Appreciation,* and Barrett's, Nuttall's, and Day and Park's *Evaluation*). It should be noted that, although the taxonomies by Bloom, Sanders, Barrett, Nuttall, and Day and Park all had categories called *Evaluation,* these categories did not share the same properties.

Nuttall's and Day and Park's *Personal Response* question types were present, and questions of this type did not fit into any of the other taxonomies.

Example *Headway Intermediate*, 1986: 44–45
Text Title: Run your way to Health
Question: What do you do to keep fit?

This question is a purely personal issue, related to the text in its theme but not its content. The *Personal Response* question types of Nuttall and Day and Park describe this type of question well. The same element can be found in another question taken from later editions of *Headway Intermediate*.

Example: *Headway Intermediate*, 1996: 80–81, and 2003: 66–67

Text Title: Who wants to be a millionaire?

Question: What for you are the answers to the questions in the last paragraph?

Text: When you next buy your lottery ticket, or do the football pools, just stop for a minute and ask yourself why you're doing it. Do you actually want to win? Or are you doing it for the excitement of thinking about winning?

The question reads 'what *for you* are the answers [...]' (my italics), which indicates that it is an individual answer, and the advice offered in the teacher's book (which provides answers to comprehension questions and advice on how to do the activities) reads: 'Students answer this for themselves.' There is no information to be inferred or evaluated, and therefore *Personal Response* suits this question type best.

Pearson and Johnson's relatively narrow distinction between *Textually Explicit* and *Textually Implicit* is not represented in the other taxonomies but accounts for subtle differences between some of the questions accompanying the texts:

Example: *Headway Intermediate*, 1986: 44–45

Text Title: Run your way to Health

Question: How did the author feel when he started running?

Text: *When I started running seven years ago, I could manage only about a quarter of a mile before I had to stop. Breathless and aching, I walked the next quarter of a mile.*

The answer to the question falls into the first level of each taxonomy – Bloom's *Knowledge*, Sanders' *Memory*, Barrett's, Nuttall's, and Day and Park's *Literal Comprehension*, and Pearson and Johnson's *Textually Explicit*, 'directly, explicitly, and precisely taken from the text' (1978: 159) – as there is a word match in the opening sentence with '*started running*' and the appropriate adjectives, '*breathless and aching*', are found in the first two words of the ensuing sentence. However, in the following example Pearson and Johnson's taxonomy better reflects the relationship between question and response:

Example: *Headway Intermediate*, 1986: 44–45

Text Title: Run your way to Health

Question: What for him are the pleasures of running?

Text: The biggest pay-off for me was – and still is – the deep relaxation that I achieve by taking exercise.

The answer to the question is in the text and does not require the reader to call on any *external* factual knowledge, which therefore places it in Bloom's *Knowledge*, Sanders' *Memory*, Barrett's, Nuttall's, and Day and Park's *Literal Comprehension* levels, but this does not reflect the difference between the wording of the question ('pleasures of running') and the wording in the text ('the biggest pay-off'), an extremely important distinction in a foreign language course. Pearson and Johnson's *Textually Implicit* question type addresses this distinction by recognizing cases when 'some sort of inference [is] necessary [...] however minor and obvious that inference may be' (1978: 159).

A question type exclusive to Nuttall, but which was present in three of my four sample units, was Nuttall's strategy-based question type '*How writers say what they mean*'. This addresses more accurately than the other taxonomies the post-reading vocabulary activities, as it encourages students to use the context of the text to infer the meaning of words rather than immediately resort to a dictionary.

Creating a new L2 reading question-type taxonomy

The outcome of my trial was that no single existing taxonomy covered all the different types of questions found even in a small sample. I therefore selected elements from the various taxonomies, both in terms of content and title, and created my own taxonomy. It is not a *cumulative* hierarchy, in the sense that the lower levels need to be mastered prior to proceeding to successive levels, although the element of scale from lower order thinking skills to higher order thinking skills is present. A new feature of my taxonomy is its division into three separate categories, which I felt better reflects the nature of what I found. The three categories are the types of questions that require the learner to understand the *Content*, the types of questions that require the learner to carry out *Language*-related tasks, and the types of questions that address learner *Affect* regarding the text.

The first category, 'Content' question types, covers the information contained in the text (who, what, where, when, how, etc.). There are three types in this category, and they are hierarchical from lower to higher order thinking. I have chosen to use Pearson and Johnson's terminology for the initial two levels, *Textually Explicit* and *Textually Implicit*, for their transparency. These names clearly indicate that the answer can be found *in the text*, that no external source is required. The distinction between these two levels is that *Textually Explicit* question types involve word matching and/or describe questions where the answer is in one place in the text whereas the *Textually Implicit* question types include questions where the answer may be worded slightly differently from the question or may be spread over several parts of the text:

Textually Explicit: Question: When did Harry *meet* Sally?
Text reads: Harry *met* Sally in 1995 or Harry *met* Sally 15 years ago.
Textually Implicit: Question: When did Harry *meet* Sally?
Text reads: Sally and Harry first *came across each other* in 1995.

For the third and final question type in the 'Content' group I have used Barrett's *Inferential Comprehension* terminology in order to capture the need for the student to understand (comprehend) what is not written but is inferred. In this category the student combines their own knowledge base and personal experiences with the information presented in the text in order to arrive at the answer. Some level of justification would be expected for the answers given.

Question: How old was Harry when he met Sally? or How long ago did Harry meet Sally?

Text reads: Harry was a final year undergraduate working part time in a local bar when Sally came in with all her friends to celebrate her birthday.

The more basic question 'When did Harry meet Sally?' would not be an *Inferential Comprehension* question type as the answer could be the *Textually Implicit* 'when he was a final-year undergraduate'. For the question to qualify as *Inferential Comprehension* in this example the reader needs to be made to draw on their background knowledge, in this case of how old, in general, final-year undergraduates are and additionally, in the second example, apply some simple mathematics.

The second category, 'Language' questions, requires the reader to *do* something with the text. These tasks focus closely on the language itself. This category also contains three types, but they are not hierarchical; they are simply different from each other. The first question type, *Reorganization*, is found in Barrett's L1 reading taxonomy and in both L2 reading taxonomies. It incorporates Sanders' *Translation* category, which is the transformation of data into parallel forms: pictures/processes can be labelled or described (or even drawn); events could be reordered (for instance, in terms of chronology); or items might be classified into appropriate categories. Actual translation tasks – that is, from English into the students' L1 (or vice versa) – would also fall into this question type. The second question type in the 'Language' category incorporates Nuttall's strategy-based category *'How writers say what they mean'* and requires the reader to guess the meaning of unknown words from the context of the text. I find Nuttall's name for this question type a little cumbersome, so I have called this question type *Lexical*. I decided on *Lexical* rather than *Vocabulary* to avoid confusion with a question type in my pre-reading question taxonomy: *Pre-Teaching Vocabulary*. The third question type in the Language category is *Form* and refers to grammar-related questions which involve learners carrying out grammatical tasks such as forming questions or negatives or providing explanations for the use of one tense over another. This question type is not found in any of the taxonomies examined previously. However, piloting revealed that such questions do indeed occur.

The final category, 'Affect' question types, involves the learner responding to the text. There are two types in this category, and they can be considered hierarchical as they require the reader to interact with the text on different levels: the first question type in this category requires responses on a purely personal level, with no 'correct' answers, whereas in the second question type in this category the response is on a deeper, evaluative level. For the 'lower' of these two levels I have retained Nuttall's and Day and Park's terminology of *Personal Response*. This question type covers all questions which call for the student 'simply to record his reaction to the text' (Nuttall, 1996: 189) in terms of like/dislike, surprise, amusement, etc. The frequent 'What do you think?' textbook reading questions are an example of this question type. The 'higher' level is *Evaluation*. The *Evaluation* question types require a considered and possibly reflective response with a reasoned justification based on evidence presented in the text and/or background knowledge or experience. The distinction between my *Personal Response* and *Evaluation* question types is illustrated by the following examples:

> Personal Response: What do you think?
> Which facts in Pizza Trivia do you find most interesting?
> Do you like Pizza?
> What are your favourite toppings?
>
> (Soars and Soars, 2003: 51)
>
> Evaluation: In the context of the 20th century and its two world wars, what message is the writer trying to make about nature and the importance of individual human beings?
>
> (Soars and Soars, 1996: 94)

All eight question types in this taxonomy are presented in their respective categories and accompanied by explanations in Figure 3.1.

Application of my taxonomy

Having created a taxonomy of text-related comprehension question types and tasks (henceforth referred to as 'comp q-types'), I applied these to every reading in each textbook in this study: four different textbook series, comprising ten different editions spread over more than 25 years. Some of the reading tasks comprise single texts, and others comprise series of texts, such as jigsaw reading activities: these latter activities consist of two or three mid-length texts (c. 200–300 words per text) on related themes such as descriptions of three different and unusual jobs, or three different types of 'artist' (e.g., a painter, a writer, and a musician), and the class is divided into three groups, with each group reading one of the texts and answering questions. Students then form new groups of three people, each having read a different text, and then they discuss, compare, and contrast what each one has read. Other readings comprise a number of mini-texts (c. 50–150 words), such as six brief newspaper stories or short biographies of famous people, and the students read one at a time. To distinguish between references to the entire reading exercise and the texts that make up a reading exercise, a 'reading' refers to the entire reading exercise, regardless of the number of

Categories	Comprehension question types	Description
Content questions	Textually Explicit	In this question type the answer to the question can be found stated directly in the text. There is word-matching between the question and the text. The information required is in sequential sentences.
	Textually Implicit	In this question type the answer to the question is stated directly in the text but is not expressed in the same language as the question (no word-matching). The information is not all in the same order. It is separated by at least one sentence.
	Inferential Comprehension	In this question type the answer to the question is not stated explicitly in the text but rather alluded to. The reader has to combine their background knowledge with the information in the text and make the necessary connections.
Language questions	Reorganization	This question type requires the reader to reorder, rearrange or transfer information in the text. – putting sequences in chronological order – transferring data into parallel forms (e.g. label pictures/maps, complete a table, translate)
	Lexical	This question type requires the reader to focus specifically on *vocabulary*, not information. Included in this category are exercises where the reader – guesses the meaning of a word or phrase from the context – matches definition A with word/phrase B – Uses a dictionary Word attack and text attack strategies are included in this level.
	Form	This question type requires the reader to focus specifically on *grammar* or *form*, not information. Examples of form questions include exercises where the reader – changes a sentence from the affirmative to the negative – forms the question that goes with a given answer – explains the use of one tense rather than another (e.g. present perfect not past simple)

Figure 3.1   The taxonomy of comprehension questions

Affect questions	Personal Response	This question type requires the reader to offer their personal reaction to the text in terms of likes/dislikes, what they found funny, surprising etc. The reader can be asked to transfer the situation in the text to their own cultural context and comment. Highly subjective, there is no 'right' answer.
	Evaluation	This question type requires the reader to make a judgement or assessment of the text/information according to some understood criteria. This criteria can be − formally recognized independent sources − teacher provided − student-set standards The reader is also expected to provide a rationale or justification for their view.

Figure 3.1   (Continued)

Table 3.1   The number of readings and texts by edition and series in the study

Textbooks		Readings per edition	Readings per series	Texts per edition	Texts per series
Cutting Edge	1998	12	24	34	70
	2005	12		36	
English File	1999	32	67	43	93
	2006	35		50	
Headway	1986	14	51	21	124
	1996	13		29	
	2003	12		29	
	2009	12		45	
Inside Out	2000	29	67	58	110
	2009	38		52	
Totals		209	209	397	397

texts that make up that reading, and 'texts' refers to the individual texts that make up an entire 'reading'. There are a total of 209 readings and 397 texts. Table 3.1 shows the number of readings and texts per edition and series.

I analysed the distribution of question types in terms of their occurrence, frequency, and range. 'Occurrence' refers to the presence or absence of a specific q-type in a reading (that is, in an entire reading exercise, which may comprise one or more irrespective of how many of that q-type there are and is calculated with reference to the number of readings in the series or edition). 'Frequency' refers to how many times each different q-type is asked in each text within the entire reading exercise. Each question is considered as an individual token, and the frequency is calculated with reference to the number of texts in the series or edition. The 'range' of q-types represents the number of different q-types accompanying a single reading in a series or edition. It is based on occurrence and is calculated out of a maximum of eight, corresponding to the number of categories in my taxonomy.

Results

I will report my findings by first looking at the entire picture of all editions of all four textbook series in the study in terms of each q-type. Then I shall compare the distribution of q-types by the three categories of Content, Language, and Affect between the series. Next I will focus on the distribution of the different q-types for each series of textbooks, comparing the original publications with their subsequent editions. Finally I shall look at the range of different q-types by series to see how many (or how few) out of the eight different q-types are present in the readings: for example, are there any readings that contain at least one instance of all eight q-types?

To calculate statistical significances comparing a specific q-type in one series with the same q-type in another series (e.g., *Explicit* q-types in *Cutting Edge* with *Explicit* q-types in *English File*) or a specific q-type in one edition with the same q-type in another edition of the same series (e.g., *Lexical* q-types in *Inside Out*, 2000, with *Lexical* q-types in *Inside Out*, 2009) I used Kruskall Wallis and Mann Whitney post-hoc paired comparisons because I have treated these comparisons as comparisons of independent groups. I have considered these two scenarios as independent groups because, in the case of comparisons between series, each series is an entirely separate entity from the other series, with no relationship between them. In the case of comparisons between editions, in most cases the texts are different and there are different numbers of texts and therefore no equal matching. To calculate statistical significances comparing one q-type with a different q-type within a series (e.g., *Activate Schemata* q-types with *Vocabulary Pre-Teaching* q-types in the *English File* series) or one q-type with a different q-type within an edition (e.g., *Implicit* q-types with *Inferential Comprehension* q-types in *Headway*, 1996) I used Friedman and Wilcoxon post-hoc paired comparisons using Holm's sequential Bonferroni adjustment (Holm, 1979: 65–70) because I have considered these comparisons as comparisons of related samples as they refer to a single series or a single edition of a series and are therefore not separate entities.

For purposes of clarity and distinction, when referring to entire series (which will include all editions of that series), I shall refer to *Cutting Edge, English File, Headway,* and *Inside Out.* When referring to individual editions of these series, I shall abbreviate these names to: *C/Edge 1* and *C/Edge 2* for the editions of the *Cutting Edge* series; *E/File 1* and *E/File 2* for the editions of the *English File* series; *HWay 1, HWay 2, HWay 3* and *HWay 4* for the editions of the *Headway* series; and *I/Out 1* and *I/Out 2* for the editions of the *Inside Out* series.

The overall picture: All question types, all series

Of the eight types of comprehension questions (comp qs) identified, their distribution across the ten textbooks in this study in terms of both occurrence and frequencies can be seen in Figure 3.2. The first three columns in each graph represent the Content category: *Explicit, Implicit* and *Inferential comprehension* q-types. The next three columns represent the Language category – *Reorganization, Lexical* and *Form* q-types – and the last two columns represent the Affect category: *Personal Response* and *Evaluation* q-types. The two graphs in Figure 3.2 contrast the number of times the comprehension question types are present at all in a reading regardless of how many there are (their occurrence), with the total number of instances of that comprehension question type –that is, how many different questions of a particular type are asked (their frequency). The figures on the bars represent the total occurrences and frequencies of that comp q-type and the proportion of that q-type out of all comp q-types.

Figure 3.2 shows that, perhaps unsurprisingly, the Content category of q-types is the greatest in terms of both occurrence and frequency. Within the Language category and Affect category, there is one q-type that is significantly more common than the other members of that group: *Lexical* q-types in Language and *Personal Response* q-types in Affect ($p < .001$ in each case). The difference in occurrence and frequency of *Lexical* q-types tells us that they may occur in fewer texts (16 per cent) but, when they are asked, are greater in number than the other question types (25 per cent).

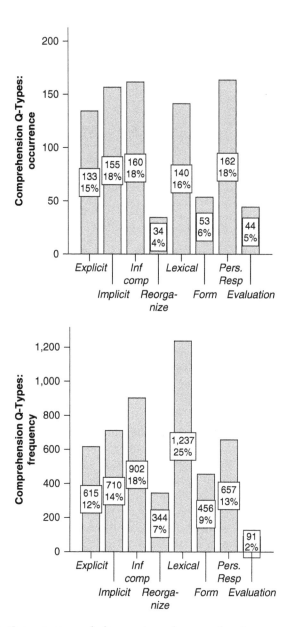

Figure 3.2 Occurrences and frequencies of comprehension questions: all editions of all series

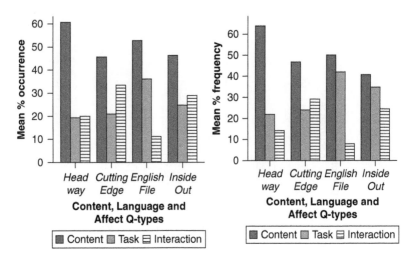

Figure 3.3 The occurrence and frequency of Content, Language, and Affect question types in all series

Series comparison: All categories (Content-Language-Affect)

This section will focus on whether the different series display any preferences for a particular comp q-type. Figure 3.3 illustrates the proportion of each of the category q-types in each series in terms of occurrence and frequency. The graphs represent the combination of all editions within each series.

As was suggested by the overall totals in Figure 3.2, Figure 3.3 shows that for each series in this study more comprehension q-types fall into the Content category (*Explicit, Implicit*, and *Inferential Comprehension*) than either the Language or Affect categories. Not only do they appear in more texts, but there are more of them than the other q-types when they do appear. Comparing the series with each other, preferences emerge. *Headway* contains significantly more Content question types than the other series (p = .005 *Cutting Edge*, p = .002 *English File*, and p < .001 *Inside Out*); *English File* favours the Language category (p = .008 *Cutting Edge* and p < .001 *Headway*), and there are significantly more Affect q-types in *Cutting Edge* than in *Headway* (p < .001) and *English File* (p = .001).

Series comparison: Individual categories

Having looked at the totals of the different categories, the following graphs illustrate the distribution of the individual q-types that make up each category. Q-types in the Content category are composed of *Explicit, Implicit,* and *Inferential Comprehension*; q-types in the Language category are composed of *Reorganization, Lexical,* and *Form*; and q-types in the Affect category are composed of *Personal Response* and *Evaluation*.

Content (Explicit – Implicit – Inferential Comprehension)

The Content category comprises information-carrying question types: information pertaining to who did what, when, and where. The three q-types that make up this category are *Explicit* (answers found directly in the text, same language as the question), *Implicit* (answers found directly in the text, different language from the question), and *Inferential Comprehension* (answers not found directly in the text, reader needs to combine information in the text with their background and/or general world knowledge). Figure 3.4 offers a closer look at this category and shows which of the three Content q-types prevail in the different series.

It is noticeable that the higher order Inferential Comprehension q-types are more prevalent in three of the four series. The occurrence graph in Figure 3.4 shows that *Inferential Comprehension* q-types are present in more readings than either *Explicit* or *Implicit* q-types, and the frequency graph shows that more *Inferential Comprehension* q-types are asked per reading than either *Explicit* or *Implicit* q-types in the *Headway, English File,* and *Inside Out* series.

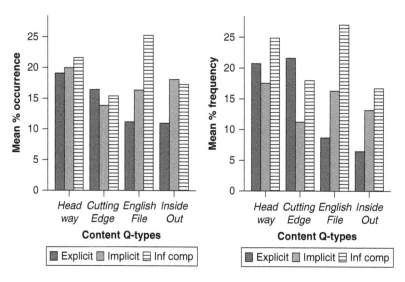

Figure 3.4   Content question types by series: occurrence and frequency

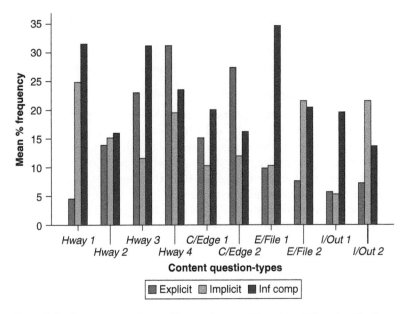

Figure 3.5 Content questions. Change from edition to edition in *Headway, Cutting Edge, English File,* and *Inside Out*

Figure 3.5 shows how the distribution of the number of Content question types (their frequency) has changed from edition to edition in all four series in this study.

In Figure 3.5 we can see the trends across the four editions of *Headway* and changes in the two editions of *Cutting Edge, English File,* and *Inside Out* of q-types in the Content category. There are some commonalities. *Inferential Comprehension* q-types are the most frequently asked in the Content category; nevertheless their number falls in each revised edition of *Cutting Edge, English File,* and *Inside Out*, although none of these falls is significant. In the case of *Headway,* the fall of this q-type between the first and second edition is significant (p = .007), as is its subsequent rise between *HWay 2* and *HWay* 3 (p = .003). The fall between the third and fourth edition is not significant.

The other notable feature of changes from edition to edition is in the *Explicit* q-types, which increase from edition to edition in three of the four series. In *Headway* there has been a significant rise in this q-type, with each subsequent edition having significantly more of this q-type than the first edition, in 1986. The significance values can be seen in Table 3.2:

Table 3.2 Significance values for *Explicit* q-types in editions of *Headway*

Explicit Q-type	HWay 1 – HWay 2	HWay 1 – HWay 3	HWay 1 – HWay 4
Sig Values	p = .002	p < .001	p < .001

The rise in *Explicit* q-types between *C/Edge 1* and *C/Edge 2* and *I/Out 1* and *I/Out 2* is not significant. In the case of *English File* the number of *Explicit* q-types actually falls, but this is not significant.

Language (Reorganization – Lexical – Form)

The Language category comprises question types which require the reader to *do* something with the information or language. The three q-types that make up this category are: *Reorganization,* which involves *reordering* information in the text (e.g., putting events in chronological order) or *transferring* information/language from the text into a chart or table; *Lexical* q-types, which focus on *vocabulary* (e.g., guessing the meaning of a word from its context in the passage); and *Form* q-types, which focus on *grammar* (e.g., identifying/justifying the use of one tense rather than another). Figure 3.6 illustrates which q-type in the Language category is most widespread.

When we examine the three different Language q-types (*Reorganization, Lexical,* and *Form*), the occurrence and frequency graphs in Figure 3.6 reveal that, of all the q-types in the Language category, the most favoured is *Lexical.* Comparing the series with each other, we can also see in the first graph in Figure 3.6 (occurrence) that *Lexical* question types occur in significantly more readings in *English File* than in the other three series (p < .001 for *Headway,* p = .002 for *Cutting Edge,* and p = .005 for *Inside Out*). The second graph (frequency) shows that the number of *Lexical* question types is also significantly higher in *English File* than *Headway* and *Cutting Edge* (p < .001 in both cases). However, a distinction between these two graphs is that, although *Lexical* q types do not occur in as many readings in the *Inside Out* series, when they do occur, there are significantly more of them than in *Headway* (p < .001) and *Cutting Edge* (p = .003).

In Figure 3.7 we can see the trends of the Language question-type category across the four editions of *Headway* and changes in the two editions of *Cutting Edge, English File,* and *Inside Out.*

When examined edition by edition, an interesting picture emerges regarding the change in focus from *Form* to *Lexical* q-types over time.

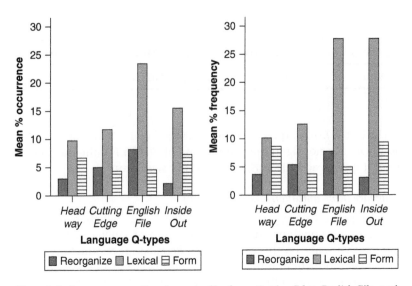

Figure 3.6 Language question types in *Headway, Cutting Edge, English File,* and *Inside Out*

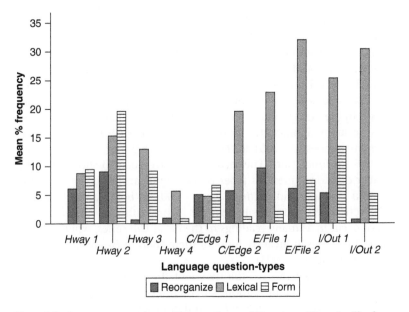

Figure 3.7 Language questions. Change from edition to edition in *Headway, Cutting Edge, English File,* and *Inside Out*

Table 3.3 Significance values for *HWay 2 Form* q-types

	HWay 1	HWay 3	HWay 4	C/Edge 1	C/Edge 2	E/File 1	E/File 2	I/Out 2
HWay 2 Sigs	p = .037	p = .027	p < .001	p = .005	p < .001	p < .001	p = .001	p < .001

Table 3.4 Significance values for *Lexical-Form* q-types in *E/File 1* and *2*, *I/Out 1* and *2*, and *C/Edge 2*

Editions	Lexical – Form	Editions	Lexical – Form	Editions	Lexical – Form
E/File 1	p < .001	I/Out 1	p = .010	C/Edge 2	P < .001
E/File 2	p < .001	I/Out 2	p = .001		

HWay 1 (1986), *HWay 2* (1996), and *C/Edge 1* (1998) all have greater numbers of *Form* q-types than *Lexical* q-types; indeed *HWay 2* has significantly more *Form* q-types than any other edition in this study except *I/Out 1* (see Table 3.3 for significance values).

However, in later textbook series (*E/File 1* and *2* 1999/2006 and *I/Out 1* and *2* 2000/2009) and the two later editions of *Headway* (2003/2009) and *C/ Edge 2* (2005), the focus on vocabulary rather than grammar in a reading becomes more apparent. In *C/Edge 1* there were more *Form* q-types than *Lexical* q-types, but in *C/Edge 2* not only had this reversed, but there was a significant increase in *Lexical* q-types (p = .001). In *E/File 1 and 2, C/Edge 2*, and *I/Out 2* there were significantly more *Lexical* q-types than *Form* q-types (see Table 3.4 for significance values), and the second editions of both *English File* and *Inside Out* saw more *Lexical* q-types asked than in their first editions, although these increases were not significant.

This pattern of more *Lexical* q-types in the second edition is also true of the *Cutting Edge* series, with a significant increase between *C/Edge 1* and *C/Edge 2* (p = .001).

Figure 3.7 also reveals that one series, *Headway*, reverses this trend and *Lexical* q-types decline steadily between *HWay 2*, *HWay 3*, and *HWay 4*.

Affect (Personal Response – Evaluation)

The Affect category comprises question types which require some kind of engagement with, response, or reaction to a reading passage. This category has two question types. *Personal Response*, the more superficial and

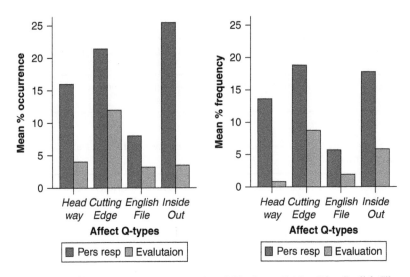

Figure 3.8   Affect question types in series of *Headway, Cutting Edge, English File,* and *Inside Out*

certainly the more subjective of the two, requires the reader to express a purely personal point of view when reacting to a text, such as preference, surprise, or amusement, to which there can be no 'correct' answer. The second category, *Evaluation*, requires a deeper, more considered response to the text, with some kind of judgement or assessment, and involves the reader applying criteria to support or justify their answer.

Figure 3.8 shows how, within the Affect category, *Personal Response* q-types clearly dominate over *Evaluation* q-types in each series, although their existence is significantly less in *English File* than in the other series ($p < .001$). The occurrence graph shows us that *Personal Response* q-types are more widely present in the readings in the *Inside Out* series than in the other series. However, in terms of frequency (how many of the q-type is asked per text) the *Cutting Edge* series has marginally more *Personal Response* q-types than *Inside Out*. Figure 3.9 illustrates the extent to which *Personal Response* q-types dominate the Affect category in each edition too.

In the Affect category, *C/Edge 1* has significantly more of both *Personal Response* q-types and *Evaluation* q-types than all the other editions. Across the board, in each edition of each series, there are significantly more *Personal Response* q-types than *Evaluation* q-types (see the significance values in Table 3.5).

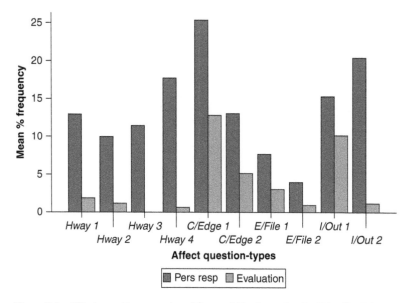

Figure 3.9 Affect question types in editions of *Headway, Cutting Edge, English File,* and *Inside Out*

Table 3.5 Significance values for *personal response – evaluation* q-types

Editions	Sig. values	Editions	Sig. values	Editions	Sig. values	Editions	Sig. values
HWay 1	p = .015	C/Edge 1	p = .006	E/File 1	p = .023	I/Out 1	p < .001
Hway 2	p < .001	C/Edge 2	p = .001	E/File 2	p = .013	I/Out 2	p < .001
HWay 3	p < .001						
Hway 4	p < .001						

E/File 1 and *E/File 2* ask substantially fewer *Personal Response* q-types than each of the other editions in this study, with this difference being significant in all cases except *E/File 1 – HWay 4, I/Out 1* and 2. The significance values can be seen in Table 3.6.

Individual series: All question types

We have seen that the Content category of q-types was more plentiful than the other two categories of Language and Affect, but that within these two other categories one specific q-type predominated. The following graphs (Figures 3.10–3.13) show the distribution of all

Table 3.6 Significance values for *E/File 1 + E/File 2 personal response* q-types compared to all other editions

	HWay 1	HWay 2	HWay 3	HWay 4	C/Edge 1	E/Edge 2	I/Out 1	I/Out 2
E/File 1	p = .037	p = .007	p = .013		p = .000	p = .004		
E/File 2	p = .005	p < .001	p = .001	p = .008	p < .001	p < .001	p = .008	p = .018

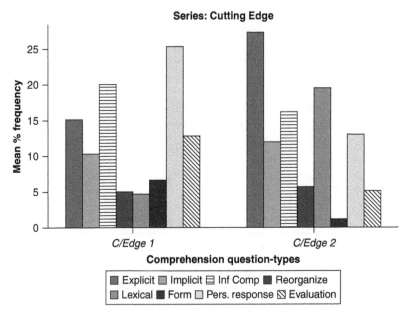

Figure 3.10 Distribution of all eight comprehension question types in *Cutting Edge*

eight question types across the four editions of *Headway* and the two editions of *Cutting Edge, English File,* and *Inside Out.* This will reveal which, if any, q-type was favoured over any other in a specific edition.

Cutting Edge

The distribution of q-types changed from *C/Edge 1* to *C/Edge 2. Explicit* and *Lexical* q-types both increased in frequency to dominate *C/Edge 2* while the *Inferential Comprehension* and *Personal Response* q-types which dominated *C/Edge 1* both fell in frequency in *C/Edge 2,* but not significantly.

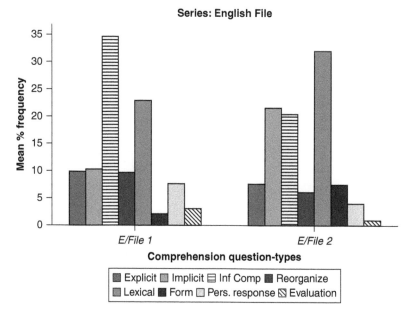

Figure 3.11 Distribution of all eight comprehension question types in *English File*

English File

The principal change between the *English File* editions is the significant increase in the *Implicit* q-types (p = .003) to share prominence with *Inferential Comprehension* in E/File 2.

Headway

Looking at all the question types across all four editions of *Headway,* it is immediately apparent that the distribution of q-types in *HWay 2* differs from the other editions. It is the only edition that is not dominated by at least two of the three q-types in the Content category. In *HWay 4* the three q-types in the Content category (*Explicit, Implicit,* and *Inferential Comprehension*) and *Personal Response* in the Affect category are all markedly more frequent than any of the q-types in the Language category and *Evaluation* q-types. Most of these differences are statistically significant with the exception of *Implicit* and *Personal Response* versus *Lexical* q-types. Table 3.7 provides the significance values.

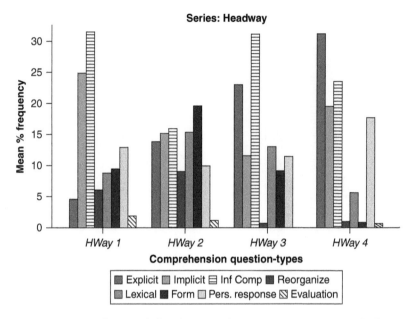

Figure 3.12 Distribution of all eight comprehension question types in *Headway*

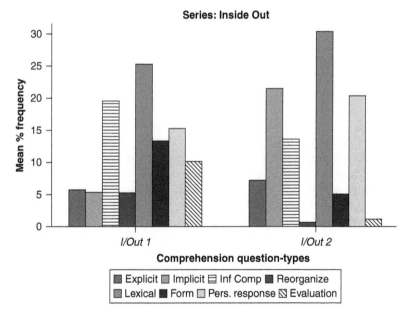

Figure 3.13 Distribution of all eight comprehension question types in *Inside Out*

Table 3.7   Significance values e*xplicit, implicit, inferential comprehension, personal response* q-types *HWay 4*

HWay 4	Reorganization	Lexical	Form	Evaluation
Explicit	$p < .001$	$p < .001$	$p < .001$	$p < .001$
Implicit	$p < .001$		$p < .001$	$p < .001$
Inferential Comprehension	$p < .001$	$p < .001$	$p < .001$	$p < .001$
Personal Response	$p < .001$		$p < .001$	$p < .001$

Inside Out

Lexical q-types dominate in both editions of *Inside Out*. There are substantially more *Implicit* q-types as well as an increase in *Personal Response* q-types in the second edition.

Range of question types

The final aspect to consider is how many different q-types out of the possible eight are used in the readings and whether there is any difference between the series. The taxonomy contains eight different types of comprehension question or task. The range shows the most and fewest different q-types out of eight used in a reading, irrespective of which type is used or how many of each type is used.

The first graph in Figure 3.14 shows the range of q-types in the four textbook series in this study (the minimum and maximum number of different q-types in any single reading). It reveals that in the *Headway* series there have been readings that contain only two out of the eight different q-types, and there have also been readings which contain six of the possible eight different q-types. Particularly noteworthy is the range in the *Cutting Edge* series, as we see that there was one instance of all eight different q-types present in a single reading: the only instance across all ten editions of textbooks in this study. The number of different q-types ranged from one to seven in *English File* and from one to six in *Inside Out*.

The second graph in Figure 3.14 is the 'repertoire', and it provides a breakdown of how many readings in each series contained only one q-type, how many readings in each series contained two types, etc. We see that out of the 51 readings in the *Headway* series, two contain only two different q-types, six readings contain three different q-types, 18 readings contain four different q-types, 15 readings contain five different q-types, and ten readings contain six different q-types. *Cutting Edge* is the only series that has a reading in which all eight q-types occur,

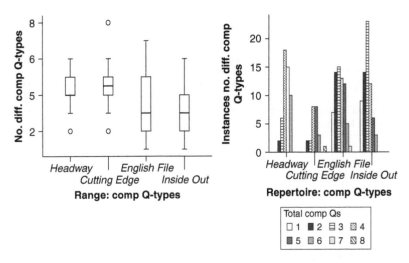

Figure 3.14   The range and repertoire of comprehension question types by series

but *English File* contains a reading in which seven of the eight different q-types occur. A noticeable distinction between the *Headway* and *Cutting Edge* series on the one hand and the *English File* and *Inside Out* series on the other is that *Headway* and *Cutting Edge* have fewer readings (approximately 12 per edition) but on average between four and five different question types accompanying them and *English File* and *Inside Out* have more readings (average 33 per edition), but more instances when only one or two different q-types accompany those readings.

Discussion

To paraphrase Littlejohn (1992), why are comprehension questions the way they are? In order to gain some insight into this question I held interviews (either face-to-face or via e-mail) with writers and/or editors of the textbooks in this study and presented each one with my taxonomy and the results of my analysis of their respective textbook series editions. I shall refer to the textbook rather than the individual when citing their views and responses in this chapter.

Given that research into teachers' beliefs has shown that 'language teachers' beliefs and understandings of teaching as well as learning play an important role in their classroom practices and in their professional growth' (Cabaroglu and Roberts, 2000; Kuzborska, 2011: 102; Richards and Rodgers, 2001), then by extension I would argue that textbook writers' beliefs regarding language teaching and learning inform their writing practices as most (if not all) are, or have been, EFL teachers.

Interviews with the writers and editors of the textbooks showed that, once the texts have been selected, the writers rely on their considerable experience of teaching and materials writing to guide their question and task writing. This process tends to be 'unscientific [...] [with] no systematic tick box type approach' (*Inside Out*). Their approach is more 'fitting your task to your text type' (*Cutting Edge*) as 'generally it's the text that suggests what type of question we're going to ask' (*Inside Out*). Consideration is given to 'the best way to get students to respond to the text' (*Cutting Edge*) and 'what mines the text most effectively [...and] support[s] students' (*Headway*). All the writers showed awareness of 'writing recipes [...] for teachers in a variety of different contexts [...] with a very different experience level' (*Cutting Edge*).

Although the writers share similar broad approaches to question writing, we can nevertheless discern the influence of their personal beliefs when applying my taxonomy to analyse the actual questions and tasks they write, since different preferences are noticeable. The view of the writers of *Cutting Edge* is that 'processing the information in the text' is an important skill and the number of *Inferential Comprehension* q-types in *C/Edge 1* shows this. However, between the 1999 edition of *C/Edge 1* and the 2005 edition of *C/Edge 2* the target audience changed, and the later, revised edition, *C/Edge 2*, 'was going more into secondary [schools... and] people thought the original *Cutting Edge* was a bit difficult'. The consequence of this response to market feedback may explain the increase of *Explicit* q-types at the expense of *Inferential Comprehension* q-types, as 'they're easier, and part of the [...] art of writing comprehension questions is to boost the confidence at the beginning' (*Cutting Edge*). While there was 'a lot of attention to collocation, word spots, that kind of thing which was newish' in *C/Edge 1*, guessing the meaning of unknown words was not focused on to a great extent in the activities accompanying the readings. The significant increase in *Lexical* q-types from *C/Edge 1* to *C/Edge 2* ($p < .001$) also reflects the extent to which market feedback contributes to revised editions, and *Lexical* q-types were incorporated into *C/Edge 2* as 'everybody feels "well I've learned something [...] I've learned six new words. Or I've used my skills to deduce the meaning of six words."' The decrease in *Personal Response* q-types was a surprise to the writers, as *Cutting Edge* felt that 'without that, it's definitely lacking'; however, the practicalities of textbook design and page layout may have accounted for this and 'the teacher ought to do it anyway, without being prompted.'

English File clearly places emphasis on the skills of inferring information from context, which accounts for the high number of *Inferential Comprehension* q-types, particularly in *E/File 1*. When compared to preteaching vocabulary and developing vocabulary inferencing skills, 'our preference is for guessing meaning from context. Students naturally have this ability from reading in their own language and it is very important for students to do this in English especially when they read extensively, rather than stopping and looking up every new word' (*English File*).

Figure 3.12, the distribution of all eight comprehension question types in each edition of the *Headway* series, showed features both at the individual edition level and trends over the course of the editions. At the individual edition level the distribution of q-types in *HWay 2* differs from the other editions. The distribution of the eight different comp q-types is more evenly spread in *HWay 2*, making it the only edition that is not dominated by at least two of the three q-types in the Content category. This was not as a result of specific planning, as the question writing process is 'organic [... beginning with] a fantastic text, and built from the text'. With regard to discernible trends, a noticeable one is the increase in the number of *Explicit* q-types in each edition of *Headway*. The change in target audience may account for this, both in terms of teachers and learners. *HWay 2*, written ten years after *HWay 1*, had a different target audience. The original 1986 edition was targeted at UK-based 'English English teachers [native-speaker teachers who] have a certain cultural knowledge already [...] which means that the text can be much more sophisticated just because they are immersed in the language'. *HWay 2*, however, experienced a 'dip in the level slightly when it became more of a global phenomenon [...] a victim of its own success' and is now used in secondary schools. Consequently learners are now younger, so the material is now written with the idea of 'keep[ing] it at thirteen plus. You're really keeping it within anyone's experience.' The following edition, *HWay 3*, contained a number of repeated texts. Figure 3.12 shows that the questions and tasks accompanying *HWay 3* texts (including those repeated) did change, with the Content category showing a further increase in the number of *Explicit* q-types and a recovery of *Inferential Comprehension* q-types after a decline in *HWay 2*. There were fewer of all Language q-types, and in the Affect category there was a marginal increase in *Personal Response* but no *Evaluation* q-types at all. The most recent edition, *HWay 4*, comprises all new texts, with accompanying q-types falling predominantly into the Content category, although the Affect q-type *Personal Response* features more in this

edition than previous editions as the ' "what do you think?" is something that we keep.' *Headway* has been sold in 126 countries worldwide
(Oxford University Press, 2006) and, as noted above, is no longer targeted towards a specific type of teacher. The approach is more 'is it
teachable? Is it *easy* to teach? Is it transparent? Is the learning objective transparent? Will anybody [...] regardless of experience, be able to
access what our main point is?' (*Headway*).

The writers of *Inside Out's* stated disinclination for Content q-types
('we're not great believers in the traditional what, who, where') is borne
out by Figures 3, 4, and 5, where we can see that they ask fewer Content
q-types than the other series. Their preference for learners encountering
'the language in context first before asking them to guess the meaning' is revealed in the prevalence of *Lexical* q-types (see Figures 6 and
7). The writer's belief that 'the meaning comes through the personalisa-
tion [...] because that's the engagement [... when] the students' heads
came up out of the worksheet and they actually spoke to each other
[...] and there was genuine communication' is reflected in the predom-
inance of *Personal Response* q-types, which can be seen in Figures 8, 9,
and 13.

The noticeable increase in *Lexical* q-types over *Form* q-types in the
more recent series, as seen in Figure 3.7, possibly reflects the increasing
value placed on vocabulary in the 2000s as 'Vocabulary acquisition has
moved from being a neglected backwater in second language acquisition
[...] to a position of some importance' (Meara, 2002: 393). Another perspective to consider is whether to teach specific vocabulary items before
reading a text or ask learners to guess the meaning from the context.
We can see in Figure 3.15 that for *English File* and *Inside Out* pre-teaching
vocabulary 'is not something we necessarily subscribe to because we
don't want to fill the texts with difficult vocabulary [... but] again it
will be dictated by the text. If there are absolutely crucial words we
might have a glossary. We prefer to have glossaries [...] than pre-teach'
(*Inside Out*). *English File* shares this stance 'as *English File* is used by many
different language groups it is difficult [...] to tell all teachers what
words they should pre-teach. A teacher of Spanish students, for example
would not think of pre-teaching '*priority*' to an intermediate class as it
is easily guessable but may think of pre-teaching something culturally
obscure like 'M and S' [Marks and Spencer, the department store]. In fact
we do sometimes add glossaries to our reading texts to cover cultural
references.' The decision by the writers of *Cutting Edge* to reduce the
pre-teaching of vocabulary and increase guessing from context in the
revised edition (*C/Edge 2*) 'was a conscious thing [...] something that

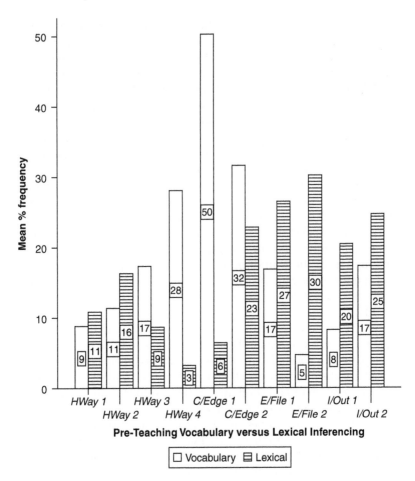

Figure 3.15   A comparison of Pre-Teaching Vocabulary question types and *Lexical* question types in all editions

did come back from the feedback [received about *C/Edge 1*]'. Regarding pre-teaching vocabulary or guessing from context, *Headway* declared 'no preference. It depends on the suitability of the vocabulary items and the text.'

Conclusion

The two principal elements of this chapter are the creation of a taxonomy of different types of questions and tasks that can be applied to any reading text and the application of this taxonomy to original and revised editions of four series of global ELT textbooks.

The rationale for the taxonomy itself is that it creates a framework for analysis and comparison of reading comprehension activities. The analysis of question types has shown certain preferences among series writers. The value of the taxonomy is manifold: it raises awareness of the different types of questions and tasks that can accompany a reading text – and each question type has its merits; it can be incorporated into a materials evaluation check list (or used independently) and can thus inform our decisions regarding choice of materials; the taxonomy can provide a basis for teacher training and professional development in materials writing as it can raise awareness of different options available once a suitable reading text has been selected, and can perhaps also provide food for thought regarding what constitutes a suitable reading text. This implies that it can (and should) play a key role in teacher training. In addition to the pedagogical benefits, there are wider benefits of this taxonomy in the research and analysis of teaching materials, expanded on further below.

Pedagogical benefits of the taxonomy

Focus on question types

There is value in raising awareness of the different possible question types. Sanders justified the creation of his taxonomy because he felt that teachers often 'overemphasize those [questions] that require students only to remember, and practically no teachers make full use of all worthwhile kinds of questions' (Sanders, 1966: 2), with the danger that this overemphasis 'may encourage students to be locaters of information rather than learners of content' (Armbruster and Ostertag, 1993: 89). It is also important to distinguish between the purposes of questions as they can 'serve two main functions [...] instructional – to promote learning [... and] to assess learning' (Armbruster and Ostertag, 1993: 69). In the context of the reading lesson in an EFL textbook I feel the questions should achieve the former, and in that regard I favour Nuttall's view that the objective of comprehension questions is 'not to test understanding, but to bring it about [... and focus on] developing, (not just demonstrating) understanding' (Nuttall, 1996: 181).

Merits of each question type

There is a rationale for each question type, and each one has its merits: the Content category conforms to both learner and teacher expectations regarding comprehension checking. The *Explicit* q-type will build confidence as it is relatively easy to get these 'right'. Further, the 'use of factual questions can be defended on the grounds that students need to know certain basic information before they can engage in higher order thinking' (Armbruster and Ostertag, 1993: 85).

The *Implicit* q-type incorporates this same ideal but reflects the language learning purpose of these classroom practices by requiring the learner to understand a single idea expressed in two different ways. The *Inferential Comprehension* q-types incorporate the higher order thinking skills.

The three q-types in the Language category involve focus on the *language* component of the texts. The *Reorganization* q-type allows for a closer examination of the text and its component parts. The *Lexical* q-type promotes 'inferencing' – using linguistic or contextual clues to access the meaning of a word (Carton, 1971), and *Form* q-types recognize the importance of the structure of language in language learning 'to develop knowledge of the language and its conventions of use [...] so that [learners] can successfully deal with any text that they may meet' (Nation, 1979: 87).

The Affect category allows for the personalization of an activity, and *Personal Response* q-types provide the opportunity for learners to relate the text to their own lives. The second q-type in this category, *Evaluation*, provides an opportunity for a deeper, more considered and thought-provoking, response to the text.

While it is not suggested here that one should strive to incorporate all eight q-types into every text, awareness of an over-reliance on one particular q-type should raise concerns with the writer and prompt them to incorporate a wider variety of activities. By the same token, if the selected texts appear only to lend themselves to a limited repertoire of these q-types, then perhaps the text choices need further consideration.

Materials evaluation

The taxonomy can contribute to textbook evaluation by illustrating question and task preferences. It facilitates comparison between textbooks, and this will enable the potential user of a textbook to make an informed decision regarding textbook selection. If we accept Richards' (2006: 7) argument that 'materials will inevitably reflect a theory of the nature of language, communication, or language use', then applying the taxonomy will help the selector to identify those views and consequently choose a book that favours their own beliefs regarding language instruction.

Materials writing

Perhaps the greatest value of the taxonomy is the support it can provide teachers in their own materials writing. Given that research has shown that the skill of writing quality material is not necessarily possessed by all (Bereiter and Scardamalia, 1993; Johnson, 2003; Tsui, 2003), and the abundance of authentic materials, particularly authentic reading materials, available to teachers nowadays, I would argue that attention needs to be given to what is done with those materials. Bearing in mind that 'writing takes a great deal of time' (Mares, 2003, p.132), I suggest that a taxonomy of this kind deserves a place in teacher-training programmes as I feel it is still true to say that 'materials design is an area of ELT training which is sometimes neglected in methodology texts and teacher-training programmes' (Block, 1991: 211).

In addition, textbook writers themselves could benefit from this taxonomy, as it was apparent from my interviews that question and task writing was an intuitive process and the existence of a checklist 'will be very useful for people to be aware of the kind of tasks [...], the kind of task types there are' (*Cutting Edge*). It is worth bearing in mind that 'the expertise required of materials writers is importantly different from that required of classroom teachers' (Allwright, 1981: 6). The same views were held by the writers I interviewed: 'you're actually preparing, you're writing recipes for teachers in a variety of different contexts which may be very different from the one you're used to [...] And I think that's part of the learning process that ELT authors have to go through' (*Cutting Edge*).

Wider research benefits of the taxonomy

If we accept Smith's (2012) observation that 'materials are a "third pillar" in most classrooms, along with the teacher and students – but a very under-researched one', then I would argue that progress in this field should encompass two elements: more analyses of teaching materials should be conducted, in terms of both breadth (a greater number of textbooks) and depth (a greater number of different aspects of textbooks). For instance, in the context of this study, a useful next step would be to analyse the comprehension questions of the readings in a wider range of textbooks as well as in textbooks of different proficiency levels, to see, for instance, whether there is any difference in the q-types found in Elementary level through to Upper Intermediate and Advanced textbooks. Then, a fruitful discussion could ensue regarding where each q-type might be placed on a scale ranging from 'of paramount importance' to 'useful' to 'quite unnecessary' and in which contexts, and whether certain q-types should receive greater emphasis than others and what proportions or distributions might be appropriate as 'the research doesn't suggest what an appropriate distribution of questions should be' (Armbruster and Ostertag, 1993: 85).

The taxonomy could also be applied to other textbook series, both past and present, to provide a clearer overall picture of the development of reading materials. Finally, yet further research could, perhaps, adapt the taxonomy for application to listening comprehension exercises in textbooks.

References

Allwright, R.L. (1981). What do we want teaching materials for? *ELT Journal*, 36, 5–18.

Armbruster, B., and Ostertag, J. (1993). Questions in elementary science and social studies textbooks. In B.K. Britton, A. Woodward, and M.R. Binkley (Eds.), *Learning from textbooks: Theory and practice* (pp.69–94). Hillsdale: Lawrence Erlbaum.

Bereiter, C. and Scardamalia, M. (1993). *Surpassing ourselves: An inquiry into the nature and implications of expertise*. La Salle: Open Court Press.

Block, D. (1991). Some thoughts on DIY materials design. *ELT Journal*, 45, 211–217.

Bloom, B.S., Engelhart, M.D., Furst, E.J., Hill, W.H., and Krathwohl, D.R. (1956). *Taxonomy of educational objectives: The classification of education goals. Handbook 1: Cognitive domain*. New York: David McKay.

Cabaroglu, N. and Roberts, J. (2000). Development in student teachers' pre-existing beliefs during a 1-year PGCE programme. *System*, 28, 387–402.

Carton, A.S. (1971). Inferencing: A process in using and learning language. In P. Pimsleur and T. Quinn (Eds.), *The psychology of second language learning* (pp. 45–58). Cambridge: Cambridge University Press.

Clymer, T. (1968). What is reading? Some current concepts. In H.M. Robinson (Ed.), *Innovation and change in reading instruction: The sixty-seventh yearbook of the national society for the study of education part II* (pp.7–29). Chicago: University of Chicago Press.

Cunningham, S. and Moor, P. (1998). *Cutting edge intermediate*. Harlow: Longman.

Cunningham, S. and Moor, P. (2005). *New cutting edge intermediate*. (2nd ed.). Harlow: Longman.

Day, R.R. and Park, J.-S. (2005). Developing reading comprehension questions. *Reading in a Foreign Language*, 17, 60–73.

Gray, W.S. (1960). The major aspects of reading. In H.M. Robinson (Ed.), *Sequential development of reading abilities* (pp.8–24). Chicago: University of Chicago Press.

Guszak, F.J. (1967). Teacher questioning and reading. *The Reading Teacher,* 21, 227–234.

Holm, S. (1979). A simple sequentially rejective multiple test procedure. *Scandinavian Journal of Statistics,* 6, 65–70.

Johnson, K. (2003). *Designing language teaching tasks.* Basingstoke: Palgrave Macmillan.

Kay, S. and Jones, V. (2000). *Inside out intermediate.* London: Macmillan.

Kay, S. and Jones, V. (2009). *New inside out intermediate.* London: Macmillan.

Kuzborska, I. (2011). Links between teachers' beliefs and practices and research on reading. *Reading in a Foreign Language,* 23, 102–128.

Littlejohn, A.P. (1992). *Why are English language teaching materials the way they are?* Unpublished PhD thesis. University of Lancaster.

Mares, C. (2003). Writing a coursebook. In B. Tomlinson (Ed.), *Developing materials for language teaching* (pp.130–140). London: Continuum.

Meara, P. (2002). The rediscovery of vocabulary. *Second Language Research,* 18, 393–407.

Nation, I.S.P. (1979). The curse of the comprehension question: Some alternatives. *Guidelines,* 2, 85–103.

Nuttall, C. (1982). *Teaching reading skills in a foreign language.* London: Heinemann.

Nuttall, C. (1996). *Teaching reading skills in a foreign language* (2nd ed.). London: Macmillan.

Oxford University Press. (2006). *The story of Headway.* Oxford: Oxford University Press.

Oxenden, C. and Latham-Koenig, C. (1999). *English file 3.* Oxford: Oxford University Press.

Oxenden, C. and Latham-Koenig, C. (2006). *New english file intermediate.* Oxford: Oxford University Press.

Pearson, P.D. and Johnson, D.D. (1978). *Teaching reading comprehension.* New York: Holt, Rinehart and Winston.

Richards, J.C. (2006). Materials development and research – making the connection. *RELC Journal,* 37, 5–26.

Richards, J.C. and Rodgers, T.S. (2001). *Approaches and methods in language teaching.* Cambridge: Cambridge University Press.

Sanders, N.M. (1966). *Classroom questions: What kinds?* New York: Harper and Row.

Schank, R.C. (1973). Identification of conceptualizations underlying natural language. In R.C. Schank and K.M. Colby (Eds.), *Computer models of thought and language* (pp.187–247). San Francisco: Freeman.

Smith, R. (2012). IATEFL research SIG: Online article discussion of B. Tomlinson (2012), materials development for language learning and teaching. *Language Teaching,* 42, 143–179. Retrieved from http://groups.yahoo.com/group/resig/messages

Smith, R.J. and Barrett, T.C. (1974). *Teaching reading in the middle grades.* Reading: Addison-Wesley.

Soars, L. and Soars, J. (1986). *Headway intermediate.* Oxford: Oxford University Press.

Soars, L. and Soars, J. (1996). *New headway intermediate.* Oxford: Oxford University Press.

Soars, L. and Soars, J. (2003). *Headway intermediate* (3rd ed.). Oxford: Oxford University Press.

Soars, L., and Soars, J. (2009). *Headway intermediate* (4th ed.). Oxford: Oxford University Press.

Tsui, A.B.M. (2003). *Understanding expertise in teaching: Case studies of second language teachers*. Cambridge: Cambridge University Press.

Waters, A. (2012). Trends and issues in ELT methods and methodology. *ELT Journal*, 66, 440–449.

4

Teaching English Reading: What's Included in the Textbooks of Pre-Service General Education Teachers?

L. Quentin Dixon, Shuang Wu, Renata Burgess-Brigham, R. Malatesha Joshi, Emily Binks-Cantrell, and Erin Washburn

Summary

With changing demographics, pre-service general education teachers in many English-speaking countries will face the challenge of effectively teaching English language learners (ELLs) when they enter the classroom. Research into how to teach English reading has emphasized the importance of five essential components as summarized by the National Reading Panel, or NRP (2000): phonemic awareness, phonics, fluency, vocabulary, and text comprehension. Other research suggests spelling and assessment are additional important components of reading instruction (Coltheart and Prior, 2007; Geva, 2000). Furthermore, pre-service teachers in countries with substantial numbers of ELLs need to learn strategies that are effective for teaching reading to ELLs (August and Shanahan, 2006).

As reading in English may be taught differently in different countries, this chapter examines what pre-service general education teachers in Australia, Canada, New Zealand, and Singapore may be learning from their textbooks assigned for courses in reading instruction. These courses, and thus the textbooks, include both the theory and practice of reading, so pre-service teachers can build both a theoretical understanding of how reading skills develop and a practical knowledge of how to implement instructional activities that will promote their future students' reading development. The chapter details the amount of inclusion of the NRP's five components, plus spelling, assessment, and English as a second language (ESL), in 39 English reading textbooks for pre-service general education teachers. Page counts quantify how much each component was covered. Results showed that spelling and assessment are included most often, followed by phonics (decoding) and text comprehension, whereas fluency is the least likely to be included. Coverage of all five NRP components ranged from 5 per cent to 59 per cent of textbook content. Regarding content specific to second language learners, 74 per cent of the textbooks included coverage, ranging from 0.2 per cent to 74 per cent of the textbook content, with most below 20 per cent coverage. With the global increase of students learning English, this chapter highlights areas needing improvement in textbooks for classes that prepare pre-service general education teachers to teach reading to their students, including ELLs.

Introduction

With an increasingly globalized economy, the importance of English language learning has grown exponentially in the 21st century. The English language is an imperative medium of international communication (Kirkpatrick, 2007; McKay, 2002). In many countries, fluency in English is associated with access to marketable educational preparation and successful career outcomes (Hirtt, 2009; Wee, 2008). This is especially true for countries in which English is an official language or the language of the majority. Building on the work of Joshi, Binks, Graham, Ocker-Dean, Smith, and Boulware-Gooden (2009) regarding the content of textbooks in the US used for pre-service general education teachers' reading courses, we examined textbook content in other English-speaking countries which have substantial numbers of English language learners (ELLs). Our focus is on the textbooks used to prepare pre-service general education teachers to teach reading to schoolchildren in Australia, Canada, New Zealand, and Singapore.

Growing numbers of English language learners

Canada, New Zealand, and Australia are currently experiencing rapid growth in immigration. The Coalition for Equal Access to Education (n.d.), using data from Statistics Canada 2005, predicts that the proportion of the population not speaking the official languages of English or French will increase from 18.5 per cent (in 2001) to between 20.8 per cent and 24.8 per cent of the total population by 2017. The Australian situation is similar to that of Canada. Using data from a nine-year cohort, the Australian Council of Educational Research (2000) reported that 10.4 per cent of Australian students speak a language other than English at home. In the case of New Zealand, there were 28,000 students in 2010 from grades 1 through 8 – about 6 per cent of the total – who were not native English speakers, mostly resulting from immigration (New Zealand Curriculum Online, 2012; New Zealand Ministry of Education, 2013).

Singapore is a special case. Unlike the other three previously mentioned countries, the majority of the school-age population consists of English language learners, as English is one of the many languages spoken there. English is the medium of instruction as well as a content area in primary and secondary schools. Thus, general education teachers teach reading and all other content areas (e.g., mathematics, science, history) in English. The number of Singaporeans over the age of five who use a language other than English most frequently at home was 67.7 per cent in 2010 (Singapore Department of Statistics, 2010). In the near future, Singapore aims for the majority of its students to reach a good level of proficiency in English, with at least 20 per cent of its students developing a high level of proficiency in the language (Ministry of Education, Singapore, 2010).

The importance of teaching reading to ELLs

For the purposes of this chapter, we term anyone who speaks a language other than English as their native language and who is in the process of acquiring the English language an English language learner (ELL). The NRP (2000) identified the skills that are paramount in children's reading development and how those skills should be taught. Learning these vital skills is especially important in the case of ELL students. Janzen (2007) states that 'reading is a complex skill that is critical to ELLs' academic achievement' (p.707). In fact, some researchers argue that extensive reading is the only way in which language proficiency can be improved (Brown, 2009). Given the complex orthographic system of the English language, learning how to read can prove to be especially difficult for ELLs, particularly when their first language uses a writing system that is not based on the Latin alphabet.

Context of reading instruction for ELLs in the four countries

Australia, Canada, New Zealand, and Singapore all participated in the Progress in International Reading Literacy Study (PIRLS) 2011.

Singapore and Canada were rated among the top-performing countries as measured by fourth-grade students' reading achievement; New
Zealand and Australia performed better than the international average but statistically significantly lower than Singapore and Canada
(Mullis, Martin, Foy, and Drucker, 2012). All four of our focal countries
demonstrated better performance in reading comprehension processes
involving 'interpreting, integrating and evaluating' (Mullis, Martin, Foy,
et al., 2012) texts than those involving 'retrieval and straightforward
inferencing' (p.93). Singapore, in particular, has shown tremendous
improvement in its PIRLS scores since 2001, moving from a little above
average to a top performer.

Of the four official languages in Singapore (Malay, Mandarin, Tamil,
and English), English is the language of administration, as well as the
language of formal school instruction. On the school level, teachers
have been adopting meaning-based instruction, emphasizing 'phonics,
word recognition, whole text, and intertextual comprehension' (Mullis,
Martin, Minnich, Drucker, and Ragan, 2012b: 572).

Different from Singapore, 75 per cent of New Zealanders speak English
only, although three languages are recognized as official: Māori, English,
and New Zealand Sign Language (Mullis, Martin, Minnich, et al., 2012b:
435). In terms of English learning, the New Zealand Curriculum focuses
on vocabulary related to literacy, comprehension, communication, and
critical literacy (Mullis, Martin, Minnich, et al., 2012b: 442). In New
Zealand's highly decentralized education system, school administrators and teachers have been given considerable freedom in adopting
teaching strategies and choosing reading texts. Students who are learning English as a second language are usually placed in mainstream
classrooms. Additional help is available through separate sessions with
specialists and a peer-support program (Mullis, Martin, Minnich, et al.,
2012b).

The linguistic situation in Canada is no less complex. In the absence
of a national curriculum, the provinces and territories develop their
own curricula and assessments (Mullis, Martin, Minnich, Drucker, and
Ragan, 2012a). English and French have been the main languages used
for school instruction. Depending on the jurisdiction, English or French
will be taught to new immigrant students by individual instruction or
in-class support. In terms of reading, classroom instruction is designed
based on 'the belief that reading must be practiced, purposeful, modeled, and supported' (Mullis, Martin, Minnich, et al., 2012a: 123). More
specifically, teachers tend to focus on scaffolding, differentiated instruction, comprehension, and explicit teaching of high-level thinking skills.

Canada also has a well-developed system for assessment, consisting of assessments at national, jurisdictional, and classroom levels (Mullis, Martin, Minnich, et al., 2012a).

In Australia, where there is no designated official language, English is the language of the majority of society, as well as the main language of school instruction. With continued emphasis on literacy and numeracy learning among primary school students, the recent national reforms, such as Literacy and Numeracy National Partnership Agreement, which commenced in 2009, also show national interest in research concerning effective teaching strategies (Mullis, Martin, Minnich, et al., 2012a). According to a major national Australian research study, *In Teachers' Hands: Effective Literacy Practices in the Early Years of Schooling*, effective instruction should be characterized by 'a highly structured approach to phonics teaching', 'clear explanations of word level structures', and 'careful scaffolding, including guided practice in a variety of contexts' (Mullis, Martin, Minnich, et al., 2012a: 51). On the state level, comprehension in the middle primary years is receiving increasing attention (Mullis, Martin, Minnich, et al., 2012a).

Teacher preparation for teaching ELLs

With increasing numbers of ELLs in many English-speaking countries, it is unrealistic to rely solely on English as a Second Language (ESL) teachers and specialists to meet the needs of ELLs who are placed in regular classes for the majority of the day; general education teachers must become knowledgeable teachers of ELLs as well (de Jong and Harper, 2005; He, Prater, and Steed, 2011). However, in reality, the majority of general education teachers are not yet ready. First, an ESL component is not always required for teacher certification. Take the US as an example. Except for New York and Florida, no states mandate ESL certification as a requirement for teaching certification (National Comprehensive Center for Teacher Quality, 2007), and only 17 per cent require any information regarding ELL education to be part of teacher preparation programs (Menken and Antunez, 2001). While acknowledging the relevance of many sound teaching practices originated for native English-speaking students from diverse cultural or ethnic backgrounds, de Jong and Harper (2005) argue that teachers need additional knowledge and skills to be effective with ELLs as well, knowledge that is often missing from mainstream teacher preparation programs.

Most teacher preparation programs fail to prepare their students for teaching ELLs in real school settings. Pre-service teachers, who may have been educated in a monolingual environment, may be quite unaware of the rapidly changing landscape in schools. Students finishing their first year of a four-year primary teacher education program in Australia revealed in reflective journals their lack of awareness of cultural diversity at school and their feelings of apprehension regarding future encounters with students from different cultures (de Courcy, 2007). Further, the course readings (journal articles and book chapters) either reinforced these pre-service teachers' deficit views of ESL students, or the students felt that reading one article equipped them fully to teach ESL children, leading de Courcy to argue that a small amount of information may actually be harmful for preparing teachers to view ELLs positively and becoming prepared to teach these students effectively.

Even in Singapore, where many students do not speak English as their main home language, literacy instruction draws from reports and techniques created for native English-speaking children (Vaish, 2012). Thus, teachers tend to apply a one-size-fits-all approach that may not serve their diverse students well (Vaish, 2012).

Requirements for effective reading instruction to ELLs

Understanding of the five components of reading

Teacher educators and pre-service teacher programs play an integral role in the literacy development of students, and they face the challenge of preparing competent teachers who can effectively mold their students into proficient readers of English. In order to accomplish this difficult feat, teachers must have a sound knowledge of the English language structure and the components of effective reading instruction. Understanding this type of knowledge, and applying it in early reading instruction, can prove to be difficult for teachers (Kelcey, 2011), especially when confounded with the lack of proper pre-service and in-service training. To make this knowledge more available to the educational community, the NRP (2000) in the US outlined five essential components of reading instruction, which were all supported by research and confirmed by similar reading committees in other English-speaking nations, such as Australia (Australian Government Department of Education, Employment, and Workplace Relations, 2005) and the UK (UK Parliament, 2004). They found that the teaching of phonemic awareness, phonics, fluency, vocabulary, and text comprehension were inextricable from quality reading instruction.

Moats and Foorman (2003) defined instruction in the five components, which will be summarized in the following. We will begin with phonics and phonemic awareness, which are highly interrelated in nature but different. While competency in phonics represents the ability to connect sounds with their written symbols, phonemic awareness is attained when a learner can discriminate and manipulate those sounds in the spoken language. Children with better phonemic awareness develop better knowledge of phonics (Scarborough, 2001), with some studies indicating a bi-directional relationship, with better phonemic awareness supporting word reading but improved word-reading skills bolstering phonemic awareness (e.g., Stuart and Coltheart, 1988; Vandervelden and Siegel, 1995). Further, explicit, systematic instruction in phonemic awareness and phonics has been shown to improve ELLs' word-reading in English, in some studies on a par with their native-speaking peers (Lesaux, Rupp, and Siegel, 2007; Lesaux and Siegel, 2003; Lipka and Siegel, 2007; Stuart, 1999, 2004).

Fluency refers to the ability to aptly identify written words with automaticity and accuracy (Moats and Foorman, 2003). For ELLs, oral English proficiency, which tends to be weaker than native speakers', plays a role in their word- and text-reading fluency (Geva and Yaghoub-Zadeh, 2006). Vocabulary knowledge – the identification of the structural and grammatical features and contextual meaning of words (Moats and Foorman, 2003) – is particularly important to ELLs, who typically display lower English vocabulary than native-speaking peers for years (Jean and Geva, 2009). Vocabulary plays a small role in predicting word recognition (Jean and Geva, 2009), but may be more critical to ELLs in the final component, text comprehension.

In order to teach text comprehension, teachers must be able 'to know and explicate such linguistic concepts as text organization, genre, inter- and intra-sentence references, figurative and idiomatic language, and the complex sentence structure found in academic discourse' (Moats and Foorman, 2003: 24). Lower knowledge of word meanings can impede ELLs' comprehension of text. Proper training in these five components is vital in any teacher preparation program (Spear-Swerling and Brucker, 2004). Without a comprehensive knowledge and implementation of the NRP's recommendations, a teacher's reading instruction will most likely be inchoate and leave much to be desired.

Knowledge of assessment and spelling instruction

Of all types of reading assessment available for ELL students, the most frequently used current practices are heavily dependent upon standardized/high-stakes testing and often occur after the student is perceived to have an oral command of English (Gersten, Baker, Shanahan, et al., 2007). For assessing the risk for reading difficulties, it is not neces-sary to wait until the student has oral English proficiency; however, the current teaching workforce is generally unaware of this, as such informa-tion was not imparted to them during their pre-service preparation and in-service professional development (Gersten et al., 2007). Synthesizing the research in this area, Gersten et al. (2007) recommended measur-ing ELL students' phonemic awareness, alphabet knowledge, phonics skills, and word-reading skills in kindergarten and grade 1, and adding a measure of word-reading fluency for grades 2 through 5. In addi-tion to these measures, Geva (2000) suggests assessing the relationship between students' reading comprehension and listening comprehen-sion to detect reading difficulties in ELLs and native English-speaking students alike. While a small gap between reading and listening com-prehension is developmentally appropriate, a large gap indicates that students are confounded by the printed representations of language, indicating a decoding disability (Geva, 2000). These assessments for reading difficulties can and should proceed, whether or not the student has developed oral language proficiency in the second language, as these assessments identify children with reading disabilities in both native speaking and ELL students (Gersten et al., 2007; Geva, 2000). A lon-gitudinal study indicated that the same skills assessed in kindergarten predicted later reading achievement for ELLs and native-speaking peers (Lesaux, Lipka, and Siegel, 2006; Lesaux, Rupp, and Siegel, 2007; Lipka and Siegel, 2007). Limbos and Geva (2001) also suggest that reading instructors should be educated on the reading development of ELLs, so that they avoid the tendency to rely on assessments measuring oral lan-guage proficiency, as research demonstrates that this is not an accurate way to measure English literacy skills in ELLs (August and Shanahan, 2006).

Like reading and the assessment of literacy skills, spelling instruc-tion should be given to all students in the first years of their reading instruction (Coltheart and Prior, 2007). Treiman (1998) argues that the early emphasis on spelling instruction can sharpen children's phonemic awareness and improve their reading. As mentioned before, Scarborough (2001) found that the ability to discriminate phonemes within words has been shown to result in better acquisition of reading skills. Treiman (1998) also argues that development of spelling skills is not automatic. Much like the NRP recommends for the teaching of phonics, spelling should be taught by means of explicit instruction (Treiman, 1998). Because of the nature of the English language, spelling instruction can be quite beneficial for young readers, especially ELLs. According to

Treiman (1998), 'even when phonological, orthographic, and morpho-logical patterns are considered, the spellings of English words are not totally predictable' (p.291). Equipping ELL students with this knowledge early on can give them a great advantage in their reading development and can possibly mitigate some of the difficulties they will encounter from the morphological nature of many words in written English.

Whether examining spelling, assessment, or any of the five NRP-established components of literacy instruction, one pervasive theme appears in the literature: general education teachers suffer from a criti-cal lack of preparation in the teaching of reading (Coltheart and Prior, 2007). Many studies show evidence that both pre-service and in-service general education teachers are unfamiliar with skills associated with early reading and are not well versed in the linguistic structure of English (Bos, Mather, Dickson, Podhajski, and Chard, 2001; Moats, 1994; Moats and Foorman, 2003; Spear-Swerling and Brucker, 2004). In addition, Bos et al. (2001) reported that the teachers themselves felt that they were not completely capable of providing the essential components of literacy instruction, specifically phonemic awareness and phonics. Although some may contend that a strong reading curriculum with instructional scripts for teachers would be adequate, research demon-strates that students whose teachers show better knowledge of reading components perform better on reading tasks (Carreker, Swank, Tillman-Doudy, Neuhaus, Monfils, Montemayor, and Johnson, 2005; Kelcey, 2011; Spear-Swerling and Brucker, 2004). If there is to be any hope at remedying this situation, we must take the logical next step to answer the following question: why are reading teachers so poorly prepared to cultivate the literacy skills of their students?

Problems with and solutions to pre-service teacher preparation

As more evidence points to inadequate preparation of reading instruc-tors, researchers have embarked upon identifying the problems with pre-service teacher preparation, as well as the solutions to these prob-lems. When professors and university instructors lack the necessary knowledge to teach reading instructional practices to pre-service teach-ers, well-designed reading textbooks could be an additional source of knowledge (Joshi, Binks, Hougen, Dahlgren, Ocker-Dean, and Smith, 2009). Moats (1994) expressed a similar opinion, that it is important for teacher education courses to provide future teachers with adequate teaching materials, such as textbooks.

Despite the scarce literature examining the textbooks used in teacher preparation, current evidence suggests that the majority of the texts used in teacher education courses devoted specifically to the teaching of reading to beginning or struggling readers failed to cover sufficiently and appropriately the five components of reading instruction deemed necessary by the NRP. By examining the 17 most popularly used textbooks in the US to prepare pre-service general education teachers to teach reading, Joshi, Binks, Graham, et al. (2009) evaluated these texts using the NRP's definitions of the five essential components of literacy instruction. Their study showed that only ten of the 17 books covered and correctly defined all five components. Except for one book, none of the books devoted more than half of its content to the NRP's components, the coverage percentage ranging from 9 per cent to 39 per cent. However, no studies have been done to determine to what extent textbooks used internationally covered essential components of reading instruction. Therefore, the present study chose to examine the content regarding reading instruction in textbooks used for general education teacher preparation in countries other than the US which have substantial numbers of ELL students.

Method

This study focused on the English reading textbooks adopted by four countries: New Zealand, Australia, Singapore, and Canada. Reading professors in major universities of each country were contacted and asked to provide details of the textbooks that reading course instructors selected to prepare pre-service teachers to teach English reading. Their book lists included nine books from three universities in New Zealand, 22 books from three Australian universities, nine books from three Canadian universities, and two books from one Singaporean university; these counts include one text that was used by two universities in Canada, and two texts that were used by two universities in New Zealand. These lists finally yielded 39 total textbooks for our analysis, because three texts were used in two countries. If the instructor noted that only one chapter was used in the preparation course, only that chapter of the book was coded. Each textbook is listed in Table 4.1. When different editions of two books were also mentioned by different instructors, each edition used was separately included in the final analysis due to the fact that different editions of the same textbook may vary considerably in content. These textbooks comprise a combination of both locally produced and internationally produced textbooks.

Table 4.1 Textbook information by inclusion of ESL, NRP components, spelling and assessment (N = 39)

Book title	Pub. date	Total page #	ESL	PA*	Phon.	Flu.	Compre.	Voca.	Spe.	Ass.	Num. of NRP components inclusion	Num. of NRP definition match
A new grammar companion for primary teachers	2011	196	8.16	0.00	0.00	0.00	6.63	3.06	0.51	4.59	2	0
A passion for poetry: Practical approaches to using poetry in the classroom	2005	140	1.43	0.00	0.00	0.00	1.43	0.00	0.00	0.00	1	0
An observation survey of early literacy achievement	2002	171	0.00	5.85	0.00	0.00	0.00	3.51	5.85	52.63	2	0
Assessment for reading instruction	2009	280	0.00	2.14	3.57	5.36	12.14	1.43	10.71	77.86	5	4
Beyond the reading wars	2006	152	7.89	3.95	13.16	5.92	3.29	7.24	2.63	11.84	5	2
Constructing critical literacies: Teaching and learning textual practice	1997	441	0.00	0.00	0.00	0.00	0.00	0.00	0.00	0.23	0	0

Table 4.1 (Continued)

Book title	Pub. date	Total page #	ESL	PA*	Phon.	Flu.	Compre.	Voca.	Spe.	Ass.	Num. of NRP components inclusion	Num. of NRP definition match
Constructing meaning: Balancing elementary language arts	2009	526	3.61	1.52	3.80	0.57	1.14	0.38	3.80	15.97	5	3
Developing early literacy: Assessment and teaching	2009	399	3.01	5.51	14.29	0.75	2.26	2.26	1.00	10.28	5	4
Developing literacy in the English classroom	2010	315	4.13	2.22	11.43	1.59	4.76	9.52	7.62	4.44	5	3
Differentiated reading instruction: Strategies for the primary grades	2007	159	1.26	10.69	13.84	9.43	13.21	11.95	10.69	25.79	5	5
Effective literacy practice in years 1–4	2003	188	0.53	2.13	4.26	0.00	6.38	3.19	7.98	10.64	4	4
Effective literacy practice in years 5–8	2006	197	12.18	3.05	1.02	10.15	10.15	3.55	4.06	15.74	5	4
Grammar and meaning: An introduction for primary teachers	2003	170	0.00	0.00	0.00	0.00	0.00	5.29	0.00	3.53	1	0

Title												
Guiding readers and writers, grades 3–6: Teaching comprehension, genre, and content literacy	2001	510	0.20	0.00	0.78	2.75	11.18	3.14	2.16	5.88	4	1
Language and learning: An introduction for teaching	2006	240	5.42	0.00	1.25	0.00	0.00	0.00	1.67	0.00	1	1
Language and learning: An introduction for teaching	2010	259	5.41	3.47	1.93	0.00	0.39	0.00	1.93	0.39	3	2
Language arts in Canadian classrooms	2012	474	2.11	1.48	2.32	1.69	5.49	2.32	4.85	14.98	5	5
Linking assessment, teaching and learning	2003	209	4.78	0.00	0.00	0.00	1.44	0.48	2.39	18.66	2	0
Literacy for the 21st century	2010	484	3.72	3.31	4.75	2.48	9.71	6.82	7.44	13.02	5	4
Literacy in the middle grades	2010	385	9.87	0.00	0.52	8.57	14.29	9.09	3.64	20.52	4	2
Literacy learning: In the early years	2000	222	11.26	0.45	2.70	0.00	0.00	0.00	5.41	12.16	2	1

Table 4.1 (Continued)

Book title	Pub. date	Total page #	ESL	PA*	Phon.	Flu.	Compre.	Voca.	Spe.	Ass.	Num. of NRP components inclusion	Num. of NRP definition match
Literacy: Reading, writing and children's literature (3rd edition)	2006	573	2.44	0.70	1.57	0.00	2.09	0.00	5.58	10.47	3	3
Literacy: Reading, writing and children's literature (4th edition)	2010	700	2.71	5.71	6.86	0.86	4.14	3.14	6.29	10.71	5	3
Making literacy real: Theories and practices for learning and teaching	2005	157	0.00	0.00	0.64	0.00	0.00	0.00	0.00	0.00	1	0
Reading and learning to read	2009	558	6.63	3.05	6.45	3.58	10.04	7.71	3.41	12.54	5	3
Reading in the primary school years	2006	244	3.69	1.23	0.00	0.00	0.00	0.00	0.00	6.15	1	0
Reading map of development: Addressing current literacy challenges	2004	305	0.98	3.61	6.56	2.30	6.56	4.59	1.31	9.84	5	3

Title	Year												
Reading power: Teaching students to think while they read	2006	144	0.00	2.08	0.00	0.69	22.92	0.69	2.08	4.17	4	0
Scaffolding language/scaffolding learning	2002	152	14.47	1.32	4.61	0.00	0.00	0.00	9.21	11.18	2	1
Speech to print: Language essentials for teachers	2010	282	0.00	2.84	1.42	0.71	0.71	2.84	15.60	0.00	5	2
Teaching children with reading difficulties	2006	173	0.00	10.40	8.67	8.67	19.65	10.98	18.50	10.40	5	4
Teaching reading in the 21st century	2011	579	8.46	3.45	1.21	6.04	11.23	8.64	4.66	20.73	5	4
Teaching reading. National inquiry into the teaching of literacy	2004	102	0.98	5.88	10.78	3.92	5.88	4.90	11.76	28.43	5	5
The literacy labyrinth	2004	381	0.00	0.00	0.79	0.00	0.79	0.00	0.00	3.41	2	1
The literacy lexicon	2003	216	0.00	0.00	0.00	0.00	0.00	0.00	0.00	8.80	0	0

Table 4.1 (Continued)

Book title	Pub. date	Total page #	ESL	PA*	Phon.	Flu.	Compre.	Voca.	Spe.	Ass.	Num. of NRP components inclusion	Num. of NRP definition match
To 'Know Papers': Aboriginal perspectives on literacy (in Portraits of Literacy)	2005	19	73.68	0.00	0.00	0.00	0.00	0.00	0.00	0.00	0	0
Turn-around pedagogies: Literacy interventions for at-risk students	2005	121	0.00	0.00	0.00	0.00	0.00	0.00	5.79	4.96	0	0
Unlocking literacy: Effective decoding and spelling instruction	2010	314	0.64	2.87	9.87	1.59	0.96	1.91	18.47	5.10	5	5
Words their way	2008	386	1.81	3.11	2.59	0.52	0.00	4.40	23.83	3.63	4	2

Each textbook was searched for the information concerning eight literacy concepts: ESL, the NRP five components (phonemic awareness, phonics, fluency, vocabulary, and text comprehension), spelling, and assessment. To be more specific, the information covered (i) the inclusion of ESL-related content; (ii) the extent to which ESL was covered in terms of page numbers; (iii) the inclusion of each of the five NRP components; (iv) the number of pages devoted to each of these five components; (v) comparison of match between the book's definition of each component and the definition given by the NRP; (vi) the inclusion of assessment and spelling; and (vii) the number of pages devoted to assessment and spelling. Key words were used for page counting: in addition to 'phonemic awareness', 'phonics', 'fluency', 'comprehension', and 'vocabulary', 'ESL', 'assessment' and 'spelling', their synonyms or related terms 'English as second language', 'English language learner', 'ELL', 'English as an additional language', 'orthography', 'encoding', 'test', 'evaluation', and 'diagnosis' were also searched. In counting pages for each book, the glossary was included, but the index, appendices, and references were excluded.

All the relevant information was located by examining the key words in the index and the table of contents. For a textbook without an index, or with an unclear table of contents, each page of the book was manually searched for the key terms. These manual searches confirmed that the search terms chosen successfully identified the content of interest. The whole page was counted even if a key term was only mentioned once on that page. When a whole chapter was identified as concerning a component, then all pages in the chapter were counted, even if the key word did not appear on every page. Pages in a single textbook could be counted more than once, as each concept was counted separately for each book. For example, a page with 'ESL assessment' on it would be counted toward both ESL and assessment.

Textbooks could include these concepts in different ways. Ideally, a textbook would give an accurate definition, explain the concept, and provide examples of the concept and specific teaching activities to build that concept. ESL was the broadest concept searched, and we simply documented the inclusion of this population and the literacy issues pertinent to it in these textbooks. Overall, ELL students need literacy instruction that includes the same concepts as native English-speaking students, but ELL students have particular needs in vocabulary and comprehension, for example. An excellent textbook would describe the process of learning to read in English for ELLs and explain how oral English proficiency can be built alongside literacy skills for ELLs.

For example, teachers should choose appropriate vocabulary to focus on orally and in literacy lessons for their ELL students.

Phonemic awareness activities typically involve teachers guiding students to be able to separate or combine sounds in words; for example, a teacher might ask students to identify the first sound in the words *bat* (/b/) or *shop* (/sh/). Phonics activities help connect these sounds to the letter or combination of letters that represent them in English. Teachers, for example, might ask students to 'sound out' a word they are trying to read (e.g., /b/-/a/-/t/), then combine the sounds to form the word (*bat*). Fluency activities work on the rapid recognition of words; for example, a teacher might ask students to read a paragraph repeatedly to increase their rate of reading while keeping up their accuracy. Vocabulary activities include students providing definitions, drawing pictures, and/or acting out new vocabulary terms, and using new vocabulary items in a variety of contexts. Comprehension instruction includes teaching specific strategies, such as making predictions about the text and reading to check whether the predictions come true. Spelling activities include introducing common spelling patterns in English, such as 'ight' as in *light, night,* and *right* or 'ear' as in *ear, near,* and *fear.* Teachers need to know appropriate measures or tasks to assess students' literacy skills, as well as how to interpret the results of these measures and use them to inform their instruction. For example, if a teacher assesses a student and finds the student is not hearing the beginning sounds in words accurately (phonemic awareness), the teacher may decide to work with that student in a small group to develop better phonemic awareness.

The percentage coverage of ESL, the five NRP components, spelling, and assessment for each textbook was calculated by dividing the total number of pages covering these elements by the total number of pages in the book and multiplying by 100. Each textbook was coded by two coders. Inter-rater agreement was calculated as 92.1 per cent (ESL), 92.1 per cent (phonemic awareness), 89.5 per cent (phonics), 94.7 per cent (fluency), 94.7 per cent (comprehension), 89.5 per cent (vocabulary), 86.8 per cent (spelling), and 81.6 per cent (assessment). When any discrepancies arose, the first author was consulted for the final decision.

Results

The results of the analysis are presented in Tables 4.1, 4.2, 4.3, and 4.4. In addition to an analysis conducted with all books, we also divided them up by country that used them, to compare reading teacher preparation trends in each nation. To account for the fact that each university assigned multiple textbooks, we also analyzed the book content according to university. By looking at content across the multiple texts assigned in a given university, we could examine whether a specific university covered all eight literacy concepts across the textbooks used. We assigned each university a number in order to provide confidentiality.

The data on how many literacy concepts and how much of each concept were included in each textbook are detailed in Table 4.1. Tables 4.2, 4.3, and 4.4 summarize these data. Concerning the number of concepts covered in the texts, all books included at least one of the eight concepts examined (see Table 4.1). Twenty-nine texts mentioned four or more concepts, and a little more than half of the texts covered at least seven concepts.

Each of the eight concepts was included by more than half of the books (see Table 4.2). More textbooks included assessment (34 texts) than any other of the eight concepts, with spelling not far behind (31 texts). Though ESL was present in 28 of the texts, only eight books had separate chapters for ESL. Of the five NRP components, phonics (28 texts), comprehension (27 texts), phonemic awareness (26 texts), and vocabulary (26 texts) were included in a similar number of textbooks. The fewest number of textbooks – only 21 – included fluency, meaning fluency was the least likely of the concepts to be mentioned, not only among the five NRP components but also among all eight concepts.

One interesting finding was that there were huge variations in coverage of ESL (ranging from 0.20 per cent to 73.68 per cent) and assessment (ranging from 0.23 per cent to 77.86 per cent). The text with the highest coverage of ESL (73.68 per cent) was a book chapter of 19 pages, which was used in Canada. Except for that one chapter, no other text included ESL in more than 20 per cent of its content. The text with the highest coverage of assessment (77.86 per cent of the book content) was a book mainly focused on assessment, which was used by one university in Australia and one university in New Zealand. Concerning assessment, the text with the next highest percentage (52.6 per cent) was used by one Australian university alone. In addition to these two texts, there were four texts with assessment coverage higher than 20 per cent: again two used in Australia, the other two in New Zealand.

The match comparison between the book's definition of each component and the definition given by the NRP was exclusively applied to books containing at least one of the five NRP components. Among the 28 texts in which phonics was included, 26 texts presented a definition of phonics that matched the NRP definition (see Table 4.2).

Table 4.2 Textbook information by inclusion of ESL, NRP components, spelling and assessment (N = 39)

Concept	Number of textbooks containing the concept	Number of textbooks containing NRP definition match	For textbooks with concept, average percentage of pages on the concept	For textbooks with concept, standard deviation of percentage of pages	For textbooks with concept, minimum percentage of pages	For textbooks with concept, maximum percentage of pages
ESL	28	N/A	7.20	13.58	.20	73.68
PA	26	18	3.54	2.56	.45	10.69
Phonics	28	26	5.06	4.41	.52	14.29
Fluency	21	15	3.72	3.23	.53	10.15
Comprehension	27	13	6.99	5.97	.39	22.92
Vocabulary	26	9	4.73	3.28	.38	11.95
Spelling	31	N/A	6.80	5.74	.51	23.83
Assessment	34	N/A	13.81	15.00	.23	77.86

Notes: PA: Phonemic awareness.

The non-matched definitions of phonics were not totally wrong but clearly incomplete, such as 'segmented or separated sounds [that] can be represented by letters' or 'letter–sound relationships; phonemes and their corresponding letters'. Twenty-seven textbooks mentioned comprehension, with only 13 definitions in each category being the same as the NRP's. In fact, although many of the textbooks mentioned comprehension, the texts often never provided an explicit definition of what comprehension is. Twenty-one of the textbooks reviewed included fluency, with 15 matching the NRP definition. Definitions of fluency were often vague and non-specific, such as 'the ability to read easily and well' or 'smooth, expressive, and rhythmic reading or writing'. Phonemic awareness showed a presence in 26 texts, 18 of which presented definitions no different from the NRP's. However, one textbook gave this incorrect definition: 'an understanding that speech is composed of a series of written sounds'. Because phonemic awareness only includes awareness of the sounds in oral speech, including the word 'written' made this definition inaccurate. Other times, phonemic awareness was defined as something more akin to phonological awareness, such as 'sensitivity to the sound structure of language'. Though phonemic awareness and vocabulary were both covered in 26 textbooks, only nine out of 26 with vocabulary presented a definition the same as NRP's. Similar to comprehension, although many of the textbooks mentioned vocabulary, the texts often never provided an explicit definition of what vocabulary is.

Examining the content of the international textbooks by the number of the five NRP components covered, only 17 texts contained all five of the components (see Table 4.3). Four textbooks did not contain any mention of any of the five NRP components and thus are excluded from this sample. Eighteen texts examined at least one component but no more than four components. In total, 35 texts covered at least one NRP component. However, an inclusion of one component did not always guarantee a corresponding definition that matched the NRP. Only four out of the 17 texts that included all five of the components contained definitions that matched the NRP for all five components. Of the five texts containing one NRP component only, merely one text provided a definition that matched the NRP.

Of all of the 39 texts examined, only two texts, one used in New Zealand and the other in Australia, devoted a little more than half of their contents to the NRP components: 59.12 per cent and 58.38 per cent respectively. It should be noted that this is a generous estimate of the books' coverage, because one page could be counted toward

Table 4.3 Textbook information by number of five NRP components included (N = 35)

Number of component(s) included	Number of textbooks containing component(s)	Average percentage of pages devoted to component(s)	Standard deviation of percentage of pages devoted to component(s)	Minimum percentage of pages devoted to component(s)	Maximum percentage of pages devoted to component(s)
5	17	27.57	14.09	7.41	59.12
4	5	20.66	8.70	10.62	32.47
3	2	5.08	1.01	4.36	5.80
2	6	5.27	3.64	1.57	9.69
1	5	1.97	1.88	.64	5.29

more than one component. If the same page, for example, discussed 'phonemic awareness' and 'phonics', the page was counted as one page for each of those components and would end up counting twice in these overall percentages. The rest of the texts had a varying degree of coverage of the components, from 0 per cent to 33.55 per cent, with most books having very low occurrences of the five components. Books with low coverage of these concepts included content on grammar, poetry, critical literacy, literacy as a social practice, different genres of literature, literacy specific to subject areas (e.g., literacy skills needed to read science texts), history of reading pedagogy, understanding images in texts, reading and playing, oral language development, reading strategies, writing process, writing conventions, identifying and responding to children's literature, drama, classroom organization, lesson planning, teacher expectations, student engagement, and teacher–parent collaboration.

Because different countries comprise their own unique combination of demographic context, history of literacy instruction, and production and use of literacy research, we decided to examine textbook content by country. Did different countries show different emphases among the eight concepts we examined? Of the four countries examined, New Zealand noticeably exceeded the other three countries in terms of the average percentage (48.36 per cent) of pages devoted to the eight concepts we examined (see Table 4.4). On average, the texts used in three countries had similar percentages of the total pages covering the eight literacy concepts: Canada (39.55 per cent), Singapore (38.84 per cent), and Australia (36.63 per cent). In texts used in New Zealand, Australia, and Singapore, the component of assessment tended to be covered by more pages than the other components. However, texts from Canada devoted more content to ESL than to the other seven concepts. In terms of the concept least covered in each country, phonemic awareness was identified for New Zealand, and fluency for the other three countries.

As shown in Table 4.4, texts used in New Zealand also ranked the highest in average percentage of pages devoted to each of the eight concepts compared with the texts used in the other countries except for ESL (covered most in Canada) and phonics (covered most in Singapore). Interestingly, the textbooks used in Singapore also ranked least in phonemic awareness (1.34 per cent), fluency (0.79 per cent), and comprehension (2.38 per cent). Vocabulary (2.52 per cent) and assessment (7.35 per cent) were mentioned least in textbooks used in Canada, and phonics least in both New Zealand and Canada (both 3.39 per cent).

Table 4.4 Average percentage of pages devoted to eight concepts by country and university (N = 39)

Country or university	Number of books analyzed	ESL	PA	Phonics	Fluency	Comprehension	Vocabulary	Spelling	Assessment	All 8 concepts together
New Zealand	9	4.10	2.85	3.39	3.52	5.98	3.51	6.99	18.02	48.36
University 1	2	6.36	2.59	2.64	5.08	8.27	3.37	6.02	13.19	47.52
University 2	4	5.44	4.78	5.01	5.39	9.32	6.21	4.25	7.56	47.96
University 3	5	2.43	1.30	2.10	2.03	3.31	1.35	10.42	31.09	54.03
Australia	22	2.94	2.21	3.37	1.80	4.17	2.89	4.96	14.31	36.63
University 1	4	4.69	2.42	5.00	1.69	3.52	4.68	2.36	7.67	32.03
University 2	17	2.70	2.29	3.18	1.93	4.57	2.63	5.52	16.42	39.24
University 3	3	1.91	3.74	7.05	0.54	2.13	1.80	3.64	8.65	30.17
Canada	9	10.64	2.29	3.39	1.26	5.70	2.52	6.40	7.35	39.55
University 1	4	20.98	1.66	2.56	1.21	8.52	2.20	2.32	8.17	47.62
University 2	3	1.45	3.00	5.35	1.59	3.79	3.86	13.84	6.04	38.92
University 3	3	2.72	2.61	4.71	1.09	2.28	1.41	8.42	6.82	30.06
Singapore	2	7.69	1.34	7.07	0.79	2.38	4.76	6.51	8.30	38.84

Notes: PA: Phonemic awareness.

On average, ESL (2.94 per cent) and spelling (4.96 per cent) were mentioned least in textbooks used in Australian universities.

We also examined whether university programs within or across countries differed in their coverage of these eight components or in their emphases on different components (see Table 4.4). When examined both by country and university, the universities of the same country varied greatly in percentage of pages devoted to ESL (Canada), spelling (Canada), and assessment (New Zealand). The greatest discrepancy between universities of the same country was found in New Zealand, where the highest university (31.09 per cent) exceeded the lowest (7.56 per cent) by a large margin in terms of average percentage coverage of assessment. Regarding the NRP components of reading instruction, percentage coverage for the five components together ranged from 10 per cent to 30 per cent, with both the lowest and the highest in New Zealand. The texts used in all three New Zealand universities covered comprehension the most and phonemic awareness the least. Of the five NRP components, the texts from Canadian and Australian universities included fluency the least, and comprehension the most.

Discussion

Despite the fact that ELL populations are large and/or growing in each of the countries examined, most of the textbooks used to prepare pre-service teachers to teach reading contain very little content regarding ELLs. Teachers, thus, are likely to be under-prepared to serve these students when they encounter them in their classrooms. Even in Singapore, where one of the two textbooks used was locally produced and thus could be customized toward the local population's language needs, a low average percentage of pages mentioning ESL was found, supporting Vaish's (2012) finding that Singaporean teachers' reading knowledge is grounded in native-language reading principles.

Further, the five components of reading instruction identified by the NRP – and confirmed by national reports in Australia and the UK – are not the focus of most of the textbooks used to prepare teachers to teach reading that we examined. Similar to the findings of Joshi, Binks, Graham, et al. (2009) among textbooks in the US, we found low coverage of these five components of reading instruction in textbooks from Australia, Canada, New Zealand, and Singapore. Thus, future reading teachers in these countries appear likely to be ill prepared to use the five components for effective literacy instruction when they arrive in classrooms.

Studies from Canada and the UK indicate that direct, explicit instruction in reading, including systematic phonemic awareness and phonics instruction, can allow ELL students to achieve in reading at similar levels to non-ELL peers (Lesaux, Rupp, and Siegel, 2007; Lesaux and Siegel, 2003; Lipka and Siegel, 2007; Stuart, 1999, 2004). In addition, spelling instruction has been found to help students develop their phonological awareness and knowledge of letter–sound correspondences (phonics), which in turn builds their reading achievement (Treiman, 1998; Weiser and Mathes, 2011). Having little coverage of these essential concepts of literacy instruction in reading instruction textbooks for pre-service teachers suggests novice teachers will not be able to deliver effective literacy instruction to their ELL students.

Further, knowledge of assessment is crucial to teachers of ELLs, as ELLs may display different oral language and literacy profiles from non-ELL peers. Being able to positively identify when ELLs are developing normally given their language background and when they need special help to counter dyslexia or other difficulties in learning to read is essential for teachers to be effective with their ELL students. Assessment was the one concept that seemed best covered on average by the textbooks from the four countries, with only two universities showing greater coverage of a different concept. However, average coverage still remained relatively low, with most universities averaging below 15 per cent coverage. With the low coverage of assessment found in this sample of textbooks, novice teachers trained at these institutions are unlikely to be prepared to assess their students appropriately and use the information to meet their students' individual needs. The exception may be one university in New Zealand, which had an average coverage of 31 per cent for assessment among its five textbooks.

We examined differences among the textbooks adopted at universities by country because support of these concepts could vary by national government. For example, Australia produced its own reading report, emphasizing the importance of the five components of reading and assessment in effective reading instruction and the need to prepare teachers to understand and be able to apply these concepts in their classrooms (Australian Government Department of Education, Employment, and Workplace Relations, 2005). Thus, we expected the textbooks adopted in Australia to have the highest coverage of these concepts. However, they did not, with only about 2–3 per cent coverage of phonemic awareness, phonics, fluency, and vocabulary; text comprehension was also low, at 4 per cent. Average coverage of assessment in the textbooks used at Australian universities was 14 per cent, with

New Zealand higher (at 18 per cent). These findings suggest that more work needs to be done to implement the teacher preparation recommendations of the Australian government report fully in all universities in Australia.

The textbooks adopted in Canadian universities had the greatest average coverage of ESL issues, which may reflect the relatively large percentage of ELLs in Canada compared with Australia and New Zealand. However, as noted above, Singapore currently contains a larger percentage of ELL students than the other countries, yet it did not give prominence to ESL issues in its teacher preparation textbooks. In summary, the reading textbooks used at universities in Australia, Canada, New Zealand, and Singapore overall do not show adequate coverage of ESL, phonemic awareness, phonics, fluency, vocabulary, comprehension, spelling, or assessment. Especially considering our methodology tends toward overestimation of the inclusion of these concepts, the fact that nearly all of these universities employed textbooks that included the eight concepts in less than half their content (with only one at 54 per cent) on average suggests that pre-service teacher training is not properly emphasizing the research-based concepts essential to effective literacy instruction for ELLs and non-ELLs alike.

Recommendations

Clearly, teacher preparation programs in the four countries studied need to re-examine the textbooks used to increase their inclusion of these eight important literacy concepts. Different, more comprehensive textbooks may be assigned, or teacher educators may demand that publishers revise current textbooks for greater inclusion of the eight concepts. Although teacher educators may supplement their textbooks with journal articles, websites, or lectures that include additional information on these eight concepts, we believe it is very important to have adequate inclusion of these eight concepts within the textbooks both because inclusion in textbooks signals the importance of the information within and because textbooks can become important references for novice teachers trying to remember what they had been taught.

Although our findings do not paint a rosy picture for teacher preparation in reading instruction, we did not obtain textbook lists from all of the universities in the contacted countries; thus, some universities may be preparing teachers better for the complex and important task of teaching children, particularly ELLs, to read. Additional research needs to be conducted regarding the extent of both pre-service and in-service teachers' knowledge of these eight concepts in these four countries and the connection between teachers' knowledge and the effectiveness of their literacy instruction, particularly with ELLs. It would be interesting to investigate, for example, whether teachers who complete the teacher preparation program at University 1 in Canada (with 21 per cent coverage of ESL) are more effective at teaching reading to their ELLs than teachers who completed programs with less content devoted to ELLs. Likewise, are teachers who graduated from University 3 in New Zealand (with 31 per cent coverage of assessment) more adept at literacy assessment than graduates from other programs?

A related question is how well versed the teacher educators in these teacher preparation programs are with the eight concepts investigated. Joshi, Binks, Hougen, et al. (2009) found that teacher educators in the US performed poorly in a survey of their knowledge of important concepts in English literacy, including the five components of literacy identified by the NRP. It may be that teacher educators in Australia, Canada, New Zealand, and Singapore are not including this content adequately because they themselves are unfamiliar with it.

Acknowledgements

The authors would like to thank the following graduate students and faculty members for either pointing us to the appropriate contact at their or other universities or providing us with a list of textbooks used at their university: Anne Cloonan, Nicole Conrad, John Dickie, Leanne Fried, Kath Jones, Blair Koefoed, Phil Lemalu, Libby Limbrick, Stefka Marinova-Todd, Sandra Martin-Chang, Alyson Simpson, and Bill Tunmer. Although in some cases we did not end up obtaining a list, we appreciate everyone's help nonetheless. We also would like to thank the following research assistants for help coding some of the textbooks: Megan Arellano, Fatma Hasan, Krystal Rivera, and Stephanie Silvia.

References

August, D. and Shanahan, T. (Eds.). (2006). *Developing reading and writing in second language learners: Lessons from the report of the national literacy panel on language-minority children and youth.* Mahwah: Erlbaum.

Australian Council of Educational Research (2000). *The measurement of language background, culture and ethnicity for the reporting of nationally comparable outcomes of schooling.* Retrieved from http://mceetya.edu.au/verve/_resources/languagebackground_file.pdf.

Australian Government Department of Education, Employment, and Workplace Relations (2005). *National inquiry into the teaching of literacy. Teaching reading:*

Report and recommendations. Retrieved from http://research.acer.edu.au/acer_history/26/.

Bos, C., Mather, N., Dickson, S., Podhajski, B., and Chard, D. (2001). Perceptions and knowledge of preservice and inservice educators about early reading instruction. *Annals of Dyslexia*, 51, 97–120.

Brown, D. (2009). Why and how textbooks should encourage extensive reading. *ELT Journal*, 63, 238–245.

Carreker, S.H., Swank, P.R., Tillman-Doudy, L., Neuhaus, G.H., Monfils, M.J., Montemayor, M.L., and Johnson, P. (2005). Language enrichment teacher preparation and practice predicts third grade reading comprehension. *Reading Psychology*, 26, 401–432.

Coalition for Equal Access to Education (n.d.). *Demographic trends.* Retrieved from http://www.eslaction.com/index.php?page=demographics.

Coltheart, M., and Prior, M. (2007). *Learning to read in Australia* (Occasional Paper 1/2007, Policy Paper #6). Retrieved from: http://www.ldaustralia.org/coltheart202620prior2020075b15d.pdf.

de Courcy, M. (2007). Disrupting preconceptions: Challenges to pre-service teachers' beliefs about ESL children. *Journal of Multilingual and Multicultural Development*, 28, 188–203.

de Jong, E.J. and Harper, C.A. (2005). Preparing mainstream teachers for English-language learners: Is being a good teacher good enough? *Teacher Education Quarterly*, 32, 101–124.

Gersten, R., Baker, S.K., Shanahan, T., Linan-Thompson, S., Collins, P., and Scarcella, R. (2007). *Effective literacy and English language instruction for English learners in the elementary grades.* (NCEE 2007–4011). Washington, DC: National Center for Education Evaluation and Regional Assistance, Institute of Education Sciences, US Department of Education. Retrieved from http://ies.ed.gov/ncee.

Geva, E. (2000). Issues in the assessment of reading disabilities in L2 children – beliefs and research evidence. *Dyslexia*, 6, 13–28.

Geva, E. and Yaghoub-Zadeh, Z. (2006). Reading efficiency in native English-speaking and English-as-a-second-language children: The role of oral proficiency and underlying cognitive-linguistic processes. *Scientific Studies of Reading*, 10, 31–57.

He, Y., Prater, K., and Steed, T. (2011). Moving beyond 'just good teaching': ESL professional development for all teachers. *Professional Development in Education*, 37, 7–18.

Hirtt, N. (2009). Markets and education in the era of globalized capitalism. In D. Hill and R. Kumar (Eds.), *Global neoliberalism and education and its consequences* (pp. 208–226). New York: Routledge.

Janzen, J. (2007). Preparing teachers of second language reading. *TESOL Quarterly*, 41, 707–729.

Jean, M., and Geva, E. (2009). The development of vocabulary in English as a second language children and its role in predicting word recognition ability. *Applied Psycholinguistics*, 30, 153–185.

Joshi, R.M., Binks, E., Graham, L., Ocker-Dean, E., Smith, D., and Boulware-Gooden, R. (2009). Do textbooks used in university reading education courses conform to the instructional recommendations of the National Reading Panel? *Journal of Learning Disabilities*, 42, 458–463.

Joshi, R.M., Binks, E., Hougen, M., Dahlgren, M.E., Ocker-Dean, E., and Smith, D. (2009). Why elementary teachers might be inadequately prepared to teach reading. *Journal of Learning Disabilities*, 42, 392–402.

Kelcey, B. (2011). Assessing the effects of teachers' reading knowledge on students' achievement using multilevel propensity score stratification. *Educational Evaluation and Policy Analysis*, 33, 458–482.

Kirkpatrick, A. (2007). *World Englishes: Implications for international communication and English language teaching*. Cambridge: Cambridge University Press.

Lesaux, N.K., Lipka, O., and Siegel, L.S. (2006). Investigating cognitive and linguistic abilities that influence the reading comprehension skills of children from diverse linguistics backgrounds. *Reading and Writing*, 19, 99–131.

Lesaux, N.K., Rupp, A.A., and Siegel, L.S. (2007). Growth in reading skills of children from diverse linguistic backgrounds: Findings from a 5-year longitudinal study. *Journal of Educational Psychology*, 99, 821–834.

Lesaux, N.K., and Siegel, L.S. (2003). The development of reading in children who speak English as a second language. *Developmental Psychology*, 39, 1005–1019.

Limbos, M., and Geva, E. (2001). Accuracy of teacher assessments of second-language students at risk for reading disability. *Journal of Learning Disabilities*, 34, 136–151.

Lipka, O., and Siegel, L.S. (2007). The development of reading skills in children with English as a second language. *Scientific Studies of Reading*, 11, 105–131.

McKay, S.L. (2002). *Teaching English as an international language: Rethinking gorals and approaches*. Oxford: Oxford University Press.

Menken, K., and Antunez, B. (2001) *An overview of the preparation and certification of teachers working with limited English proficiency (LEP) students*. Washington, DC: National Clearinghouse for Bilingual Education. Retrieved from http://www.usc.edu/dept/education/CMMR/FullText/teacherprep.pdf.

Ministry of Education, Singapore (2010). English language syllabus 2010: Primary and secondary (express/ normal [academic]). Retrieved from http://www.moe.edu.sg/education/syllabuses/languages-and-literature/files/english-primary-secondary-express-normal-academic.pdf.

Moats, L.C. (1994). The missing foundation in teacher education: Knowledge of the structure of spoken and written language. *Annals of Dyslexia*, 44, 81–102.

Moats, L.C. and Foorman, B.R. (2003). Measuring teachers' content knowledge of language and reading. *Annals of Dyslexia*, 53, 23–45.

Mullis, I.V.S., Martin, M.O., Foy, P., and Drucker, K.T. (2012). *PIRLS 2011 international results in reading*. Chestnut Hill: TIMSS and PIRLS International Study Center, Boston College.

Mullis, I.V.S., Martin, M.O., Minnich, C.A., Drucker, K.T., and Ragan, M.A. (Eds.) (2012a). *PIRLS 2011 encyclopedia: Education policy and curriculum in reading* (Vol. 1). Chestnut Hill: TIMSS and PIRLS international Study Center.

Mullis, I.V.S., Martin, M.O., Minnich, C.A., Drucker, K.T., and Ragan, M.A. (Eds.) (2012b). *PIRLS 2011 encyclopedia: Education policy and curriculum in reading* (Vol. 2). Chestnut Hill: TIMSS and PIRLS international Study Center.

National Comprehensive Center for Teacher Quality (2007). *Teacher preparation state policy database – undergraduate programs*. Retrieved from http://www2.tqsource.org/mb2dev/reports/reportTQ.aspx?id=1139.

National Reading Panel (2000). *Teaching children to read: An evidence-based assessment of the scientific research literature on reading and its implications for reading instruction*. Retrieved from http://www.nichd.nih.gov/publications/pubs/nrp/pages/smallbook.aspx.

New Zealand Curriculum Online (2012). *Fact sheet 9: English language learners*. Retrieved from http://nzcurriculum.tki.org.nz/National-Standards/Key-information/Fact-sheets/English-language-learners.

New Zealand Ministry of Education (2013). *Time Series Data for Trend Analysis 2000–2012*. Retrieved from http://www.educationcounts.govt.nz/statistics/schooling/july_school_roll_returns/6028.

Scarborough, H.S. (2001). Connecting early language and literacy to later reading (dis)abilities: Evidence, theory, and practice. In S.B. Neuman and D.K. Dickinson (Eds.) *Handbook of early literacy research* (pp. 97–110). New York: Guilford.

Singapore Department of Statistics (2010). *Census of population 2010: Demographic characteristics, education, language and religion*. Retrieved from http://www.singstat.gov.sg/pubn/popn/c2010sr1/cop2010sr1.pdf.

Spear-Swerling, L., and Brucker, P.O. (2004). Preparing novice teachers to develop basic reading and spelling skills in children. *Annals of Dyslexia*, 54, 332–364.

Stuart, M. (1999). Getting ready for reading: Early phoneme awareness and phonics teaching improves reading and spelling in inner-city second language learners. *British Journal of Educational Psychology*, 69, 587–605.

Stuart, M. (2004). Getting ready for reading: A follow-up study of inner city second language learners at the end of Key Stage I. *British Journal of Educational Psychology*, 74, 15–36.

Stuart, M. and Coltheart, M. (1988). Does reading develop in a sequence of stages? *Cognition*, 30, 139–181.

Treiman, R. (1998). Why spelling?: The benefits of incorporating spelling into beginning reading instruction. In J. Metsala and L. Ehri (Eds.), *Word recognition in beginning literacy* (pp.289–313). Mahwah: Erlbaum.

UK Parliament (2004). *Select committee on education and skills eighth report*. Retrieved from http://www.publications.parliament.uk/pa/cm200405/cmselect/cmeduski/121/12104.htm.

Vaish, V. (2012). Teacher beliefs regarding bilingualism in an English medium reading program. *International Journal of Bilingual Education and Bilingualism*, 15, 53–69.

Vandervelden, M.C. and Siegel, L.S. (1995). Phonological recoding and phoneme awareness in early literacy: A developmental approach. *Reading Research Quarterly*, 30, 854–875.

Wee, L. (2008). Linguistic instrumentalism in Singapore. In P.K.W. Tan and R. Rubdy (Eds.), *Language as commodity: Global structures, local market places* (pp. 31–43). New York: Continuum.

Weiser, B. and Mathes, P. (2011). Using encoding instruction to improve the reading and spelling performances of elementary students at risk for literacy difficulties: A best-evidence synthesis. *Review of Educational Research*, 81, 170–200.

Part II

Studies of Textbook Consumption

5
Teachers' Conceptualization and Use of the Textbook on a Medical English Course

Ahlam Menkabu and Nigel Harwood

Summary

While there have been numerous analyses of second language (L2) English language textbook material, there has been far less research conducted on how teachers use this material in class, and why. This chapter duly focuses on seven English language teachers' conceptualizations of, and adherence to, their prescribed textbook. The teachers were teaching English to medical students on an English for Specific Purposes (ESP) course at a Saudi Arabian university. Classroom observations were followed up by qualitative interviews to explore teachers' textbook use and motivations underlying their practices. Teachers held varying views of the textbook, with some describing it using metaphors associated with constraint or tedium while others conceptualized it in more positive terms, using metaphors associated with guidance. Although the textbook played a central role in all the teachers' lessons, there were variations in the ways teachers adapted the materials to meet their learners' needs and to best satisfy their own pedagogical preferences and priorities. However, a perceived lack of subject specialist knowledge, a shortage of time, and an exam-driven syllabus all negatively impacted on teachers' use of and attitudes towards the textbook. The implications of this study are explored, particularly for teacher development within ESP contexts.

Introduction

Much of the English language teaching to L2 speakers that occurs throughout the world today is conducted through the medium of textbooks; hence, the quality and appropriateness of the language and content of these commercially produced materials have been the focus of many studies (e.g., Barbieri and Eckhardt, 2007; Boxer and Pickering, 1995; Cullen and Kuo, 2007; Gray, 2010a; Levis, 1999; Porreca, 1984; Römer, 2004; Williams, 1988, among many others). However, little is known about how such materials are used: these analyses are confined to the textbook page, and do not include investigations of how the materials are exploited in class. This is a vital aspect to consider, since although many teachers may not be in a position to select the textbooks they use in class, they may still adapt them in order to ensure an optimum match between the materials, their learners' needs, and their own pedagogical preferences (Harwood, 2010; Islam and Mares, 2003; McDonough and Shaw, 2003; McGrath, 2002; Samuda, 2005). A number of studies from first language education show that teachers' use of the materials can vary considerably and can be exploited to attain different aims (e.g., Alvermann, 1987); and although there are some studies of second language contexts which draw similar conclusions (e.g., Wette, 2010), there have been fewer investigations into L2 contexts generally and into English for Academic or Specific Purposes (EAP/ESP) contexts in particular: teachers with different learners, but also different experiences, teaching styles, and areas of expertise, may make different use of the same materials, experiencing different degrees of ease or difficulty in utilizing them. The results of such investigations will have profound implications for how teacher education programmes address trainees' use of textbooks in general, and their adaptations of materials in particular. We are not aware of any published studies of textbook use in the Arab world, and the present study therefore focuses on textbook use in an ESP course in Saudi Arabia for students of medicine, investigating the teachers' conceptualizations of, and adherence to, the prescribed materials.

The role of textbooks

There has been a long-running debate about the desirability of L2 textbooks, and about their effects on teachers and learners (see Hadley, this volume; Harwood, 2005, 2010). Those who are suspicious of textbooks and prescribed teaching materials may see these resources as tools of institutional control, and/or believe that the routines described by the materials leave teachers with almost nothing to decide on, as they merely act out pre-planned procedures and are de-skilled (Apple and Jungck, 1990; Shannon, 1987). For others, the role of textbooks is potentially more positive, providing guidance and structure, and saving busy teachers a great deal of time that would be otherwise spent preparing materials from scratch (Freebairn, 2000; Hutchinson and Torres, 1994; O'Neill, 1982). Although textbooks can never fully meet the needs of individual students and teachers in diverse classrooms and institutions around the world, teachers can artfully manipulate the materials to suit their context (Allwright, 1981; Bell and Gower, 1998; Gray, 2000; McGrath, 2002; Samuda, 2005; Stodolsky, 1989). Teachers will make decisions about which parts of a book to use, which to adapt, and which to abandon, although such an art will need to be developed, perhaps as part of pre- or in-service training (McGrath, 2002; Richards, 1993; Tomlinson, 2003).

What is conspicuously lacking from much of this theorizing about the merits and demerits of textbooks, however, are the voices of teachers, although McGrath's (2006) study is a notable exception. McGrath (2006) studied 75 Hong Kong secondary school teachers' attitudes to textbooks by having them complete the statement 'A coursebook is...' with a metaphor or simile of their choice. McGrath (2006) classified the teachers' images for textbooks according to four themes: guidance (e.g., 'map', 'path'), support (e.g., 'blind man's stick', 'scaffolding'), resource (e.g., 'convenience store', 'menu'), and constraint (e.g., 'road block', 'straitjacket'), the latter being the only negative category. It seems that metaphor/simile description is a useful heuristic to uncover teachers' views of textbook roles, and the same technique was used in this research to uncover informants' conceptualizations of their textbooks.

Methods of textbook adaptation

The main purpose of textbook/materials adaptation is, as McDonough and Shaw (2003: 76) state, 'to maximise the appropriacy of teaching materials in context, by changing some of the internal characteristics of a coursebook to suit our particular circumstances better'. McDonough and Shaw provide an inventory of methods that may be used to achieve this, as follows:

Adding: the teacher can supplement or extend the original material. For instance, extra practice activities of a language point learners are likely to find tricky can be inserted. These additions can be of a purely quantitative nature, providing more of the same exercises as those which are already to be found in the textbook; alternatively, the changes can be qualitative, by introducing a new skill or language practice component to that which already features.

Deleting: McDonough and Shaw (2003) note that omissions can also be quantitative or qualitative in this category. Whereas the former type simply consists of reducing the amount of materials, focusing on a particular skill or language point if it is felt that learners do not need the volume of practice envisaged by the textbook writer, a qualitative deletion may mean that discussion activities are omitted entirely for reasons such as syllabus constraints, a lack of time, or because achieving oral proficiency is not a priority for learners.

Modifying: McDonough and Shaw's (2003) Modifying category is subdivided into (i) rewriting and (ii) restructuring. Rewriting 'may relate activities more closely to learners' own backgrounds and interests' (p.81), or perhaps make the book's problem-solving tasks less predictable. Rewriting may also involve simplifying a textbook activity the teacher feels is too complex for his/her learners in its current form. Restructuring is carried out for reasons of classroom management, and may come about if, for instance, the textbook suggests role-playing when the size of the class would make this problematic.

Reordering: the teacher may decide to sequence activities differently for reasons of logic or pedagogical effectiveness.

Our informants' textbook adaptations were investigated using McDonough and Shaw's framework.

Research on textbook use

While a number of content analyses of L2 textbooks are available (e.g., Barbieri and Eckhardt, 2007; Boxer and Pickering, 1995; Jiang, 2006; Römer, 2004; Shardakova and Pavlenko, 2004; Williams, 1988), the obvious limitation of such studies is that they are not anchored to a classroom context: since they only analyse the textbooks' pages, there is no coverage of how teachers use them and how learners receive them. Thus situated studies investigating teachers' use of textbooks deserve more attention. Key studies from both L2 and L1 education are now reviewed, with two L1 studies included because of their methodological rigour and their connections with the present study.

Studying ten teachers working in UK language schools, Shawer (2010a, 2010b) drew on teacher and student interviews as well as multiple classroom observations to examine how the teachers used L2 textbooks and materials. Teachers were native speakers, all highly experienced and mostly well qualified (e.g., holding TEFL diplomas). Despite the similar teaching profiles, there were very significant differences in the ways informants taught and used materials, and three categories of teacher emerged from the data: curriculum-transmitters, curriculum-developers, and curriculum-makers. Curriculum-transmitters treated the textbook as a script, moving from each task and exercise in a linear sequence, making few if any adaptations. In contrast, curriculum-developers adapted, supplemented, and expanded the curriculum and textbook with their class in mind, using the book as a springboard. Finally, curriculum-makers invariably conducted a needs analysis at the start of the course to find out what topics would engage learners, creating a curriculum around the results of this analysis. Much or all of the time the textbook was abandoned.

How can we account for these variations in textbook usage? Hutchinson's (1996) study, discussed more fully in Harwood (this volume) and Grammatosi and Harwood (this volume), provides a framework with which to do so. Since Hutchinson's framework emerged out of an EAP teaching situation, it is also relevant for our purposes because of the specialized, rather than general, nature of the English being taught. The different patterns of textbook usage associated with two of the teachers in Hutchinson's study, Nancy and Marcia, appear to be connected with the teachers' experience of EAP and degree of content knowledge (relating to English for fisheries). Nancy's lack of EAP experience/training meant she depended heavily on the textbook. Although there was some evidence of selection of materials in class – her lack of specialist fisheries knowledge meant that Nancy chose units from the textbook which seemed to her the easiest in terms of their content, and she made occasional decisions to add or omit materials – she always followed the recommended sequence of tasks, and generally adhered closely to the textbook script. In contrast, being more assured than Nancy in terms of her pedagogical know-how and content knowledge, Marcia adapted the textbook more extensively, supplementing it with other materials. Hutchinson concludes that textbook use is influenced by a complex mix of factors, including (i) the textbook (e.g., its content, difficulty level, length, etc.); (ii) the teacher (profile, beliefs, experience, training, etc.); (iii) the learners (profile, beliefs, aptitude, etc.); and (iv) the classroom and institutional context (e.g., class layout, timetabling constraints, attitudes towards textbook use by authorities, etc.) (pp.333–334).

All of the factors Hutchinson mentions as influencing textbook use can be identified in other studies, such as Lee and Bathmaker (2007), a study of English language teachers' perceptions and use of their textbooks in a Singaporean context, where teachers were working with Normal Technical (NT) students, considered to be academically the weakest of the three secondary-school streams. The study sought to determine the extent to which teachers relied on textbooks to teach literacy skills, and was based on responses to a semi-structured questionnaire by 23 teachers from 11 schools, complemented by telephone interviews with some informants. Although the study reported that teachers used the prescribed textbook to teach different language skills, they modified, omitted, and/or supplemented this material at times for a variety of reasons. For instance, teachers added additional materials which they judged to be suitable for the learners' modest levels of proficiency. They also reported using their textbooks least for pair work or group discussions in an attempt to avoid disciplinary problems, disruption, and noise. And they were reluctant to teach students the reading and writing strategies included in the textbooks, being unconvinced that these strategies would benefit their low-level students. Perhaps most significantly in this context, however, there was evidence that teachers were preoccupied with 'teaching to the test', attempting to meet the exam-driven learning needs of their students by supplementing the textbook with practice tests.

As in Hutchinson and Lee and Bathmaker, Wette's (2010) study shows how what she calls low-, medium-, and high-constraint contexts, in which teachers can exercise greater or lesser autonomy in their choice of curricula and materials, can impact on teachers' practices. This is also something which is of interest in our research, since Wette's high constraint environment, like our context, is exam-driven, with a rigidly prescribed syllabus and textbook. Using interviews, Wette focuses on EFL teachers' planning and the changes teachers make to their plans (and therefore their curricula and materials) before and during class. Wette found that teachers' plans were provisional and open to modification in the light of learners' performances and preferences. Teachers carefully monitored the classroom climate by assessing learners' reactions to the materials (e.g., by learners' (in)ability to perform activities successfully, or by their (lack of) involvement); and by inviting explicit feedback on the materials, including feedback about whether additional work on a particular topic was required. Hence greater or lesser additions to curricula and materials were made, although time and context constraints sometimes hampered these learner requests for changes or additions. For instance, one of the types of adaptation Wette itemizes is a change of instructional pace, often a slowing down due to learners' difficulties. However, the teacher in the high-constraint, exam-driven context reported that she was unable to slow the pace as much as she would have liked due to the requirement to get through a set amount of textbook material each week. Nonetheless, it is clear that plans, curricula, and usage of materials shifted considerably.

Two more EFL studies are discussed here because they show the influence of the teaching context in general, and examinations in particular, on teachers' use of materials. Cheng (1997) studied the washback effect of the revised Hong Kong Certificate of Education Examination (HKCEE) in Hong Kong secondary schools using questionnaires, interviews, and classroom observations. The changes to the HKCEE syllabus led to a marked shift in teachers' lessons in terms of focus. For instance, the old syllabus emphasized reading aloud, an activity which featured in teachers' old syllabus classes. However, the emphasis of the new syllabus shifted to more communicative oral activities such as role-playing and discussions, activities which featured in the new syllabus textbooks, and which duly started to feature in new syllabus classes. Cheng's interviews with teachers revealed how they associated their role with exam success ('I am very exam-oriented. And I will do whatever I can to get my students fully prepared for this public examination'), and the 'guilt' they would feel if students were unfamiliar with the exam format (p.49). This was because of the high-stakes nature of the exam, which would play a large part in determining students' futures. Exam-driven textbook use is also found in Pelly and Allison (2000), who investigated 58 Singaporean primary school teachers' views of assessment influences on their teaching practices by means of a questionnaire and conducted semi-structured interviews with four of these teachers. They found that 79 per cent of respondents reported that their teaching was determined 'to a large/very large extent' by tests. All four interviewees said that they 'teach to the test': that is, they taught only the parts of the textbook expected to come up in the examinations, although they deplored the necessity of operating in this way.

Two important L1 textbook studies are reviewed here which similarly highlight the factors identified by Hutchinson (1996) as impacting on textbook use. Stodolsky (1989) is an investigation of 12 experienced teachers' use of textbooks across various schools in US elementary fifth-grade school mathematics and social studies classes by means of classroom observation. She found that teachers varied considerably in their textbook use, with practices ranging from 'close adherence' to the textbook to 'extreme autonomy' (i.e., non-dependence on the textbook; p.170), but in general, teachers exhibited considerable independence from their textbooks, being extremely selective in what parts of the textbooks they taught. The manner in which teachers used the material must be understood against the backdrop of the institutional contexts, with teachers' schools granting them the freedom to exercise this control over the materials. However, there was a suggestion that two teachers in the study who referred to the textbook to a greater degree than their peers may have done so because their school required teachers to keep to the same schedule of topics covered. In sum, then, rather than unthinking adherence to textbooks, Stodolsky uncovered much calculated variation in usage of materials

> that seems to result from teachers' own convictions and preferences, the nature of the materials they use, the school context in which they teach, the particular students in their class, and the subject matter and grade level they are teaching. (p.180)

Nevertheless, it is worth stressing that Stodolsky's teachers were highly experienced, which might explain why most of her participants seemed to be comfortable using and adapting the textbooks to suit their purposes in a way that less experienced teachers might not have been (cf. Tsui, 2003, which found differences between the way expert and novice teachers use textbooks, with the novice teacher sticking to the textbook script).

Hinchman (1987) is an ethnographic study focused on the use of textbooks by three US secondary school teachers' who were identified by colleagues as being good at their job. Informants were from different subject areas: social studies, biology, and English. Repeated observations of the teachers' lessons over a period of three years were complemented by field notes, qualitative interviews, and analysis of the materials used in class. Hinchman found the three teachers used their textbooks to differing degrees and in different ways, and placed her informants on a cline of textbook adherence. At one end was Mary, whose textbook use 'reflects methodical coverage of her curriculum' (p.259). Susan was situated in the middle of the cline, introducing more supplementary material into her lessons than Mary, while Kevin was at the opposite end of the cline, since he and his learners selected texts to read based on the results of in-class discussions, rather than sticking to a pre-ordained order and coverage of material. Interviews revealed that teachers' need to cover the curriculum, the (un)availability of supplementary materials, and pedagogical beliefs all helped explain this variation. For instance, Mary explained how her use of materials was heavily influenced by the final examinations students would have to take. In contrast, Kevin claimed these exams did not really influence the way he taught. While the influence of the curriculum and state examinations is apparent in this study, it is clear from the teachers' use of the textbook material that they still retain flexibility over their handling of materials, and that they have the time to supplement the textbook: even Mary, the teacher who stuck most closely to the textbook and was preoccupied with the end-of-course exams, explained that she was able to intersperse teaching of items from the textbook that would likely appear in the exams with 'things of interest to the kids' (p.258).

The final part of this discussion of previous studies is devoted to L2 textbook research by Gray (2000, 2010b), which has a more specific focus than the research reviewed above. Gray's attention is on the cultural dimension of textbooks and is included here because this cultural aspect was also found salient to our informants. The 22 teacher interviewees in Gray's (2010b) book-length study reported that the cultural setting in which the materials were to be used impacted profoundly on the success or failure of their implementation. Teachers varied in their reactions to materials which they felt perpetuated cultural stereotypes: while some informants said they would avoid using them because of the danger that their learners would believe the teachers endorsed the stereotypes, others said such materials could generate lively discussions. In an earlier publication, Gray (2000) reports that all 12 of his native-speaker English teachers working in Barcelona had sometimes been uncomfortable with the cultural messages they felt were transmitted by textbook activities. Eleven out of 12 teachers had omitted or adapted materials on topics which they felt were inappropriate for discussion in the language classroom: for example, materials about alcohol and sexually promiscuous teenagers. Gray (2010b) argues that teacher education programmes need to equip teachers to critically evaluate and adapt textbook materials to make them fit for purpose in their contexts. One possibility is a cross-cultural approach to culturally alien materials, 'where students are encouraged to make comparisons between their own culture and those represented in the coursebook' (Gray, 2000: 280). Although he sees the textbook as 'a bearer of [cultural] messages' (p.281), teachers and learners can engage critically with these messages; and hence textbooks 'can become a useful instrument for provoking cultural debate and [...] a genuine educational tool' (2000: 281).

In sum, the literature demonstrates that textbooks play a vital role in second language classrooms all over the world (Hutchinson and Torres, 1994). However, using textbooks can be far from straightforward, especially for less experienced practitioners (Ball and Feiman-Nemser, 1988; Tsui, 2003). While they enhance our understanding of what is a neglected area, studies such as those by Lee and Bathmaker (2007) are limited in that they rely wholly on interview-based accounts of how teachers exploit textbooks in class, rather than examining the extent to which these reported practices actually occur. Hence the present study adopted a design that features both interviews and classroom observation, in an attempt to determine whether reports and practices coincide. Our research questions were as follows:

1. How do teachers conceptualize their textbook? Why?
2. To what extent do teachers adhere to their textbook? Why?
3. What adaptations do teachers make to their textbook? Why?

Methodology

The context

The English Language Centre (ELC) of the Saudi Arabian university where this study is situated provides a two-term English language programme for all students in their first year at the university. This programme is compulsory for all medical students since all medical college courses (i.e., courses in the College of Pharmacy, College of Medicine, College of Dentistry, and College of Medical Applied Sciences) are English-medium. The programme consists of two English language courses: a course of English for General Purposes (EGP) is offered in the first semester, its main goal being to ensure that all medical students reach an intermediate proficiency threshold from which they can begin the English for Specific Purposes (ESP) course in the second semester, the focus of the current study.

Teaching material

The general English language textbooks *Elementary New Headway Plus* and *Pre-Intermediate New Headway Plus* (Soars and Soars, 2006a, 2006b) are covered in the first semester. In the second semester, the *Nursing 1* (Grice and Greenan, 2007) and *Nursing 2* (Grice and Greenan, 2008) textbooks are taught for 14 weeks, 12 hours per week. Designed for students of a pre-intermediate to intermediate level, these books deliver a specialist course for students preparing for a nursing career. Each book consists of 15 units focusing on (i) career skills knowledge; (ii) language skills; and (iii) language knowledge (grammar, vocabulary, and pronunciation). The institution requires that teachers teach 2–3 units per week in order to cover all 30 units during the semester. Since the university offers a range of medical programmes one may wonder why textbooks focusing specifically on English for nurses were used with all medical students. In fact, it was originally intended that students from the Colleges of Medicine, Pharmacy, and Dentistry would use different books from the same textbook series specifically related to English for medicine. However, some of the institution's most experienced English teachers believed the other books would be too difficult for the students (in terms of the language presented) and also for the teachers (in terms of the specialist content). Hence the more general, less challenging, *Nursing 1* and 2 books were preferred for all medical students.

Assessment procedures

Students were assessed principally on the basis of an examination set by two English teachers chosen by the director of the programme. The exam featured a multiple-choice format, focusing primarily on medical terminology, and was based on the textbooks' content. It evaluated students on their listening, reading, and grammar only, with neither speaking nor writing skills being tested. In order to pass the English course, students needed to score at least 60 per cent. If a student failed, they could be given the opportunity to re-sit the exam during the summer semester, and if they failed again they could be asked to leave the college, although the various colleges had different procedures regarding failing students. What is clear, however, is that the English exam is high-stakes.

Participants

In Saudi Arabia, education is segregated according to gender, and all participants in this study were female, with data being collected by the first author. Eight of the 12 ELC teachers agreed to take part in the study. Upon signing consent forms and receiving information sheets about the project, it was stressed that participation was voluntary and teachers were free to withdraw from the study at any time without giving reasons for doing so; and in fact one participant did drop out of the study, so we were left with seven informants. Most teachers held Master's degrees. The participants' teaching EFL experience ranged from three to 12 years, and their ESP teaching experience ranged from one to nine years. Details are summarized in Table 5.1, with teachers being referred to as E1–E7.

Only five informants, while doing their undergraduate degrees, had completed the required teacher training to be appointed as language teachers, in that they took some courses on teaching English methodology, followed by a period of one or two semesters of pre-service training at a school. As can be seen from Table 5.1, however, this training took place some time ago. Teachers explained that this pre-service training

Table 5.1 Informants' profiles

Teacher	Teacher training	TEFL experience (years)	ESP teaching experience (years)
E1	Yes: 14 years ago	3	1½
E2	Yes: 13 years ago	12	3
E3	No	3	1½
E4	Yes: 14 years ago	7	3
E5	Yes: 13 years ago	10	2
E6	No	7	5
E7	Yes: 12 years ago	12	9

had been less than adequate, in that it did not provide them with sufficient knowledge and skills to adapt and make efficient use of the materials available. When asked what they had been told about the use of textbooks, some teachers in fact reported that they could not remember if they were told anything of particular interest or significance. Neither of the two remaining teachers had had teacher training.[1] Relevant in-service workshops or seminars on materials and textbook usage were also lacking, the exception being a three-day workshop on using the general English *Headway* textbooks, rather than ESP materials.

Data collection instruments

It was felt that a qualitative approach would be suitable for the present study, as we were seeking to collect data on teachers' practices in their natural settings (Creswell, 2007; Dörnyei, 2007). Since the present study focused on how teachers actually used the textbook in their lessons and the reasons behind these choices, classroom observations and interviews were appropriate. Observations were useful because they allowed us to record the participants' behaviours in a naturalistic environment while interviews 'allow the researcher access to the participants' motivations for their behaviors and actions' (Mackey and Gass, 2005: 176). However, mismatches between beliefs and reported practices are not uncommon (see Borg, 2003), and so it was important to triangulate the two sources of data.

Observations

Observation offers a researcher the opportunity to collect 'live' data from real situations (Cohen, Manion, and Morrison, 2007: 396). That is, it 'can help demystify what is actually going on as opposed to what one might hope or assume or what a participant says is happening'

(Anderson, Herr, and Nihlen, 2007: 185; Dörnyei, 2007). For the purposes of the present research, anything which related to the role of the ESP materials in the teachers' lessons was considered significant: that is, the extent to which teachers used and adhered to the textbook in their lessons, and any adaptations that were made to the materials were the principal concerns. However, other features of the observed lessons which were felt to relate to our research questions were also recorded: for instance, learners' reactions to the materials and the effect these were perceived to have had on the teachers' lesson plan.

Hence, after gaining access to the research site and obtaining consent, the first author undertook classroom observations for a period of two weeks, observing two consecutive two-hour classes of each of the seven teachers during this time, enough to observe how each participant taught one complete unit of textbook material. In order to arrive at a fuller understanding of why such behaviour occurred, interviews were then held with informants about what had been observed.

Interviews

Qualitative interviews can allow researchers to examine phenomena that are not directly observable – for instance, teachers' attitudes – and to do so in depth (Dörnyei, 2007; Mackey and Gass, 2005). Because interviews are interactive, interviewers can press for complete, clear answers and can also probe into any emerging topics (Cohen et al., 2007; Mackey and Gass, 2005). A semi-structured interview format allowed us to investigate how teachers used the textbook, revealing the teachers' attitudes towards these books to understand what lay behind their behaviours. Interviews lasted between 60 and 100 minutes.

The interview schedule was divided into five sections (see Appendix A). The first section consisted of background questions covering qualifications, teaching experience, and pre- and in-service training. The second and third sections focused on teachers' behaviours, opinions, and feelings towards the use of the textbook. In order to obtain more precise answers, participants were asked to think of a particular unit they had taught from the book and then to compare their teaching of that unit with their teaching in general. Prompt cards were also used in these two sections, with participants commenting on their use of *Nursing 2* in relation to quotes by two imaginary teachers who proffered opposing views about the need to adapt their textbooks. Another prompt card used the same technique to elicit informants' views as to how constrained or free they felt when using the textbook. Teachers were also asked about their use of various types of textbook adaptations which drew on McDonough and Shaw's (2003) inventory. And there was a question about teachers' preferred metaphors for describing textbooks which drew on McGrath's (2006) study. The fourth part of the interview was devoted to questions arising from the observations of the interviewees' classroom, investigating the motivations underlying specific behaviours that the first author had witnessed relating to teachers' use of the textbook materials. For instance, it was observed that most teachers ignored the textbook instructions to have students work in pairs, and so teachers were asked to comment on this. In the last part of the interview schedule the participants were invited to add or comment on anything that might or might not have been discussed relating to materials and to textbooks.

The interview was piloted with two teachers with similar profiles to the participants who were to take part in the main study, and the schedule was modified as a result.

Transcribing and coding the interview data

All interviews were transcribed and coded. Drawing on techniques in Creswell (2007) and Hammersley and Atkinson (2007), the transcripts were examined to obtain a sense of the overall data before a start list (Miles and Huberman, 1994) of codes was compiled. Having analysed and re-analysed the data several times, four overarching categories were identified affecting textbook conceptualization and use: (i) factors related to learners, such as language proficiency and motivation; (ii) factors related to physical environment, such as class size and facilities; (iii) factors related to teachers, such as their knowledge of the subject matter and teaching preferences; and (iv) factors related to institutional constraints, such as the classroom contact time available and the exam-oriented system of assessment.

Results

How do teachers conceptualize their textbook in metaphorical terms?

In order to better understand the teachers' attitudes to the textbooks, participants were invited to describe their feelings about using the *Nursing 2* student's book by choosing from a list of metaphors, which were drawn from McGrath (2006). Three teachers reported feeling constrained by the textbook because it was full of medical information and terminology. E1 pictured the textbook as a *straitjacket* ('we can't do much [...] just follow what's in the book'). For E6, *sleeping pills* was the metaphor that spoke of the boredom she felt most of the time when using the textbook. And E5 selected *nightmares* and *straitjacket* to aid her description:

> Most of the time I feel that I don't have the freedom to do and teach what I really want [...] If I have the freedom, then that means I can teach what is in this book and I can also add other kinds of activities. I can't do that here. This book is full of new terms and information and I have to cover all skills and many different activities. It is exhausting just to prepare for one lecture.

Then she referred to the difficulty of covering the book in the allotted time:

> This book is a nightmare. I'm afraid I would drop out of the rhythm and won't be able to teach all units before the final exam. Then I'll feel guilty.

In contrast, the other teachers said they did not feel constrained by the textbook: E2, E3, and E7 described it in terms of metaphors associated with guidance (*path, compass*). E4 used metaphors to give the book mixed reviews, saying that it could be likened to a *parachute* that gave support but sometimes it was like a 'toothache': although the book was useful, it featured too many medical terms, and sometimes she worried about not pronouncing these terms correctly in class.

This range of images selected by our teachers differed from those chosen by McGrath's (2006) participants, whose metaphors were predominantly positive. Conversely, some of our teachers chose textbook metaphors relating to constraint, boredom and anxiety/fear. However, it is noteworthy that McGrath's informants were not in an ESP teaching situation, unlike the teachers here, and it appears that a limited amount of medical background knowledge on the part of some teachers led to less favourable descriptions of the textbook. This lack of specialized knowledge was a recurring theme in the data, as we shall see below, where we examine teachers' use of the textbook, together with the adaptations they made to the textbook materials.

To what extent do teachers adhere to the textbook?

Data from classroom observations indicated that the *Nursing 2* student's book was the only textbook material used in teachers' lessons. Each textbook unit focused on three main areas: career skills knowledge, language skills, and language knowledge. Table 5.2 shows these different

Table 5.2 Teachers' use of the main components of a *Nursing 2* unit

Teachers	Career skills and knowledge			Language skills				Language knowledge		
	It's my job/ Patient care	Signs and symptoms/ Body bits/ Tests	Project	Listening	Reading	Speaking	Writing	Language Spot	Vocabulary	Pronunciation
E1	Used	Used	Not used	Used	Used	Not used	Used	Used	Used	Used
E2	Used	Used	Used	Used	Used	Used	Used	Used	Used	Used
E3	Used	Used	Used	Used	Used	Used	Used	Used	Used	Used
E4	Used	Used	Used	Used	Used	Used	Used	Used	Used	Used
E5	Used	Used	Not used	Used	Used	Used	Not used	Used	Used	Used
E6	Used	Used	Used	Used	Used	Used	Not used	Used	Used	Used
E7	Used	Used	Used	Used	Used	Used	Used	Used	Used	N/A

Note: N/A signifies that no pronunciation activity featured in the textbook unit observed.

sections, the activities comprising each section, and teachers' use/non-use of each section. As can be seen, a high proportion of the materials were drawn on in each of the teachers' lessons.

In summary, it should be clear that the textbook had a central role in the teachers' lessons. This was not surprising, given the institutional requirement to cover the book in its entirety, and given that exams were set by drawing on textbook content. And yet while these conditions undoubtedly constrained the teachers, obliging them to cover virtually every part of the book, they were able to make their own decisions about which sections to focus on particularly, in response to their students' needs and their own preferences and beliefs, as we shall see in the next section. Some teachers believed that the most pressing need for their students was to pass the exam. However, other teachers felt students should be equipped with the English they might need later on irrespective of the exam syllabus, and so covered all the skills. Consequently there was some divergence in teachers' use of the materials.

What adaptations do teachers make to their textbook?

The observations revealed that adding, reordering, modifying, and deleting textbook exercises occurred in the data, although to varying degrees and for various reasons. We now describe the various kinds of adaptations teachers made and report their rationale for doing so.

Adding

In all observed classes, teachers devoted time to explaining grammar rules and presenting additional examples of these rules in action before doing the textbook exercises because they all agreed that these were insufficient, particularly given what they perceived as their students' modest proficiency level in English.

In fact it turned out that more than just grammar activities were added to the textbook offerings. There were a number of activities presenting what teachers anticipated would be unknown terms to the learners, and E7 was observed to supplement the textbook by introducing some related prefixes, suffixes, and stems into a vocabulary activity, also encouraging students to generate additional terms of their own. For her part, E6 explained that she added material in accordance with her students' needs as determined by their responses to her questions in class:

> When I asked them about the meaning of 'lump' students confused it with 'lamb', it was obvious that they had problems with vowels and the /p/ and /b/ sounds. We discussed the differences in meaning and

pronunciation. So we ended up talking about three words instead of one: 'lump', 'lamb' and 'lamp'.

(Distinguishing between /p/ and /b/ causes problems for many L1 Arabic speakers.)

Lastly, E2 added information about the functions of the different areas in the brain and kinds of aphasia in a lesson focusing on neurology, since she felt that her students were always keen to know more than was in the book, and because she herself was interested in medical issues.

In sum, then, both the observation and interview data suggested that adding was the most common adaptation technique deployed by the teachers. Although all the participants emphasized the time constraints they operated under and the fact that the textbook was loaded with medical and specialized terms, teachers found it imperative to add activities and information to enhance students' understanding at the level of both language and content, to facilitate learning, to maintain their students' interest, and to satisfy their own preferences.

Deleting

Observations revealed that it was rare to delete a section from a unit completely. Teachers' motivations for deletion were connected with time constraints and the need to teach to the exam. E1 argued that there was no time for students to make an oral presentation in class, so why ask them to do the research which the textbook envisages will be the subject of the presentation? For her part, E5 pointed out that the research topics suggested by the textbook were specialized and medically oriented – for example, the task of researching types of suicide – and said she felt unqualified to discuss such topics; if the students misunderstood or misrepresented the topic, she would be unable to correct them. E5 and E6 also deleted writing activities, reasoning that, while writing takes time if done properly in class, their students seemed to have no interest in spending time on it because exams do not include writing assessment tasks.

When it came to speaking activities, however, all seven teachers believed it important for students to voice their opinions about the different topics covered in the book. Nonetheless, the classroom observations revealed that neither E3 nor E4 retained all the book's discussions. For instance, they deleted a discussion about smoking and alcohol, with E4 explaining during interview that she did not like discussing topics that are culturally or religiously alien: hence topics related to boyfriends, girlfriends, and sex were always omitted. E6 agreed that there were topics that were inappropriate for discussion in class and which made her uncomfortable, and which were thus deleted. On the other hand, E3 explained how she had decided not to discuss smoking and alcohol in her class only because it had been covered in a previous book, making it clear that she opposed the idea of deleting topics for cultural reasons, irrespective of her own feelings on the issues in question:

There was an activity talking about a female patient who was sexually abused as a child and then she went [in]to prostitution. I tried not to shy away from these things. I tried to let them see the difference in Islam. We don't drink but people drink and bad things happen because of it. [...] I don't think we should hide. I mean they are going to see strange patients in their life so they have to be prepared for [a] different society.

The other four teachers (E1, E2, E5, E7) were of the same opinion, E1 for instance explaining that she and her students enjoyed discussing the differences between cultures so that they could learn from and about them.

Reordering

Although reordering was identified in most observations, interviewees claimed they rarely changed the sequence of the sections in a unit or within an individual activity. E3 was the only participant who stated that she reordered quite often. She explained that she decided to tackle a pronunciation activity before a reading comprehension (in contrast to the order suggested in the textbook) because students looked tired and she felt the reading exercise was a bit heavy. She believed the pronunciation activity would lighten things up, allowing her to save the reading comprehension for the start of the following class. E3 also explained how she frequently reordered material which she felt was organized in an illogical fashion:

So for example in the unit we talk about a kidney. And then we go to relative clauses, then talk about the functions of a kidney. It seemed silly to go to grammar and then back to what the kidney does. We'd already started talking about the kidney so we continued with what the kidney does and then afterwards we went back to talk about grammar.

Additional motivations for reordering were associated with classroom resources, or lack of them: since the institution's language lab was not fully equipped, E7 opted to do the textbook listening exercises in her classroom instead. However, the unit's exercises were reordered so that they could all be done in one session because of the preparation time required to set the equipment up. Other activities were reordered because of the time teachers anticipated they would take to complete. Hence E6 delayed a grammar exercise until the beginning of the following class because she felt the time that remained was insufficient to do the activity justice. Her students' anticipated lack of content knowledge also led E6 to reorder in the hope that the revised sequence would make a speaking activity more productive:

> I assumed that students have no background knowledge about nursing children with head injuries. So I preferred that they read the text first, then we could discuss it together.

Modifying

Although not a great deal of modifying was observed in teachers' lessons, during interview all informants claimed they modified frequently in their lessons. For example, E3, who used the same textbook with a group who were studying another medical field rather than nursing, explained how she would modify those activities that required students to imagine being a nurse in a given situation or required them to talk about the most challenging aspect of the job, so she could relate them to her students' interests. Similarly, E2 described how she modified activities to ensure they matched students' needs (in relation to exam requirements), while also being maximally time-efficient. Another example of E2's modifying due to time constraints can be seen in the way she consistently asked students to present their research findings in written form rather than in the five-minute oral mode recommended in all units of the book:

> Five minutes for oral presentation as suggested by the book is far less than what our students need to present their research findings in the class. I know from experience [...]

E3 claimed during interview that she often modified activities, illustrating her approach by referring to a recent lesson which had not been observed:

> Yesterday they had this unit, there's speaking at the end. The students were tired because they'd had an exam. Actually [the speaking activity is] very depressing, talking about whether they should switch

off this [life support] machine, this mother and daughter, it's just so depressing. And so in fact I stopped halfway through and then we started talking about ethics and things [...] because I feel as long as they're using the vocabulary and the concept it doesn't really matter whether they answered these particular questions.

So in this instance the textbook was modified because of the students' energy levels and because of the subject matter.

In sum, then, the data indicated that there were numerous reasons why teachers used and adapted the prescribed textbook the way they did, ranging from factors related to the classroom environment, such as a lack of facilities, to factors related to students' lack of scientific and linguistic knowledge, from factors connected to institutional demands to teachers' limited knowledge of the subject matter. As reported above, a constant complaint was the time pressures teachers were under because of the institutional requirement to cover two books in one term. The institution's exams also impacted on teachers' textbook use. Given the multiple-choice format of the exam, which excluded writing, teachers believed that getting students to learn good writing skills was challenging. All of this meant that most teachers admitted sometimes neglecting what they considered important for students to learn while spending time on things they did not perceive as so significant because these were likely to come up in the exam. Another prominent concern was teachers' limited knowledge of the subject matter, which is discussed below at length given its centrality in the data, and given this issue is central to ESP debates.

Teachers' subject matter knowledge

It was clear that informants' subject matter knowledge had a major impact on how they perceived and used the textbook. E2 had been teaching ESP for three years, and possessed some knowledge of and interest in the subject matter. Similarly, although E3 had been teaching ESP for only three semesters, she had a solid background in science. Both teachers evaluated the textbook more critically and displayed more autonomy and flexibility in teaching, as seen through their adaptations.

On the other hand, E6, who described the book using the sleeping pills (i.e., boring) metaphor, adhered closely to the textbook because her grasp of its disciplinary content was more tenuous:

I don't and I can't make many changes in the book because everything is related to [students'] field. Everything is about science and

I'm not a science teacher. I'm an English teacher. If they ask me about English then yes I can do what is needed. But with science I prefer following the book.

The other teachers (E1, E4, and E5) who, like E6, appeared to stick more closely to the textbook script than E2 or E3, expressed their liking for the book but also referred to the content-related difficulties they experienced when preparing a lesson, either in terms of difficulties with the pronunciation of some of the medical terms or more general difficulties relating to their lack of relevant knowledge. E5's example below is typical:

In unit 12, it was mentioned that polio is an infectious disease. In the class the students kept asking me how that is. They kept asking and wondering and I felt like saying 'No more questions please, don't go into details. I can only explain what is in the book.'

This lack of in-depth knowledge therefore led to discomfort, causing teachers either to delete sections or to follow them to the letter. Moreover, some of the teachers also indicated that they were not interested in acquiring content-specific knowledge beyond what was provided in the book.

Discussion and conclusion

This study confirms the findings of previous studies of L2 textbook use (e.g., Hutchinson, 1996; Lee and Bathmaker, 2007), in that it is clear that different teachers use and adapt textbook materials in different ways, being influenced by their students' needs and by their own pedagogical beliefs and priorities, although, like previous studies of teachers' beliefs and practices, reported and actual behaviour did not always coincide (see Borg, 2003). Our informants adapted their materials and sometimes added external material, although their adaptations were fairly conservative, albeit not as conservative as those of Shawer's curriculum-transmitters, who rarely if ever departed from the textbook script. In fact, like Shawer's curriculum-developers and makers but unlike the curriculum-transmitters, our informants had in mind their learners' needs when implementing the materials. While the most obvious needs were exam-related, sometimes teachers spoke of addressing learners' future needs as they understood them – for instance the likelihood that learners would eventually need to deal with patients from non-Muslim cultures – leading to a discussion around cultural and lifestyle choices, and a departure from the textbook script. As in Gray's (2010b) research, then, our informants reacted to what they felt to be culturally inappropriate material in different ways, but most chose to engage with it rather than delete it. Departures from the script occurred too when teachers felt the textbook grammar coverage was too advanced for their class. So while informants' adaptations may have been modest compared with Wette's (2010) expert teachers' adaptations, to those of the teachers in Hinchman (1987) and Stodolsky (1989), who regularly and radically departed from the textbook script, and compared with those of Shawer's curriculum-developers and makers, the rigidity and linearity which characterized the practices of his curriculum-transmitters do not accurately describe the practices of our informants, even in their acutely exam-oriented environment.

In fact, there were three major contextual issues emerging from our data, all of which impacted negatively upon teachers' conceptualization and use of the textbook. These were (i) the lack of classroom time to get through the large volume of material; (ii) the high-stakes exam, whose content was derived from the textbook; and (iii) teachers' lack of content knowledge. The pressure to get through the material meant that informants were sometimes simply focused on deleting activities rather than creatively supplementing the textbook. The fact that most teachers had no input in the exam content but were aware that exam materials could be taken from any part of *Nursing 1* and 2 made them feel there was no option but to cover a large swathe of material. However, the exam did not include a spoken or written component, so these two skills, particularly the latter, were neglected as a result. This connects to studies of washback (the influence of testing on learning and teaching) in general, and the impact of high-stakes exam situations on teacher behaviour in particular (e.g., Cheng, 1997; Wall and Alderson, 1993). Cheng (1997) is of particular relevance here, because of the impact examinations were found to exert on textbooks and teachers' use of the teaching materials they were provided with, sticking closely to the exam syllabus. In contrast, although Wette's (2010) teachers working in high-constraint conditions similarly found their room for manoeuvre limited, they seem to have resisted these conditions to a greater degree, slowing down the pace of their classes despite the pressure to cover the required number of textbook units each week, albeit not to the extent they would have wished. In both studies, though, the pressure of exam-related contexts and the impact these conditions can have on teachers' use of materials are clear. Lastly, the third context-related issue concerns subject knowledge. The fact that informants were teaching medical rather than general English led to difficulties pronouncing and understanding specialist terminology and with answering students' content-related questions, difficulties similar to those experienced by the teachers in Hutchinson's (1996) study, and by Wu and Badger's (2009) Chinese college teachers of maritime English, who felt students would lose 'respect' for them if it was clear that they lacked subject-specific knowledge. It will be recalled that the nursing English textbooks were specifically chosen because it was felt their discipline-specific content would be less problematic for teachers, but clearly content-related issues remain an issue, and our teachers' lack of specialized knowledge led some informants to conceptualize the materials in terms of anxiety/fear.

The findings regarding informants' content knowledge are pertinent to the ongoing debate in EAP/ESP circles about how and to what extent English language classes should relate to the discipline-specific content students are studying on their degree programmes. Some researchers, such as Spack (1988), argue that ESP teachers should limit themselves to focusing on commonalities across academic genres, and 'general' academic English. Hyland (2002), on the other hand, contends that taking a more discipline-specific approach to ESP will lead to more relevant programmes. However, our study illustrates that acquiring the subject-specific knowledge which a more specific approach to ESP will likely require can cause formidable difficulties for teachers, who, like E6, may not identify with such a specific role. We suggest that these difficulties could be combated by means of (i) in-depth pre- and in-service ESP training programmes which include a component on textbook adaptation and use, informed by the results of studies such as this one; and (ii) cooperation and collaboration with discipline specialists in preparing materials, and in classroom instruction. We now explore these two proposals in more detail.

Both Wette (2010) and Shawer (2010a) argue that their findings about teachers' curricula and materials implementation have implications for teacher education. Wette (2010) recommends that foundation-level teacher-training books begin to feature case studies which raise trainees' awareness of how their plans for materials use will change according to classroom conditions; while Shawer (2010a) recommends that pre- and in-service teacher training programmes describe the different approaches to curricula/textbooks that his studies revealed (transmission, development, and creation) to raise awareness of the repertoire of different behaviours possible when it comes to using materials.

Shawer (2010b) argued that his curriculum-developers and -makers were delivering superior lessons compared to the curriculum-transmitters. The curriculum-developers and curriculum-makers' linguistic knowledge increased, for instance, where they felt the textbook handled a target grammatical feature badly or inappropriately for their learners, since they reported then consulting other sources and gaining a better understanding of the language in question (p.607). These teachers also modified their lessons based on how successful their previous approaches to the materials were. In contrast, irrespective of the perceived quality of the material or the needs of the particular class, the curriculum-transmitters simply proceeded step by step, line by line, through their textbook, a practice hardly encouraging reflection or criticality. Shawer therefore also suggests that school administrators should allow and encourage teachers to depart from their textbooks so as to tailor the curriculum as closely as possible to their learners' needs, and to become more thoughtful and more proficient users of materials. It will be recalled that in our context there are currently no training or development programmes in place, and we argue that a rigorous programme is urgently needed which features some or all of Wette and Shawer's proposals. Although the EAP course in focus in the present study is not specifically for nursing students but for medical students generally, we can gain many useful pointers on EAP curriculum design from exemplary accounts of developing EAP nursing materials and curricula in other institutions, as described by Bosher (2010), Bosher and Smalkoski (2002), and Hussin (2002), where the EAP practitioners are acutely aware of students' precise needs, having been encouraged by nursing faculty to observe nursing lectures and placements and to interview all parties concerned, and who work closely in and out of the classroom with content lecturers to ensure these needs are addressed. These accounts contrast starkly with our context, where communication between ESP teachers and content lecturers is non-existent. In addition, we believe the findings of this study highlight the need for reform of the ELC's system of assessment. Other studies of nursing students' needs (Bosher, 2010; Bosher and Smalkoski, 2002; Hussin, 2002; McCullagh, 2010) highlight various written and spoken skills and genres that learners require and experience serious difficulties in mastering, and we therefore argue that the in-house exam should include all four skills. Lastly, we believe the idea that the textbooks constitute the exam syllabus should be discouraged: instead, cooperation with subject specialists would ensure assessment tasks are maximally relevant for students' content-related studies.

Appendix A

Semi-structured interview schedule

Informant's details

First I'd like to ask a few background questions...

Name:
Native language:
Qualifications:
Teacher Training: • Can you tell me about the training you've had as a teacher?   • Have you attended any workshops, conferences, or seminars which covered materials design or how to use textbooks?   • Did you attend the workshop 'Oxford University Press *Headway* Training' which was held in this institution last semester? If so, can you tell me about it?
Total number of years' TEFL experience:
For how long have you been teaching ESP?
Have you ever taught English in other institutions prior to here? Where?   • How similar was the way you used textbooks in these other institutions compared with the way you use textbooks here?

The student's book

Now let's talk about teaching this *Nursing 2* textbook... Please try to think of a specific unit you have taught in the last week or two...

1. When you prepared for that lesson, did you FIRST refer to the student's book or the teacher's book? Why?

   • Did you use any external references? Why/why not?

2. How much use did you make of the student's book in that lesson?

   • Is the same true of your teaching in general?

3. Here is a list of the basic methods of textbook adaptations. [Show informants prompt card 1]

Prompt card (1)

Methods of adapting textbook

(i) *Deleting* (i.e., not covering an activity or skill in the textbook)
(ii) *Editing* (i.e., making changes to an activity that is given to you in the textbook)
(iii) *Reordering* (i.e., adjusting the sequence of presentation within a unit)
(iv) *Adding* (e.g., before a listening activity that may contain new vocabulary, the teacher adds an activity to introduce this vocabulary. Similar examples could include a prediction activity before reading)

- Did you make any of these adaptations in your lesson? If yes,
- What kind of adaptations did you make and Why?
- Which kind of adaptation did you make the most and which one did you make the least?
- Are the TYPES and the FREQUENCY of adaptation you made in this lesson typical of the types and the frequency of adaptation you make in your teaching in general?
- About the adaptation methods on the card which WEREN'T used in this lesson, have they been used/will they be used in other lessons? If yes, when and why? Or why not?

---

4. Here are two quotes by two teachers about adapting textbooks. [Show informants prompt card 2]

Prompt card (2)

Two quotes by teachers about adapting textbooks:

Reem: *'I need to make lots of adaptations to the textbook.'*

> Rasha: *'I rarely adapt the textbook and often make no adaptations at all.'*
>
> - *Which quote is closer to your own experiences of using* Nursing 2, *explaining how and why?*

5. Again I have two quotes by teachers about using textbooks. [Show informants prompt card 3]

Prompt card (3)

Two quotes by teachers about using textbooks:

Aisha: 'I feel constrained by the textbook, like I don't have the freedom to teach what I want.'
Hala: 'I don't feel constrained by the textbook; I have the freedom to teach whatever I want.'

- *With whom do you most agree? Explain how and why.*

---

6. Here are some metaphors teachers have used to describe the textbook. [Show informants prompt card 4]

Prompt card (4)

messenger	time machine	a great mind
supermarket	key to exam	a locker
a friend	teacher's parachute	pillow
map	compass	path
a wall	road block	professional killer
sleeping pills	toxic (like CO2)	rubbish bin
blank paper	nothing	nightmares
toothache	a devil	straitjacket (a special coat for mentally ill people)

(i) *Could you please pick up to 3 metaphors which REFLECT your opinion of the* Nursing 2 *textbook, explaining why; and*
(ii) *Please pick up to 3 metaphors that do NOT reflect your opinion of the* Nursing 2 *textbook, explaining why.*

The Teacher's book

Now let's talk about the teacher's resource book...

If we continue thinking about the unit you taught before...and we were discussing earlier...

7. How much use did you make of the teacher's resource book when planning your lesson?

   - Which suggestions did you take into account and which ones did you ignore? Why?
   - Is the same true of your use of the teacher's reference book in general?

8. How would you describe the teacher's resource book?
9. Here is a list of potentially constraining factors which may limit and affect the use of the teacher's book. [Show informants prompt card 5]

Prompt card (5)

Potentially constraining factors when teaching

- Students' proficiency level
- Students' needs
- Time constraints
- Large classes
- Institutional constraints
- Limited knowledge of the subject matter
- Limited years of teaching experience
- Workload
- Seating arrangements (some classes are equipped in a way that makes it difficult for students to move and work in pairs or groups)
- The unified exam (the exam is set by someone other than the teachers themselves)
- Students' attitudes toward learning English language
- Which of these factors most affect your use of the teacher's book? How?
- Any other constraining factors you like to add to the list, explaining *how and why?*

---

10. Here are two quotes by teachers about the way they use the teacher's resource book. [Show informants prompt card 6]

Prompt card (6)

Two quotes by teachers about the teacher's resource book:

Fatima: 'I sometimes do things differently to what is recommended in the teacher's book.'
Nadya: 'I never do things differently to what is recommended in the teacher's book.'

- So, *what about your use of the teacher's book? (And why?)*

Observations

Now I'd like to move on and talk about some of the incidents that I noticed during the classroom observations and that caught my interest...

....
....
....

To close

Finally, was there anything you wanted to comment on about using the textbook and the teacher's book which we haven't discussed?

Acknowledgements

We are grateful to Dr Bojana Petrić for her comments on an earlier version of this chapter.

Note

1. More specific profiles/educational backgrounds of informants are omitted to ensure anonymity.

References

Allwright, R.L. (1981). What do we want teaching materials for? *ELT Journal*, 36, 5–17.

Alvermann, D.E. (1987). The role of textbooks in teachers' interactive decision making. *Reading Research and Instruction*, 26, 115–127.

Anderson, G., Herr, K., and Nihlen, A. (2007). *Studying your own school*. Thousand Oaks: Corwin Press.

Apple, M.W. and Jungck, S. (1990). 'You don't have to be a teacher to teach this unit': Teaching, technology, and gender in the classroom. *American Educational Research Journal*, 27, 227–251.

Ball, D.L. and Feiman-Nemser, S. (1988). Using textbooks and teachers' guides: A dilemma for beginning teachers and teacher educators. *Curriculum Inquiry*, 18, 401–423.

Barbieri, F. and Eckhardt, S.E.B. (2007). Applying corpus-based findings to form-focused instruction: The case of reported speech. *Language Teaching Research*, 11, 319–346.

Bell, J. and Gower, R. (1998). Writing course materials for the world: A great compromise. In B. Tomlinson (Ed.), *Materials development in language teaching* (pp.116–129). Cambridge: Cambridge University Press.

Borg, S. (2003). Teacher cognition in language teaching: A review of research on what language teachers think, know, believe, and do. *Language Teaching*, 36, 81–109.

Bosher, S. (2010). English for nursing: Developing discipline-specific materials. In N. Harwood (Ed.), *English language teaching materials: Theory and practice* (pp.346–372). New York: Cambridge University Press.

Bosher, S. and Smalkoski, K. (2002). From needs analysis to curriculum development: Designing a course in health-care communication for immigrant students in the USA. *English for Specific Purposes*, 21, 59–79.

Boxer, D. and Pickering, L. (1995). Problems in the presentation of speech acts in ELT materials: The case of complaints. *ELT Journal*, 49, 44–58.

Cheng, L. (1997). How does washback influence teaching? Implications for Hong Kong. *Language and Education*, 11, 38–54.

Cohen, L., Manion, L., and Morrison, K. (2007). *Research methods in education* (6th ed.). London: RoutledgeFalmer.

Creswell, J. W. (2007). *Qualitative inquiry and research design: Choosing among five approaches* (2nd ed.). Thousand Oaks: Sage.

Cullen, R. and Kuo, I.-C. (2007). Spoken grammar and ELT course materials: A missing link? *TESOL Quarterly*, 41, 361–386.

Dörnyei, Z. (2007). *Research methods in applied linguistics: Quantitative, qualitative, and mixed methodologies*. Oxford: Oxford University Press.

Freebairn, I. (2000). The coursebook – future continuous or past? *English Teaching Professional*, 15 (April), 3–5.

Gray, J. (2000). The ELT course book as cultural artefact: How teachers censor and adapt. *ELT Journal*, 54, 274–283.

Gray, J. (2010a). The branding of English and the culture of the new capitalism: Representations of the world of work in English language textbooks. *Applied Linguistics*, 31, 714–733.

Gray, J. (2010b). *The construction of English: Culture, consumerism and promotion in the ELT global coursebook*. Basingstoke: Palgrave Macmillan.

Grice, T. and Greenan, J. (2007). *Nursing 1 student's book*. Oxford: Oxford University Press.

Grice, T. and Greenan, J. (2008). *Nursing 2 student's book.* Oxford: Oxford University Press.

Hammersley, M. and Atkinson, P. (2007). *Ethnography: Principles in practice.* London: Routledge.

Harwood, N. (2005). What do we want EAP teaching materials for? *Journal of English for Academic Purposes*, 4, 149–161.

Harwood, N. (2010). Issues in materials development and design. In N. Harwood (Ed.), *English language teaching materials: Theory and practice* (pp.3–30). New York: Cambridge University Press.

Hinchman, K. (1987). The textbook and three content-area teachers. *Reading Research and Instruction*, 26, 247–262.

Hussin, V. (2002). An ESP program for students of nursing. In T. Orr (Ed.), *English for specific purposes* (pp.25–39). Alexandria: TESOL.

Hutchinson, E.G. (1996). What do teachers and learners actually do with textbooks? Teacher and learner use of a fisheries-based ELT textbook in the Philippines. Unpublished PhD thesis, Lancaster University.

Hutchinson, T. and Torres, E. (1994). The textbook as agent of change. *ELT Journal*, 48, 315–328.

Hyland, K. (2002). Specificity revisited: How far should we go now? *English for Specific Purposes*, 21, 385–395.

Islam, C. and Mares, C. (2003). Adapting classroom materials. In B. Tomlinson (Ed.), *Developing materials for language teaching* (pp.86–100). London: Continuum.

Jiang, X. (2006). Suggestions: What should ESL students know? *System*, 34, 36–54.

Lee, R.N.F. and Bathmaker, A.-M. (2007). The use of English textbooks for teaching English to 'vocational' students in Singapore secondary schools: A survey of teachers' beliefs. *RELC Journal*, 38, 350–374.

Levis, J.M. (1999). Intonation in theory and practice, revisited. *TESOL Quarterly*, 33, 37–63.

Mackey, A. and Gass, S. (2005). *Second language research: Methodology and design.* Mahwah: Lawrence Erlbaum.

McCullagh, M. (2010). An initial evaluation of the effectiveness of a set of published materials for medical English. In B. Tomlinson and H. Masuhara (Eds.), *Research for materials development in language teaching: Evidence for best practice* (pp.381–393). London: Continuum.

McDonough, J. and Shaw, C. (2003). *Materials and methods in ELT: A teacher's guide.* London: Blackwell.

McGrath, I. (2002). *Materials evaluation and design for language teaching.* Edinburgh: Edinburgh University Press.

McGrath, I. (2006). Teachers' and learners' images for course books. *ELT Journal*, 60, 171–180.

Miles, M.B. and Huberman, A.M. (1994). *Qualitative data analysis: An expanded sourcebook* (2nd ed.). Thousand Oaks: Sage.

O'Neill, R. (1982). Why use textbooks? *ELT Journal*, 36, 104–111.

Pelly, C.P. and Allison, D. (2000). Investigating the views of teachers on assessment of English language learning in the Singapore education system. *Hong Kong Journal of Applied Linguistics*, 5, 81–106.

Porreca, K.L. (1984). Sexism in current ESL textbooks. *TESOL Quarterly*, 18, 705–724.

Richards, J.C. (1993). Beyond the textbook: The role of commercial materials in language teaching. *RELC Journal*, 24(1), 1–14.

Römer, U. (2004). A corpus-driven approach to modal auxiliaries and their didactics. In J. Sinclair (Ed.), *How to use corpora in language teaching* (pp.185–199). Amsterdam: John Benjamins.

Samuda, V. (2005). Expertise in pedagogic task design. In K. Johnson (Ed.), *Expertise in second language learning and teaching* (pp.230–254). Basingstoke: Palgrave Macmillan.

Shannon, P. (1987). Commercial reading materials, a technological ideology, and the deskilling of teachers. *The Elementary School Journal*, 87, 307–329.

Shardakova, M. and Pavlenko, A. (2004). Identity options in Russian textbooks. *Journal of Language, Identity, and Education*, 3, 25–46.

Shawer, S. (2010a). Classroom-level curriculum development: EFL teachers as curriculum-developers, curriculum-makers and curriculum-transmitters. *Teaching and Teacher Education*, 26, 173–184.

Shawer, S. (2010b). Classroom-level teacher professional development and satisfaction: Teachers learn in the context of classroom-level curriculum development. *Professional Development in Education*, 36, 597–620.

Soars, L. and Soars, J. (2006a). *New Headway plus elementary student's book with interactive CD-ROM*. Oxford: Oxford University Press.

Soars, L. and Soars, J. (2006b). *New Headway plus pre-intermediate student's book with interactive CD-ROM*. Oxford: Oxford University Press.

Spack, R. (1988). Initiating ESL students into the academic discourse community: How far should we go? *TESOL Quarterly*, 22, 29–52.

Stodolsky, S.S. (1989). Is teaching really by the book? In P.W. Jackson and S. Haroutunian-Gordon (Eds.), *From Socrates to software: The teacher as text and the text as teacher* (pp.159–184). Chicago: National Society for the Study of Education.

Tomlinson, B. (2003). Materials development courses. In B. Tomlinson (Ed.), *Developing materials for language teaching* (pp.445–461). London: Continuum.

Tsui, A.M. (2003). *Understanding expertise in teaching: Case studies of second language teachers*. Cambridge: Cambridge University Press.

Wall, D. and Alderson, J.C. (1993). Examining washback: The Sri Lankan impact study. *Language Testing*, 10, 41–69.

Wette, R. (2010). Professional knowledge in action: How experienced ESOL teachers respond to feedback from learners within syllabus and contextual constraints. *System*, 38, 569–579.

Williams, M. (1988) Language taught for meetings and language used in meetings: Is there anything in common? *Applied Linguistics*, 9, 45–58.

Wu, H. and Badger, R.G. (2009). In a strange and uncharted land: ESP teachers' strategies for dealing with unpredicted problems in subject knowledge during class. *English for Specific Purposes*, 28, 19–32.

6

An Experienced Teacher's Use of the Textbook on an Academic English Course: A Case Study

Fotini Grammatosi and Nigel Harwood

Summary

Although the textbook enjoys a prominent role in many ELT classrooms, empirical research investigating textbook usage in classroom contexts is lacking. Using a repeating cycle of classroom observations and pre- and post-interviews over the course of a semester, this qualitative descriptive case study focused on the way John, an experienced teacher, used the mandated textbook, and his explanations for these behaviours as he sometimes adapted, but frequently abandoned, the book. The study was situated in a UK university, on an English course to prepare students for academic study; and although the textbook was supposed to constitute the syllabus, John enjoyed considerable freedom and autonomy in choosing what was covered in class, and how. Results revealed that John's decisions regarding the use of the textbook were influenced by his evaluation of the quality of the textbook and its lack of alignment with his preferred pedagogical approach, but also by contextual factors, such as: John's views on the lack of fit between the textbook material and the needs, abilities, and interests of his students; course logistics, with new students enrolling halfway through the course; and his course director's refusal to allow him to replace the mandated textbook with an alternative title which John felt was at a more appropriate level. Our findings echo those of mainstream education research, which conclude that textbook usage patterns are context-bound and mediated, and also suggest that Eunice Hutchinson's (1996) framework for describing the factors affecting textbook use is valid. We end the chapter by proposing various textbook consumption projects for future research of a more evaluative bent.

Introduction

What factors impact upon teachers' patterns of textbook use? Why do teachers use the textbook in the way they do? These questions are addressed in this case study of a single teacher. The argument for studying and understanding textbook consumption has been made elsewhere (Harwood, this volume; also Menkabu and Harwood, this volume), and it was pointed out that we have a good deal of evidence from the mainstream education literature showing that teachers may use textbooks in different ways, and may depart considerably from the content of their textbooks, for different reasons and purposes (e.g., Behm and Lloyd, 2009; Collopy, 2003; Davis, Beyer, Forbes, and Stevens, 2011; Manouchehri and Goodman, 1998; Nicol and Crespo, 2006; Remillard and Bryans, 2004; Smagorinsky, Cook, Moore, Jackson, and Fry, 2004; Smagorinsky, Lakly, and Johnson, 2002). And although ELT-related textbook consumption studies are much thinner on the ground, we have Shawer's studies (Shawer, 2010a, 2010b; also Shawer, Gilmore, and Banks-Joseph, 2009) as evidence that this is also the case in our field. Based on repeated classroom observations, Shawer found his teacher participants could be categorized according to their fidelity or lack of fidelity to the textbook as follows:

(i) *Curriculum-makers* rarely if ever used a textbook, creating their own materials. They began the course by conducting an initial needs analysis which suggested a syllabus, and then created materials accordingly. Although much of the subject matter they used did not appear in the textbook, sometimes the book and its table of contents were used as inspiration to create these materials.

(ii) *Curriculum-developers* freely adapted the textbook to best suit their learners. They also created their own materials if they felt the textbook fell short, but not on the scale of the curriculum-makers.

(iii) *Curriculum-transmitters* strictly adhered to their textbook, proceeding exercise by exercise, page by page, rarely if ever even changing the task order. (Shawer, 2010a, 2010b; Shawer et al., 2009)

More can be found in both the ELT and mainstream education literature regarding the various ways in which teachers can use or abandon the textbook. A much-used framework from the ELT literature to describe textbook use or non-use is that of McDonough and Shaw (2003), who speak of teachers maximizing the fit between textbook and learners by means of adding, deleting, modifying, and reordering materials. And a mainstream education researcher who theorizes teachers' textbook use is Brown (2009). Likening teachers' textbook usage to jazz musicians improvising from a musical score, Brown argues that teachers are designers who craft, 'adapt and improvise [textbook content] in response to local factors and creative ability' (p.22). It is noteworthy here that Brown explains teachers' patterns of textbook consumption not only in terms of learners' needs and the teacher's perception of these needs: the 'creative ability' he speaks of means that the teacher's 'skills, knowledge and beliefs' (p.22) will also play their part in how the teacher understands and implements textbook material. Brown specifies five ways in which teachers interact with materials, and this taxonomy duly references teachers' skills, knowledge, and beliefs. First, teachers *select* from the pages of a textbook, choosing whether the materials are more or less faithfully implemented, used more selectively, or resisted and abandoned. Second, they *interpret* materials while planning and teaching, this interpretation being influenced by the teacher's pedagogical and content knowledge (that is, by what the teacher knows about teaching and the subject matter), and also by their contextual conditions. Teachers then *reconcile* their own goals and their contextual constraints with what they see as the intended goals of the materials. Fourth, they factor in or *accommodate* their students' profile – their interests, abilities, experiences, etc. Finally, the teacher *adds, modifies,* or *omits* the materials as s/he sees fit. Hence the teacher and the textbook influence each other: the textbook influences the teacher, since Brown views textbooks as artefacts (in the sense of tools which help accomplish some kind of action) which can both afford and constrain teachers as they design and craft their lessons; and the teacher influences the textbook and its content, in that the knowledge s/he brings to the materials, as well as how this knowledge is applied to shape the materials for his/her purposes, will affect the materials for better or worse. In relation to this, Brown (2009) coins the term *pedagogical design capacity* to speak of the teacher's skills in 'perceiving the affordances of the materials and making decisions about how to use them to [...] achieve her goals' (p.29).

In order to account for what Brown sees as teachers' design decisions, then, we need a framework which takes into account the profiles of the teacher and learners, the micro and macro context, and the textbook and materials. Hutchinson's (1996) simple but powerful framework does so, having emerged from a situated study of a textbook in use. Her study of EAP teachers suggested that the following factors impact on the teacher–textbook interaction:

(i) the textbook (its content);

(ii) the teacher (e.g., beliefs, training, pedagogical and content knowledge, experience, preferred teaching style, perception and evaluation of the textbook, attitude towards top-down mandates (e.g., school/state syllabus, directives from school principal));

(iii) the learners (e.g., level, aptitude, previous learning experiences, preferred learning styles);

(iv) the classroom (e.g., physical layout); and

(v) the school (e.g., timetable constraints, principal's attitudes towards textbook use and to EFL as a subject). (pp.47–48, 99–100)

We felt Hutchinson's framework would likely prove a useful starting point for our own analysis, since it captures the context-bound, mediated nature of textbook consumption also foregrounded by Brown.

Methodology

Context

The research took place in a UK university language centre, on a preparatory English programme for international students who needed to improve their general and academic English language skills. All students on the programme held conditional offers for places on undergraduate or postgraduate degrees from various UK universities, guaranteeing a place on the degree scheme provided the students achieved the required IELTS score. The course ran throughout the whole year (over four ten-week terms) and was divided into five-week study blocks. It consisted of only three levels: elementary, intermediate, and advanced. Students were assigned a level on the basis of an initial placement test; progress to the next level depended upon their performance. According to the amount of progress required to attain the prerequisite IELTS score, students attended the programme for between five and 40 weeks. As a result, the make-up of classes changed frequently, and students were permitted to enrol in a class mid-term.

Classes were typically small, comprising six–nine students in each class, and the focal class in this study was at the elementary level, the lowest level on the programme. It comprised six students from the Arab world (four females, two males) whose actual language level was judged by their teacher to be between false beginners and upper-elementary and to be a mixed-ability class. Indeed, such were the differences in terms of ability that our teacher participant and the course director had discussed giving the two stronger female students the option to move up to the next-level class before finally deciding not to. Other challenges included the fact that one of the students was pregnant and was said to become easily fatigued and to lose concentration, and patchy class attendance, with only two of the six students turning up regularly (as was the case when our participant was teaching the second of the textbook units we focus on below).

The programme was intensive, with 26 hours of instruction each week. This included 16 hours of grammar and vocabulary instruction, which were taught using a textbook that was chosen by the language centre, *Elementary Language Leader* (Lebeau and Rees, 2008). The textbook constituted the syllabus, and teachers had access to all its components, including the teacher's guide. However, teachers were permitted the freedom to adapt and/or supplement the textbook with their own or other published materials, but not to substitute it with another textbook. A copy of the textbook was provided to each student by the language centre. For the remaining ten hours per week, students were taught academic writing, reading, listening, and speaking, for which the teachers were free to choose any materials they thought suitable from the centre's bank of resources or elsewhere. It is the grammar and vocabulary part of the course, with its mandated textbook, that is the focus here.

Participant

The dataset in this chapter is taken from a larger study by the first author of five teachers who all worked on the same programme, but here we focus on one teacher, 'John' (a pseudonym). At the time of data collection, John had been teaching on the programme for three years. He was experienced, with 12 years of teaching in different contexts in Europe and Asia, and held a first degree and an initial teacher-training qualification (the Certificate in Teaching English to Speakers of Other Languages (CELTA)). The reason we decided to focus on John in particular in this chapter is connected to his professed attitudes towards and use of textbooks in general and his mandated textbook on the grammar and vocabulary course in particular: while he did not describe himself as an anti-textbook teacher, he used textbook materials very sparingly in his classes during the time of the study, mostly relying on his own worksheets or materials from other sources such as resource books and websites. This piqued our interest and motivated the present case study of John.

Procedure

The case study methodology was deemed suitable for our purposes since it enables intense, in-depth examination of a small number of participants in a specific context (see Duff, 2008; Merriam, 1998). Specifically, we wished to identify and investigate the factors which impacted upon the teacher–textbook interaction, and, in connection with this, the reasons for which John either used or (more commonly) abandoned the mandated textbook.

In order to accomplish this, it was essential to study John and his textbook (non-)use in the classroom, collecting 'live' data (Cohen, Manion, and Morrison, 2007: 396), and the central methods employed were classroom observations and semi-structured pre- and post-observation interviews. Additional information was also collected from John's lesson plans, as well as from the materials, both published and unpublished, that John drew on to supplement and replace the materials in the set textbook. Initially the use of think-aloud protocols was also considered with the aim of gathering richer pre-observation data, since the think-alouds would have provided further insights into John's lesson-planning processes. However, this did not prove possible, as John argued that his lesson-planning was ongoing and did not take place in a fixed location or at a specific time, and so attempts to supplement observation and pre- and post-observation interview data were eventually abandoned.

John was observed for ten consecutive teaching periods of 50 minutes each. Before the first observation John and the students were assured that the research was focused on the use of materials and not on the teacher's or students' performance; in other words, it was made clear that the focus of the study was descriptive rather than evaluative.

During the pre-observation interviews John went through his lesson plan, explaining how he envisaged each stage of the lesson and its aims, describing the materials he planned to use, and elaborating on the reasons for his choice of materials and tasks. The questions for the pre-observation interviews derived from John's lesson plan and materials. Below follows an extract from a pre-observation interview where John explained the reasons why the order in which he had originally planned to use his handouts changed:

John: [...and thirdly] I'm going to give them worksheet 2, which is from onestopenglish.com [...] and it's going to be them looking at some adjectives. Some of it might be new for them, but most of them there they should be quite familiar with [...] And then that's going to just consolidate what they have just focused on [...] in the grammar focus part of the lesson. [...]

Int: Since it follows on from the warm-up, why do you give it third and not second?

John: Because I wanted to do the grammar focus first. I wanted to do the grammar focus at the beginning of the lesson so they are clear and then move on to a more meaty part.

The lesson plan that John had provided served as an observation guide, inasmuch as the first author noted whether and to what extent John adhered to the plan. And during the post-observation interview John was asked to reflect on his practice and to comment on the reasons he made any changes to the way he had originally envisaged the lesson and the uses to which the materials were put, as previously explained in the pre-observation interview.

Data codes and coding

Both of us independently and collaboratively summarized several interview and observation transcripts and drew up a start list (Miles and Huberman, 1994; see also Smagorinsky, 2008) of codes as a result, before making further refinements as a result of continuing to try out the codes on John's data and the data of other teachers in the larger study. Like the coding process, the analysis of John's data was done both independently and then collaboratively. Full details of the coding and analytical procedures, including a complete list of codes, can be found in Grammatosi (in preparation).

Results

An overview of John's textbook use

During the period of data collection, in Shawer's terms John's patterns of textbook use were closest to those of the curriculum-maker, a curriculum-maker being the type of teacher who rarely if ever uses a textbook, creating his/her own materials on the basis of the learners' needs. Like Shawer's curriculum-makers, John also reports using the grammar points covered by each unit of the textbook as a general guide and a source of inspiration for the focus of the materials he creates or takes from elsewhere (other textbooks, websites, etc.), so that he loosely adheres to the textbook's language syllabus. He also reports 'sometimes' adopting the same strategy regarding coverage of the textbook's vocabulary syllabus, although he often chose a different topic and associated vocabulary around which to present the grammar, judging this to be more interesting or diverting for learners, and his vocabulary focus to be more useful and relevant to the learners' everyday lives.

It should be made clear, however, that John says that this curriculum-making behaviour is not his customary practice; he claims instead to normally take a greater proportion of materials from the textbook, being more of a curriculum-developer than a curriculum-maker in Shawer's terms. John's decision to use the textbook much more sparingly than usual during the time of the study is explained by his unfavourable evaluation of the book, his view that it was unsuitable for his class, particularly for the weaker students, and the fact he was denied permission to replace the textbook with an alternative of his choice. John had previously taught from his preferred alternative textbook and judged it to be a better fit for his learners, but the course director felt the book was too low-level. However, the director *did* give John licence to depart from the book during the initial stages of the course should he deem it necessary, as the following extract shows:

> [...] we had these really weak students and [the course director's] advice was 'Don't do the book, then [during the initial stages of the course]', because the book was a bit too high for them until the new girls came. That's why I didn't do the book from the beginning [...]

As stated above, John had a rather low opinion of the mandated textbook. He felt the textbook materials failed to provide sufficient amounts of practice of the grammar in focus, such practice as there was being evaluated as 'bitty' or 'bits and pieces' ('the book isn't very thorough [...] there aren't enough exercises in the book'). And the fact that John perceived the book to be too challenging for his two weakest learners was a serious problem, given that the class consisted of only four regular attendees, including these two students. Crucially, John's evaluation was based on bitter experience: he reported having attempted unsuccessfully to use the textbook in his first class (before data collection began), attributing his lack of success to the difficulty of the materials ('it was too hard for them'). In sum, then, John found the book to be too difficult, to focus on some topics which his learners would likely find uninteresting, to be inconsistent in terms of quality in its presentation, and also to lack coherence, clarity, and relevance:

> I find the book really unclear, lots of different things going on, on the page [...] The book [...] floated from grammar point to grammar point and some of the exercises in each unit or on each page weren't relevant enough or were too vague or were hit-and-miss, and I really wanted to focus my students on specific points in the best way in my opinion that I knew how, which was to focus it with my own materials, to get it more concise than the pages in the book.

> [The textbook] doesn't link things well enough for my liking [...] But I like personally a lot of the time to link and focus on the same topic using the four skills.

Moreover, John explained how he had recently been 'experimenting' with abandoning the textbook in class, and that, although he had 'always felt guilty for not using the book', one of his colleagues (who presumably had no qualms about textbook abandonment and being a curriculum-maker) told John that his sense of guilt was misplaced. Given the difficult circumstances, then, specifically the perceived lack of fit between textbook and class, John resolved to draw far less on the textbook than normal:

> [...] and this term I've just decided, well, with only four students and with the disparity in their level as well and the book was too hard for them really, for two of them [...], I thought blow it, I'm not going to use the book for once in my whole life [...], but I did feel guilty not using the book, like I'm not doing something properly [...]

John's judgement that the textbook features a number of uninspiring and irrelevant topics can be seen in his comments on and use of the first of two textbook units we focus on here, a unit devoted to the topic of inventors and their inventions.

John's use of the inventors and inventions unit

The unit on inventors and their inventions begins with pictures of Alfred Nobel, Leonardo da Vinci, and Levi Strauss, asking students how much they know about Nobel, da Vinci, and Strauss, before leading in to a reading about da Vinci. The reading is used to introduce the past simple, contextualizing this with examples such as *Leonardo worked as an engineer for 32 years*. The unit then turns to inventions and innovations in the field of medicine, both old and new, including acupuncture needles, false teeth, the microscope, and the MRI scanner. John deemed this topic to be particularly unsuitable and difficult for his class, and so omitted all of the textbook materials, using alternative materials of his own creation, as well as materials from other textbooks, grammar books, and websites to teach the past simple grammar focus. Hence the textbook's grammar point was covered, but by using none of the materials in the book.

Commenting on the inventions unit, John felt there was a mismatch between the level of general knowledge required (particularly general knowledge of the West), and the knowledge of his students. He also doubted the relevance of this topic to the learners' lives:

> [...] look at the book [...], for example, 'inventions'. I look at that, and it's a quite an off-putting topic, I think. And it is difficult to talk about as well with these students, with some of them, plus their age, as well. They are 20 years old, some of them, the oldest is 25 [...] Difficult for them to talk about inventions and some of these names you know, irrelevant, Greek philosopher. I don't find it very useful.

John therefore judged that he could cover the past tense, the grammar focus of this unit, 'in a more interesting or a more relevant way' instead of centring the grammar around the inventions topic. The perceived inappropriacy of this topic contrasts with another topic in the book, shopping, which John used rather than omitted (prior to data collection), because 'it is an everyday useful topic which the girls are interested in'.

John also believed the level of difficulty of the material to be excessive with regard to the topic in general and the unit's reading in particular. Neither did he feel the vocabulary which features would be useful to the learners:

> [...] and I think the topic inventions isn't very good for this level [...] it's not just because it is Leonardo da Vinci, Levi Strauss, it's because of the topic inventions, which is a very hard topic to talk about as a false beginner, for Arabic students. They are not going to be able to tell me about these people or even about people who they know in their own country. They probably won't know anybody. It is very hard in your own language to know about people who invented something and discuss it in detail, let alone in a foreign language. I didn't like the topic.

> [The grammar focus] was past tense which [was] very new [for the learners] [...] This is too difficult for them [...] [Flicking through the textbook pages and singling out vocabulary from elsewhere in the unit] 'Acupuncture', 'scalpel', they are not useful words that [learners] are going to use at this level. This is high-level vocabulary I think [...]

In his own vocabulary materials, then, John tried to 'include new words which are useful rather than random words which [learners] will probably never need to use'.

John specific comments on the unit's warm-up activity were consistent with the perceived shortcomings he identified above. The book shows learners portraits of Nobel, da Vinci, and Strauss, and asks them to discuss with a partner what they know about these three figures and their inventions. Again John felt there was a mismatch between his learners' interests/knowledge and the topic, and added that the textbook presents the material in an unattractive manner:

> [...] the pictures aren't very appetizing. They are very black and white. They are non-contemporary inventors. [...] This lesson [...] would be very useful if they were European teenagers. They *would* know who Leonardo da Vinci is, it would be interesting. Or Levi Strauss or somebody else. But they are Arabic students who are not interested *at all* in anything European, about ancient history, they're not interested, it is just obvious. I've been teaching [Arab students] for three years now. They haven't got a clue who most people are and they don't care, to be frank. They don't care.

To sum up then, although the textbook material was abandoned, John nonetheless covered the unit's grammar focus of the past tense. But rather than inventions, he organized this work around the theme of holidays, a theme 'which everybody loves and can talk about'.

John's use of the money unit

Our second textbook unit in focus is themed around the topic of money. Beginning with a warm-up picture showing a jar full of coins and the heading *Keeping it safe*, this is followed by a vocabulary activity on the same theme (e.g., teaching/eliciting *PIN number, wallet, purse*, etc.), and then reading and listening activities with a similar subject, giving advice to international students living in the UK on how to keep their money safe. This advice-giving is effected by the grammar focus of the unit, *should/shouldn't*, and gap-fills highlight and practise this language, followed by speaking and writing activities which also require students to give advice and continue to use *should/shouldn't*.

Unlike the inventions theme, John was positive about this money unit. Although he had omitted all of the previous three units of textbook material, merely covering the textbook's grammar syllabus from these three units in his own way, the money theme enthuses him, and it initially appeared he would now adhere much more closely to the textbook material:

> [...] I don't usually use the book but as we've covered the last three units without the book completely I thought [...] the topic money was quite interesting for them, there are some good vocabulary words in there which are quite relevant to everyday use, even at low level [...]

John believed the topic and associated vocabulary would prove to be both interesting and relevant to the learners. However, it was also noticeable that John spoke not only of the anticipated interests of his learners, but also his *own* interests, and what *he* found interesting to teach:

> [...] and I just thought, well, I haven't used the book at all [since the beginning of the course] and I just decided, well this is actually interesting because I like money and it is important to know the vocabulary for money [...]

Despite this willingness to use the textbook unit, however, it turned out that John made very substantial adaptations to the material, as well as supplementing and replacing it with his own exercises, finally using just one activity from the entire unit in an unadapted form, a listening exercise. Other activities were radically altered or omitted altogether.

We begin our closer examination of John's materials with the textbook's warm-up picture of a jar of coins, which John believes to lack mileage as a starter activity, and which he feels his learners will be unable to exploit:

> [...] I didn't need the picture money with a bowl of money, I didn't need that – very irrelevant, just coins. I taught that anyway later

with my own worksheets, the word 'coins' [...] There is nothing to speculate from that picture, apart from maybe three words and the students were false beginners, they had no imagination in English. It was such a bland picture.

John began the lesson instead with an interactive speaking game of his own design which led into the topic by having learners produce money-related vocabulary:

I'm probably just going to elicit their knowledge, get them to stand up, and I'm going to go around the room and play a little speaking game, and they've got five seconds to say any word they can think of associated with the word money, with the topic money, and if they can't think of a word or if they repeat a word that someone else has said, then they're out.

John then proceeded with an adapted version of the next textbook activity in the unit, a vocabulary exercise (see Appendix A). The textbook lists eight words/phrases associated with money and has learners look up any unknown items in dictionaries. However, John's own version was lengthier, teaching/checking more vocabulary items, and began to prepare the class for a later activity, the listening:

[...] not just for three or four [words] like in the book but for the 14 words I had [...] and all those words were the difficult words I thought that were relevant for the listening [...]

So here we see how John replaced textbook materials to address what he saw as the insufficient volume of grammar and vocabulary practice it contains. He also perceived his own vocabulary activity as more pedagogically effective and efficient than the book's, since it introduced vocabulary students would encounter later in the listening transcript.

Unlike the textbook's starter activity and vocabulary exercise, the listening activity was evaluated positively by John, since it enabled him to vary the type of listening learners would be exposed to, as he had not used a textbook audio recording up to this point:

[...] also I thought I wanted to do a listening not from me, not from my own story, me reading it. I wanted to give them a different voice and a different context and a longer story maybe, and a different intonation, different nuances in their voice, and just a more

natural conversation between two people rather than just me reading [a] dialogue. I thought it was also quite lengthy as well, I thought
that would be nice to hear a longer story, and that's why I used the
book for that listening task, because it interested me. I thought the
vocabulary was useful and it was a different voice, different nuance,
different intonation, different dialogue and we changed, we used the
book for once [...]

Again we see John speaking of the material for inclusion interesting *him*,
as well as his class.

The listening activity above aside, we have seen that generally, on
the few occasions where John elected to use textbook material, this was
often heavily adapted to meet the needs of his learners as he understood
them. And yet we do not want to leave readers with the misleading
impression that where John used his own materials, these were not subject to adaptations also: the observations revealed that John frequently
departed from his original lesson plans, and was always prepared to
adapt and omit his own materials in response to the way things were
progressing during the lesson. In fact, during the planning stage John
intentionally prepared a variety of materials and activities because he
wished to keep his options open as to what exactly would be covered;
so a considerable amount of his materials were only ever reserve activities and John's lesson plans were characterized by a certain degree of
flexibility. And further flexibility was introduced as John began to put
the plans into action in the classroom; the learners and their consumption of the materials had a profound impact on the flow of the lesson,
and on the choice and use of these materials. To give a flavour of this,
we now present some data relating to two of John's own activities as he
departed once more from the textbook materials yet continued with the
textbook's money theme and the grammar point found in the textbook
money unit, *should/shouldn't*. What we refer to here as Activity 1 was
a card/matching game John took from the Internet which consisted of
problem cards and their corresponding solutions. The activity as John
had planned it comprised two parts: the first part involved reading and
dictionary work, with learners ensuring they understood each of the
problem cards by consulting dictionaries as and when necessary, and
then writing advice to solve the problems. In the second part John was
to give the learners another set of solution cards which learners would
then match to the appropriate problem cards, racing against each other
to be the first to do so. John expressed doubts about whether he would
actually use this activity in the pre-observation interview ('but that's

quite hard, so I am not totally decided on that activity') and, as we shall see, finally decided not to use the activity at all. Activity 2 also focuses on *should/shouldn't* to give advice, but is a board game which John obtained from another ELT website which again gives students imaginary situations their partners have to respond to (e.g., Situation: *My best friend is very angry with me*; Solution: *You should talk to her and apologize*). So the emphasis this time is on oral production. Here is how John responded to a question in the post-observation interview asking why he ended up omitting Activity 1 but retaining Activity 2:

> [...] I actually missed out the card game, the matching game [i.e., Activity 1], I think it was getting a bit tedious. [The learners] were tired and hungry and maybe a little bit bored, but tired and hungry especially. And I thought with two [learners only in the class] it wasn't very much fun, and also the pregnant girl doesn't want to stand up, so how's she going to enjoy, she's just sick so. And that card game was actually quite difficult vocabulary, so I was going to skip that I knew but I thought, this will take a long time as well I thought [...] I just thought, time, timing, energy levels, the girl was visibly not very well, was she? Remember she was sick and she has been sick all term actually, so I just thought well, let's cut to the chase, so I just skipped [Activity 1] 'cos it was quite hard for them anyway. So I got straight to the speaking [Activity 2] 'cos I thought that the speaking is quite practical [...] And only two students and one is quite weak as well and not very motivated just generally [...] And I was also worried because I think the other girl was getting frustrated [with her weaker classmate] too, even though they are friendly, she is thinking 'Come on' [...] Even though I know she's sick it was getting frustrating, so I just thought, well, let's cut something out and make it a bit easier [...]

We therefore see John evaluating how the learners are feeling, how well they will perform the task, and the likely effect of following his original plan. John's judgement that the learners were fatigued, coupled with the challenging level of difficulty of the activity and the difference in ability levels between the two learners, caused him to omit Activity 1.

Finally, we discuss another exercise providing extra written practice using *should/shouldn't*, where students had to read and give advice on 12 problems. John began by eliciting answers to half of the situations and set the remainder as homework. Although John designed this worksheet himself, he drew on an existing consolidation exercise from the textbook in order to do so (see Appendix B for John's worksheet). This re-design of the original textbook exercise was due to the make-up of John's class. He explained below how he felt unable to use this exercise as it appears in the textbook because two of the learners in the class had previously covered it. While he was of the opinion that the whole class would benefit from the activity, then, John also felt the need to rewrite it so that everyone would be working with fresh mate-rial. In addition, John also felt his own version was 'clearer' and 'less confusing' than the textbook version in terms of presentation, and that his own material provided a greater volume of practice:

> Handout number two is my own creation but I've actually adapted it from the back of the textbook which is called *Extra Practice* of unit 10, and the reason why I haven't used that from the book, the rea-son I've made my own is because I just think, I like to take them away from the book, number one, rather than giving them the text, it is quite confusing [...My own handout] looks more clear but also because I know that two of the students have done it before, because I've done it with them before, last term. And so I've changed it so it won't be the same material for those two students [...] And also there's only five [practice sentences in the textbook material...], and I haven't given an example. There is an example in the book which is a waste. I will do the example on the board maybe first. So it is basically because they have done it before, two of them, and so I've changed it totally to consider them.

John also evaluated the textbook activity as likely to be too difficult for the class. His own replacement activity was pitched at a level he believed learners could more readily cope with, and covered only the vocabulary encountered in class. Hence its perceived superiority in terms of appro-priacy. In the extract below John explained how he was teaching the lowest-level class, and so there was no possibility of transferring the weakest students to an easier group. They were therefore stuck with a book that was, in John's eyes, too challenging for them, accounting for his preoccupation with ensuring his own replacement materials were less intimidating:

> [...] my class was the lowest level. There was no lower level. And also to follow up on the point I made earlier about why didn't I use the book, this is the perfect example, because I [...] thought the book was too difficult for them and [...] too many new words and too

long text sentences, so I made it more concise, I used, I adapted the book, I used my own materials [...] which was more suited for the level, in a bigger font, less daunting. The book was too difficult [...] the text font was too small for them. Some of them were struggling to read English in that font [...] so I made it a bigger font for them, font 14 [...]

Afterthoughts on textbook use

Having been observed and interviewed about his curriculum-making behaviour, John was asked for his views in general about adherence to the textbook. John argued that the book should not be wholly abandoned in the manner of some of Shawer's curriculum-makers, since it can provide a course with structure and the learners with a resource to consult out of class:

> [Teachers] should use the book as a guide perhaps and follow the curriculum maybe of the book, but I think it's also very useful to be flexible and to use your own resources, materials and supplement a lot if you want to do that. [...] Also the students [...] can follow something step by step [...], rather than handouts and pieces of paper [...] and which they can refer to [the book] later on which is bound together.

Elsewhere John explained that even when he used no textbook materials, the book's syllabus (table of contents) made it 'easier to plan [...] and link my lessons', and that a book gave learners 'something [to follow] from beginning to end [...] all in one place'. However, he also claimed that it was important for teachers to have the freedom to tailor their course to the learners and the context, in order to 'improve on what the book is trying to do'. In the extract below, we see how John argued that this freedom enabled him to improve on what he saw as a textbook of varying quality and coherence; but it also allowed him to produce materials with which he was comfortable and hence to enhance the quality of his teaching, and to fulfil the creative urge he had to produce materials which address learners' needs:

> I feel more comfortable knowing what I'm doing with my own materials. I know exactly where I'm going and how to do it much more easily than if I'm following a book which can be hit and miss and jump and be a bit confusing, and maybe have too much unnecessary waffle, or exercises which may be too easy or too difficult. I can make

my materials, which I enjoy doing, and aim it to suit what exactly they need for the level [...], and I know exactly where I'm going with it when I am teaching it as well, and so it's better for me as a teacher.

Discussion

Given the non-evaluative nature of our study, some readers may ask how much value a purely descriptive study such as this one has: what is to be gained from simply focusing on the factors which influence the teacher–textbook interaction and the reasons why John uses the textbook in the way he does, rather than focusing on how (in)effective this use is? There are several ways in which we believe our study moves ELT textbook research forward. Like the consumption studies from mainstream education (e.g., Behm and Lloyd, 2009; Collopy, 2003; Davis et al., 2011; Manouchehri and Goodman, 1998; Nicol and Crespo, 2006; Remillard and Bryans, 2004; Smagorinsky et al., 2002, 2004), this study highlights the context-bound, mediated nature of textbook use, reaffirming that content analyses will only take textbook research so far, and that textbooks cannot be studied in a classroom-free vacuum: it is abundantly clear that John radically transformed the textbook material *in situ*, a pattern of behaviour that both of us have noticed, having worked in EFL for a number of years in various countries, as we have observed classes and talked to teachers about their textbook use, and one which we believe to be not uncommon. As Shawer (2010a, 2010b) and Brown (2009) claim, then, different teachers in different contextual conditions use textbooks in different ways, and our study helps explain how and why this is so, and why, in Shawer's terms, there was something of the curriculum-maker rather than a curriculum-developer or curriculum-transmitter about John during the period of data collection and why, according to John, his behaviour has been closer to that of the curriculum-developer in other situations.

Our study also has implications for the way future consumption studies are designed and analysed: we found that pre-observation interviews alone would have proved inadequate in helping us to describe and understand John's behaviour as his constant monitoring of the students' progress and response to the materials in class led to frequent and wholesale adaptations of and departures from the original plan. Hence we feel repeating cycles of pre-/post-observation interviews and classroom observations are necessary for this type of research. If supplementary think-alouds could be added to the research design, as we had originally intended, this would provide further insights into the teacher's decision-making and patterns of textbook use, as would logs or diaries in which teachers describe, explain, and comment on their design decisions. (See Hadfield, this volume, for a fascinating example of the use of logs.)

With regard to our analysis, the factors which impacted upon John's use of the textbook map onto Hutchinson's framework, as well as onto a more complex framework from mainstream education by Remillard (2005), suggesting these schemes provide researchers with valid instruments for investigating textbook consumption. Recall that Hutchinson's framework posits textbook use can be accounted for by exploring five factors: (i) the textbook; (ii) the teacher; (iii) the learners; (iv) the classroom; and (v) the school. In our case, only the influence of category (iv), the classroom, by which Hutchinson referred to physical characteristics of the instructional setting (e.g., seating layout, temperature, etc.), was absent from the data. However, the other factors were certainly present: the textbook impacted upon what was covered in the class and how, as did John's evaluation of and beliefs about the textbook, and his views on teaching and learning. His understanding of the students' abilities and interests had a profound effect on his consumption of the textbook (and helps account for his decision to omit the inventions unit in its entirety). Lastly, data relating to the school context included the course director's refusal to allow John to use the textbook of his choice, which meant that John was asked to work with materials he believed were beyond the capabilities of at least some of the students in the class. Under these conditions John felt what he described as the 'experiment' of largely abandoning the textbook was one worth attempting.

We mention Remillard's work above and now say a little more about how this may serve to complement or replace Hutchinson's analytical framework in lengthier, more fine-grained consumption studies than we have had the space to develop here. Based on a longitudinal study of two US elementary-level mathematics teachers' use of a textbook, Remillard (1999) formulated a model to describe the factors influencing this use which she claims can also be applied to the teaching of other subjects. Her model features:

(i) *the design area*, where teachers choose, adapt, and/or design tasks for learners. This, then, is planning during the pre-classroom stage. The form and enactment of these materials enable us to understand 'the teacher's assumptions about content (what students should learn) and pedagogy (how they should learn it)' (p.323).

(ii) *the construction area*, where these materials are enacted in class and adapted in response to learners' reactions and performances (for instance, as learners struggle to grasp what is required of them or to accomplish the task). Hence unplanned adaptation of the materials comes to the fore here, and Remillard captures the essence of this stage by describing the teacher as an 'improviser' (p.332); the textbook activities are mere proposals that the teacher enacts so as to cater to the learners. This stage also includes the beginnings of teacher reflection on the materials and the lesson which feeds into the final stage.

(iii) *the mapping area*, where, outside the class, teachers decide on the overall content and order of the topics and concepts/skills to be covered in the programme. Remillard exemplifies this by pointing out that teachers may decide to omit a textbook unit altogether, or to spend much more/less time on one unit or topic than on another. Clearly teachers' views about what is appropriate and important to learn will have an impact on this planning, as will their content knowledge and confidence in this knowledge, which may result in their departure from the book or a more extended treatment of the topic should they feel capable of delivering this. However, once again contextual factors help account for the differences between teachers' behaviours that Remillard identified at this stage: one of Remillard's teachers knew she would be teaching the same students for three years, and so did not feel obliged to cover the textbook in its entirety, presumably feeling she would be able to cover any content not delivered by the end of the year later on. In contrast, the other teacher felt she had to get through the book by the end of the year.

We see this model as complementing rather than replacing Hutchinson's, as it allows the factors which Hutchinson identified to be studied in the pre-, during-, and post-use stages of consumption, and it is easy to see how Remillard's model would enable us, for instance, systematically to examine the extent to which John's behaviour, beliefs, and intentions during the design stage (i.e., during lesson planning) corresponded with those of the construction stage (i.e., his consumption during the lesson).

The second model by Remillard (2005) that we mention here is derived from her meta-analysis of 25 years of research (over 70 studies) on maths curricula/materials usage. It is similar to Hutchinson's framework, in that, like hers, teacher, textbook, students, and context figure prominently, but it is more complex and so may feasibly replace Hutchinson's model in certain cases. We reiterate that we found Hutchinson's framework suitable for our purposes and appreciate its elegance and ready usability, but we anticipate that Remillard's model, which includes components such as the teacher's identity, his/her tolerance for discomfort, and capacity to design materials, may enable the analyst to capture the complexity of consumption and design decisions more successfully.

Issues for future research

We have made it clear throughout that this case study is descriptive rather than evaluative: we have focused here on the factors which influence the teacher–textbook interaction, and why John uses the textbook in the way he does, rather than focusing on how effective this use is, and how valid his reasons which motivate these usage patterns are. However, in presenting our results at two international conferences, we have found both post-presentation discussions have had something of an evaluative flavour, with questions and comments regarding the quality of John's teaching, materials, and instructional decisions. Accordingly, a number of projects for further research which come to mind involve an evaluative element.

First, we may wish to try to determine the effectiveness or otherwise with which a teacher uses his/her materials/textbook, as well as evaluating the quality of the materials themselves. In addition to soliciting data from teacher and learners and including multiple classroom observations, such a project could feature a pre-/post-test design to evaluate learners' proficiency gains having used the materials in question (for an example of this, see Hadley, this volume).

Other obvious avenues to explore in future research concern the links between teachers' decision-making and lesson planning and their use of textbooks and materials. In fact John's frequent references to learners' needs and wants (as he understood them) in accounting for his use of materials bring to mind Wette's (2009, 2010, 2011) expert teachers' preoccupation with their students' needs, and whose lesson planning was found to be somewhat sketchy and provisional, since plans were then modified during lessons in response to how they were playing out, similar to the findings of an earlier study by Bailey (1996). So too John's original plans evolved as the lessons unfolded; during the pre-observation interviews John was often clear that his plans were of a provisional nature and that he would be able to establish exactly what materials were to be used and how only as the lesson progressed and the learners' responses could be gauged. While this type of study could simply be descriptive, evaluative work of this type could seek to identify how expert teachers' planning, decision-making, and textbook consumption are differentiated from that of less expert colleagues.

Another evaluative project would involve exploring John's theoretical knowledge base and his theories about teaching and learning, and then comparing all of this with the theories of learning espoused in the materials he adopts, adapts, or designs himself, to determine the extent to which his personal pedagogy and the materials he uses align in their aims. The elements informing a teacher's knowledge base as proposed by Shulman (1987) could be adapted for analytical purposes.

Drawing inspiration from Peacock's work (e.g., Peacock, 1997, 1998), other projects could collect data from the students' perspective. For instance, John explained how he adapted or abandoned the textbook for reasons connected to his own and his learners' perceived ease of use and it would be well worth having his learners evaluate John's teaching in general and his materials and his use of these materials in particular, and indeed student perspectives could be more routinely included in future textbook consumption research. Another student-facing idea for further research focuses on the learners' role in selecting and shaping the materials used: in common with every teacher, John makes judgements regarding learners' needs, abilities, and interests when choosing materials, but to what extent did John also consult the learners about what they wanted and needed, and, if he had done so to a larger degree than appears to have been the case here, what impact would this have had on his choice of materials, and on how they were received by his learners? In other words, future researchers could explore the extent to which teachers negotiate the syllabus with their learners when consuming materials. The problems associated with syllabus negotiation are well documented (cf. Boon, 2011; Breen and Littlejohn, 2000; Clarke, 1991), and we therefore envisage interesting design decisions would emerge when the impact of these negotiations on the textbook and materials was explored.

Textbook consumption research can also inform teacher education and development. We believe that the take-home message of our study – that textbook use is mediated and context-driven – is a fundamental tenet and a good starting point in textbook education. But the results of the evaluative studies proposed above would provide pre- and in-service trainers with rich teacher education resources, enabling them to expose trainees to examples of effective and ineffective textbook use which could be used as evaluative-reflective case studies in an attempt to develop trainees' pedagogical reasoning (see Shulman, 1987).

A very different avenue for future research in contrast to those proposed above is non-evaluative, like our own study. During John's accounts of how and why he chose the materials he did, how he planned to use them, and, post-observation, how and why these plans worked out the way they did in practice, we got more than a glimpse of John's self-image and self-identity as a teacher, although we have not reproduced or discussed data pertaining to this very much in the present chapter – there is a sense of the duty of care John feels towards his students, as well as his own doubts and insecurities about his content and pedagogical knowledge. We suggest, then, that teacher identity researchers will find talking with teachers about the materials selected and used in class a potentially fruitful avenue of exploration, and could draw inspiration from Smagorinsky et al.'s (2002, 2004) work in mainstream education, which does something similar – and indeed we noted above how Remillard's (2005) consumption framework features teacher identity as one of its components.

In closing, although we explained earlier that textbook abandonment is something with which we are both familiar, one teacher's patterns, practices, and motivations cannot be used to make generalizations about other teachers' practices (see Duff, 2008, on generalization and the case study), and indeed we suspect that some, perhaps many, readers will have reflected upon and compared their own textbook use with John's as they worked their way through this chapter and concluded that their own behaviour and its causes are very different. Yet we believe Hutchinson's framework will provide a basis for describing other patterns of use, and hope to see similar studies of textbook consumption begin to appear in the field of ELT. We make a case, then, for further studies to follow in our wake, as textbook consumption studies are sorely lacking in the ELT literature at present.

Acknowledgement

We presented a version of this chapter at the British Association of Lecturers in English for Academic Purposes (BALEAP) 2013 conference in Nottingham, and would like to thank the audience for their comments, which helped us improve and refine our work in general, and the discussion and issues for further research sections in particular. We also thank Dr Bojana Petrić for her comments, which were similarly helpful.

Appendix A

John's money replacement vocabulary activity

Pre-listening task. Use your dictionary to match the description to the words. Good luck!!!

a) pickpocket b) wallet c) debit card d) PIN number e) cashpoint f) coins g) note h) traveller's cheques i) cash j) money belt k) cheque l) steal m) thief n) purse

1) You go to this machine in the wall to take out money.   ___
2) Women use this to carry their money and cards.   ___
3) This is a person who steals things from other people.   ___
4) You need to remember this number to take money from the cashpoint.   ___
5) This is another word for money.   ___
6) This round money is made of metal.   ___
7) These are safe to take on holiday and exchange in a bank for cash.   ___
8) You wear this around your waist to keep money and a passport in.   ___
9) This is paper money. For example £10.   ___
10) This is a person who steals wallets from people's jeans.   ___
11) This is similar to a credit card, but you don't borrow the money.   ___
12) This piece of paper isn't money, but I can pay with it.   ___
13) Men carry their cash, credit and debit cards in this.   ___
14) This verb means to take something from someone.   ___

Appendix B

John's extra practice activity
Should/Shouldn't

A) Can you write some advice for these problems? Use *should* or *shouldn't*. Good luck!!!

1) He eats too much meat. (he /eat/more vegetables)
2) I live in a noisy neighbourhood. (you/move/quieter)
3) A pickpocket stole my wallet. (you/put/wallet/back pocket)
4) I am worried about my money on holiday. (you/take/traveller's cheques)

5) She always feels tired in the mornings. (she/go/bed/early)
6) He watches 6 hours of TV every day. (he/watch/so much)

B) Can you write 2 sentences for these problems? Use *shouldn't* in the first sentence. Invent the second piece of advice using *should*. Good luck!!!

1) I always go to bed very late.
2) John carries his wallet in his back pocket.
3) The students often chat when the teacher is talking.
4) Maria spends too much money on weekends.
5) I drink too much alcohol.
6) He smokes 2 packets of cigarettes a day.

References

Bailey, K.M. (1996). The best laid plans: Teachers' in-class decisions to depart from their lesson plans. In K.M. Bailey and D. Nunan (Eds.), *Voices from the language classroom: Qualitative research in second language education* (pp.15–40). Cambridge: Cambridge University Press.

Behm, S.L. and Lloyd, G.M. (2009). Factors influencing student teachers' use of mathematics curriculum materials. In J.T. Remillard, B.A. Herbel-Eisenmann, and G.M. Lloyd (Eds.), *Mathematics teachers at work: Connecting curriculum materials and classroom instruction* (pp.205–222). New York: Routledge.

Boon, A. (2011). Negotiated syllabuses: Do you want to? In J. Macalister and I.S.P. Nation (Eds.), *Case studies in language curriculum design: Concepts and approaches in action around the world* (pp.166–177). Abingdon: Routledge.

Breen, M.P. and Littlejohn, A. (2000). *Classroom decision-making: Negotiation and process syllabuses in practice*. Cambridge: Cambridge University Press.

Brown, M.W. (2009). The teacher-tool relationship: Theorizing the design and use of curriculum materials. In J.T. Remillard, B.A. Herbel-Eisenmann, and G.M. Lloyd (Eds.), *Mathematics teachers at work: Connecting curriculum materials and classroom instruction* (pp.17–36). New York: Routledge.

Clarke, D.F. (1991). The negotiated syllabus: What is it and how likely is it to work? *Applied Linguistics*, 12, 13–28.

Cohen, L., Manion, L., and Morrison, K. (2007). *Research methods in education* (6th ed.). Abingdon: Routledge.

Collopy, R. (2003). Curriculum materials as a professional development tool: How a mathematics textbook affected two teachers' learning. *The Elementary School Journal*, 103, 287–311.

Davis, E.A., Beyer, C., Forbes, C.T., and Stevens, S. (2011). Understanding pedagogical design capacity through teachers' narratives. *Teaching and Teacher Education*, 27, 797–810.

Duff, P.A. (2008). *Case study research in applied linguistics*. New York: Lawrence Erlbaum.

Grammatosi, F. (in preparation). English language teachers and teaching materials: A situated study of textbook use. Unpublished PhD thesis, University of Essex.

Hutchinson, E.G. (1996). What do teachers and learners actually do with textbooks? Teacher and learner use of a fisheries-based ELT textbook in the Philippines. Unpublished PhD thesis, Lancaster University.

Lebeau, I. and Rees, G. (2008). *Elementary language leader coursebook*. Harlow: Pearson Education.

Manouchehri, A. and Goodman, T. (1998). Mathematics curriculum reform and teachers: Understanding the connections. *Journal of Educational Research*, 92, 27–41.

McDonough, J. and Shaw, C. (2003). *Materials and methods in ELT: A teacher's guide* (2nd ed.). London: Blackwell.

Merriam, S. (1998). *Qualitative research and case study applications in education* (2nd ed.). San Francisco: Jossey-Bass.

Miles, M.B. and Huberman, A.M. (1994). *Qualitative data analysis: An expanded sourcebook* (2nd ed.). Thousand Oaks: Sage.

Nicol, C.C. and Crespo, S.M. (2006). Learning to teach with mathematics textbooks: How preservice teachers interpret and use curriculum materials. *Educational Studies in Mathematics*, 62, 331–355.

Peacock, M. (1997). The effect of authentic materials on the motivation of EFL learners. *ELT Journal*, 51, 144–156.

Peacock, M. (1998). Exploring the gap between teachers' and learners' beliefs about 'useful' activities for EFL. *International Journal of Applied Linguistics*, 8, 233–250.

Remillard, J.T. (1999). Curriculum materials in mathematics education reform: A framework for examining teachers' curriculum development. *Curriculum Inquiry*, 29, 315–342.

Remillard, J.T. (2005). Examining key concepts in research on teachers' use of mathematics curricula. *Review of Educational Research*, 75, 211–246.

Remillard, J.T. and Bryans, M.B. (2004). Teachers' orientations toward mathematics curriculum materials: Implications for teacher learning. *Journal for Research in Mathematics Education*, 35, 352–388.

Shawer, S. (2010a). Classroom-level curriculum development: EFL teachers as curriculum-developers, curriculum-makers and curriculum-transmitters. *Teaching and Teacher Education*, 26, 173–184.

Shawer, S. (2010b). Classroom-level teacher professional development and satisfaction: Teachers learn in the context of classroom-level curriculum development. *Professional Development in Education*, 36, 597–620.

Shawer, S., Gilmore, D., and Banks-Joseph, S. (2009). Learner-driven EFL curriculum development at the classroom level. *International Journal of Teaching and Learning in Higher Education*, 20, 125–143.

Shulman, L.S. (1987). Knowledge and teaching: Foundations of the new reform. *Harvard Educational Review*, 57, 1–22.

Smagorinsky, P. (2008). The method section as conceptual epicenter in constructing social science research reports. *Written Communication*, 25, 389–411.

Smagorinsky, P., Cook, L.S., Moore, C., Jackson, A.Y., and Fry, P.G. (2004). Tensions in learning to teach: Accommodation and the development of a teaching identity. *Journal of Teacher Education*, 55, 8–24.

Smagorinsky, P., Lakly, A., and Johnson, T.S. (2002). Acquiescence, accommodation, and resistance in learning to teach within a prescribed curriculum. *English Education*, 34, 187–213.

Wette, R. (2009). Making the instructional curriculum as an interactive, contextualized process: Case studies of seven ESOL teachers. *Language Teaching Research*, 13, 337–365.

Wette, R. (2010). Professional knowledge in action: How experienced ESOL teachers respond to feedback from learners within syllabus and contextual constraints. *System*, 38, 569–579.

Wette, R. (2011). Meeting curriculum, learning and settlement needs: Teachers' use of materials in courses for adult migrants. *TESOL in Context*, 21, 59–77.

7
Global Textbooks in Local Contexts: An Empirical Investigation of Effectiveness

Gregory Hadley

Summary

Global textbooks (GTs) – full-featured English language teaching materials containing a range of workbooks, videos, CD-ROMs, and online materials – have become a major feature of Teaching English to Speakers of Other Languages (TESOL) pedagogy in the 21st century. However, they are much maligned by some scholars as tools of cultural imperialism that damage local cultures and contribute to the learners' failure to acquire proficiency in English as a Foreign Language. This chapter uncovers a number of the sociopolitical dynamics that give rise to GT opposition, and questions some of the more strident claims of anti-GT scholars. The chapter then presents a six-year empirical study conducted at a university English language program in Japan, where nearly 700 students have used a GT as the core material. Drawing from both qualitative and statistical analyses, this chapter concludes that GTs have significant potential for becoming an effective resource for second language learning, but the greatest chance of pedagogical improvement seems most likely in language programs where major institutional stakeholders achieve an acceptable degree of political equilibrium.

Introduction

The industry of English language teaching (ELT) textbook publishing is not only big business; it is a major driver of the global economy. A recent article in *The Sunday Times* found that in the year 2011 alone, among the top four publishers of ELT textbooks, total sales were in excess of £1 billion (Tryhorn, 2011). At Cambridge University Press and Oxford University Press, even during these recent years of global economic austerity, internal reports reveal that annual sales in ELT textbooks and related learning materials have continued to increase by between 9 and 12 per cent, and make up 40–50 per cent of their total profits (Cambridge University Press Annual Report, 2010; Cambridge University Press Annual Report and Accounts, 2011; Cambridge University Press Performance Study, 2010; Oxford Annual Report of the Delegates of the University Press, 2010/2011). Many ELT textbooks sold every year are what some (Gray, 2010; Tomlinson, 2008; Wallace, 2002) have called global coursebooks or, as they will be referred to in this chapter, GTs. GTs are comprehensive pedagogical packages containing a student textbook, a teacher's book, workbooks, computer CD-ROMs, DVDs, and accompanying websites that serve as an 'e-learning platform' (Cambridge University Press Annual Report, 2010: 70). While GTs are beginning to be seen in English for Academic Purposes classrooms of Anglophone countries, they have been found in secondary and tertiary classrooms of the 'outer circle' countries (Kachru, 1982) such as Brazil, Iran, South Korea, or Japan, where English is spoken neither as a native language nor in any of the major socio-linguistic domains outside the area of education (Hadley, 1997; Tollefson, 1981). Examples of GTs can be seen in multiple-level series such as *Top Notch* (Saslow and Ascher, 2006), *Interchange Third Edition: Full Contact* (Richards, Hull, Proctor, and Shields, 2005), and *New Headway* (Soars and Soars, 2000), which is in its fourth edition and has sold over 100 million copies (Oxford Annual Report of the Delegates of the University Press, 2010/2011: 7).

However, in the wake of this significant economic and, one would hope, pedagogical activity, the international TESOL community has become increasingly polarized on the issue of such materials. While Nunan (1991: 209) noted this trend over a generation ago, Harwood (2005: 150–153) explains that, at present, TESOL professionals fall into two groups, one being an anti-textbook community (with its respective 'strong' and 'weak' camps) and the other a pro-textbook faction.

Arguably better represented in the literature, those who argue against GTs portray them as 'highly wrought [...] carriers of cultural messages' (Gray, 2002: 152), as having 'serious theoretical problems, design flaws, and practical shortcomings' (Litz, 2005: 8). The weak anti-textbook camp also view GTs as defective but resign themselves to the notion that their presence in the second language classroom is often unavoidable (Allwright, 1981; Harwood, 2010). Even those supporting the use of GTs are less than inspiring in their defense, framing them either as valuable time-savers for tired teachers or as helpful guides for those too inexperienced to develop their own materials (Gabrielatos, 2004: 28; Harmer, 1998: 116–117; Ur, 2000: 182; Woodward, 2001: 146).

The scholarly debate surrounding GTs leaves one with the impression that, for many language teachers, GTs have taken on a role similar to a fraught relationship where people find themselves inextricably bound to someone they both hate to love and love to hate (Sheldon, 1988: 237). Yet beyond the rhetoric and hyperbole, pressing questions remain that are related to the efficacy of such materials. Is it true that, as Tomlinson claims, 'ELT materials (especially global coursebooks) currently make a significant contribution to the failure of many learners of English' (2008: 3), or can they, as Richards (1993: 6) argues, serve as 'an authoritative and accessible tool which can both facilitate learning and make it more enjoyable'? Is there any empirical evidence of GTs succeeding in local contexts, and if so, under what conditions? Increasingly, language teachers find themselves in places where GTs are used either because they are the only option for staving off professional burn-out from crushing course loads. Can language teachers in such environments return home at the end of the day with a measure of confidence that their use of GTs has been effective in helping their learners in their language studies?

I wish to explore these issues, first by addressing some of the sociopolitical dynamics that contribute to the anti-GT stance of some in the ELT community. I will then shift to an empirical, mixed-methods study of how one GT, *Interchange Third Edition: Full Contact* (Richards, Hull, Proctor, and Shields, 2005, referred to hereafter as *Interchange*), was implemented in the local context of a private Japanese university. Drawing from Ellis (1997: 37; 2011: 215), who distinguishes between macro-evaluations of language programs and micro-evaluations of specific teaching methods, I will present a macro-evaluative insider account explaining the rationale for how this GT has been utilized. This chapter will also present something that is rare in the debate on GTs: several years of statistical data generated from nearly 700 participants investigating the effectiveness of *Interchange*. Near the end, I will discuss the implications of this empirical study, reflect upon the issue of GTs in local contexts, and offer some tentative answers to the questions posed throughout.

Contextualizing the opposition to GTs: A sociopolitical survey

What has given rise to the view among some scholars (e.g., Meddings and Thornbury, 2011: 12) that GTs represent a stiflingly oppressive presence in the second language classroom? Such attitudes stem in part, I believe, from a reaction to several sociopolitical dynamics that have affected the role and status of Higher Educational Institutions (HEIs) in Anglophone, European and East Asian nations. Often associated with 'globalization', three factors that have had the most bearing on attitudes regarding GTs and changes in tertiary-level ELT are corporatization, massification, and the steady deconstruction of 'culture' following the end of the Cold War.

'Corporatization' refers to when the organizational culture and practices of universities are transformed to emulate aspects of the service and manufacturing industries (Castree and Sparke, 2000; Donoghue, 2008; Jarvis, 2001; McKenzie and Scheurich, 2004; Silvey, 2002; Steck, 2003; Tuchman, 2009; Washburn, 2005; Woolgar, 2007; Yamamoto, 2004). This trend first started in the US over 30 years ago, when national funding for higher education began shrinking, due to a combination of a declining tax base and a change in the attitudes of policymakers about the overall purpose of HE. Faced with yearly reductions in public support, Stanley Aronowitz (2000: 83) writes that American HEIs rapidly began 'retreating from the ideals of liberal arts and the leading-edge research it always has cherished' in favor of a corporate model. 'By the mid-1990s', he continues, 'the corporate university had become the standard for nearly all private and public schools' in the US, and has now expanded internationally. Policymakers in the UK, Japan, the EU, and even Scandinavian countries, such as Norway and Iceland, have implemented similar versions of America's Corporate University Model (Baber and Linsday, 2006; Block, 2002; Bocock, Baston, Scott, and Smith, 2003; Hubball and Gold, 2007; Itoh, 2002; Kinnell, 1989; Power and Whitty, 1999; Stanley and Patrick, 1998; Tjeldvoll, 1996; Welle-Strand, 2000; Yamamoto, 2004; Yonezawa, 2002).

The term 'massification' in educational discourse refers to the process by which governments seek to reduce the number of unemployed while encouraging innovation and economic growth through greater participation in higher education (Alexander, 2000; Fox, 2002; Guri-Rosenblit, Sebkova, and Teichler, 2007; Kitagawa and Oba, 2010; Smeby, 2003; Teichler, 1998). HEIs undergoing massification tend to experience larger classes, limits on hiring new teachers, and significant increases in teaching loads. Japan features an extreme form of massification called universalization (Kwiek, 2001; Mori, 2002). In the past 20 years, over 200 new HEIs (ostensibly labeled as 'universities') have been established, bringing the total number of universities to 783. Because the population of college-age students is continuing to shrink, today there are more places on undergraduate courses than there are students ('Relaxed Rules Led to Too Many Universities', 2013). These issues had a significant bearing upon the study that will be discussed later in this chapter.

In terms of the deconstruction of culture, Readings (1996) notes that this trend emerged following the end of the Cold War, when national governments no longer needed universities to serve as the ideological arm of the state. During the Cold War, higher education was seen in both the Western and Soviet Blocs as an intellectual bulwark in the national defense strategies against each other (Mauk and Oakland, 2002: 252); the study of foreign languages often highlighted national and local cultural ideals, as this served to foster identities that were both distinct from and resistant to enemy propaganda. However, the idealization of national or local culture concerns, whatever else they may have meant to educators, were increasingly downplayed by policymakers after the Cold War, as these could become potential obstacles in forming a globalized society. Corporate-style concepts such as quality and excellence began entering the discourse of universities, with the goal of exposing formerly protected universities to the forces of globalization and to prepare learners for participation in the international marketplace. Today in 'managed' universities, it is not uncommon to find EAP program administrators seeking to de-emphasize the unique aspects of the local culture in the curriculum.

The convergence of the above sociopolitical dynamics has implications for language teacher identity and the emergence of GTs, especially at universities whose organizational cultures now feature entrepreneurialism, a focus on the global over the local, and authoritarian central control of teachers – what Deem (1998, 2001) has called the 'new managerialism'. Whereas previously many language teachers, to borrow liberally from anthropologist Paul Friedrich (1988, 1989), were linguacultural artisans who initiated students into many aspects of the host culture through tailor-made materials designed to improve their language proficiency, the new managerialist ethic of corporate universities has transformed their professional identities into that of linguistic service technicians – those who are charged with fixing broken language and maintaining a streamlined system of course delivery (Giroux, 2004: 206). The experience of language teachers today is often one of diminished classroom autonomy and of being managed by business-savvy administrators. Within the matrix of increasingly large class sizes structured for cost performance, students are to be treated as knowledge consumers, and language teachers are expected to successfully deliver a standardized language content that results in measurable, often marketable, improvement. GTs thrive in these environments, partly because such pre-packaged material is seen both as already quality-tested on a wide range of learners, and partly because GTs, which have been created by large corporations that espouse a worldview often similar to the new managers of corporatized universities, have sought to strike a balance between the needs of administrators, language teachers, and learners (as an example, see interviews with managers of ELT publishing companies in Crewe, 2011: 60–78). The result is that GTs are rapidly becoming what Sheldon foresaw as 'the route map' of many an ELT program around the world, 'laying bare its shape, structure and destination' (Sheldon, 1988: 238).

Understanding and addressing the critical response to GTs

It should be noted that even the more outspoken critics of GTs are not against ELT textbooks per se, since some develop their own textbook materials or encourage materials that emulate pedagogical values hearkening back to those days when most language teachers were still linguacultural artisans, who were free to address local concerns in their classrooms (e.g., Bolitho and Tomlinson, 2005). However, the deconstruction of Cold War ideals at most universities after the collapse of the Soviet Union, combined with the aggressive rise of a neoliberal form of globalization, are sociopolitical changes that have led to the problematization of GTs. For those resistant to what is seen as the spread of neoliberalism in the face of retreating liberal humanist ideals in HE, GTs are fearsome tools by which language teachers are de-skilled and recast as mere deliverers of course content (Apple and Jungck, 1990; Bax, 2003: 283; Shannon, 1987). Allman states:

> Many feel that they are no longer educationalists – professional educators – but technicians whose intellectual and creative skills have been incorporated into learning packages the consumption of which they now only disseminate, manage and assess.
>
> (Allman, 2001: 71)

Accordingly, GTs are 'Trojan Horses' (Littlejohn, 2011) used to engineer second language classrooms on a global scale: artifacts of a pervasive form of neoliberal globalization that erode the pedagogy of tertiary-level TESOL in outer-circle countries by isolating learners from the concerns of their local contexts (Frank, 2005: 276; Gray, 2010: 730).

It should be further noted that I share many of concerns voiced by opponents of GTs. Criticisms about the blandness of the course content of GTs, and of the need to challenge learners to think critically about the underlying values communicated in GTs, raise issues that we should take seriously (Kramsch and Sullivan, 1996; Kubota, 1998; Wette and Barkhuizen, 2009). Nevertheless, current attempts to problematize GTs appear to have several shortcomings, which can be better understood if viewed through a well-established framework that was developed by the American sociologist and Symbolic Interactionist Herbert Blumer (1971). Blumer observed that claims-makers can progressively convince larger groups and academic communities that certain issues are problematic, but only if they have successfully completed the following five stages: (i) identifying the emergence of a certain empirical change as problematic; (ii) legitimizing the problem; (iii) mobilizing action; (iv) creating an action plan; and (v) implementing the action plan (Blumer, 1971: 301).

According to Blumer's framework, the faction currently opposed to the implementation of GTs in second language classrooms has certainly identified the emergence of a problem. The sociopolitical changes discussed earlier violate their constructs about how the pedagogy of TESOL should function. They have also successfully legitimated these claims through the publication of scholarly books and journal articles (e.g., Block, 2002; Gray, 2002; Masuhara and Tomlinson, 2008; Meddings and Thornbury, 2011; Tomlinson, 2011). However, the final stages, those of creating a movement with the conviction both to form an action plan and to implement it, have not been forthcoming. As an example, Block (2002) denounces task-based language teaching and learning (which publishers claim to be the operative pedagogy for virtually every GT on the market) as a major feature of the way second language pedagogy has become pre-packaged, predictable, and controllable, something he calls the McDonaldization of language teaching. However, he offers alternatives that are sufficient for no more than a few class sessions and which would require language teachers to devote even more time to developing lessons. Another example is in Meddings and Thornbury's (2011) 'Dogme ELT', which eschews the types of resources usually provided by GTs. They call on teachers and students to unplug from the topics of their textbooks, to focus instead on local concerns, and to talk to each other in a framework similar to that of improvised drama, thereby allowing language to emerge in a natural way. Their instructions on how to accomplish this are enthusiastic and helpful, but seem more appropriate to low-risk classes in private language schools than to large university classes of risk-averse learners. In corporatized HEIs, time and the freedom to develop such materials and techniques are resources that, as Harwood (2010: 4) acknowledges, many language teachers lack: 'Time is short, teaching schedules are heavy, and practitioners are sometimes not permitted to deviate from a rigid syllabus by introducing their own materials.'

There are obvious challenges in creating such action groups which could provide alternatives to GTs, especially in a community as diverse as TESOL, but I believe there are at least three reasons why anti-GT proponents have failed either to stimulate action against GTs or to formulate viable solutions.

The first has been their inability to convince a significant number of second language learners to reject GTs. A number of studies investigating student perceptions of their language texts suggest that most are not as dissatisfied with GTs as some of their teachers, though for reasons that are not always pedagogical in nature (Harmer, 2001: 117; Hawkey, 2006; Litz, 2005; Peacock, 1998). In addition, the lack of voice afforded to students on both sides of the GT debate creates what Ardener (1997) has defined as a muted group. Second language learners have been relegated to the periphery of the discourse surrounding GTs. They have little input, and claims-makers on both sides can represent the learners however they see fit, or in crafting questionnaires that may, on a subconscious level, encourage learners to supply claims-makers with the data needed to further their agenda (see Toivonen and Imoto, 2012: 17). Gaining the support of more learners and allowing their voices to be heard would certainly aid in developing action groups that would garner the attention of publishing companies as well as administrative managers and policymakers.

Another reason has been the clear preference of GT critics for ideological issues over those of pedagogical concerns. While White, Martin, Stimson, and Hodge (1995: 169) rightly note that all formal education is an expression of a particular ideology, and that language teaching is not immune to this tendency, the difficulty, as Waters (2009) observes, is that a Critical Social Theory perspective has so pervaded Applied Linguistics that papers dealing specifically with pedagogical concerns are dwindling in number. Rowland and Barrs (2013) as well as Menkabu and Harwood in this volume have also recognized this trend, and with specific reference to GTs, Crewe (2011) states wryly: 'For a subject so central to the practice of ELT there are relatively few examples that focus directly upon it' (p.7). Harwood (2010: 18) is correct in suggesting that it is easier to critique pedagogical materials in an abstract manner than to predict their potential success or failure in the class-room, but I would add that an ideology of critical theory is also a major influence.

Interrelated with the issue of ideology is the third reason, that of subjective and incomplete forms of analysis. By 'subjective', I mean that many studies can be found of teachers who have either evaluated the materials based upon their experience of what they feel might or might not work in their classes, or through conducting questionnaires investigating only teacher and student impressions about the materials rather than actually measuring the effectiveness of the materials in facilitating acquisition (see Shannon, 1987; W. C. Wang, Lin, and Lee, 2011; Wette and Barkhuizen, 2009; Wong, 2011). Some reports do study the actual use of commercial materials in second language classrooms, but investigations were conducted primarily through qual-itative diary studies or ethnographic observation (e.g., Canagarajah, 1993; Rowland and Barrs, 2013; Yakhontova, 2001). I am not sug-gesting that there is anything inherently wrong with these forms of qualitative inquiry. The concern I have is about the lack of evi-dence that the findings of these studies were triangulated or further interrogated by other forms of inquiry and datasets. This measure of incompleteness leads to questions about whether the problems which have been observed have more to do with the personal constructs of the researcher than the concerns of other stakeholders, such as stu-dents and administrators (Berger and Luckmann, 1967; Spector and Kitsuse, 2006; Williamson, 2006). This is why specialists in qualita-tive research methodology (Charmaz, 2001, 2006; Glaser, 1978, 1992) encourage the use of multiple sources of data and suggest that close attention should be given to events that contradict the developing ideas that researchers form through field observations. The goal is to challenge the researcher to rethink observed events in multiple ways and to help readers define the limits of the researcher's conclusions. These features are not readily apparent in many, if not most, of the published studies of commercial ELT textbooks in second language classrooms.

This disturbing lack of criticality and subjectivity has long been embraced by scholars who have problematized GTs or other commer-cial textbook materials, explaining that it is 'something of a "black art"' (Low, 1989: 153) and 'fundamentally a subjective, rule-of-thumb activity' (Sheldon, 1988: 245). Masuhara and Tomlinson (2008: 23), citing their '70 years of experience using ELT materials', explain that their research on the effectiveness of seven GTs is 'subjective and can do no more than reflect our own personal views of what facilitates language acquisition', and represents what they 'intuitively feel' about the potential success or failure of GTs in local contexts.

One must respect the level of expertise represented in such statements, and impressionistic evaluations of GTs from scholars and classroom practitioners most certainly contain many insights and interesting observations. The concern, however, is that a confirmation bias springing from attitudes and dispositions about the globalized encroachment of corporate power may have colored the conclusions of many textbook studies. Because GTs are known to be created by for-profit, multinational corporations, it is no surprise that some critics who have relied on observation and personal reflection find such materials to be either pedagogically faulty (Block, 2002; Gray, 2002; Phillipson, 2001; Sheldon, 1988: 239; Tomlinson, 2008: 7), damaging to the local concerns of language teachers and learners (Asgari, 2011; Bax, 2003; Frank, 2005; McKay, 2003; Meddings and Thornbury, 2011; Ur, 2000: 185; Zarei and Khalessi, 2011), or simply incompatible with their style of teaching. In the spirit of the linguacultural artisan of an earlier age, these teachers prefer instead to use textbooks and classroom materials that have been crafted in their intellectual workshop, as these are seen as inherently superior to GTs:

> Global coursebooks from English-speaking countries [...] seemed impressive, with more fashionable approaches promising success, but their contents seemed too alien to be imported directly in my classrooms. The only time that adoption was minimal was when I had tailor-made the materials myself.
>
> (Masuhara, 2011: 236)

Given the sentiments of the community engaged in anti-GT discourse, it is not surprising to find more intemperate pronouncements emerging, such as the claim by Tomlinson (2008: 3) mentioned at the beginning of this chapter, which criticizes GTs (and by implication, the teachers who use them) as contributing to the failure of their learners, or by Meddings and Thornbury (2011: 11–12), who write approvingly of a 'visionary' teacher who consigned all of her language textbooks to her school's incinerator.

I would suggest, however, that such subjective and implicitly biased critiques do little in the way of offering hopeful solutions for the large numbers of TESOL teachers working in today's corporatized HEIs, many of whom have neither the time nor the freedom to choose classroom materials. There needs to be more empirical evidence provided that would give credence to the claims that GTs damage local cultures, de-skill teachers, or are unusable, or that they are detrimental to the second language acquisition of learners. There seems to be, at least in my reading of the literature, a paucity of such evidence. Additionally, the question of whether GTs have the potential to be pedagogically effective seems to have been lost in the ideological discussion.

McDonough and Shaw (2003) have called for more post-course evaluations of such teaching materials, arguing: 'We must bear in mind that their ultimate success and failure can only be determined after trying them in the classroom with real learners' (p.71). Smiley and Masui (2008: 247) add that, in the context of evaluating textbooks, 'statistical tools to place subjective knowledge within a broader framework of objective fact' are needed, especially when the 'individual author's impressions underpinned a great many of the statements' of observational or diary study research. Such data could objectively support or refute the claims made by those in the GT debate, including any claims that I would wish to make in this chapter.

This discussion brings us full circle to the question posed at the beginning of this chapter: is successful second language learning possible with GTs? If so, under what sorts of conditions, and if not, why not? I will now turn my attention to a six-year study of a Japanese tertiary-level TESOL program that implemented GTs as part of its curriculum.

A macro-evaluation of GT implementation in localized Japanese settings

Ellis (1997, 2011) states that macro-evaluations of the type which is to follow should consider not only the choice of teaching materials but also the issues surrounding administration, teachers, and students. He adds that a mixed-methods approach consisting of both qualitative description and quantitative investigation can enhance the overall quality of the report (Ellis, 2011: 219–222). Therefore, so that readers can better contextualize this investigation, I will highlight features suggested by Woodward (2001: 19–20) and Masuhara and Tomlinson (2008: 21) to provide a qualitative account of the background settings, institution, students, teachers, and program features that contributed to the reasons for choosing a GT over the alternative of using teacher-generated materials. This will be followed by a quantitative investigation to determine whether statistically significant improvement took place among the majority of language learners in the program.

Contextual factors

The story begins with my appointment as a tenured lecturer and coordinator of the Intensive English Program (IEP) at Nippon University of Global Studies (NUGS), a small, private, four-year undergraduate institution located about 300 km north of Tokyo on the coast of the Japan Sea.[1] Although I was still working at another college and would not start at NUGS for another four months, I was contacted by members of the IEP steering committee. They expected me to develop all aspects of the IEP before starting at NUGS the following April. In my free time I began conducting a preliminary needs analysis, designing a curriculum, recruiting teachers, and considering the selection of teaching materials.

The needs assessment was conducted through interviews and e-mail exchanges with committee members and adjunct faculty. I discovered a very typical mix of political, ideological, and structural issues of the type that could have been found at any number of the small, private universities formed during the Japanese higher educational massification drive of the 1990s (Arimoto, 2007). NUGS had been created from the combined support of national, prefectural, and city funding, grants from local industries, and support from a conservative political faction that had been at their height of power during the Nakasone-Reagan-Thatcher era. From these interconnected networks emerged the key members of the administration, some of whom had been former bureaucrats serving under a past Japanese Minister of Health and Welfare, while others who had connections with construction and farming concerns that had supported the minister during his time in office. It soon became clear in my interviews that the administration were major stakeholders around whom all others orbited.

The IEP committee represented the largest of stakeholder satellites. They espoused a mixture of ideological beliefs and structural aspirations that had a bearing upon later pedagogical decisions. The language program envisaged had clear links with the work of Japanese right-wing scholars such as Takao Suzuki (2000). Other courses at the university were taught in Japanese, but the medium of instruction in IEP was to be English, and more specifically, 'International English'. International English for the committee was less about accents or regional lexis than about avoiding the discussion of iconic images or cultural features found in Anglophone countries, such as Guy Fawkes Day or North American Thanksgiving celebrations. Instead, they wanted students to be encouraged to study English in English, but using Japanese cultural images and concepts. The hope was that students would eventually be able to engage foreigners confidently, to further a positive image of Japan, and to help Japan to maintain its place in a global economy where English is the mode of communication. While aspects of the IEP Committee wish list complemented concerns of Global English advocates (Canagarajah, 1999; Modiano, 2001; Phillipson, 1993; Wagi'alla, 1996), other features of their ideological aims were more in line with prewar nationalist traditions, which led to the creation of English language curricula that sought to replace all Western references with references to Japanese people and cultural symbols. Similar to the concerns of the committee, the goal, then, was also to design a curriculum that would equip Japanese to hold its own in a world that they saw as increasingly dominated by Anglo-American power (Hino, 1988; Lincicome, 1999).

Structurally, the committee wanted six classes of 18–20 students, each of which was to be streamed according to language proficiency. Classes for first-year students were to be graduation requirements, and to run concurrently five days a week, divided over two semesters for a total of 30–32 weeks per year. Similar to Tudor (2001), classes were envisaged as places where students were actively 'doing things', but it was also important for them to communicate in a controlled environment that molded them into socialized Japanese citizens.

Over 90 per cent of the first-year students at NUGS come from the local community, where they continue to live at home with their parents and commute to school. Parents send what they see as their adolescent children to NUGS in order to be socially refined and so that they can find gainful employment (Warrington, 2006). Toivonen and Imoto (2012) here explain such views are common throughout Japan; undergraduate university students are 'no longer "children" but not yet "adults" or "full members of society" (shakaijin in Japanese) [. . .] youth are frequently viewed as a threat to the established order, as unstable agents, and as insufficiently socialized "semi-citizens" who need further training and molding in order to play adult roles' (p.17). Learners become regularly accustomed to passively allowing authority figures at various institutions to tell them what to do, and learners rely on teachers to do all manner of things on their behalf. Research in this area also finds that many university students in Japan have unclear goals and expectations for TESOL courses (Irie, 2003; O'Donnell, 2003; Riley, 2006), making needs analysis difficult to conduct. This was confirmed later, after I started at NUGS and began to talk with learners. Few had any goals with regard to their English studies apart from some day traveling to an English-speaking country, making a friend in English, or passing the course.

Two other dynamics in Japanese society have created additional challenges with undergraduate learners. One has been the effect of an educational policy known as 'Relaxed Education' (yutori kyōiku), which was introduced during the 1990s in secondary schools by the Ministry of Education, Culture, Sports Science, and Technology (MEXT). This was intended to replace the focus on testing with a broader curriculum giving students more free time to explore and develop into well-rounded individuals. Unfortunately, due to its misapplication at the local level, this policy has resulted in large numbers of learners entering university lacking the basic study skills and competencies of earlier student generations. The other dynamic has been the decline in the number of college-aged learners, which, due to the creation of hundreds of post-secondary institutions in the 1990s, has created a situation where there are now more university places than students. Fierce competition still exists for places in the small number of top universities, but presently in Japan the vast majority of secondary students can under-achieve and still easily enter other colleges and universities such as NUGS (Arimoto, 2007; Goodman, 2012: 165–167; Kariya and Rosenbaum, 2003: 53).

In my role as a recruiter of teachers I wanted people on a permanent basis, but administrative management was adamant about IEP teachers being kept on a term-limit, non-tenured status. Both administration and the IEP committee wanted me to find enthusiastic, engaging individuals who could both thrill and inspire learners. This concern was partly due to the imbrication of student assessment upon university teachers, which has complicated the attitudes of university students as immature adolescents. I was to seek people who were willing to walk the dangerous tightrope of requiring students to study something they might not naturally enjoy, and who could make such study engaging enough so that they would give positive endorsements that could in turn be used by the university administration for recruitment drives. However, I wanted to set my sights higher than this by recommending teachers who had lived in Japan for several years, who had recently finished one of several distance MA in TESOL programs available in Japan (Dunkley, 1997, 2007), and who were interested in either publishing research in language teaching journals or in giving presentations at teachers' conferences. I eventually succeeded in finding enthusiastic teachers who were committed to teaching in Japan and experienced in working with today's Japanese undergraduates, and who were developing their professional credentials through publications and presentations, so that whatever length of time they decided to stay at NUGS, they would take the opportunity to enhance their professional knowledge and practices during this period.

Selecting materials

The major stakeholders wanted a language program that could process a large number of students with a small number of teachers. The faculty committee wanted me and the two new teachers to develop in-house materials that would last for 150 sessions (five classes a week for two 15-week semesters), and to create six different proficiency levels that would be taught, in tandem, to a yearly cohort of 120–30 first-year learners. There would be no provision of time for materials development: the committee expected that the two teachers and I should easily be able to produce materials either just before or during the time we taught in the program.

Those who have taught tertiary-level TESOL or EAP for any amount of time will know that it is not uncommon to encounter colleagues who, although they have never taught English themselves, still feel eminently qualified, due to their ability to speak English with some proficiency, to make decisions affecting the practices of language teachers and the development of materials. While hurriedly creating hundreds of untried lessons in a piecemeal manner with a team of new teachers might have been exciting, there was also the risk of confusion, teacher burn-out, conflict, and program failure. Faced with these circumstances, a GT seemed relevant to the pedagogical environment, since it would provide ready-made materials similar to those that the IEP teachers and I would have probably created, had we had the time (Harwood, 2005: 152–153; Nunan, 1991: 209; Williams, 1983).

I approached the committee and soon found myself enmeshed in heated negotiations, as there were ideological misgivings about using materials produced by large American or British publishers. However, realizing that many on the committee were equally risk-averse, due to the high profile they planned on giving IEP in upcoming recruitment drives, I pointed out the danger of making large amounts of in-house materials without time for careful development and trialing. Along the lines of Nunan (1991: 219), Bell and Gower (2011: 138), and Crewe (2011: 61), I explained that, given the conditions and impending time limits, a commercial textbook might entail fewer risks, because, as mentioned earlier in this chapter, large publishing companies often invest major resources into matching GTs to the needs of students, teachers, and university administrators, and also trial the materials in classrooms (although not always, as Amrani (2011) reveals).

In the end a compromise was reached: I would be free to choose commercial teaching materials for the required first-year courses so long as I avoided any emphasis on things unique to Anglo-American cultures, and if I encouraged students to discuss issues from a Japanese perspective. The IEP teachers and I would use a GT as the core material for the course but also design a system of content delivery that would satisfy the sometimes nationalist concerns of the corporate-style management structure in NUGS. In exchange, we would have the freedom later on to develop in-house materials and work with smaller numbers of learners who would elect to study English in their second, third, and fourth years.

New Interchange Levels 1, 2 and 3 (Richards, Hull, and Proctor, 1997), was chosen for the first-year courses. Popular throughout Eastern Asia, it is a four-skills GT, though greater emphasis is on listening, speaking, and reading. The series was written in American English, but 'the course reflects the fact that English is the major language of international communication and is not limited to any one country, region or culture' (Richards, et al., 1997: iv). This point, and the diversity of races, nationalities, and role representations, seeking to overturn gender stereotypes, as well as the variety of accents in the listening materials, were appreciated by the committee. Importantly, the series had enough material to fill 30–32 weeks of instruction, and it had a placement test (Turner, Laurens, Stevens, and Titterington, 1997) which could be used to stream students into their proper classes. Video materials, a workbook, and a teacher's book with expansion materials were also available for all the textbook levels.

McDonough and Shaw (2003: 60) note that, once a textbook is chosen, it will likely become core program material for many years. This has been the case in the IEP, and we have used *New Interchange* through two of its incarnations. Confusingly, the word 'new' is no longer in the title, and the most recent version of the series that we been using for the past several years has been *Interchange Third Edition: Full Contact* (Richards, Hull, Proctor, and Shields, 2005). This GT incorporates the student book, workbook, and video textbook in one volume. On the inside of the back cover, there are CD-ROMs for Levels 1 and 2 (but not for Level 3) and an accompanying flash-based website providing extension work for all of the levels. The Teacher's Book contains additional expansion activities, and the Teacher's Resource Book (Richards, Hull, Proctor, Cory-Wright, Dorado, and Pianco, 2005) provides additional material for recycling grammar and vocabulary. The series continues to have a placement test

(Lesley, Hansen, and Zukowski/Faust, 2005), which is virtually identical to the previous version.

Each level has 16 chapters covering general conversational topics (e.g., introductions, occupations, emotional states) that have specific grammatical and lexical targets similar to other GTs on the market. *Interchange* comes either as a 16-chapter textbook or as eight-unit split editions. The eight-unit version provided greater flexibility, because students often move to courses of different levels of proficiency after the first semester. Split editions allow the purchase of a new textbook at the beginning of the second semester without the waste of having to discard a half-finished textbook containing all 16 chapters.

Materials adaptation and implementation

Despite the pre-packaged nature of GTs, '[t]hey are never intended to be a straitjacket for a teaching programme in which a teacher makes no decisions to add, to animate, or to delete' (Bell and Gower, 2011: 138). GTs are tools to be used judiciously (Williams, 1983). Adaptation, therefore, is an important part of implementation and entails a careful consideration not only of the learners, but also the political, managerial, administrative, and educational context (McDonough and Shaw, 2003: 85). As I was to be the one held responsible for failure, I was also the one who directed most of the decisions in the way *Interchange* would be adapted. Adaptation was, however, minimal. I did not simplify, add, or delete any of the *Interchange* materials, mainly because I was interested in learning whether the materials would work as they had been designed. Bell and Gower's (2011: 138–139) assertion is that many of the criticisms in GTs stem from teacher misuse, so I saw major adaptations as an unwanted variable in investigating the potential effectiveness of the teaching materials. The only real adaptations were of pair work and group work tasks, where learners were encouraged to consider discussion topics in the GT from their perspective as Japanese youths, and in sequencing the order in which students encountered the GT materials. Based upon what was then ten years of experience with teaching Japanese university first-year students, I knew that most craved a presentation—practice—production (PPP) approach, one in which vocabulary and grammar were presented before listening and speaking tasks were to be undertaken. I decided that reading, grammar, and vocabulary would be presented in the classes at the beginning of the week, listening tasks would be in the middle, and the end of the week would culminate with an emphasis on oral communication tasks. I hoped that these modifications would serve as a scaffold for the GT and allow students to get the maximum amount of language practice, and through the tightly managed system that is explained below, equip a small number of teachers to deliver the material to large numbers of learners. Implementing these adaptations consisted first of streaming students according to their levels of language proficiency and then designing pedagogical cycles of repeated instruction, testing, and assessment.

In the first semester of the academic year, all first-year students would take the *Interchange* placement test (Lesley et al., 2005), which lasts for 50 minutes and consists of 70 multiple-choice items divided into three sections that assess listening (20 items), reading (20 items), and grammatical knowledge (30 items). We had used the earlier version of this test (Turner, et al., 1997), but shifted to the most current version in 2004, when the Japan office of Cambridge University Press asked whether IEP would participate with programs at several other universities around the world in assessing the reliability and validity of the new placement test. We agreed and conducted two unpublished investigations using a test-retest design for reliability with two groups of learners at NUGS ($n = 118$ and $n = 113$). We found reliability coefficients for the *Interchange* placement test to be adequate across two three-month intervals ($r > .75$, $p < 0.05$ and $r > .79$, $p < 0.05$ respectively).

Subsequent years have confirmed that the placement test is generally consistent in matching learners to appropriate textbook levels. Content validity is high because the placement test has been specifically designed to complement the textbooks. Construct validity is more problematic since only reading, grammatical knowledge, and listening are assessed (Wall, Clapham, and Alderson, 1994: 327–328). The placement test package includes a speaking assessment module, but it has never been possible to use it due to a lack of space, time, and staff needed to administer the test during the beginning of term, and also because of the difficulties of insuring the inter-rater reliability within the interview format of the placement package. Therefore we have had to rely upon the listening portion of the placement test as a rough indicator of the students' spoken proficiency. This is not ideal, but we take solace in the fact that some studies do suggest a moderate correlation between second language speaking and listening proficiencies (e.g., Feyten, 1991; Hirai, 2002; Liao, Qu, and Morgan, 2010).

Based on the placement test, most of the students are streamed to Level 1, 2, or 3 of the textbooks. There are often times when between three and eight students place slightly higher or lower than the levels of the textbooks. These learners are placed in the classes with the highest and lowest levels. This is an unfortunate result of massification and new managerialism, in that with the number of students, the limits on teachers, ever growing numbers of courses added to the curriculum, and administrative concerns about reaping the highest possible cost performance between class size and facility use all made it impossible to create classes with specialized material for groups of two to six learners. In addition, while there are six classes in IEP, we effectively consolidated them into three proficiency levels according to the design of the textbook series. Once streamed, students work with the materials of their proficiency levels in series of three-week lesson cycles. During each of the four cycles within a semester, learners study two units from the text (Figure 7.1). After two weeks, all students are given listening and speaking tests. In four cycles, learners study all eight units of the split edition.

Constant student assessment was another feature of the classroom management scaffold. All marks from tests, homework, classroom participation, and in-class assessment were stored in Excel and updated on a weekly basis. We monitored the progress of all learners and quickly identified those who were having difficulties. The database allowed us to provide students with progress reports after every cycle so that could know how they were faring and, if necessary, speak with a teacher.

Quantitative investigation

Despite the daily hum of activity in the first-year IEP program, was language learning taking place? To find out, from 2006 until 2011, a two-tail paired sample t-test was conducted with six separate groups to analyze the pre-test and post-test means of all first-year students who had completed the program. The *Interchange* placement test was used because, as noted earlier, it was a sufficiently reliable and valid way of assessing the learners' language proficiency, at least in terms of matching learners to the appropriate textbooks. Each year the investigation was conducted as follows.

Learners took the pre-test during the first week of April, and the post-test was administered in the second week of January the following year. Administration of the test was in three stages, with the listening section given first, followed by reading, and then grammatical knowledge. Students had 15 minutes to complete the listening section, 20 minutes for the reading section, and 15 minutes to complete the grammatical knowledge section, for a total time of 50 minutes. The tests were graded and then double-checked by the IEP teachers and myself. The results for

IEP 1 NIC 2 Cycle 3

Unit 5 Going places

Topics	What to say
• Travel	• describing vacation plans
• Vacations	• giving travel advice
• Plans	• planning a vacation

Unit 6 Sure. No problem!

Topics	What to say
• Complaints	• making requests
• Household Chores	• accepting requests
• Requests	• refusing requests
• Excuses	• complaining
• Apologies	• apologizing
	• giving excuses

NIC 2	Monday	Tuesday	Wednesday	Thursday	Friday
Week 1 June 11th	No homework	Check Homework Ex 3ab p 31 **(IC Unit 5)**	Check Homework Ex 4a p 32 Ex 7ab p 33 **(IC Unit 5)**	Check Homework Ex 1-2 p 18 **(IV Unit 5)**	No Homework
	Classwork Ex 12 p 35 Workbook Unit5 Vocabulary Log 5 Reading Quiz 5	Classwork Ex 2 p 30 Ex 1 p 30 Ex 3c p 31 **(IC Unit 5)**	Classwork Ex 6 p 32 Ex 9 p 34 Ex 7c p 33 Ex 11 p 34 **(IC Unit 5)**	Classwork Ex 3-5 p 19 Ex 8 p 21 Ex 6-7 p 20 Ex 9 p 21 **(IV Unit 5)**	Activity day Review test **(Unit 5)**
Week 2 June 18th	No homework	Check Homework Ex 3a p 37 Ex 5ab p 38 **(IC Unit 6)**	Check Homework Ex 8a p 39 **(IC Unit 6)**	Check Homework Ex 1-2a p 22 Ex 9a p 25 **(IV Unit 6)**	No Homework
	Classwork Ex 12 p 41 Workbook Unit6 Vocabulary Log 6 Reading Quiz 6	Classwork Ex 2 p 36 Ex 3b p 37 Ex 1 p 36 Ex 6 p 38 Ex 5c p 38 **(IC Unit 6)**	Classwork Ex 7 p 39 Ex 8bc p 39 Ex 9 p 40 **(IC Unit 6)**	Classwork Ex 3-6 p 23-24 Ex 8 p 25 Ex 7 p 24 Ex 2b p 22 Ex 9b p 25 **(IV Unit 6)**	Activity day Review test **(Unit 6)**
Week 3 June 25th	No Homework	No Homework	Speaking Test Practice Questions	No Homework	No Homework
	Computer day Room 252-253	Listening Test	Practice for Speaking Test	Speaking Test	Speaking Test

Figure 7.1 Three-week cycle implemented as a localized scaffold for *Interchange* (IC) and the *Interchange* video materials (IV). Copies of each cycle are provided as a PDF download for students and teachers

the listening, reading, and grammar sections were then entered into an Excel spreadsheet, where they were calculated and transformed arithmetically to a 100-point scale, zero being the lowest possible score and 100 being the highest. The pre-test scores of any students who had dropped out of the course, or who had been absent from the post-test, were excluded from data analysis. The number of students excluded from the study ranged from five to eight, out of an average cohort of 117 students.

The null hypothesis of either no significant difference in the means or of a post-test mean lower than that of the pre-test was adopted. The level of significance was initially set at 95 per cent probability ($\alpha < 0.05$) in order to strike a middle ground between risks of Type I and Type II errors (Larson-Hall, 2010: 101–103), but 99 per cent probability ($\alpha < 0.01$) was also investigated.

Effect Size (ES), a mode of power analysis, is used when the null hypothesis can be rejected. It indicates whether the statistically significant findings affected a large or small number of the subjects. ES factors, which are not affected by either large or small numbers of subjects, can enhance the interpretive power of meta-analyses using statistical research that explore issues in second language learning (Larson-Hall, 2010: 114–115). A variety of statistical tools can be used to determine ES, but Cohen's d (Cohen, 1988: 20–21) is a popular, accessible, and clearly benchmarked means of determining the ES of t-tests. Low effect sizes have scores of around 0.2, medium are around 0.5, and a large ES is 0.8 or above (Cohen, 1992: 158). Several versions of Cohen's d can be applied to different types of t-tests, and Dunlap, Cortina, Vaslow, and Burke (1996: 175) found that for paired samples t-tests, the means of the pre-test and post-test should be used with their standard deviations instead of using the t value.

The Analysis ToolPak in Microsoft Excel was used to calculate the statistics for this study. The use of Excel as a tool for statistical research has both its detractors and its supporters. For those engaged in complex statistical studies, Excel has been criticized as being both inflexible and inaccurate (McCullough and Heiser, 2008). However, for relatively simple statistical studies, such as those that were used in this meta-evaluation, calculations derived from Excel have been found to be accurate, appropriate, and an economical alternative to more expensive software packages such as SPSS (Warner and Meehan, 2001). There is admittedly a clear preference for the use of SPSS in Applied Linguistics research, but examples of studies in refereed journals, where Excel was used to analyze t-tests investigating pedagogical issues related to TESOL, also exist (Ekkens and Winke, 2009; Kim and Craig, 2012; Meiron and Schick, 2000; Y. H. Wang and Wang, 2010).

A more pragmatic reason for using the Analysis ToolPak in Excel relates to the corporatized nature of NUGS. Administrative managers and faculty use Excel on an almost daily basis, but many were unfamiliar with SPSS. My experience in Japan has been that, at times, administrative managers can question data generated from programs they do not recognize. Mediating analyses through Excel meant presenting data in a program that administrators trusted, understood, and could verify on their own computers. This point will be taken up again near the end of this chapter, but for the moment I shall focus on the pedagogical findings of this study.

Findings and discussion

At both 95 per cent and 99 per cent levels of statistical probability, the means of the post-tests were significantly higher than those of the pre-test at the beginning of each year (Table 7.1), thus allowing for the rejection of the null hypothesis. In five instances of this six-year investigation, effect sizes (d) were moderate to large among all of the learners. Despite statistical significance, the effect size in 2008 was quite small $(t(111) = 13.21, p < 0.05, d = 0.31)$. Understanding some of the possible causes sheds light on the level of support and effort needed to ensure that GTs such as *Interchange* work as effective tools for second language learning.

A closer examination of the findings from 2008 found that one grouping of learners scored considerably lower on the post-test, another scored significantly higher, but the largest concentration of learners improved by only a few points. The students even began at a slightly higher level of proficiency than in other years (average of means = 44.2, $n = 699$). However, even though the GT and other program features were the same as before, variables related to implementation may have affected the result.

During that academic year, one of the IEP teachers was hired for a tenured university post and gave notice long after the traditional autumn recruitment season in Japan. I was faced with searching for a replacement teacher during a time when only a limited pool of possible candidates is available. The teacher hired was later discovered to harbor deep misgivings about the manner in which IEP had been developed. Such occurrences are common in TESOL and EAP units, or wherever there are educated people with valid reasons for differing opinions.

Table 7.1 Descriptive statistics for two-tail paired sample t-tests of Communicative English Program pre-test and post-tests from 2006 to 2011

Year	df	Pre-test Mean	SD	Post-test mean	SD	t Stat	t Critical two-tail (.05)	t Critical two-tail (.01)	p-value	d
2006	111	38.5	11.5	49.9	12.1	15.73	2.360	2.864	<0.001	0.96
2007	125	44.1	13.0	52.8	14.5	12.02	2.356	2.857	<0.001	0.62
2008	111	48.9	12.0	52.8	13.0	5.98	2.360	2.864	<0.001	0.31
2009	111	40.9	12.1	51.3	12.3	13.21	2.360	2.864	<0.001	0.85
2010	120	47.0	13.2	58.8	13.3	17.77	2.357	2.859	<0.001	0.88
2011	115	46.0	15.4	54.6	14.5	11.43	2.359	2.862	<0.001	0.57

Unfortunately in this case, the cycle system was not followed by the dissenting teacher, textbook use was at times rather unsystematic, and there was a return to a form of leniency reminiscent of the 'relaxed education' policy that learners experienced before entering university. The situation soon developed into one where students knew in which classes study would be required and which class had the high probability of a free pass. Other reasons for the low effect are indeed possible, such as students only going through the motions of study without learning, or the sequencing and method of classroom management not being appropriate for these learners, or simply the textbook materials not working. Nevertheless, this anecdote suggests that no GT, regardless of how varied the materials, careful the modifications in sequencing, or organized in terms of classroom management, will succeed if teacher cooperation is lacking. Program administrators forget this point at their peril.

The t-tests analyzed the results on a placement test that assesses only receptive skills. High-impact, statistically significant results were found in two-tail t-tests of the paired means of the raw pre-test and post-test scores of the listening component of the placement test (e.g., Year 2006: $t(111) = 9.97$, $p < 0.05$, $d = 0.91$). Because, as noted earlier in this chapter, listening proficiency moderately correlates with oral proficiency, these are tantalizing hints that improvements in the students' speaking skills have taken place. Direct observation of students in classes and during speaking tests suggests that most do improve over the year. Nevertheless, the findings of this study cannot be directly applied to questions about the potential effectiveness of GTs in improving learners' spoken proficiency.

Accepting for the moment that these statistical findings are an indication of something positive having taken place in terms of student learning, a question that must be asked is whether the cause of improvement was found in the GT, the system of classroom management, the teachers, or the students? The most likely answer is that combinations of all these elements were needed for significant improvement to take place. The system of classroom management gave teachers a handle on working with large numbers of students and helped to track student progress. The majority of the teachers taught from the GT in a coordinated manner and maintained the cycles of repeated assessment. The students, through being held accountable for their studies, became accustomed to regular study before entering the classroom, which aided their ability to interact in an active manner once classes commenced. This is significant because, despite the availability of English via the Internet and other media sources, surprisingly few Japanese undergraduates attending middle- to low-status univer-sities will access English in a meaningful way outside the classroom. Apart from that highly motivated minority who seek out additional resources, most seem to be satisfied with carrying a required textbook to class and to study from it only after the class has started. In addition to these factors, the role of *Interchange* was crucial not only in provid-ing study materials but also for the considerable number of IEP students with ambiguous goals and variable levels of motivation; *Interchange* was a resource that they could hold in their hands – something that, in tandem with teacher encouragement and the classroom management structure, gave them a concrete sense of 'clarity, direction and progress' (Woodward, 2001: 146).

The limits of this study did not allow for an exploration of other ques-tions, such as the effectiveness of GTs as opposed to teacher-generated materials or anti-textbook approaches using no materials at all (e.g., Meddings and Thornbury, 2011). Questions such as these present fresh opportunities for teacher-researchers interested in carrying out empiri-cal research and meta-evaluations within their own pedagogical venues. Doing so will not only provide objective data; it will also serve as a sig-nificant contribution to the ongoing debate associated with GTs in local contexts.

A common question that has been raised by some colleagues is that, given the level of control in classroom management in this study, would not the use of another GT have been just as effective? Again, the lim-its of this research precluded a comparative study of GTs. This would be an interesting area of investigation, and indeed I feel such empir-ical research is necessary so that language teachers can better discern whether GTs are suitable for their specific contexts.

Others have questioned whether the choice of a GT in itself suggests an implicit bias in favor of such materials, thereby coloring the entire study. *Interchange* was chosen only because it was one of the very few GT packages that can provide material for over 150 lessons running concurrently at three distinct proficiency levels, but if, after years of sta-tistical and qualitative research, the results had suggested that, along the lines of Tomlinson, the GT in this study had either damaged the learn-ers or contributed to their failure to acquire the target language better, it would have been my duty to report such findings to the ELT community as well.

This, however, is not what emerged from this study. While other vari-ables and limitations to this study should not be minimized, the fact that the groups in this study spent five classes a week for over 30 weeks with *Interchange* as the core study material suggests that, far from being detrimental, the GT appears to have played a major role in the students' improvement.

The findings of this study also have important political implications for the local context in which it was situated. Returning to the point mentioned earlier about providing stakeholders with empirical evidence of student improvement in a computer format they both trust and understand, this has also been helpful when entrepreneurial faculty, for reasons other than pedagogical, propose during faculty meetings to revamp IEP completely and package it as a 'new and improved' product in order to help in recruiting high school students. When working with colleagues in corporatized HEIs who are seeking to make educational decisions about language programs either for reasons of ideology or because they see the marketing of change as a way to bring fiscal rewards to a university, rational arguments do not work. However, in universities that act like businesses, numbers communicate. Over the past few years, the yearly findings of this research has been a major help in insulating the IEP from the ambitions of faculty who would want to demonstrate their entrepreneurial potential to the managing administration, because the majority of faculty and administrative stakeholders are not willing to change the current program when students are showing signs of measurable improvement.

Conclusion

Can GTs facilitate language learning, or do they contribute to the failure of learners to acquire the language? While the research in this chapter cannot claim to provide the definitive answer, based upon six years of empirical testing with nearly 700 learners, there are strong indications that GTs can play an important role in helping, and not harming, second language learning.

This conclusion also comes with a caveat. Even with the large amount of teaching materials in GT packages, a considerable investment of time and effort is needed to make them work. GTs will not serve as a panacea for teaching environments where there is either a loosely structured curriculum, uncoordinated management, teacher disdain for the materials, uninformed eclecticism in the way the GT is used, or where learners need not study the GT in a consistent, meaningful manner over a prolonged period of time. Educators and language program coordinators should keep this in mind while wandering among the publisher booths at language teacher conferences, and as they wrestle with the question of whether a GT might work in their classes.

Another question raised by this study is whether conscientious language teachers can survive with their professional identities intact while working in the corrosive climates of calculating corporatized HEIs – places where the institutional values aspire more to those of the City than to those of the Dreaming Spires. Given the heavy course loads and lack of teacher autonomy in such environments, can language teachers and students still cling to the prospect that, at the end of the day, the commercial materials they are using can aid in fostering language improvement? Certainly, more studies of GTs used in other HEIs and teaching environments are needed before stronger statements can be made, but the answer from this study seems to be a hopeful yes.

It is this possibility of hope that is especially important for teachers of TESOL in corporatized HEIs, many of whom find themselves in an almost daily struggle against despair. Such despair is often further propagated by enthusiastic and well-meaning scholars who, this chapter has suggested, have sought to problematize GTs on ideological grounds, and who have unwittingly taken on a role similar to protesters burning flags on CNN: their words and actions make a statement; there is a certain satisfaction within the catharsis of protest; but in the end, their anti-textbook pronouncements do not change anything. Those in the corridors of power, those who make far-reaching decisions affecting tertiary programs in TESOL, are unfazed. TESOL educators must still return to the grind of factory-like language programs and endure the terrors of assessment. In such institutions, language teachers can still equip learners to acquire the language. In the process, they can encourage their learners to question, to think, and perhaps to become part of a generation of new policymakers who deconstruct the current neoliberal machinations affecting tertiary-level TESOL and higher education in general. As we look to that day when regime change may be possible, this chapter urges the use of empirical data, rather than ideology, as a prime mover for positive change.

Note

1. All place names and program designations have been anonymized.

References

Alexander, F. (2000). The changing face of accountability: Monitoring and assessing institutional performance in higher education. *Journal of Higher Education*, 71, 411–431.

Allman, P. (2001). *Revolutionary social transformation: Democratic hopes, political possibilities and critical education*. Westport: Bergin and Garvey.

Allwright, R. L. (1981). What do we want teaching materials for? *ELT Journal*, 36, 5–18.

Amrani, F. (2011). The process of evaluation: A publisher's view. In B. Tomlinson (Ed.), *Materials development in second language teaching* (2nd ed.) (pp.267–295). Cambridge: Cambridge University Press.

Apple, M. and Jungck, S. (1990). 'You don't have to be a teacher to teach this unit': Teaching, technology, and gender in the classroom. *American Educational Research Journal*, 27, 227–251.

Ardener, S. (1997). *Women and space: Ground rules and social maps*. Oxford: Berg.

Arimoto, A. (2007). Thirty years in higher education research: A retrospective review and perspective. *Higher Education Research in Japan*, 4, 1–30.

Aronowitz, S. (2000). *The knowledge factory*. Boston: Beacon Press.

Asgari, A. (2011). The compatibility of cultural value in Iranian EFL textbooks. *Journal of Language Teaching and Research*, 2, 887–894.

Baber, L. and Linsday, B. (2006). Analytical reflections on access in English higher education: Transnational lessons across the pond. *Research in Comparative and International Education*, 1, 146–155.

Bax, S. (2003). The end of CLT: A context approach to language teaching. *ELT Journal*, 57, 278–287.

Bell, J. and Gower, R. (2011). Writing course materials for the world: A great compromise. In B. Tomlinson (Ed.), *Materials development in language teaching* (2nd ed.) (pp.135–150). Cambridge: Cambridge University Press.

Berger, P. and Luckmann, T. (1967). *The social construction of reality* (3rd ed.). London: Penguin.

Block, D. (2002). 'McCommunication': A problem in the frame for SLA. In D. Block and D. Cameron (Eds.), *Globalization and language teaching* (pp.117–133). London: Routledge.

Blumer, H. (1971). Social problems as collective behavior. *Social Problems*, 18, 298–306.

Bocock, J., Baston, L., Scott, P., and Smith, D. (2003). American influence on British higher education: Science, technology, and the problem of university expansion, 1945–1963. *Minerva*, 41, 327–346.

Bolitho, R. and Tomlinson, B. (2005). *Discover English: Language analysis for teachers*. Oxford: Macmillan Education.

Cambridge University Press Annual Report (2010). Cambridge: Cambridge University Press.

Cambridge University Press Annual Report and Accounts (2011). Cambridge: Cambridge University Press.

Cambridge University Press Performance Study (2010). Cambridge: Cambridge University Press.

Canagarajah, A. (1993). Critical ethnography of a Sri Lankan classroom: Ambiguities in student opposition to reproduction through ESOL. *TESOL Quarterly*, 27, 601–626.

Canagarajah, A. (1999). *Resisting linguistic imperialism in English teaching*. Oxford: Oxford University Press.

Castree, N. and Sparke, M. (2000). Professional geography and the corporatization of the university: Experiences, evaluations, and engagements. *Antipode*, 32, 222–229.

Charmaz, K. (2001). Qualitative interviewing and grounded theory analysis. In J. Gubrium and J. Holstein (Eds.), *Handbook of interview research: Context and method* (pp.675–696). Thousand Oaks: Sage.

Charmaz, K. (2006). *Constructing grounded theory*. London: Sage.

Cohen, J. (1988). *Statistical power analysis for the behavioral sciences*. Hillsdale: Lawrence Erlbaum.

Cohen, J. (1992). A power primer. *Psychological Bulletin*, 112, 155–159.

Crewe, J. (2011). *How far do 'global' ELT coursebooks realize key principles of Communicative Language Teaching (CLT) and enable effective teaching-learning?* Unpublished MA dissertation, University of Birmingham.

Deem, R. (1998). 'New Managerialism' and higher education: The management of performances and cultures in universities in the United Kingdom. *International Studies in Sociology of Education*, 8, 47–70.

Deem, R. (2001). Globalisation, new managerialism, academic capitalism and entrepreneurialism in universities: Is the local dimension still important? *Comparative Education*, 37, 7–20.

Donoghue, F. (2008). *The last professors: The corporate university and the fate of the humanities*. New York: Fordham University Press.

Dunkley, D. (1997). A guide to British master's degrees in TESOL by distance learning. *The Language Teacher*, 21, 7–12.

Dunkley, D. (2007). 21st century distance learning in TESOL. *Foreign Languages and Literature of Aichi Gakuin University Center of Linguistic Research*, 32, 103–115.

Dunlap, W., Cortina, J., Vaslow, J., and Burke, M. (1996). Meta-analysis of experiments with matched groups or repeated measures designs. *Psychological Methods*, 1, 170–177.

Ekkens, K. and Winke, P. (2009). Evaluating workplace English language programs. *Language Assessment Quarterly*, 6, 265–287.

Ellis, R. (1997). The empirical evaluation of language teaching materials. *ELT Journal*, 51, 36–42.

Ellis, R. (2011). Macro- and micro-evaluations of task-based teaching. In B. Tomlinson (Ed.), *Materials development in language teaching* (2nd ed.) (pp.212–235). Cambridge: Cambridge University Press.

Feyten, C. (1991). The power of listening ability: An overlooked dimension in language acquisition. *Modern Language Journal*, 75, 173–180.

Fox, C. (2002). The massification of higher education. In D. Hayes and R. Wynyard (Eds.), *The McDonaldization of higher education* (pp.129–142). London: Bergin and Garvey.

Frank, M. (2005). The Shibata project: A Freirean approach to community-based research in the EFL classroom. *Keiwa College Research Journal*, 14, 275–287.

Friedrich, P. (1988). Multiplicity and pluralism in anthropological construction/synthesis. *Anthropological Quarterly*, 61, 103–112.

Friedrich, P. (1989). Language, ideology, and political economy. *American Anthropologist*, 91, 295–312.

Gabrielatos, C. (2004). Session plan: The coursebook as a flexible tool. *IATEFL Teacher Trainers and Educators SIG Newsletter*, 1, 26–31.

Giroux, H. (2004). Teachers as transformative intellectuals. In A. Canestrari and B. Marlowe (Eds.), *Educational foundations: An anthology of critical readings* (pp.205–214). Thousand Oaks: Sage.

Glaser, B. (1978). *Theoretical sensitivity: Advances in the methodology of grounded theory*. Mill Valley: Sociology Press.

Glaser, B. (1992). *Basics of grounded theory analysis*. Mill Valley: Sociology Press.

Goodman, R. (2012). Shifting landscapes: The social context of youth problems in an ageing nation. In R. Goodman, Y. Imoto, and T. Toivonen (Eds.), *A sociology of Japanese youth: From returnees to NEETs* (pp.159–173). London: Routledge.

Gray, J. (2002). The global coursebook in English Language Teaching. In D. Block and D. Cameron (Eds.), *Globalization and language teaching* (pp.151–167). London: Routledge.

Gray, J. (2010). The branding of English and the culture of the new capitalism: Representations of the world of work in English Language textbooks. *Applied Linguistics*, 31, 714–733.

Guri-Rosenblit, S., Sebkova, H., and Teichler, U. (2007). Massification and diversity of higher education systems: Interplay of complex dimensions. *Higher Education Policy*, 20, 373–389.

Hadley, G. (1997). A survey of cultural influences in Japanese ELT. *Bulletin of Keiwa College*, 6, 61–87.

Harmer, J. (1998). *How to teach English: An introduction to the practice of English language teaching*. Harlow: Longman.

Harmer, J. (2001). *The practice of English language teaching*. Harlow: Longman Pearson Education.

Harwood, N. (2005). What do we want EAP teaching materials for? *Journal of English for Academic Purposes*, 4, 149–161.

Harwood, N. (2010). *English language teaching materials: Theory and practice*. New York: Cambridge University Press.

Hawkey, R. (2006). Teacher and learner perceptions of language learning activity. *ELT Journal*, 60, 242–252.

Hino, N. (1988). Nationalism and English as an international language: The history of English textbooks in Japan. *World Englishes*, 7, 309–314.

Hirai, M. (2002). Correlations between active skill and passive skill test scores. *Shiken: JALT Testing and Evaluation SIG Newsletter*, 6, 2–8.

Hubball, H. and Gold, N. (2007). The scholarship of curriculum practice and undergraduate program reform: Integrating theory into practice. *New Directions for Teaching and Learning*, 112, 5–14.

Irie, K. (2003). What do we know about the language learning motivation of university students in Japan? Some patterns in survey studies. *JALT Journal*, 25, 86–100.

Itoh, A. (2002). Higher education reform in perspective: The Japanese experience. *Higher Education*, 43, 7–25.

Jarvis, P. (2001). *Universities and corporate universities: The higher learning industry in global society*. London: Routledge.

Kachru, B. (1982). *The other tongue: English across cultures*. Urbana: University of Illinois Press.

Kariya, T. and Rosenbaum, J. (2003). Stratified incentives and life course behaviors. In J. Mortimer and M. Shanahan (Eds.), *Handbook of the life course* (pp.51–78). New York: Kluwer Academic/Plenum Publishers.

Kim, J. and Craig, D. (2012). Validation of a videoconferenced speaking test. *Computer Assisted Language Learning*, 25, 257–275.

Kinnell, M. (1989). International marketing in UK higher education: Some issues in relation to marketing educational programmes to overseas students. *European Journal of Marketing*, 23, 7–21.

Kitagawa, F. and Oba, J. (2010). Managing differentiation of higher education system in Japan: Connecting excellence and diversity. *Higher Education*, 59, 507–524.

Kramsch, C. and Sullivan, P. (1996). Appropriate pedagogy. *ELT Journal*, 50, 199–212.

Kubota, R. (1998). Ideologies of English in Japan. *World Englishes*, 17, 295–306.

Kwiek, M. (2001). Globalization and higher education. *Higher Education in Europe*, 26, 27–38.

Larson-Hall, J. (2010). *A guide to doing statistics in second language research using SPSS*. London: Routledge.

Lesley, T., Hansen, C., and Zukowski/Faust, J. (2005). *Interchange third edition passages placement and evaluation package*. New York: Cambridge University Press.

Liao, C.W., Qu, Y.X., and Morgan, R. (2010). The relationships of test scores measured by the TOEIC®listening and reading test and TOEIC®speaking and writing tests. In *TOEIC Compendium 10*, 13, 1–15.

Lincicome, M. (1999). Nationalism, imperialism, and the international education movement in early twentieth-century Japan. *The Journal of Asian Studies*, 58, 338–360.

Littlejohn, A. (2011). The analysis of language teaching materials: Inside the Trojan horse. In B. Tomlinson (Ed.), *Materials development in language teaching* (2nd ed.) (pp.179–211). Cambridge: Cambridge University Press.

Litz, D. (2005). Textbook evaluation and ELT management: A South Korean case study. *Asian EFL Journal*, 48, 1–53.

Low, G. (1989). Appropriate design: The internal organisation of course units. In R. Johnson (Ed.), *The second language curriculum* (pp.136–154). Cambridge: Cambridge University Press.

Masuhara, H. (2011). What do teachers really want from coursebooks? In B. Tomlinson (Ed.), *Materials development in language teaching* (2nd ed.) (pp.236–266). Cambridge: Cambridge University Press.

Masuhara, H. and Tomlinson, B. (2008). Materials for general English. In B. Tomlinson (Ed.), *English language learning materials: A critical review* (pp.17–37). London: Continuum.

Mauk, D. and Oakland, J. (2002). *American civilization: An introduction* (3rd ed.). New York: Routledge.

McCullough, B. and Heiser, D. (2008). On the accuracy of statistical procedures in Microsoft Excel 2007. *Computational Statistics and Data Analysis*, 52, 4570–4578.

McDonough, J. and Shaw, C. (2003). *Materials and methods in ELT: A teacher's guide*. Malden: Blackwell.

McKay, S. (2003). Teaching English as an international language: The Chilean context. *ELT Journal*, 57, 139–148.

McKenzie, K. and Scheurich, J. (2004). The corporatization and privatization of schooling: A call for grounded critical praxis. *Educational Theory*, 54, 431–443.

Meddings, L. and Thornbury, S. (2011). *Teaching unplugged: Dogme in English language teaching*. Peaslake and New Delhi: Delta ELT Publishing and Viva Books.

Meiron, B. and Schick, L. (2000). Ratings, raters and test performance: An exploratory study. In A. Kunnan (Ed.), *Fairness and validation in language assessment (Vol. 9: Selected papers from the 19th language testing research colloquium, Orlando, Florida)* (pp.153–176). New York: Cambridge University Press.

Modiano, M. (2001). Linguistic imperialism, cultural integrity, and EIL. *ELT Journal*, 55, 339–347.

Mori, R. (2002). Entrance examinations and remedial education in Japanese higher education. *Higher Education*, 43, 27–42.

Nunan, D. (1991). *Language teaching methodology: A textbook for teachers.* Englewood Cliffs: Prentice Hall.

O'Donnell, K. (2003). Uncovering first year students' language learning experiences, their attitudes, and motivations in a context of change at the tertiary level of education. *JALT Journal*, 25, 31–62.

Oxford Annual Report of the Delegates of the University Press (2010/2011). Oxford: Oxford University Press.

Peacock, M. (1998). Exploring the gap between teachers' and learners' beliefs about 'useful' activities for EFL. *International Journal of Applied Linguistics*, 8, 233–248.

Phillipson, R. (1993). *Linguistic imperialism.* Oxford: Oxford University Press.

Phillipson, R. (2001). English for globalisation or for the world's people? *International Review of Education*, 47, 185–200.

Power, S. and Whitty, G. (1999). Market forces and school cultures. In J. Prosser (Ed.), *School culture* (pp.15–29). London: Paul Chapman Publishing.

Readings, B. (1996). *The university in ruins.* Cambridge: Harvard University Press.

Relaxed Rules Led to Too Many Universities. (2013). *The Yomiuri Shimbun Online* (4 November). Retrieved from http://www.yomiuri.co.jp/dy/national/T121103002195.htm

Richards, J. (1993). Beyond the text book: The role of commercial materials in language teaching. *RELC Journal*, 24, 1–14.

Richards, J., Hull, J., and Proctor, S. (1997). *New interchange series levels 1, 2 and 3.* Cambridge: Cambridge University Press.

Richards, J., Hull, J., Proctor, S., Cory-Wright, K., Dorado, E., and Pianco, S. (2005). *Interchange 3rd edition teachers resource book levels 1, 2, and 3.* New York: Cambridge University Press.

Richards, J., Hull, J., Proctor, S., and Shields, C. (2005). *Interchange third edition: Full contact. Student's book 1, 2 and 3.* New York: Cambridge University Press.

Riley, P. (2006). The beliefs of first year Japanese university students towards the learning of English. Unpublished Doctor of Education (EdD) Thesis, Faculty of Education, University of Southern Queensland.

Rowland, L. and Barrs, K. (2013). Working with textbooks: Reconceptualising student and teacher roles in the classroom. *Innovation in Language Learning and Teaching*, 7, 57–71.

Saslow, J. and Ascher, A. (2006). *Top notch.* Harlow: Pearson ELT.

Shannon, P. (1987). Commercial reading materials, a technological ideology, and the deskilling of teachers. *The Elementary School Journal*, 87, 307–329.

Sheldon, L. (1988). Evaluating ELT textbooks and materials. *ELT Journal*, 42, 237–246.

Silvey, R. (2002). Sweatshops and the corporatization of the university. *Gender, Place and Culture*, 9, 201–207.

Smeby, J. (2003). The impact of massification on university research. *Tertiary Education and Management*, 9, 131–144.

Smiley, J. and Masui, M. (2008). Materials in Japan: Coexisting traditions. In B. Tomlinson (Ed.), *English language learning materials: A critical review* (pp.245–262). London: Continuum.

Soars, J. and Soars, L. (2000). *New headway*. Oxford: Oxford University Press.

Spector, M. and Kitsuse, J. (2006). *Constructing social problems*. New Brunswick: Transaction.

Stanley, E. and Patrick, W. (1998). Quality assurance in American and British higher education: A comparison. *New Directions for Institutional Research*, 99, 39–56.

Steck, H. (2003). Corporatization of the university: Seeking conceptual clarity. *The ANNALS of the American Academy of Political and Social Science*, 585, 66–83.

Suzuki, T. (2000). *Nihonjin wa naze Eigo ga dekinai ka (Why Can't Japanese Master English?)*. Tokyo: Iwanami Shoten.

Teichler, U. (1998). Massification: A challenge for institutions of higher education. *Tertiary Education and Management*, 4, 17–27.

Tjeldvoll, A. (1996). Recent developments in Scandinavian higher education. *International Higher Education*, 6, 13–14.

Toivonen, T. and Imoto, Y. (2012). Making sense of youth problems. In R. Goodman, Y. Imoto, and T. Toivonen (Eds.), *A sociology of Japanese youth: From returnees to NEETs* (pp.1–29). London: Routledge.

Tollefson, J. (1981). The role of language planning in second language acquisition. *Language Learning*, 31, 337–348.

Tomlinson, B. (2008). *English language learning materials: A critical review*. London: Continuum.

Tomlinson, B. (2011). *Materials development in language teaching* (2nd ed.). Cambridge: Cambridge University Press.

Tryhorn, C. (2011). English language turns into big business asset. *The Sunday Times*, 1 May, 2011. Retrieved from http://www.thesundaytimes.co.uk/sto/public/roadtorecovery/article615630.ece

Tuchman, G. (2009). *Wannabe u: Inside the corporate university*. Chicago: University of Chicago Press.

Tudor, I. (2001). *The dynamics of the language classroom*. Cambridge: Cambridge University Press.

Turner, J., Laurens, S., Stevens, R., and Titterington, T. (1997). *New interchange/passages English for international communication placement test*. New York: Cambridge University Press.

Ur, P. (2000). *A course in language teaching: Practice and theory*. Cambridge: Cambridge University Press.

Wagi'alla, A. (1996). English in Sudan. In J. Fishman, A. Conrad, and A. Rubal-Lopez (Eds.), *Post-Imperial English: Status change in former British and American colonies, 1940–1990* (pp.339–356). Berlin: Mouton de Gruyter.

Wall, D., Clapham, C., and Alderson, J. (1994). Evaluating a placement test. *Language Testing*, 11, 321–344.

Wallace, C. (2002). Local literacies and global literacy. In D. Block and D. Cameron (Eds.), *Globalization and language teaching* (pp.101–114). London: Routledge.

Wang, W.C., Lin, C.H., and Lee, C.C. (2011). Thinking of the textbook in the ESL/EFL classroom. *English Language Teaching*, 4, 91–96.

Wang, Y.H. and Wang, C.N. (2010). Exploring EFL Taiwanese university students' perceptions of a collaborative CALL environment. In J.-S. Pan, S.-M. Chen, and N.-T. Nguyen (Eds.), *Computational collective intelligence. Technologies and applications* (pp.421–432). Berlin: Springer.

Warner, C. and Meehan, A. (2001). Microsoft Excel(tm) as a tool for teaching basic statistics. *Teaching of Psychology*, 28, 295–298.

Warrington, S. (2006). The time in between: Socialization training as a learning priority for Japanese university students. *Asian EFL Journal*, 12, 1–14.

Washburn, J. (2005). *University, inc.: The corporate corruption of American higher education.* New York: Basic Books.

Waters, A. (2009). Ideology in applied linguistics for language teaching. *Applied Linguistics*, 30, 138–143.

Welle-Strand, A. (2000). Knowledge production, service and quality: Higher education tensions in Norway. *Quality in Higher Education*, 6, 219–230.

Wette, R. and Barkhuizen, G. (2009). Teaching the book and educating the person: Challenges for university English language teachers in China. *Asia Pacific Journal of Education*, 29, 195–212.

White, R., Martin, M., Stimson, M., and Hodge, R. (1995). *Management in English language teaching.* Cambridge: Cambridge University Press.

Williams, D. (1983). Developing criteria for textbook evaluation. *ELT Journal*, 37, 251–255.

Williamson, K. (2006). Research in constructivist frameworks using ethnographic techniques. *Library Trends*, 55, 83–101.

Wong, P.W.L. (2011). Textbook evaluation: A framework for evaluating the fitness of the Hong Kong New Secondary School (NSS) curriculum. Unpublished MA dissertation, Hong Kong: City University of Hong Kong.

Woodward, T. (2001). *Planning lessons and courses: Designing sequences of work for the language classroom.* Cambridge: Cambridge University Press.

Woolgar, L. (2007). New institutional policies for university-industry links in Japan. *Research Policy*, 36, 1261–1274.

Yakhontova, T. (2001). Textbooks, contexts, and learners. *English for Specific Purposes*, 20, 397–415.

Yamamoto, K. (2004). Corporatization of national universities in Japan: Revolution for governance or rhetoric for downsizing? *Financial Accountability and Management*, 20, 153–181.

Yonezawa, A. (2002). The quality assurance system and market forces in Japanese higher education. *Higher Education*, 43, 127–139.

Zarei, G.R. and Khalessi, M. (2011). Cultural load in English language textbooks: An analysis of *Interchange* series. *Procedia – Social and Behavioral Sciences*, 15, 294–301.

Part III
Studies of Textbook Production

8
Writing Materials for Publication: Questions Raised and Lessons Learned

Ivor Timmis

Summary

This chapter discusses the process of writing materials for publication, with a particular emphasis on what happens when the principles of the materials writer conflict in some respects with the views and wishes of other stakeholders in the process, such as publishers and education authorities. The chapter describes a particular instance of this process, outlining the key methodological principles of the materials writer and the difficulty of applying these principles in the light of feedback from the publishers. Specific examples are given of potentially problematic feedback from the publishers, along with examples of how the problems were negotiated. The main issue of the chapter is how far and on what basis we should attenuate principles we have drawn from language teaching research in response to the traditions, expectations, wishes, and constraints of a particular educational context. The chapter argues that in a discipline such as applied linguistics the views of practitioners and other stakeholders are a part of the theoretical equation and that some kind of compromise between research-based principles and local realities is, therefore, not only necessary but also desirable. For such compromise to be principled and constructive, however, we need a set of principles to help us to mediate between theory and practice in materials design. The chapter concludes by proposing some principles which might help us to achieve principled compromise rather than compromised principles.

Introduction

Mediated and unmediated materials writing

Up until a few years ago my experience of materials writing had been similar, I suspect, to that of many English language teachers in that I had written supplementary materials for my own classes, and occasionally specific materials for short courses. This chapter, however, focuses on my first experience of writing materials for publication. Specifically, it deals with the transition from writing 'unmediated' materials, where nobody intervenes between the writer and the learners, to writing published materials, where a range of stakeholders can intervene in the process. Potential intermediaries include: the internal leader of the writing team; the publisher's editor; the end-user teachers; the local education authority; the ministry of education; the project evaluator; and even parents.

The materials writing case study which is the focus of this chapter differed from my teacher/materials writer experience in four important ways:

(i) I was writing as part of a team.
(ii) The team leader had articulated an explicit set of methodological principles to guide and facilitate the materials writing process.
(iii) The materials were for publication.
(iv) The materials were to be used in the state education system of another country of which I had no experience.

These four factors brought into play a number of the potential intermediaries listed above, most notably the team leader, the publisher's editor, and the ministry of education. It should also be noted that these intermediaries sometimes claim to speak on behalf of other stakeholders, such as teachers and parents. Bell and Gower (2011) present an interesting case study of the compromises necessary when taking into account the views of such intermediaries, while Mares (2003) discusses in general terms the need for coursebook writers to empathise with the publisher's requirements. However, whereas Bell and Gower (2011) and Mares (2003) were discussing materials for a global market, in this chapter I discuss writing materials for a *specific cultural context*, and I would like to focus more closely on challenges presented by local mediation in the materials writing process when a writer is part of a team writing materials to a given set of theoretical principles. I would also like to discuss whether we can distinguish between compromise which is purely pragmatic and compromise which is principled.

Background to the materials writing project

The main materials writing project I will be referring to in this chapter is a project I was involved in a few years ago to write textbooks for use in secondary schools in a south-east Asian country. One of the aims of the textbook was to prepare learners for a specific examination in English. The contract for the materials was between the publisher in this south-east Asian country and our university. The contract was probably awarded to us partly because of the reputation of our team leader, who had worked for a number of years in the country in question and published articles and books about materials development. Those of us selected for the writing team had taken a short course in materials development taught by the team leader and taught on the MA in Materials Development which the university ran at the time. Personally, I had no experience and little knowledge of the country in question, and at the time I had never even visited south-east Asia. My experience of teaching teenagers was also very limited, and my knowledge of the local educational culture was close to zero. This meant, for example, that I didn't know anything about the training, English level, or methodological preferences of the end-user teachers. I also knew very little about the examination for which the book was preparing the learners, though it was not too difficult to acquaint myself with this during the materials writing process. I was, then, very dependent on the team leader, and on desk research, to plug some of these gaps, and, to give myself some credit, I made a sincere effort to do this. It has to be said, however, that this desk research focused very much on 'general knowledge' topics such as the history, geography, and institutions of the country in question. I still knew very little about the attributes and preferences of the end-user teachers.

The writing brief

Suggested content

The contract stipulated that we were to write two books of 12 units each, with accompanying workbooks. These books would constitute one level of an existing series. We received an initial briefing document from the publisher, which was quite short and did not seem to be too restrictive or onerous.

The key specifications in the briefing document were that the writing team should:

- identify a topical focus for each unit;
- include three or four texts for each unit, which should be different text types to develop the learners' awareness of genre;
- include exam-type comprehension exercises for two of the texts;
- include a focus on study skills;
- include a focus on critical literacy;
- use graphic organisers to 'scaffold thinking/comprehension tasks'.

This all seemed eminently reasonable, and the publisher suggested some topics for the units. They noted that the ministry of education was keen in general terms to promote an interest in life sciences and economic literacy and made the following specific suggestions for topics:

 (i) consumerism/poverty;
 (ii) cinema;
 (iii) Internet/communications;
 (iv) travel;
 (v) extreme sports;
 (vi) depressed teenagers/self-mutilation;
 (vii) business (create your own/entrepreneurial);
(viii) natural disasters;
 (ix) United Nations High Commissioner for Refugees;
 (x) epidemics.

It was useful to have some guidance on topics, though (vi), (ix), and (x) were not topics which would have occurred to me: (ix) and (x) in particular did not seem obviously attractive to teenagers. A further topic emerged during the writing process: the need to focus on the country's official national values throughout the materials, a topic which was very remote from the informal materials writing experience I had and the published textbooks with which I was familiar.

The feedback process

In terms of the process of writing the materials, the publisher suggested that we should send them the texts and a table of contents for the unit before writing the complete unit. Feedback was then given after each draft unit had been submitted. It is also important to note that feedback was given on the draft units by the internal team leader before they were submitted to the publisher. This seemed a sensible way to pre-empt unnecessary and time-consuming revision of units at a later date. At this point, the publisher's design specifications, particularly with the emphasis on texts, seemed to be compatible with our approach to materials writing. In retrospect, these guidelines seem quite skeletal, and it could be argued that we should have sought closer design specifications before setting out to write the textbooks. As we will see, the apparent openness of these initial guidelines was to prove problematic, and to lead to conflict which I had not envisaged. Before looking in detail at the process of negotiating our approach with other intermediaries in the process, I will outline the key features and principles of our approach to this materials writing project.

Our approach to writing the materials

The need for a framework

If you are writing materials for publication, particularly if you are writing as part of a team, you are probably going to need to draw up a set of design specifications and/or a set of methodological principles to ensure quality and consistency. You will also need a set of layout and presentation conventions unless this aspect of the work is to be done by the publisher's editor. In our case, we worked from a text-driven framework devised by our team leader. In a sense, this framework combines both design specifications and methodological principles, as it has implications both for the structure of a unit and the nature of the learning/teaching activities to be included. It is important to look at an overview of this framework to see how it influenced our writing and the subsequent discussions with the publishers (for a detailed description and explanation of this framework, see Tomlinson, 2003). We will look first at the type and sequence of activities suggested by the framework and then at the methodological principles the framework entails.

Tomlinson's materials writing framework

The sequence of activities

In Tomlinson's (2003) framework the materials writing process begins with *text selection*. The writer selects a spoken or written text with the potential to engage the target learners. The writer then devises *readiness activities* with the aim of helping learners 'achieve mental readiness for experiencing the text' (Tomlinson, 2003: 119, 120). The next step in the process is to develop *experiential activities*, activities that learners do while listening or reading. These activities encourage learners to enjoy the experience of the text rather than to study it. The materials writer then designs *intake response activities*, which encourage learners to talk about what they have taken from the text. This emphasis on starting with what the learners have got from the text, rather than exposing what they have not got, is, for me, one of the distinctive features of Tomlinson's framework and one which has influenced the way I write materials. Intake response activities are followed by *development activities*, where learners use what they taken from the text as a basis for oral or written language production. Finally, *input response tasks* take learners back to the text to study the way language is used in the text: this may involve a focus on grammar, lexis, discourse, or pragmatics. The framework is meant to be applied flexibly and allows the writer some freedom to change the sequence of activities or to omit certain activities. Importantly for our purposes, the framework also allows the writer considerable freedom in selecting which language to focus on in the texts we used.

Methodological principles

This framework acted as a template for the structure of a unit, and my experience was that working to such a framework does indeed contribute to the speed and efficiency of the materials writing process and, to some extent, to the consistency of the final product. As I have argued above, however, this framework is not just a template for the structure of a unit; it also involves certain important methodological principles. Since these principles played an important role in the process of producing the materials and getting them published, we will look now at these principles and their implications for practice. This chapter is a case study, so this is not the place for a detailed theoretical justification of the principles, but I have given a brief rationale for the key principles which influenced the way I wrote my units for the project.

The syllabus in a course of materials should be text-driven.

Rationale

Given that we know from second language acquisition research that learners don't necessarily learn the language items we teach in the order we teach them, it can be argued that an itemised language syllabus with a fixed sequence seems at best of limited value, and at worst counter-productive (Tomlinson, 2003; Willis, 2003). Considering that we also know that exposure and motivation are important factors in second language acquisition (e.g., Tomlinson, 2011), a syllabus of varied and interesting spoken and written texts seems, on the face of it, to be a legitimate point of departure for materials writing. A text-based approach rests on the assumption that some of the input of the texts – the language that learners are exposed to – will become intake – the language that becomes part of the learners' repertoire – and that the transformation of input into intake will be more efficient if learners are engaged with the content of the text.

Implications

If we apply this principle in an undiluted way, then the starting point for writing a course of materials should be a collection of spoken and written texts which will at least provide wider exposure to the language than is typically found in textbooks. It is also important that these texts should be selected for their intrinsic motivational and interest value for the target learners rather than because they exemplify particular language features. Selecting texts which engage a particular audience cognitively and/or affectively is of paramount importance. The cognitive and linguistic level of the texts and their cultural appropriateness will also come into play as important but subsidiary criteria.

Texts should be used as a basis for language work on selected lexical, grammatical, or discourse features.

Rationale

While motivation and exposure are crucial for language acquisition, second language acquisition research suggests that motivation and exposure alone are generally not enough for efficient acquisition (Ellis, 1997). Learners benefit from selective focus on form, though the benefit may well be delayed (Ellis, 1990). A premise of a text-based approach is that learners will be better able to see the purpose of this language focus, and thus more disposed to learn an item, if the focus is on items they have encountered in texts (or text-based tasks) in the materials (Tomlinson, 2011). This approach to language work also has the advantage that learners will already have experienced the items selected for study in a communicative context (Willis, 2003).

Implications

An important task for materials writers is to analyse the texts they have chosen for lexical, grammatical, and discourse features which they think will be useful for the group of learners and which they think the group are ready to learn. If texts are to determine what language points are taught, and if texts are selected on non-linguistic criteria such as motivational value, a text-based approach seems at first sight to be incompatible with the sort of pre-planned language syllabus that schools, education authorities, and exam boards traditionally employ. The possibility exists, however, as Tomlinson (2003) argues, that texts selected on non-linguistic criteria can then be matched against an inventory of language items required by a specific syllabus. Where gaps are noticed, texts can be found to plug these gaps. Willis (2003) has also suggested that the problem of developing a syllabus which is both text-based and systematic can be addressed by building a 'pedagogic corpus' consisting of all the spoken and written texts in the coursebook and any supplementary texts added by the teacher. The corpus would be built text by text as the learners experienced them in class and then used for retrospective language work on points selected by the teacher. Both of these solutions have something to commend them in terms of principled flexibility, but neither seems easy to sell to teachers, publishers, or education authorities looking for packages which offer transparent and convenient accountability and 'testability', even if what is tested offers only a very limited view of overall progress in the language. It can be argued that *ad hoc* selection of language points from texts presents the materials writer with a considerable challenge. Decisions have to be made about what language points in a text are potentially useful for a given group of learners at a given stage and how what is selected in a particular unit relates to points taught in other units. Given that some of these decisions are likely to be based on previous teaching experience, it is an approach which may well favour (and suit) the experienced teacher.

Tasks which facilitate comprehension should precede text analysis tasks.

Rationale

One of the basic tenets of Communicative Language Teaching is that the four skills are not just different ways of practising grammar and vocabulary but skills in their own right which need to be systematically developed (e.g., Harmer, 2007). One way to develop these skills is to model tasks on the processes we use in the four skills in our first language. Tasks which facilitate comprehension should precede text analysis tasks, as 'tasks which require simultaneous processing of meaning [and form] may overload the learner's system, leading to less intake rather than more' (Van Patten, 1990, cited in Batstone, 1996: 273).

Implications

We need tasks which *facilitate* global understanding of the text and tasks which *encourage* the learner to make a personal response to the text, before we *test* comprehension or focus on particular items of language.

Language focus work should reflect what we know about the nature of language.

Rationale

In recent years, corpus linguists have produced many new descriptive insights into the language. A consistent theme to emerge from these insights is that lexis and grammar are more closely linked than had been previously thought and that lexis is more important than grammar in the production and reception of language. Widdowson (1989: 135), among others (Sinclair, 1990; Willis, 2003), has relegated grammar from a generative role to a 'subservient' role:

> communicative competence is not a matter of knowing rules for the composition of sentences [...] It is much more a matter of knowing a stock of partially pre-assembled patterns, formulaic frameworks, and a kit of rules, so to speak, and being able to apply the rules and make whatever adjustments are necessary according to contextual demands. Communicative competence in this view is essentially a matter of adaptation, and rules are not generative but regulative and subservient.

Lewis (1993) and Willis (2003) both cast doubt on the validity and/or value of much of the grammar traditionally taught in coursebooks.

Implications

We must first acknowledge that there is never an automatic transfer from description to pedagogy. Larsen-Freeman (2002) has spoken of 'the reflex fallacy': the (mistaken) idea that because a language feature exists, it must be taught. Harwood (2010) also discusses the question of how far it is desirable for language presented in materials to be faithful to what corpora are telling us about authentic language use. If, however, descriptive insights are telling us something about the nature of language and language processing, it would seem to be negligent to ignore them completely. The recommendations below are, I would argue, consistent with recent descriptive insights into the language and, as such, would seem at the very least to be worth considering:

- There should be greater emphasis in language work on identifying lexical features such as collocations, fixed phrases, and sentence stems.
- There should be less emphasis on forms which are difficult but infrequent.
- We should focus on forms which are useful rather than forms which are easily packaged.
- We should avoid teaching 'rules' which are not supported by the evidence, such as some/any, or backshift rules for reported speech.
- There should be more focus than is conventionally the case in textbooks on how words behave grammatically: for example, verb patterns such as verb + object + infinitive, or adjective + preposition combinations.

Language tasks should focus on discovery and 'noticing' rather than production.

Rationale

In recent years, given the evidence from second language acquisition (SLA) research of the rather indirect relationship between teaching and learning, the efficacy of traditional, explicit ways of teaching grammar such as the present-practise-produce (PPP) paradigm has been called into question (Ellis, 2006). However, as we noted above, there is evidence that some form of selective focus on language items does accelerate the acquisition process. As a result of these findings, there has been more of an emphasis, at least in language teaching literature, on implicit approaches which emphasise noticing and discovery (Tomlinson, 2011). The value of controlled practice of discrete language items has also been thrown into question (Tomlinson, 2011), and our team leader certainly subscribed to the view that such practice was of doubtful value. However, changes recommended in theoretical literature are rarely implemented quickly in textbooks, if they are implemented at all, and Nitta and Gardner (2005) showed that the theoretical emphasis on noticing and discovery had made little significant impact on textbooks. Similarly, Waters (2012), in a comparative study of 1996 and 2009 versions of the influential textbook series *Headway*, shows that grammar presentation has remained a prominent feature of the book and may even have become more prominent.

There are various terms for approaches which value noticing: discovery (Tomlinson, 2011), noticing (Batstone, 1996), consciousness-raising (Willis and Willis, 1996), and language awareness (Bolitho, Carter, Hughes, Ivanič, Masuhara, and Tomlinson, 2003). If we look at that these different terms, however, we see that they overlap more than they differ:

- There is an emphasis on drawing students' attention to a contextualised target feature and asking them to 'discover' its form, meaning and use.
- There is an assumption that the effort involved in discovering a feature will lead to more durable learning.
- Students are not necessarily required to produce the target form.

Such a guided discovery approach – the term I will use henceforward – appears to be admirably suited to a text-driven approach to course design. In a very literal sense there should be no great need for *presentation* of language in a text-driven approach, as the language is already there (in the texts) waiting to be discovered.

Implications

There will be an emphasis on guided discovery tasks which involve processes such as identifying and comparing language features and inferring the meaning of language features from context. There will be little room for practice tasks which involve only the mechanical manipulation or repetition of given forms.

Principles, practice, and publication

Challenging feedback

While these five key principles were, in a sense, inherited from Tomlinson's (2003) framework, they were not incompatible with my own beliefs and practice. While I certainly did not regard these principles as inviolate and beyond question when we began the writing process (and nor do I now), they seemed to provide a good basis for practical and principled materials writing. Armed with this framework, which appeared to be in sympathy with the publisher's emphasis on texts, we set out to write the materials. To paraphrase Churchill, we 'took up our task with buoyancy and with hope'.

In this section I will refer to and discuss some of the feedback we received from the publisher (and from the Ministry via the publisher) which made it difficult to implement our principles in the way we had envisaged. It is important to note that it is not at all my intention to lay all the blame for difficulties encountered in the writing procedure on the publisher, though, as we shall see, greater clarity on what they required and greater understanding of our approach from the outset would certainly have expedited the process. By the same token, as I make clear in the conclusion, if I were involved in a similar project again, I would approach the task in a different way. Indeed, looking back on the experience a few years on, I am struck by the naïvety of my approach and reactions. In this section I simply want to illustrate the challenges presented by mediated materials writing and to describe how these challenges were negotiated. We will look at each of the principles in turn, the potentially problematic feedback we received in relation to that principle, and the way we responded.

Principles questioned

The syllabus in a course of materials should be text-driven

The grammar question. As we started to send in the draft units, word came back from the publisher that 'there should be three grammar points per unit'. It would have been helpful if we had been aware of this apparently arbitrary figure from the outset, and selecting a fixed number of grammar points was somewhat at variance with our principle that texts should determine what we teach: we couldn't necessarily guarantee that the texts would contain three useful grammar points suitable for the level. It would also have been useful to have had an explanation of why *three* grammar points per unit were necessary. If we had been adopting an uncompromising text-based approach, we might have insisted that principled selection of language teaching points could only be done by teachers on the spot, who would have a better idea of learners' degree of readiness for a particular point. It seemed reasonable, however, to give teachers unused to this approach to language work some 'scaffolding' to begin with. It also has to be said that, in practice, it was not too problematic to accommodate this demand for three language points, at least on the surface.

The nature and role of grammar in the materials were, as we shall see, a key area of debate between the publishers and the writing team, so it is worth making some observations about this debate at this point. One thing I learned from this process was not to underestimate the hold that grammar has on many intermediaries in the materials writing process. There may be a question of 'face validity' here, in that materials which do not overtly address grammar may not be taken seriously by teachers and, indeed, may be rejected by publishers. The case of including explicit grammar work, however, is not simply a question of face validity: this debate also made me wonder whether, when English is being taught in a school context, there may be some value in the teaching and learning of grammar *even if it doesn't make the learners more communicative.* The traditional argument that learning grammar is a form of mental training may have been overemphasised in the past, but that doesn't mean that this aspect of language learning should be completely neglected. In a secondary-school context an argument can be made that language learning should be part of broader educational development rather than focused on the utilitarian goal of practical communicative ability.

Cultural appropriateness.   We also received feedback in relation to the cultural appropriateness of the texts we had selected, and I would like to give three examples, as this was another key area of debate:

(i)   One of the texts I chose was about Irish teenagers and contained some references to drug use and heavy drinking, though it was far from an advertisement for these practices. The publisher informed me that the Ministry liked to think that teenagers in their country didn't talk about these things. I was a bit surprised by this, as one of the recommended topics had been depression and self-mutilation, but I deferred to local knowledge and excised references to alcohol and drugs. This exchange underlined to me that some of the intermediaries can be very influential, particularly in relation to matters of the cultural appropriateness of materials.

(ii)   In one unit I focused on the lives of Nelson Mandela and Martin Luther King. It was suggested to me that I could replace one of them with Aung San Suu Kyi, giving the unit more of an Asian focus. To be fair to the publisher, this was only made as a suggestion and I didn't act on it in this case, as I felt Mandela and King were international figures. More practically, I had also completed the unit and didn't want to do a major rewrite. I did, however, use an interview with Aung San Suu Kyi in a subsequent unit.

(iii)   I used an interview with the Asian pop star Coco Lee in one unit. The appropriateness of this text was challenged on the grounds that she had, in effect, turned her back on Asia and embraced Western values. I pointed out that these very issues were brought out in a subsequent role play task where one of the partners was briefed to criticise her adoption of Western values. She was presented as a role play rather than a role model. The text survived.

Gray (2000, 2010) has stressed that textbooks are 'cultural artefacts' and 'sources not only of grammar, lexis, and activities for language practice, but, like Levi's jeans and Coca Cola, commodities which are imbued with cultural promise' (Gray, 2000: 274). More specifically, Mukundan (2008) has drawn attention to the way Malaysian school ELT textbooks are designed to promote specific state agendas, particularly the Five National Principles. The state policy to promote science and technology, for example, is reflected in one unit when a 13-year-old boy is taken to the National Science Museum as a birthday treat. Similarly, Mukundan (2008) observes, the state agenda to promote inter-racial harmony is reflected in units where representatives of different ethnic groups come together to resolve a problem. I must confess to my naïvety here: I had never considered the role of English language textbooks in promoting national values, perhaps because most of my experience had been with global textbooks and multilingual classes of adult students. As we noted above, national values were meant to be a recurrent theme in the syllabus for these materials, and the textbook was seen in part as a vehicle for a certain view of the national identity. This was a revelation to me.

Texts should be used as a basis for language work on selected lexical, grammatical, or discourse features

We were selecting language points strictly from the texts we had chosen, rather than creating texts or creating contexts as a vehicle for focusing on a particular language point. There was inevitably a danger of overlap in this process. The publisher, quite rightly, drew our attention to the fact that the passive was focused on by three different writers in three different units. As we noted above, combining a systematic syllabus with a text-driven approach presents difficulties. We had to go back and find different points, but I must confess that at times I was struggling to find a worthwhile grammar point to teach which arose reasonably naturally from the texts in the unit, especially as the publisher seemed to see grammar as the 'big structures' of the verb phrase which have traditionally dominated the language syllabus.

Tasks which facilitate comprehension should precede text analysis tasks

As a 'reading for gist' task to go with the Aung San Suu Kyi interview, the learners were asked, after reading the interview, to match the questions with excerpts from the answers without looking back at the complete interview. I thought this was an efficient and user-friendly way to check that the learners had got the main points of the interview. The feedback from the publisher, however, was that 'the text about Aung San Suu Kyi needs a comprehension check'. After an exchange of e-mails it tran-spired that what the publisher required was exam-type comprehension practice, even though this was not one of the two texts per unit which were supposed to be accompanied by exam-type work. Rather than challenge what appeared to be a new specification, I supplied a more tra-ditional comprehension check, with a heavy heart, on the proviso that it was used after the matching task. Including tasks which test com-prehension alongside tasks which facilitate comprehension seemed to me to be a reasonable compromise as, in a school setting, teachers may need some tasks which can be marked/graded quickly and used as one component of assessment. Preferably, in our view, the comprehension testing tasks would be done after the facilitative tasks.

Language focus work should reflect what we know about the nature of language

It was probably in this area more than any other that I put my own stamp on the framework in the units for which I was responsible. I have a long-standing interest in the lexical approach (Lewis, 1993), and this came through in the language work in my units with a focus on colloca-tions and chunks. One of my tasks involved matching the two parts of collocations which had been in the text the learners had read. The pub-lisher's comment about this task was that 'there needs to be a teaching point'. This comment, I feel, revealed much about our different views of language teaching: there are, in my view, things which need to be learned that cannot easily be taught. In this case I argued that colloca-tions are highly important and that they are a matter of convention, not rules, or at least not rules which are easily accessible to either learners or teachers. The task survived.

Our different conceptions of grammar also came out through more general feedback on the unit: 'There are not enough grammar points in this unit.' I pointed out that there were arguably six grammar items in the unit, with four items in one task: infinitive vs. gerund; adjective + preposition combinations; verb + preposition combinations; noun + preposition combinations. At this stage the publisher was com-menting on draft materials for the student's book. We did not feel it would be useful to label all these points in the student's book, particu-larly if we were trying to adopt a discovery approach, but as a compro-mise I 'signposted' these points as grammar points in the teacher's book.

Cunningsworth and Kusel (1991) have argued that teacher's books can play an important training role, and this experience seems to reinforce their argument.

Language tasks should focus on discovery and 'noticing' rather than production

The following feedback comment, as the publisher acknowledged, became something of a mantra: 'The grammar points need to be explicitly taught.' There was also an insistence on production activities for every language point. The publisher never sought to justify why explicit teaching of grammar points was needed, but it seems reasonable to suppose that this kind of teaching would meet the expectations of teachers, learners, and the Ministry. The excerpt below, from an e-mail I sent at the time, captures the feeling of frustration which arose from time to time from this process of negotiating with the publisher:

> I have tried to make the teaching points more explicit, but, on this occasion, I confess, with a heavy heart. The awareness tasks allowed for explicit teaching by the teacher as they stood. With the explicit guidance now given the activities are less challenging and do not develop the habit of 'noticing'.

In response to this feedback, we tended to adopt a 'belt and braces' approach by having guided discovery tasks *and* explicit teaching.

The explicit/implicit debate did give me pause for thought and raised four important questions:

(i) How convincing is the argument that implicit learning is more effective than explicit teaching? Might it be the case, as Willis (2003) argues, that some language points lend themselves better to discovery work and some to explicit teaching? Might it also be the case that some learners learn more effectively through explicit teaching than others? The view that learners are not willing to analyse language for its own sake and that language analysis is the exclusive domain of teachers and applied linguists is no less elitist than the view that learners should focus exclusively on grammar.

(ii) Should there be a blanket ban on controlled practice activities, or could activities be devised which provide fluency practice *and* a focus on a particular form?

(iii) If we see English as a school subject as well as a means of communication, doesn't part of the value of learning the language lie in the development of analytical skills and other cognitive skills?

(iv) In deciding on an approach to teaching grammar, how far do we need to take into account the training, experience, expectations, and beliefs of the teachers who are going to use the materials, especially if these expectations and beliefs conflict with our own? This kind of consideration does not only apply to grammar teaching, of course, but it was a salient area of difference in this project. Mares (2003: 131) offers an interesting perspective on the process of writing materials for other teachers to use: 'When I first began to write commercial materials, I was subconsciously writing for clones of myself, teachers who had chosen to take a further degree to better their understanding of language teaching and learning, teachers who were familiar with the principles of language acquisition.'

Principles for compromise

Thus far I have outlined the principles we were trying to apply in our materials writing, the feedback we got from other intermediaries in the process, and our response to the feedback, but I have skirted round the big question: 'Should you attenuate your principles in response to feedback from other intermediaries in the process? If so, how far should you attenuate them?' It is to this question that we now turn. The cynical answer would be that, if you are writing materials commercially, you should definitely compromise your principles and give the 'customers' what they want. I think I can fairly claim that we didn't take that attitude. There are, however, two theoretical reasons why the views of other intermediaries should be taken into account:

(i) There isn't enough relevant theoretical evidence to justify the unquestioning application of theory to practice. We can base our principles on second language acquisition, but, as Sheen (2003) points out, not much work has been done on *classroom-based* acquisition. That does not mean that we should disregard second language acquisition research; it means, rather, that we can only expect a 'balance of probabilities verdict' rather than a 'beyond reasonable doubt' verdict.

(ii) Language and language teaching are *complex human* activities and are difficult to account for in a unified theory (Cook and Seidlhofer, 1995a, 1995b). A crucial human factor is 'teacher plausibility'

(Prabhu, 1990): can teachers be convinced that materials, methods, or approaches which are perhaps unfamiliar are workable for them in their context?

There are, then, persuasive theoretical reasons why we should amend our principles in response to feedback from other intermediaries. That is helpful up to a point, but it doesn't tell us what criteria we should apply in deciding whether and how far to compromise a particular principle. If we simply implemented all the changes suggested to us, we would merely be perpetuating the status quo, and if the local intermediaries are satisfied with the status quo, why are they contracting an external agency to write the materials? An answer to that question would take us into the realms of cultural politics, which is beyond the scope of this chapter, but it is worth noting in passing that there have been other projects where the design specifications have been so detailed and so stringently applied that we have asked ourselves: 'If you know so clearly what you want, why are you asking us to write the materials?'

Conclusion

In this chapter I have tried to describe the process of writing materials for publication, the challenges presented by this process, and the way we met these challenges.

I would like now to outline the questions we might ask ourselves before deciding whether to attenuate our principles in response to feedback from intermediaries:

(i) Is the feedback based on evidence from actual practice?
     If there is consistent evidence that the materials have not worked well in practice, you can't keep blaming the learners, the teachers, or the system. A theoretical principle, as we have argued above, needs to take into account the context of use.
(ii) How confident can you be that your principle is sound?
     What empirical evidence is there to support your methodological predilections? The feedback we received made me question, for example, my views on explicit teaching and controlled practice. Questioning your principles does not necessarily mean abandoning or compromising them – they may emerge stronger from the process – but it is, I would argue, a salutary process. A visit to

another Asian country as part of a different project writing materials for primary schools showed my naïvety in writing materials for publication in stark relief. One of the consistent complaints from the teachers was that the dialogues in our materials were too long. I couldn't understand why they were too long until a teacher explained that they expected the learners to memorise them, a thought that had never entered my head. When I later had the opportunity to observe classes in this country, the issue of how far one should compromise principles, of how far context should govern what we do in class, came sharply to the fore. As I listened to the choral repetition which was a dominant feature of the class I was observing, my initial reaction was that it was far more effective than my training and experience would have led me to believe. However, as the choral repetition went on and on and on, my strong instinctive reaction was, 'This is excessive by any standards'. I could see that in this context choral repetition could play a more useful role than it might play elsewhere, but even in that context it seemed to be used to a counter-productive level.

(iii) Is the feedback based on reliable local knowledge?

If the publisher or some other intermediary tells you that the materials are in some way unsuitable for the learners and teachers, then there is a case for adapting your principles. This is, however, a tricky area, because these judgements by intermediaries on behalf of other stakeholders are not always accurate. In this project, for example, we were told that football would not be a popular topic, though there is a huge football merchandise shop in the country. On a different project we received a damning report on the materials we had written from a project evaluator, though it should be noted that this evaluator was not local to the country where the materials were being used. Fortunately, we had received feedback 'on the record' from local users which was very positive. There is no real substitute for going to the place yourself to assess the context, but that is not always possible.

(iv) Can you incorporate the feedback, whether you like it or not, without serious detriment to the principles?

I referred above to examples of including implicit and explicit work on the same language point and including both comprehension testing tasks and facilitative comprehension tasks.

When I looked at the published version of the units, I noticed the differences between the version I had written and the final published version. I was pleasantly surprised by my reaction: the final product seemed to me to be a good compromise between continuity and change, between familiarity and innovation. The process, as I have shown above, was difficult and sometimes tense, but the end product was worthwhile. Ron Carter (personal communication) described materials writing as 'the ultimate applied linguistic challenge'. Judging from this experience, he was right.

References

Batstone, R. (1996). Key concepts in ELT: Noticing. *ELT Journal*, 50, 273.

Bell, J. and Gower, R. (2011). Writing materials for the world: A great compromise. In B. Tomlinson (Ed.), *Materials development in language teaching* (2nd ed.) (pp.131–151). Cambridge: Cambridge University Press.

Bolitho, R., Carter, R., Hughes, R., Ivanič, R., Masuhara, H., and Tomlinson, B. (2003). Ten questions about language awareness. *ELT Journal*, 57, 251–259.

Cook, G. and Seidlhofer, B. (1995a). *Principle and practice in applied linguistics: Studies in honour of H.G. Widdowson*. Oxford: Oxford University Press.

Cook, G. and Seidlhofer, B. (1995b). An applied linguist in principle and practice. In G. Cook and B. Seidlhofer (Eds.), *Principle and practice in applied linguistics: Studies in honour of H.G. Widdowson* (pp.1–26). Oxford: Oxford University Press.

Cunningsworth, A. and Kusel, P. (1991). Evaluating teachers' guides. *ELT Journal*, 45, 128–39.

Ellis, R. (1990). *Instructed second language acquisition*. Oxford: Blackwell.

Ellis, R. (1997). *Second language acquisition*. Oxford: Oxford University Press.

Ellis, R. (2006). Current issues in the teaching of grammar: An SLA perspective. *TESOL Quarterly*, 40, 83–107.

Gray, J. (2000). The ELT coursebook as cultural artefact: How teachers censor and adapt. *ELT Journal*, 54, 274–283.

Gray, J. (2010). *The construction of English: Culture, consumerism and promotion in the ELT global coursebook*. Basingstoke: Palgrave Macmillan.

Harmer, J. (2007). *The practice of English language teaching* (4th ed.). Harlow: Pearson Education.

Harwood, N. (2010). Issues in materials development and design. In N. Harwood (Ed.), *English language teaching materials: Theory and practice* (pp.3–30). New York: Cambridge University Press.

Larsen-Freeman, D. (2002). The E of TESOL. Unpublished colloquium paper, TESOL, Salt Lake City.

Lewis, M. (1993). *The lexical approach*. Hove: Language Teaching Publications.

Mares, C. (2003). Writing a coursebook. In B. Tomlinson (Ed.), *Developing materials for language teaching* (pp.130–140). London: Continuum.

Mukundan, J. (2008). Agendas of the state in developing world English language textbooks. *Folio*, 12, 17–19.

Nitta, R. and Gardner, S. (2005). Consciousness-raising and practice in ELT coursebooks. *ELT Journal*, 59, 3–13.

Prabhu, N. (1990). There is no best method – why? *TESOL Quarterly*, 24, 161–176.

Sheen, R. (2003). Focus on form – a myth in the making. *ELT Journal,* 57, 255–233.

Sinclair, J. (1990). *Collins cobuild English grammar.* London: HarperCollins.

Tomlinson, B. (2003). Developing principled frameworks for materials development. In B. Tomlinson (Ed.), *Developing materials for language teaching* (pp.107–130). London: Continuum.

Tomlinson, B. (2011). Introduction: Principles and procedures of materials development. In B. Tomlinson (Ed.), *Materials development in language teaching* (2nd ed.) (pp.1–31). Cambridge: Cambridge University Press.

Van Patten, B. (1990). Attending to form and content in the input. *Studies in Second Language Acquisition,* 12, 287–301.

Widdowson, H. (1989). Knowledge of language and ability for use. *Applied Linguistics,* 12, 128–137.

Willis, D. (2003). *Rules, patterns and words: Grammar and lexis in ELT.* Cambridge: Cambridge University Press.

Waters, A. (2012). Trends and issues in ELT methods and methodology. *ELT Journal,* 66, 440–449.

Willis, J. and Willis, D. (1996). *Challenge and change in language teaching.* Oxford: Heinemann.

9
An Interdisciplinary Textbook Project: Charting the Paths Taken

Fredricka L. Stoller and Marin S. Robinson

Summary

Advanced-level literacy textbooks, written for students who are transitioning from 'general' academic English to the English of their academic disciplines, are not often discipline-specific, nor are they written by teams of authors who bring in both language and disciplinary expertise. In this chapter, we showcase an interdisciplinary textbook development project that brought together professionals from two disparate fields: applied linguistics and chemistry. Specifically, we explain the complex and iterative process that led to the publication of Write like a Chemist, *a textbook that assists university-level chemistry students (native and nonnative speakers of English) develop discipline-specific reading and writing skills. To explain why the textbook looks the way it does, we chart the various paths taken during the writing process. After providing background on the project and identifying the textbook's defining characteristics, we highlight numerous (and intertwined) steps that led to its development and final publication. We comment on these steps sequentially, even though most occurred in a non-linear fashion, influencing and informing one another throughout the multi-year project. We depict the following steps in the textbook-development process: (i) articulating priorities and principles; (ii) scaffolding the instructional approach; (iii) selecting target genres, compiling corpora with full-length text exemplars, and analyzing them using tools from corpus linguistics and discourse, genre, and move analyses; (iv) converting analytical findings into instructional materials; (v) piloting and assessing materials; and (vi) using feedback to improve materials. To describe the textbook publication process, we focus on steps taken to (i) find a publisher; (ii) secure copyright permissions; (iii) select a title; (iv) acknowledge contributors; and (v) finalize copy. We conclude with suggestions for language professionals who wish to pursue interdisciplinary textbook endeavors in other content areas or with different skill emphases.*

It is uncommon for language professionals to partner with experts in other fields to write textbooks that focus on the development of advanced language abilities. In this chapter, we showcase an interdisciplinary textbook project[1] that brought together professionals from two disparate fields: applied linguistics and chemistry. The partnership allowed for a true intersection of ideas that led to the vision, design, and completion of Write like a Chemist: A Guide and Resource (Robinson, Stoller, Costanza-Robinson, and Jones, 2008), a textbook that aims to assist university-level students (native and nonnative speakers of English) in making the transition from 'general' academic reading and writing to more advanced discipline-specific literacy skills. To chart the multiple-year path that led to the publication of the textbook, we highlight key steps taken by the interdisciplinary team to analyze the language of chemistry and convert findings into an instructional approach and textbook that could be used by chemistry faculty and their students. To frame our discussion, we provide background on our textbook project and describe the overarching organization and defining characteristics of the final product. From there we focus on the textbook development and publication process. We conclude with suggestions for language professionals who wish to pursue interdisciplinary textbook endeavors in other content areas or with different skill emphases.

Project background

The *Write like a Chemist* project was initially motivated by a Northern Arizona University (NAU) mandate to address third-year undergraduate students' writing; the mandate represented a university-wide acknowledgement of students' need for improved writing abilities. To provide students with more explicit writing instruction as they progress in their studies, university departments were given the option of developing (and offering) their own writing-intensive courses or requiring their students to take one of two third-year courses developed by the English Department: Writing in Disciplinary Communities or Technical Writing. Although students from multiple disciplines are simultaneously enrolled in these courses, class assignments require that students write for their own disciplines (to the best of their abilities). In the Writing in Disciplinary Communities course, as an example, students are asked to interview a professor from their major department about writing and use insights gained to write a paper modeled on a genre in their discipline.

Despite the fact that chemistry students can opt to take one of these two English Department courses, the second author of this chapter strongly advocated the development of a chemistry-specific writing course, taught by a chemistry faculty member. To begin the course-development process she initiated a 'cross-disciplinary alliance' (Wardle, 2004) with an applied linguist in the English Department (the first author of this chapter). This unconventional interdisciplinary partnership, together with the different areas of expertise it afforded, contributed greatly to the project's success. The chemist contributed knowledge of chemistry content, familiarity with chemistry curricula, insights into the literacy demands of various chemistry courses, and personal experience with writing and writing conventions across the discipline (e.g., in research articles, grant proposals, and scientific posters). The applied linguist offered language expertise, a knowledge of approaches to literacy skills instruction, a familiarity with second language student populations and the language-related challenges that they face in university classrooms, and a commitment to solving language-related problems, the latter a distinguishing attribute of the field. Together, our two viewpoints led to innovations that we would not have been able to dream of alone. The partnership evolved as the project broadened in scope and later moved beyond the confines of our home institution. (See Swales and Feak, 2001, for reflections on collaborative practice in English for Academic Purposes materials production.)

It is worth noting that to be an effective interdisciplinary team we had to develop a shared vocabulary that we could use to discuss: project goals; the expectations we had of each other; instructional priorities and practices; language, in general, and language features, more specifically; content-area subject matter; genre, genre analysis, and genre-analysis findings; and classroom expectations – to name just some of the areas that required shared terminology (see Horn, Stoller, and Robinson, 2008).

In the subsections that follow, we provide additional background information that further contextualizes our case study. We focus on general assumptions, the formative assessment components of the project, and project transformations that took place during the life of the project.

General assumptions

From the onset our two target audiences were chemistry students, at the time in their studies when they are transitioning to disciplinary genres, and their chemistry instructors, who often have little training (or motivation) to teach writing (but often find themselves doing so anyway). We also made a dual commitment to disciplinary reading and writing in our course (and materials), even though the university mandate only specified writing. We simply could not imagine teaching students to write for the discipline without asking them to read authentic texts from the discipline as well. Furthermore, we knew that we would need (i) to target select chemistry genres for textual analysis and instruction; and (ii) to write our own materials, because those available commercially at that time did not meet our students' chemistry-specific literacy needs (e.g., Alley, 1996; Beall and Trimbur, 2001; Kovac and Sherwood, 2001; Moriarty, 1997). Moreover, unlike most textbook efforts in English language teaching (ELT), our reality required that we seek grant funding because chemistry faculty are under pressure to support their scholarly efforts with external grants. We applied for and received two US National Science Foundation (NSF) grants[2] for our project. The first was a 'proof-of-concept' grant, which supported a short-term project, typically carried out at the home institution, designed to test and demonstrate the feasibility and usefulness of an anticipated long-term project. In our case this entailed demonstrating the feasibility of not only the development of a prototype for a writing-intensive chemistry-specific course but also our interdisciplinary collaboration, a novel partnership in the eyes of the NSF. The second grant (a 'full-development' grant, meant to build upon the proof-of-concept grant and expand to include other institutions) supported our textbook development project. During the last two years of our second grant, which lasted four years, we extended our efforts beyond our home institution and systematically piloted textbook materials in chemistry classes of different types at 16 other US tertiary institutions. The second grant included funding for chemistry-faculty piloters to attend summer training workshops at NAU. The grant also supported chemistry faculty ($n = 15$) who served as external evaluators, a post-doctoral fellow in chemistry, a project-assessment coordinator (an NSF requirement), two graduate students in applied linguistics, and one graduate student in chemistry.

Formative assessment

Ongoing formative evaluation of textbook materials (including extensive piloting) played an integral role in the development and refinement of textbook materials. Two major impetuses drove our materials assessment activities. First, we were mindful of our funding agency's assessment and accountability expectations; the NSF views evaluation as an essential component of curriculum and materials development processes, rather than an activity conducted solely at the end of a project (Frechtling Westat, 2002). Furthermore, as recipients of NSF support, we were obliged to submit annual reports. Our assessment activities – including the collection of (i) qualitative data from pilot-site participants and external evaluators and (ii) quantitative pre- and post-course student ability measures – facilitated the annual reporting process (and also our materials development efforts). The second impetus was the perceived (and later confirmed) value of input, from various stakeholders, that could inform the ongoing process of materials creation, revision, and improvement. Because our materials were designed for use by chemistry faculty and students both within and beyond our home institution, we devised data collection instruments (following recommendations by Dudley-Evans and St. John, 1998; Tomlinson, 2003) from which we could gain an understanding of (i) how materials were used and adapted by chemistry faculty in different instructional settings and course contexts (i.e., chemistry writing-intensive courses, lab courses, and seminars); (ii) what specific activities and sections of the textbook were and were not used (and for what reasons); and (iii) how different user groups (students and faculty alike) judged the overall effectiveness of the materials. (See Stoller, Horn, Grabe, and Robinson, 2005, 2006, for more details on the development of assessment instruments and the evaluative review process.) In the sections below we comment on aspects of our formal piloting and the data collection instruments that helped us refine our materials (and report back to the NSF).

Piloting

Our systematic piloting efforts – over numerous years, in various classroom settings, and with different stakeholder groups – helped us improve our textbook materials in innumerable ways. For example, piloting enabled us to assess the suitability of the overall scope, approach, level, organization, and sequencing of textbook content and tasks. Piloting also revealed appropriateness (and inappropriateness), ease of use, and fit in different classroom settings (see Donovan,

1998; Littlejohn, 1998). One example that stands out in our memories showcases the appropriateness/inappropriateness dichotomy that was revealed through piloting. In a fairly early version of our textbook materials we had a task in Chapter 1 that was designed to demonstrate how writing conventions (and subject matter) change for different audiences. We provided an example that juxtaposed how writing about *knitting* for avid knitters would differ from a passage trying to communicate with those unfamiliar with knitting:

> *Written for an experienced knitter*: Sock pattern: Use U.S. 5 dpn, CO 6 sts. With 2 sts on each dpn, join, and K two rnds.

> *Written for a friend who has never knitted before*: Double-pointed needles (dpn) allow you to knit continuously in a circle, essentially to knit a tube, like for socks or mittens. It's probably a good idea to start with a knitting project that *doesn't* require dpns; they're a bit more difficult to use than regular needles.

Although we believed that our knitting examples were illustrative, our target audiences were, for the most part, uninterested in knitting. Thus, to better communicate with our target audiences, we changed the examples to chess, which resonated better with our own targeted textbook audiences.

Piloting also served to build camaraderie among chemistry faculty regarding the struggles of teaching chemistry students to write. For example, during a summer training session we were all relieved to learn that students nationwide struggle with *it's/its* and *affect/effect*. We commiserated over how novice writers often begin research papers with (inappropriate) phrases such as 'In this experiment, I will prove [...]' and how, in their Experimental (i.e., Methods) sections, they often mention KimWipes, a popular disposable wiper used for laboratory cleaning. Students include KimWipes (and other items such as beakers, thermometers, and test tubes) because when they prepare for an instructional lab, they are expected to generate a list of equipment that they will need for that lab. They have not yet learned that such details are unnecessary (and inappropriate) in a journal article, which is written for an expert audience. Conversations such as these revealed aspects of writing that we decided to address explicitly in the textbook. Piloters also helped us expand our Language Tips section of the textbook; for example, it was piloters who recommended that we add *since/because* and *while/although* to our list of troublesome word pairs and that we address both hyphenated two-word modifiers and split infinitives.

Another valuable (yet frustrating) outcome of the piloting process was our deepened realization that so many variations exist in chemistry writing, even among experts, and that each subdiscipline of chemistry (organic, analytical, inorganic, physical, and biochemistry) clearly has its own writing preferences. Although the chemistry author was aware of some of these differences before piloting, the piloting process raised her awareness of these differences considerably. As a result, we went back and revised the textbook to state more explicitly that such variations do exist. Finally, the piloting process increased our optimism that the number of chemistry faculty interested in writing was increasing, although most piloters indicated that only a few chemistry faculty at their home institutions would actually be willing to teach a writing course.

Materials were piloted at NAU for six years in a third-year, chemistry-specific writing course (CHM 300W). In addition, we conducted two rounds of piloting beyond our own campus, during two back-to-back academic years. Those pilots were conducted in chemistry classes of different types (i.e., designated writing-intensive courses, labs, and seminars), in a total of 16 different tertiary institutions, of six different Carnegie classifications.[3] Sixteen chemistry faculty and 200 chemistry students participated. These institutions were identified through an e-mail request sent to roughly 100 chairs of chemistry departments nationwide. All respondents were included in the pilot.

Grant funds provided the monetary resources needed to bring pilot faculty to our campus the summer before each pilot period. Our two-day summer orientations introduced piloters to the overall project, our read-analyze-write approach (discussed in more detail below), key features of our materials, and our expectations of them and their students. It is worth mentioning that our publisher was pleased to learn about our piloting because it provided evidence of chemistry faculty interest in the materials, chemistry students' needs for improved disciplinary writing, and our willingness to adjust materials in response to piloter feedback from a range of institution types. What dismayed the publisher about the piloting, required by our granting agency, was that it 'slowed down' textbook development by two years.

Data collection instruments

Numerous data collection instruments were developed to collect information that, over time, informed the textbook development process.

We designed surveys to collect demographic information from pilot students in addition to semi-structured telephone interview protocols, pilot course evaluation forms, and textbook material evaluation forms to solicit feedback on textbook materials from pilot faculty and students. We also developed (i) pre-tests and post-tests that were administered to pilot students and (ii) scoring rubrics, which we comment on below. Pilot faculty also submitted to us all participating students' mock journal articles, written as part of the Journal Article Module. All sources of data, which provided useful information of different types, guided us in refining textbook materials over time.

Pre- and post-tests for pilot students

The pre- and post-tests developed for the project included four tasks: writing a methods section, preparing a table for a results section, proofreading and writing concisely, and writing a reflective essay, in which students commented on their own strengths and weaknesses as scientific writers (in the pre-test) and on their experience with *Write like a Chemist* materials (in the post-test). Pre-tests helped us ascertain students' needs and initial abilities; post-tests permitted us to evaluate the effectiveness of our materials, revealed in part by changes in pilot students' abilities.

Holistic and analytic rubrics

In collaboration with our project assessment coordinator and PhD student research assistant, we developed and validated a set of analytic rating scales to assist instructors in providing their students with feedback on major course writing assignments (i.e., target genres written in pilot courses). Holistic rating scales were designed, validated, and used for socializing pilot faculty during pre-pilot summer orientations and for preparing external evaluators to assess students' writing outcomes (from across all pilot sites), the latter serving as one indicator of the overall effectiveness of the textbook project. As part of the rubric development process, we spent a considerable amount of time agreeing upon a set of student writing samples that could serve as scale anchors (see Stoller, Horn, Grabe, and Robinson, 2005, for details).

Project transformation

What began as an in-house course development project, accompanied by the development of instructional materials, gradually transformed itself into something much larger. Classroom handouts grew into spiral-bound 'course packs', which became thicker and more 'textbook like' (with side-bars that included definitions of key terms and reminders about important points, consecutively numbered tasks, interesting findings from our own analyses of the language of chemistry) each semester. With each iteration items were added, modified to better reach our target audiences, consolidated to minimize repetition, and improved upon based on our own reflective practices and on the feedback that we received from piloters at NAU and nationwide. Midway through the project we had to radically rewrite many of our materials, including two entire chapters that dealt with in-text citations, references, and the formatting of tables and figures, to reflect disciplinary conventions specified in the *new* edition of *The ACS* (American Chemical Society) *Style Guide* (Coghill and Garson, 2006). (Although those revisions were laborious, in part because they required that we first familiarize ourselves with new disciplinary conventions, we were fortunate that the third edition of the *Style Guide* did not come out a year *after* our textbook was published. That unfortunate timing would have invalidated many of our textbook materials.)

In early stages some materials were discarded in their entirety. For example, in our first year of the project we developed materials to guide students in writing a paper about a scientific topic for the layperson (i.e., a scientifically curious but not a scientifically educated audience). We were aiming for something akin to a *Science News* entry (http://www. sciencenews.org/). As it turns out, such popularizations of science are rarely, if ever, written by scientists; rather, they are written by science writers. Although the applied linguists on the project team found students' popularizations of science to be interesting and accessible, this genre did not meet our course (or materials development) goals, which centered around preparing students for the genres that they themselves would be reading and writing.

Throughout the multiple-year process (see Figure 9.1), our materials and instructional approach evolved as a result of systematic piloting, trial and error, reflection, changed expectations in the field of chemistry, outcomes of students' pre- and post-tests, weekly meetings among course and materials development team members, and end-of-semester focus groups with students in pilot courses on our own campus. Over the years we presented phases of our work to professionals interested in English for Specific Purposes at the meetings of Teachers of English to Speakers of Other Languages (TESOL), American Association for Applied Linguistics (AAAL), and ACS. Questions asked and comments made by

Year							
1	2	3	4	5	6	7	8+
University mandate	Proof-of-concept grant		Textbook-development grant				Completion of textbook and publication
Materials (and textbook) development							
	Initial course and materials development		Continued materials development and refinement				
Corpus and genre analyses							
	WLAC corpus creation and analyses						
			Use of ACS Journal Search data-base for corpus analyses: http://pubs.acs.org				
Formative assessment							
	Piloting in-house; assessment of student writing by external evaluators						
					Piloting at 16 other institutions; assessment of student writing by external evaluators		
Publisher-related tasks							
			Secure publisher and contract		Copyright permissions		
			Communicate with publisher				

Figure 9.1   Milestones in the multiple-year *Write like a Chemist* textbook project

our audiences were illuminating and led to modifications in our materials as well. Finally, our materials were transformed into a published textbook (of 698 pages), with support materials on the web.

Milestones that propelled us from our initial course development efforts and single-page handouts to a published textbook are described in the sections that follow. Instead of proceeding in chronological order, we start 'at the end', with a description of the final product. We then turn our attention to the multi-faceted and iterative process of textbook development. At times, however, we blend our discussions of product and process, when the two topics are difficult to separate.

Write like a Chemist: The final product

To describe the *Write like a Chemist* (*WLAC*) textbook, we begin with a description of its overall organization and defining characteristics. Later in the chapter we highlight steps that we took to achieve the final product.

Broad organization of the textbook

We start with a snapshot of the broad organization of the textbook. As shown in Figure 9.2, the textbook is divided into two major sections. Chapter 1 serves as an introduction to the book, to our read-analyze-write approach to writing instruction (described in more detail below), and to important terminology (e.g., *genre, genre analysis, audience, moves*) that is assumed to be brand new to our two target audiences. Section 1 is then divided into three multiple-chapter modules, each one corresponding to a targeted genre: the journal article (Module 1), the conference abstract–poster genre chain (Module 2), and the research proposal (Module 3).

It is worth noting here that we sequenced the chapters in the journal article module not in the order in which the sections of a journal article are published and often read, but rather in the order in which they are typically written. We begin with the Methods section (followed by Results, Discussion, Introduction, Abstract, and Title). Consensus among the chemists on our materials development team, piloters, and external evaluators suggests that the Methods section is typically written first by chemists because it describes what chemists know best: that is, the procedures that they have repeated many times to conduct their work. Furthermore, the Methods section is often somewhat formulaic, hence the easiest to introduce, and students are usually best prepared to write it. We made similar sequencing decisions in our other modules after seeing how effective it was in the journal article module.

Section 2 focuses on writing conventions and practices that run across our target genres. Chapter 16 centers on the formatting of tables and figures. Chapter 17 explores disciplinary expectations with regard to in-text citations and references. Chapter 18 guides students in finalizing

Section 1 Writing modules	Section 2 Graphics, references, and final stages of writing

Ch1: Learning to write like a chemist
 	
Module 1: The journal article
  Ch2: Overview
  Ch3: Writing the methods section
  Ch4: Writing the results section
  Ch5: Writing the discussion section
  Ch6: Writing the introduction section
  Ch7: Writing the abstract and title
 	
Module 2: The scientific poster and
       conference abstract
  Ch8: Writing the conference abstract
      and title
  Ch9: Writing the poster text
  Ch10: Designing the poster
 	
Module 3: The research proposal
  Ch11: Overview
  Ch12: Writing the goals and importance
       section
  Ch13: Writing the experimental
       approach section
  Ch14: Writing the outcomes and
       impacts section
  Ch15: Writing the project summary
       and title
	Ch16: Formatting figures,
	      tables, and schemes
	Ch17: Formatting citations and
	      references
	Ch18: Finalizing your written
	      work

	Appendix A **Language Tips (Self-Study)**
	Audience and purpose Writing conventions Grammar and mechanics Word usage
	Appendix B **Move Structures**
	[Replication of move structures introduced throughout Section 1, Modules 1–3.]

Figure 9.2   Overview of *Write like a Chemist: A Guide and Resource* (Robinson et al., 2008)

their written work through revision and proofreading. (Early in the project all of these elements were incorporated into *each* chapter in Section 1. At a certain point in the project, after a lot of writing had been done, we realized that the repetition was unnecessary. That realization led to the conceptualization of Section 2 of the textbook and a lot of revisions.)

Appendix A comprises self-study materials in language areas that were troublesome for pilot students (as revealed in pre-/post-tests and students' written work) and chemistry-faculty pet peeves (i.e., student errors observed repeatedly by the second author of this chapter and corroborated by other chemistry faculty). Language areas targeted for self-study include easily confused words (such as *effect/affect*), hedging, nominalizations, conciseness, active and passive voice, scientific plurals, punctuation, parallelism, and subject–verb agreement. Each language tip includes explanatory notes, exercises, and an answer key. Excerpts from the chemistry literature are used throughout to showcase targeted features, but our language tips did not start out that way. In fact, drafts of our very first (small) set of language tips used everyday language and content to illustrate key points. Students did not see the value of those tips until we embedded the targeted language items into sentences and paragraphs using chemistry content. This change required the applied linguist on the materials development team to learn to use the ACS Journals Search web site (http://pubs.acs.org/) to find authentic language samples and then confer with the chemist on the team to ascertain whether students could actually understand the content of the excerpts. Thus what would be fairly straightforward for ELT textbook writers (e.g., the *between/among* distinction) became a more laborious task. Appendix B replicates the move structures (which provide easy-to-interpret visual displays of organizational conventions for each section of our target genres) introduced in Section 1.

Accompanying the textbook is the *Write like a Chemist* website (http://www.oup.com/us/writelikeachemist), which includes supplementary resources. For students we include textbook exercises that require editing and revision. Placing these exercises on the web allows students to copy and paste passages, rather than retype them, so that they can focus their energies on actual editing and revising. Also included for students are peer-review guides, which assist students in reviewing peers' written work and providing 'actionable' suggestions for revisions. Moreover, for chemistry students who do not have a sufficiently robust research project to write about, datasets and relevant background information, for fictitious but realistic research projects, are posted on the website. And finally, to cut down on textbook-publication costs, color versions of the gray-scale scientific posters included in Module 2 are posted on the *WLAC* website for student consultation.

For chemistry faculty, who gain access to this part of the website with a publisher-provided password, we include answer keys and sample grading rubrics (analytic and holistic) for major assignments (i.e., mock journal article, poster, research proposal). In addition, we include guidelines for using the textbook and practical tips for teaching writing (e.g., suggestions for helping students with writer's block, instructional techniques for working with mixed-ability groups, and reminders that general discussions about writing are less effective than hands-on writing experiences).

A hard-copy instructor's manual was not considered for this textbook project because such manuals are not part of the 'chemistry textbook culture'. Chemistry faculty are, however, accustomed to consulting online 'solution manuals' (with answer keys for odd or even numbered textbook problems). Even though teaching tips are not customarily included in web-based solution manuals for chemistry faculty, we chose to include teaching tips for *WLAC* adopters on our website for two major reasons: (i) chemistry faculty are accustomed to seeking information on the web; and (ii) chemistry faculty are not trained to teach writing, so we felt that they might appreciate the tips. Many of the tips that we offer would probably be viewed as standard fare among English language teachers (e.g., 'Do not assume that one correction or one reminder will lead to automatic improvement'; 'Some mistakes are likely to persist, at least for a while'; 'Learning to write like a chemist is a long-term process'). Nonetheless, such tips seemed appropriate for our chemistry faculty audience. We did not include these tips in the front matter of the textbook itself, in a Note to the Teacher section, such as one might see in an ELT textbook, because chemistry faculty would not typically think to look there for tips. The web was the most logical mechanism for reaching our target audience.

Defining characteristics of the textbook

Write like a Chemist mirrors the priorities of many English for Specific Purposes materials with its commitment to authenticity of purpose, task, and texts. To this end, the book provides students with models of targeted genres and guides their discovery of chemistry-specific writing conventions. Additionally, the materials strive to engage students actively in authentic writing, problem solving, and self-reflection (the latter a novelty in chemistry curricula). As we developed our materials, guided by these priorities, three features emerged that ultimately defined our textbook and set it apart from other writing guides for chemists: (i) the use of analytic methods from the fields of discourse analysis (Paltridge, 2006) and corpus linguistics (Biber, Connor, and Upton, 2007) to identify notable linguistic and non-linguistic features of chemistry writing in our target genres; (ii) a read-analyze-write approach to writing instruction; and (iii) a 'five components' orientation to genre analysis.

Our commitment to using tools from discourse analysis and corpus linguistics was linked to our desire to center instruction on the practices of real chemists writing for real audiences, not on intuitions (or hypotheses) about the language of chemistry. The read-analyze-write approach developed as a way to underscore our commitment to authentic texts and to introduce students to lifelong analytical skills. This approach was defined for readers in Chapter 1 as follows:

> Many effective writers develop their discipline-specific writing skills by reading and analyzing the works of others in their fields. Learning to write in chemistry is no exception; chemistry-specific writing skills are developed by reading and analyzing the writing of chemists. We coined the phrase 'read-analyze-write' to describe this approach and promote this process through the textbook.
>
> (Robinson et al., 2008: 5)

Our five-components approach to genre analysis allowed us to showcase the elements of writing that the book would address and to focus students' attention, in an intentionally repetitive manner, on these elements. These components also focused *our* attention and became checkpoints for consistency as we wrote each new chapter and module. The approach is introduced to readers in prose and a table, again in Chapter 1, as follows:

> At the core of the read-analyze-write approach is genre analysis, a systematic way to read and analyze writing. Through genre analysis, you will identify and examine essential components of a genre, thereby facilitating your ability to write effectively in that genre. This textbook focuses on five such components: audience and purpose, organization, writing conventions, grammar and mechanics, and science content. As shown in [Table 9.1], each component can be further divided into two or more subcomponents. Our goal is to teach you to analyze chemistry-specific writing according to these components and subcomponents.
>
> (Robinson et al., 2008: 7)

We explore in more detail the read-analyze-write approach and the five components of genre analysis in the next two sections.

Read-analyze-write

Our shared commitment to an integrated reading and writing approach was strengthened by the explicit addition of *analysis* to our instructional framework, thereby creating a read-analyze-write approach. In fact, this approach mirrors the way in which many chemists learn to write in their discipline (in part because chemistry-specific writing instruction is still relatively uncommon). The chemist author of *WLAC*

Table 9.1   Components of genre analysis addressed in *Write like a Chemist*[a]

Audience and purpose	Organization	Writing conventions	Grammar and mechanics	Science content
Conciseness	Broad structure	Abbreviations and acronyms	Parallelism	Graphics
Level of detail	Fine structure	Formatting	Punctuation	Text
Level of formality	('moves')	Verb tense	Subject–verb agreement	
Word choice		Voice	Word usage	

Note:[a] p.7: Table 1.1 from *Write like a Chemist: A Guide and Resource* by Robinson, Stoller, Costanza-Robinson, and Jones (2008), by permission of Oxford University Press, US.

(Robinson) remembered writing her first two first-authored manuscripts as a graduate student: the first required substantial revisions, while the second was accepted with only minor changes. The key difference between the two manuscripts (with respect to writing) was the use of a template. The more successful paper was modeled on a similar paper published in the targeted journal. Why not use an analogous approach to teach chemistry students to write? Such an approach would be familiar to most chemists, even those untrained in teaching writing, and superior to the 'red pen' approach, a method that is often frustrating for students and instructors alike. Not surprisingly, this template-based approach also appealed to the applied linguistics author of *WLAC* (Stoller). Thus the decision was made to commit to the use of authentic texts (in their entirety and as excerpts) throughout the textbook and to center read-analyze-write tasks around them.

Excerpts from authentic texts were incorporated into textbook Modules 1–3 (and elsewhere). ACS journal articles were used in Module 1. Conference abstracts published in the 2007 ACS National Meeting program were used for Module 2. Because posters are not published, authentic posters were not available for that part of Module 2. Nonetheless, examples of posters, following disciplinary conventions, were created for read-analyze-write tasks; posters without color (gray scale) were included in the book, while their corresponding color versions were posted on the *WLAC* website. For Module 3, research proposals were obtained from chemistry faculty who were recipients of NSF CAREER[4] awards. Authentic passages from our target genres were also included in exercises throughout textbook chapters and the language tips in Appendix A. (Details about securing copyright permissions are included later in this chapter.)

The read-analyze-write approach also directed the organization of key instructional textbook chapters. For example, in Module 1, each chapter begins with a section entitled 'Reading and Analyzing Writing', where students are provided an authentic excerpt to read and analyze in a guided exercise. By the end of the module, students have read and analyzed the entire article, section by section. 'Writing on Your Own' tasks guide students from what they have learned from reading and analyzing authentic texts to writing on their own. With the repeated practice that comes from our volume-wide commitment to the read-analyze-write sequence, we believe that students develop skills that they can apply well beyond their experience with *WLAC*, in new situations, with new genres, across different journals, and as conventions change, as they are likely to do over time.

Because our focus was on teaching writing, not science, we intentionally selected excerpts with content accessible to most third-year university chemistry students. (Determinations of content accessibility were made by the chemists on the team, who were familiar with students' disciplinary knowledge.) That said, as students learned to read and analyze texts for writing, their confidence and ability to read them for science also improved. Similarly, as students learned to read different genres, they also learned where to look in these genres for specific types of information, another skill that translates into improved scientific literacy.

Our commitment to authentic texts is also evidenced in our decision to write a chemistry-specific textbook, rather than a more general textbook on science writing. Although initially encouraged by our publisher to consider broadening the scope of the book (by, for example, addressing writing in biology as well), presumably to promote sales, we resisted because of what we perceived to be the vital importance of a singular focus on chemistry. It is worth noting here that we were lucky to have a harmonious relationship with our publisher. Oxford University Press (OUP) was on board with the project early on. Fortunately, during the time we were working with OUP, there was little turnover of important OUP personnel (an all too common phenomenon in ELT publishing divisions). Thus, we did not experience requests for radical (or even minor) changes in textbook goals, target audiences, or content emphases, which could have happened had a new acquisitions editor been assigned to the project.

Five components of genre analysis

Our five-components approach to genre analyses ultimately resulted in focusing students' attention on audience and purpose, organization, discipline- and genre-specific writing conventions, grammar and mechanics, and science content (Table 9.1). Our materials guide students in analyzing writing either move by move or across targeted sections based on these five components. For example, when analyzing for audience and purpose, students are asked to discover for themselves, in guided exercises, what details to include for an expert audience (fewer than they typically guess), how experienced writers achieve concise writing (e.g., by using 'respectively'; nominalizations; statistical symbols; abbreviations for units of measure [mL for milliliters], chemical structures [Tris for tris(hydroxymethyl)aminomethane], common instrumental techniques [SPME for solid-phase microextraction], common terms [mp for melting point, m/z for mass-to-charge ratio, LD_{50} instead of 'dose that is lethal to 50 per cent of subjects']), and what word choices are most appropriate for a specific audience (e.g., the words 'truth' and 'prove' are rare in chemistry writing; verbs such as 'withdraw' are more appropriate than phrasal verbs such as 'take away'; verbs such as 'investigate' and 'determine' are more appropriate than 'see if' or 'look into'; 'In this work' is more appropriate than 'In this experiment' because a published work describes the results of many experiments). When analyzing for organization, students are directed to analyze both the genre as a whole (broad organization) and individual moves (and sub-moves) within each section (following the seminal work of Swales, 1990, 2004, and others). Move structures (developed as flow-chart-like visuals) are included in each of the writing module chapters (chapters 2–15) to illustrate common moves and sub-moves. When analyzing for writing conventions that are both widely used in chemistry writing, as determined by our own genre analyses, and endorsed by *The ACS Style Guide* (Coghill and Garson, 2006), students are directed to analyze passages for conventions related to abbreviations and acronyms, formatting of tables and figures, numbers and units, verb tense and voice, among other conventions. When analyzing for grammar and mechanics, students examine authentic texts for examples of parallelism in complex sentences, subject–verb agreement, and troublesome words (e.g., 'fewer' and 'less'). Finally, students examine authentic texts for science content and the way(s) in which it is presented, in text or graphics.

These distinguishing features, in addition to other textbook elements that are introduced in the next section of this chapter, provide the explicit instruction, repeated exposures, practice, feedback, and time that students need to gradually develop an understanding of valued disciplinary genres and their layers of complexity (Tardy, 2009). The end-result is intended to improve students' reading, analytic, and writing skills and offer them initial access to and control of discipline-specific practices.

The process: Textbook development and publication

Writing our textbook was a multi-faceted and iterative process. For clarity, we have divided this process into two parts, textbook development and textbook publication, even though these parts did overlap considerably. The textbook development process required that we (i) articulate priorities and principles; (ii) scaffold our instructional approach; (iii) select and analyze target genres; (iv) incorporate analytical findings into our instructional materials; and (v) pilot and assess materials (and use this feedback to improve materials). The textbook publication process required us to (i) find a publisher; (ii) secure copyright permissions; (iii) select a title; (iv) acknowledge contributors; and (v) finalize copy. (See Figure 9.3 for a schematic representation of these parallel processes.) We comment on these steps sequentially, even though most components occurred in a non-linear fashion, influencing and informing one another throughout the multi-year project. (See Samuda, 2005, for more on the complex, recursive, and 'often messy' (p.243) process associated with task design.) Nonetheless, our discussion should give readers of this chapter a sense of the many issues that needed to coalesce for our textbook project to be successful.

Textbook development process

Articulate priorities

Early in the project, we identified the priorities and principles that would guide the materials development process. For example, we selected our four target genres (mentioned above) and agreed to use authentic texts (in their entirety and as excerpts) throughout the textbook as illustrations of common disciplinary practices and springboards for instructional tasks. We agreed to limit our scope to the writing conventions endorsed by *The ACS Style Guide* (Coghill and Garson, 2006) and also evidenced in our own genre analyses. Because variations within genres are inevitable, and because disciplinary expectations change over time (even *The ACS Style Guide* went from its second to third edition during our project), we also committed ourselves to providing students with the analytic tools and practice required to discover writing conventions on their own. In this way, students would develop analytic abilities that could carry over into their future studies and professional lives. To this end, we endorsed a learning-by-doing philosophy, translated to

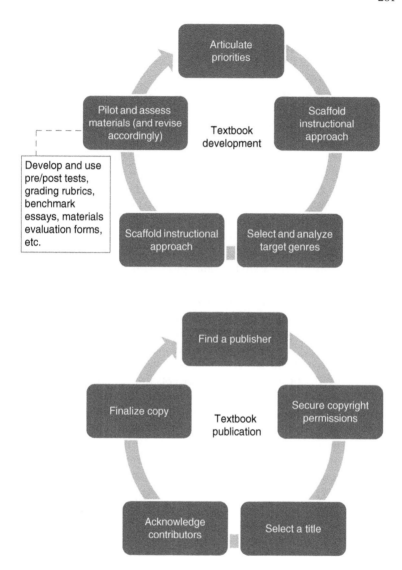

Figure 9.3 Schematic representation of the parallel processes that led to the successful completion of our textbook

mean that users of the textbook would be actively engaged in examining model texts (through reading and analysis) and writing, instead of just reading about writing, the latter approach simply too passive for our purposes.

Scaffold instructional approach

To reach our target audiences (who would have little, if any, experience with discipline-specific writing instruction), we knew that we would have to introduce key concepts and terminology, including audience (expert, scientific, student, and general), word usage vs. word choice, genre, genre analysis, and organization (in terms of moves and what we called sub-moves), following the work of Swales (1990, 2004). We bring these key concepts and terminology alive by having students compare texts written for different audiences. In a very early iteration we had students compare a methods section in a familiar chemistry genre (the lab report, written for a student audience) with a methods section in a not yet familiar chemistry genre, specifically the journal article, written for an expert audience. Ultimately, we modified the approach by starting with common everyday genres and then transitioning to familiar and less familiar disciplinary genres. This more gradual approach seemed to work better. To begin, students are guided in their analyses of familiar, non-chemistry, genres (jokes, letters, and newspaper used-car ads), thereby bringing relevant concepts to the conscious attention of our readers without scaring them away! From everyday genres we move to two chemistry genres, one that is familiar to most students (the Materials Safety Data Sheet) and one that is less familiar but easy to read (i.e., journal article acknowledgments). We then transition to two papers on the same chemistry topic, one written by a science writer for a general audience (complete with direct quotations, a catchy title, and an elementary drawing of ethane) and the other written for an expert audience. Students compare the two papers to identify differences and similarities. From this point on, students are ready to embark upon the read-analyze-write approach developed for the textbook (and our target genres).

To add some light-hearted fun to the textbook, and to help students contrast distinct genres, we include a poem that pokes fun at chemistry seminars written by Roald Hoffmann, who shared the Nobel Prize in Chemistry in 1981. In an exercise, students are asked to examine the poem for purpose, audience, organization, writing conventions, grammar and mechanics, and science content, once again bringing to their conscious attention the many elements of writing that are needed for successful communication. Our incorporation of four Snoopy comic strips with poignant messages about the challenges of writing serves a similar purpose: that is, to lighten things up.

Scaffolding is also used in peer-review activities; students practice peer review using text samples manipulated by us to include many of the same errors that were made by students in our pilot classes. We ultimately numbered the lines of these text samples in the textbook to facilitate class discussion. The practice and the accompanying classroom discussion prepare students to engage in authentic peer review using the peer-review guides found on the *WLAC* website. As a final example of scaffolding, key instructional chapters include sequential Writing on Your Own tasks, designed to guide students, step by step, in writing sections of the genre being studied.

Select and analyze target genres

Our target genres, selected for textual analysis and explicit instruction, were chosen for different reasons. The *journal article* is the primary means by which new scientific claims and the certification of those claims (Berkenkotter and Huckin, 1995) are disseminated in chemistry. It is not uncommon, as confirmed by NAU practices and our 16 pilot faculty, for third-year chemistry students to begin reading the primary literature (including peer-reviewed journal articles) and contribute to the writing of journal articles in their research groups. *Posters* typify the way in which chemistry students and professionals alike disseminate their newest, pre-published research findings at conferences. (At most chemistry meetings, the number of poster presentations far exceeds the number of oral presentations.) To have a poster accepted for presentation requires the prior submission of a *conference abstract* (thus the earlier abstract–poster genre chain designation). The *research proposal* represents the most common way for chemists (including students) to solicit research support.

Target genres were analyzed using tools from (i) corpus linguistics and (ii) genre and move analyses. For three of the four genres (journal articles, conference abstracts, and research proposals), a set of full-length 'text exemplars' (i.e., corpora) was systematically compiled for analysis and later use in materials development efforts (see also Feak and Swales, 2010). In Stoller and Robinson (2013), we describe the steps taken to select chemistry journals and articles within them as an illustration of the process. We also made extensive use of the ACS Journals Search, which provides easy access to a large database[5] of chemistry journal articles; we learned to use the ACS Journals Search for linguistic analyses, though such analyses are not the intended purpose of the database. Tools from corpus linguistics and genre analysis helped us identify lexico-grammatical usage and frequencies, contexts in which particular words and structures occur, generalizable linguistic patterns, standard and optional moves and their variations in sections of each genre, in addition to the language features aligned with the five perspectives noted in Table 9.1.

Unlike these emergent findings, we also looked for examples of predetermined discourse characteristics, in particular conciseness, a common theme in *The ACS Style Guide* (Coghill and Garson, 2006), which reminds authors to 'write economically' (p.54), precisely, and concisely. Similarly, in chemistry-journal Information for Authors documents, the 'be complete but concise' reminder is ubiquitous (e.g., http://pubs.acs. org/paragonplus/submission/esthag/esthag_authguide.pdf). To achieve conciseness, chemists, like other scientists (Hyland, 1998), often use nominalizations. Thus, we looked for patterns related to their use as well (see below).

As part of our move analyses, we aimed to determine the communicative functions of moves and sub-moves, the boundaries between them, and their sequencing, preferential patterns, obligatory and optional components, linkages, and potentially repeating parts. Analyses continued until teachable, familiar patterns (with some variations) became evident (e.g., Table 9.2), as agreed upon by team members and chemistry piloters of our instructional materials.

The results of our analyses (and manner of presentation) were reviewed and validated by our 30 piloters and external evaluators, all representatives of the target discipline. These validation efforts occurred at various junctures during textbook development (e.g., while creating grading rubrics with our assessment team; during piloter training and piloting, external-evaluator reviews of textbook materials and students' written work), thereby adding an important (and unique) dimension to our validation efforts (Stoller, Horn, Grabe, and Robinson, 2005; Stoller and Robinson, 2013).

Incorporate analytical findings

It came as no surprise that chemistry faculty and students appreciated the objectivity that results from systematic text analyses; after all, the scientific method used by many chemists is, by design, an objective approach. Hence, we were motivated to include findings from our

Table 9.2 Common functions of different tense–voice combinations in journal article discussion sections[a]

Function	Tense–Voice combination	Example
To remind readers about what was studied in the current work	Past (active or passive)	In this work, three Cr^{3+} compounds *were examined* for their impact on genotoxicity and cell proliferation in vitro (From Plaper et al., 2002) (past-passive)
To remind readers about/summarize specific result(s) in the current work	Past (active or passive)	Similar to regular garlic, regular broccoli florets *reduced* the incidence of mammary tumors (From Finley et al., 2001) (past-active)
To share corroborating or conflicting results from others' works	Past (active or passive)	Uptake of dissolved organic carbon by zebra mussels *was* also *reported* by Roditi et al. (30). (Adapted from Voets et al., 2004) (past-passive)
To interpret results presented in the current work	Present-active	The 0.5 TU threshold *is* arbitrary but *suggests* a strong likelihood that the analyte *makes* a substantial contribution to the observed mortality. (From Weston et al., 2004)
To propose 'truths' based on the current work and others' works	Present-active	The data in this paper *are* consistent with a wealth of evidence showing that dietary Se consumed in excess of the Recommended Dietary Allowance *lowers* the risk of several important cancers (*2, 13, 26, 27*). (From Finley et al., 2001)
To present the take-home message of the current work	Present-active	In summary, (R)-phenylglycine amide **1** *is* an excellent chiral auxiliary in the asymmetric Strecker reaction with pivaldehyde or 3,4-dimethoxyphenyl-acetone. (From Boesten et al., 2001)

Table 9.2 (Continued)

Function	Tense–Voice combination	Example
To suggest overall implications and/or applications of the current work	Present-active	The good sensitivity, excellent selectivity, and simplicity of use of the DNA biosensor *make* it more compatible for integrating with on-chip PCR reactors than other DNA biosensors of which we are aware. (Adapted from Wong and Gooding, 2006)

Note: [a] p.189: Table 5.1 from *Write like a Chemist: A Guide and Resource* by Robinson, Stoller, Costanza-Robinson, and Jones (2008), by permission of Oxford University Press, US.

Table 9.3 Common nominalizations used in chemistry writing[a]

absorption	concentration	extraction	presence
activation	conductivity	formation	purification
addition	conversion	intensity	reaction
aggregation	dependence	interaction	reactivity
agreement	diffusion	luminescence	reduction
analysis	efficiency	measurement	synthesis
calculation	emission	oxidation	treatment
comparison	excitation	preparation	

Note: Nominalizations determined through a computer-based search of 200 chemistry journal articles. [a]p.41: Table 2.2 from *Write like a Chemist: A Guide and Resource* by Robinson, Stoller, Costanza-Robinson, and Jones (2008), by permission of Oxford University Press, US.

analyses in the textbook, some of which are showcased in the sections that follow.

Select genre-analysis results. Conciseness, as mentioned earlier, is highly valued by chemists. We found that chemists frequently use nominalizations to achieve this goal (even though the term 'nominalization' is unfamiliar to many chemists). To illustrate this practice in the textbook, corpus analysis tools were used to search 200 chemistry journal articles, from which a list of 31 commonly used nominalizations was generated (Table 9.3).

Corpus analyses were also used to examine active and passive voice. Common lore among chemists (as reported by chemistry materials development team members) is that active voice using the word 'we' is generally discouraged. *The ACS Style Guide*, in fact, advises against using the phrases 'we believe', 'we feel', and 'we can see' (Coghill and Garson, 2006: 44). We investigated uses of 'we' using the ACS Journals Search. We learned that 'we' is used sparingly (three in 1,000 words), but it was observed in 85 per cent of the journals analyzed. 'We' did not appear in Methods sections, but it was used predictably at the end of Introductions to introduce the current work ('In this work, we...'), in Results sections (though not often) to highlight human decisions, and in Discussion sections to indicate decisions or courses of action, compare findings with previous works, offer an interpretation, or summarize findings. Of particular interest was our analysis of the changing frequency of 'we' over time (Figure 9.4). We also used the ACS Journals Search to find examples of the passive voice to illustrate when and where it is used (i) to shift the focus from the scientist to the science and (ii) to convey objectivity (i.e., that the results are not influenced by the person doing the work), two common practices in chemistry writing.

Journal article titles provide a final example of how findings from corpus analyses were incorporated into our textbook. After analyzing

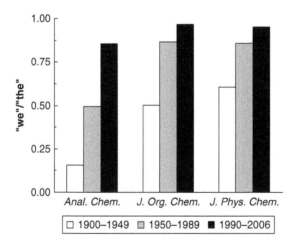

Figure 9.4 The documents using 'we' at least once (relative to the number using 'the') over three time periods, determined using the ACS Journals Search. (Note: *Journal of Physical Chemistry* includes *Journal of Physical Chemistry A* and *B* after 1996)

Note: p.149: Figure. 4.2 from *Write like a Chemist: A Guide and Resource* by Robinson, Stoller, Costanza-Robinson, and Jones (2008), by permission of Oxford University Press, US.

Table 9.4   Common examples of the x of y by z pattern found in journal article titles

X (optional)		Y (required)		Z (optional)
A nominalization (e.g., Determination, Investigation, Analysis Measurement) A phrase that refers to, describes, or modifies Y	of in for to ...	What was studied	on in via by using at from ...	Target of Y or what was impacted by Y Method used (or detail of method used) to study Y
[a]Preparation	of	5-Substituted 1*H*-Tetrazoles	from	Nitriles in Water
[b]Heteronuclear Recoupling	in	Solid-State Magic-Angle-Spinning NMR	via	Overtone Irradiation
[c]Cancer-Protective Properties	of	High-Selenium Broccoli		
		[d]A Class II Aldolase Mimic		

Note: Titles are from [a]Demko and Sharpless (2001), [b]Wi and Frydman (2006), [c]Finley, Ip, Lisk, Davis, Hintze, and Whanger (2001), and [d]Hedin-Dahlström, Rosengren-Holmberg, Legrand, Wikman, and Nicholls (2006).
Adaptation of pp.246–247: Table 7.1 from *Write like a Chemist: A Guide and Resource* by Robinson, Stoller, Costanza-Robinson, and Jones (2008), by permission of Oxford University Press, US.

numerous titles, we created a formula-like pattern that would guide students in constructing their own titles (Table 9.4).

Select move-analysis results.   Move analyses led to useful findings about the broad organization of our target genres and the moves and sub-moves (referred to as 'steps' by Swales and others) within them. For the textbook, we converted findings into flow-chart like visual depictions, unlike the ways in which moves and steps are commonly reported to applied linguists (see Appendix A). Our manner of presentation, like the representative sample in Figure 9.5, has been well received by our target chemistry audiences for its simplicity, ease of interpretation, and familiar numbering system (3, 3.1, 3.2...). Early depictions of our findings, however, were more complicated and cluttered. Early on, as shown in Appendix B, we boxed moves and sub-moves, and used arrows to highlight information flow. We even attempted to indicate the typical

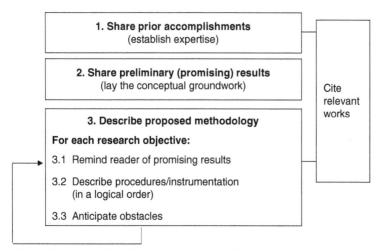

Repeat (as needed) for different research objectives

Figure 9.5   A move structure depicting the organization of a typical experimental approach section in the project description part of a research proposal
Note: p.437, Figure. 13.1 from *Write like a Chemist: A Guide and Resource*, by Robinson, Stoller, Costanza-Robinson, and Jones (2008), by permission of Oxford University Press, US.

length of each 'stretch of text' (Swales and Feak, 2009: 5) by placing (i) shorter moves and sub-moves in more shallow boxes and (ii) longer moves and sub-moves in deeper boxes. We also attempted to show changing levels of specificity (drawing upon Hill, Soppelsa, and West, 1982; Swales, 1990, 2004) with the width of our boxes; moves with more general information (such as the early moves in Introductions and Abstracts) were placed in wider boxes; moves with more specificity (such as those at the end of Introductions and beginning of Discussions) were placed in more narrow boxes. Feedback from chemistry students and faculty at various points in the project (about, e.g., the superfluous downward arrows, the distracting subtleties such as the gradually narrowing boxes) led to the streamlined model shown in Figure 9.5. (See Stoller and Robinson, 2013, for more on the evolution of our move structures.)

In textbook Module 1, a move structure is introduced for each section of each target genre. Accompanying each move structure is at least one activity that obliges students to use the move structure to read and analyze authentic texts. For example, activities direct students (i) to find phrases, sentences, and/or paragraphs corresponding to moves and sub-moves; (ii) to identify the ways in which writers transition from one move to the next; and (iii) to locate variations in organization as a way to reinforce the notion that the move structures are frameworks of conventionalized practices, not rigid templates. Additional types of textbook activities that involve move structures are itemized in Table 9.5.

Table 9.5 A sampling of textbook activities that center on organization and move structures (adapted from Robinson et al., 2008)

Instructional task	Sample activity
Propose a move structure	Read through the 'Beer Analysis' Discussion section in Excerpt A. What moves do you see in this excerpt? Propose a move structure for the Discussion section, with at least one move for each paragraph.
Examine an excerpt in relation to an already introduced move structure	Reread Excerpt B. How well does it adhere to the move structure in Figure X? How do the authors use subheadings to help the reader locate the moves? Can you equate each subheading with one of the moves? Are any moves left out? If so, which one(s)?
Assign a move to sentences taken from excerpts	These sentences were taken from different journal article Results sections. By reading just the selected sentences, can you determine what move(s) or sub-move(s) are accomplished?
Sequence scrambled sentences to match a move structure	The following three sentences appear in the Introduction of an article on asbestos. Based on content and language, which is likely to be the first sentence of the Introduction? Based on the move structure in Figure X, predict the order of all three sentences.
Find variations in organization	Excerpt C includes the Discussion section from a 2001 issue of the *Journal of Agricultural and Food Chemistry*. Read the excerpt and complete the following tasks: (a) Identify each of the moves and sub-moves. Does this Discussion section follow the typical move structure presented in Figure X? (b) Do the authors of this Discussion section both interpret results and apply them to a larger context?
Compare move structures in different chemistry sub-fields	Consider how the move structure in Figure X applies across different fields of chemistry. (a) Find two articles in the *Journal of Organic Chemistry* and two articles in *Organic Letters*. How are methods presented in these articles? What subheadings are used? Do they adhere to the move structure suggested in Figure X? Explain.

	(b) Find two articles with the word 'theoretical' or 'computational' in their titles. How are methods presented in these articles? What subheadings are used? Do they adhere to the move structure suggested in Figure X? Explain.
Consult a move structure to complete a simulation	Concentrations of lead in lakebed sediments can be used to estimate concentrations in the atmosphere as far back as the 17th century. Imagine that you are writing a journal article that shows how lead concentrations in North American lakebed cores varied over the past 100 years (1900–1999). Your data show that lead concentrations peaked between 1955 and 1975, which you attribute to the use of lead additives in gasoline. Write an opening paragraph for your paper that (a) introduces your topic, (b) emphasizes its importance, and (c) summarizes study results (jotted down below). Use the move structure in Figure X to guide you.

Textbook publication process

Find a publisher

We sought a publisher shortly after we received notification that our second NSF grant was funded. We did so at the urging of the NSF panel that reviewed our proposal. (On our own, we likely would have waited until the book was further developed.) We both agreed on Oxford University Press (OUP) as the ideal publisher because of its excellent reputation in ELT and its recent acquisition of the copyright for *The ACS Style Guide* (formerly published by the ACS), a pairing that was ideal for our project. We reviewed submission requirements on the OUP website and submitted the requisite materials including an outline, two sample chapters, and marketing information regarding our target audience and competition. The acquisitions editor in the OUP chemistry division demonstrated an interest in our proposal and sent out our sample materials for blind review. Reviews were favorable, and a contract was signed. During contract negotiations, we requested more time (four years) to bring the book to press so that we could (i) complete off-campus piloting and (ii) make meaningful changes to the textbook based on piloter feedback. This request and a few others were granted; the entire process took less than four months. In retrospect, the NSF panel was absolutely right to urge us to find a publisher early in the project.

Secure copyright permissions

Because of our commitment to incorporate authentic passages throughout the textbook, securing copyright permissions was non-trivial.

Excerpted materials fell into several categories: (i) articles published in ACS journals; (ii) NSF CAREER proposals and one ACS Division of Analytical Chemistry Graduate Fellowship proposal; (iii) conference abstracts from the 2007 *Proceedings of the 233rd American Chemical Society National Meeting*; (iv) Snoopy cartoons; and (v) the poem written by Nobel Laureate Roald Hoffmann. We began seeking permissions early in the writing process. We worked closely with the ACS copyright manager to obtain permissions to use excerpts from approximately 260 published ACS journal articles. For research proposals, copyright belongs to the principal investigator (PI); thus we contacted PIs for permissions. All PIs were acknowledged by name in the book. A similar process was used for ACS conference abstracts, where again copyright is owned by the author. The four Snoopy cartoons required a copyright fee[6] to be paid to PEANUTS: @ United Feature Syndicate, Inc. Permission for Hoffmann's poem was granted by the author.

Select a title

The publishers liked our proposed title (*Write like a Chemist*) from the start for its succinctness and subtle humor. (We later heard stories of chemists coming up to the OUP booth at ACS conferences and asking 'Really? Write like a *Chemist?*') We did debate with the publisher over the subtitle (*A Guide and Resource*). We wanted the word 'textbook' in the subtitle because the book was designed to be used in chemistry-specific writing courses, but the publisher believed that the 'textbook' designation would limit marketability. It turns out that the publisher was probably right because the book is being used on its own by motivated post-docs and practicing chemists who want to improve their professional writing.

Acknowledge contributors

Bringing any book to press requires decisions about authorship and royalties. At different points we invited a variety of individuals (including graduate students, a post-doctoral fellow, and faculty with interests in royalties and authorship) to contribute to the project. Thus we saw a need to be explicit about intellectual property rights. To this end, we developed a Memo of Understanding, in consultation with university personnel associated with the Office of the Vice President for Research and the Provost, that spelled out how participants would be compensated for their efforts (e.g., through a stipend or salary) and how they would be acknowledged in the book (e.g., as a co-author or in the Acknowledgments).

Finalize copy

When the textbook was nearly complete, we created an index and worked with a copy editor to finalize the manuscript, deciding, for example, where to place icons, how to cite excerpts, and how to format graphics. Because OUP and ACS use different formatting conventions, it was decided that (i) OUP conventions would be followed in our own prose and graphics; and (ii) ACS guidelines would be followed in excerpted materials. We were surprised to learn that we had to strip our final manuscript of all its formatting at this stage (e.g., font sizes and bolding), indicating our preferences instead by inserting publisher symbols in the margins (a laborious and tedious task). The final step was to add page numbers to the index and Table of Contents. Then (at last) the book went to press.

Concluding remarks

In this case study of an interdisciplinary textbook project, we have tried to explain why the textbook, in its final published form, looks the way it does. To chart the complex and iterative process of textbook development, we highlighted the contributions of numerous intertwined steps. These include: articulating instructional priorities and principles; scaffolding our instructional approach; selecting and analyzing the language of chemistry in four genres; converting findings into materials; piloting systematically and using piloters' feedback to improve materials; finding a publisher; securing copyright permissions; and seeing the book through the final stages of publication.

What would we do differently if we had the chance to do so? We would likely divide our 698-page book into a set of shorter volumes, as Feak and Swales have done with some of their works (e.g., Swales and Feak, 2009). In this way instructors and students could select the genre(s) that they are most interested in, and the overall size of the textbook would not be as intimidating. We would also ask the publisher to consider an online version of the textbook, in response to the contemporary university student's comfort with and preference for all things electronic (including books). Similarly, chemistry faculty are typically comfortable using online resources (e.g., online dictionaries), so a natural extension would be to have *Write like a Chemist* in electronic form too. Furthermore, we would be more proactive in raising the consciousness of chemistry faculty, and the field at large, about the importance of discipline-specific writing instruction. While the field of ELT has many journals dedicated to literacy issues and instruction (including *English for Specific Purposes, TESOL Quarterly, TESOL Journal, Journal of Second Language Writing, Reading in a Foreign Language*), the field of chemistry lacks such journals. Nor do premier professional chemistry associations have special interest groups that focus on disciplinary reading or writing. We have discussed the value of establishing a network of faculty interested in chemistry-specific writing, creating a listserv to facilitate communication among such professionals, working with ACS conference program chairs to promote regularly scheduled sessions on writing at ACS conferences, and communicating with editors of the *Journal of Chemical Education* to explore the feasibility of publishing a special topics issue on chemistry writing. Sadly, our efforts to secure post-publication grant support for such activities have not succeeded.

What would we do in a similar manner? Quite a bit. We conclude this chapter by delineating some of these practices, with the hope that they serve as guides for others involved in interdisciplinary textbook projects. First, take care in establishing an interdisciplinary partnership; respect each member's viewpoints, capitalize on each member's expertise, and expect to gain a broader vision of the project as a result. Second, take the time to develop a shared vocabulary and commitment to the project. Third, resist intuitions about the language of the discipline; be systematic in analyzing the language of target genres. Fourth, be willing to abandon materials that have taken 'an eternity' to develop (Johnson, 2003) if they no longer complement the textbook as it evolves over time or if improvements are possible. Fifth, be willing to write, rewrite, and rewrite again. Sixth, take the time to engage in systematic piloting and make use of insights gained to improve materials, even if that signifies major changes. Seventh, expect to encounter competing demands (see Harwood, 2010). And finally, celebrate small accomplishments.

Appendix A

Common manner of presentation of moves among applied linguists (from Kanoksilapatham, 2005, p.290)

Partial move structure for biochemistry research articles

Move/step	Frequency of occurrence (%)
Introduction	
Move 1: Announcing the importance of the field	100.00
By Step 1: Claiming the centrality of the topic	

By Step 2: Making topic generalizations
By Step 3: Reviewing previous research

Move 2: Preparing for the present study   66.66
    By Step 1: Indicating a gap
    By Step 2: Raising a question

Appendix B

An early (later abandoned) move structure for a chemistry journal article introduction (from Stoller and Robinson, 2013, p.55)

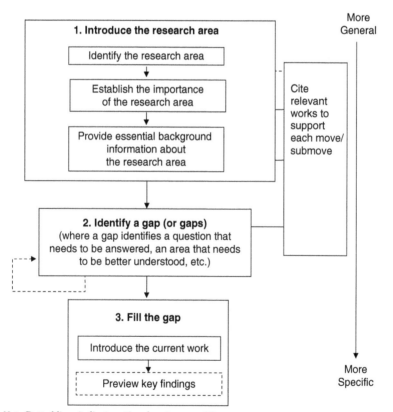

Note: Dotted lines indicate optional parts or repetitions.

Notes

1. The US National Science Foundation (NSF) supported the *Write like a Chemist* project with grants DUE 0087570 and 0230913. Opinions, findings, conclusions, and recommendations expressed here are those of the authors; they do not necessarily reflect the views of the NSF.
2. We received two NSF Course, Curriculum, and Laboratory Instruction (CCLI) grants. At the time of writing this chapter, CCLI grants no longer exist. In their place, the NSF seeks proposals for Transforming Undergraduate Education in Science, Technology, Engineering, and Mathematics (TUES) grants.
3. The Carnegie Classification [http://classifications.carnegiefoundation.org/] is a widely used framework for recognizing, describing, and distinguishing among higher education institutions in the US. Each institution is classified based on a combination of factors, including its undergraduate and graduate programs, student enrolment profiles, size and setting, degrees granted, type and amount of research conducted, etc. For example, Northern Arizona University is classified partially as follows: RU/H (Research University/High research activity); L4/R (large four-year, primarily residential); HU (High Undergraduate); prof+A&S/SGC (Professions plus arts and sciences, some graduate coexistence).
4. The US National Science Foundation's prestigious Faculty Early Career Development (CAREER) grants offer support to teacher scholars, early in their careers (pre-tenure), for projects that integrate research and educational endeavors.
5. When *Write like a Chemist* was published, in 2008, the ACS Journals Search 1996-to-Current Issue database included 45+ journals and more than 395,000 articles.
6. Permissions for Snoopy comic strips were paid for with grant monies.

References

Alley, M. (1996). *The craft of scientific writing* (3rd ed.). New York: Springer.

Beall, H. and Trimbur, J. (2001). *A short guide to writing about chemistry* (2nd ed.). New York: Pearson Education.

Berkenkotter, C. and Huckin, T.N. (1995). *Genre knowledge in disciplinary communication: Cognition/culture/power*. Hillsdale: Lawrence Erlbaum.

Biber, D., Connor, U., and Upton, T.A. (2007). *Discourse on the move: Using corpus analysis to describe discourse structure*. Philadelphia: John Benjamins.

Coghill, A.M. and Garson, L.R. (Eds.). (2006). *The ACS style guide: Effective communication of scientific information* (3rd ed.). Washington, DC: American Chemical Society.

Demko, Z.P. and Sharpless, K.B. (2001). Preparation of 5-substituted 1H-tetrazoles from nitriles in water. *Journal of Organic Chemistry*, 66, 7945–7950.

Donovan, P. (1998). Piloting – A publisher's view. In B. Tomlinson (Ed.), *Materials development in language teaching* (pp.149–189). New York: Cambridge University Press.

Dudley-Evans, T. and St. John, M.J. (1998). *Developments in English for specific purposes: A multi-disciplinary approach*. New York: Cambridge University Press.

Feak, C.B. and Swales, J.M. (2010). Writing for publication: Corpus-informed materials for postdoctoral fellows in perinatology. In N. Harwood (Ed.), *English language teaching materials: Theory and practice* (pp.279 –300). New York: Cambridge University Press.

Finley, J.W., Ip, C., Lisk, D.J., Davis, C.D., Hintze, K.J., and Whanger, P.D. (2001). Cancer-protective properties of high-selenium broccoli. *Journal of Agricultural and Food Chemistry*, 49, 2679–2683.

Frechtling Westat, J. (2002). *The 2002 user friendly handbook for project evaluation.* Arlington: National Science Foundation.

Harwood, N. (2010). Issues in materials development and design. In N. Harwood (Ed.), *English language teaching materials: Theory and practice* (pp.3–30). New York: Cambridge University Press.

Hedin-Dahlström, J., Rosengren-Holmberg, J.P., Legrand, S., Wikman, S., and Nicholls, I.A. (2006). A class II aldolase mimic. *Journal of Organic Chemistry*, 71, 4845–4853.

Hill, S.S., Soppelsa, B.F., and West, G.K. (1982). Teaching ESL students to read and write experimental-research papers. *TESOL Quarterly*, 16, 333–347.

Horn, B., Stoller, F.L., and Robinson, M.S. (2008). Interdisciplinary collaboration: Two heads are better than one. *English Teaching Forum*, 42, 2–13.

Hyland, K. (1998). *Hedging in scientific research articles.* Amsterdam: John Benjamins.

Johnson, K. (2003). *Designing language teaching tasks.* Basingstoke: Palgrave Macmillan.

Kanoksilapatham, B. (2005). Rhetorical structure of biochemistry research articles. *English for Specific Purposes*, 24, 269–292.

Kovac, J. and Sherwood, D.W. (2001). *Writing across the chemistry curriculum: An instructor's handbook.* Upper Saddle River: Pearson Education.

Littlejohn, A. (1998). The analysis of language teaching materials: Inside the Trojan Horse. In B. Tomlinson (Ed.), *Materials development in language teaching* (pp.190–216). New York: Cambridge University Press.

Moriarty, M.F. (1997). *Writing science through critical thinking.* Sudbury: Jones and Barlett.

Paltridge, B. (2006). *Discourse analysis: An introduction.* New York: Continuum.

Robinson, M.S., Stoller, F.L., Costanza-Robinson, M.S., and Jones, J.K. (2008). *Write like a chemist: A guide and resource.* New York: Oxford University Press.

Samuda, V. (2005). Expertise in pedagogic task design. In K. Johnson (Ed.), *Expertise in second language learning and teaching* (pp.230–254). Basingstoke: Palgrave Macmillan.

Stoller, F.L., Horn, B., Grabe, W., and Robinson, M.S. (2005). Creating and validating assessment instruments for a discipline-specific writing course: An interdisciplinary approach. *Journal of Applied Linguistics*, 2, 75–104.

Stoller, F.L., Horn, B., Grabe, W., and Robinson, M.S. (2006). Evaluative review in materials development. *Journal of English for Academic Purposes*, 5, 174–192.

Stoller, F.L. and Robinson, M.S. (2013). Chemistry journal articles: An interdisciplinary approach to move analysis with pedagogical aims. *English for Specific Purposes*, 32, 45–57.

Swales, J.M. (1990). *Genre analysis: English in academic and research settings.* Cambridge: Cambridge University Press.

Swales, J.M. (2004). *Research genres: Exploration and applications.* Cambridge: Cambridge University Press.

Swales, J.M. and Feak, C.B. (2001). Reflections on collaborative practice in EAP materials production. In M. Hewings (Ed.), *Academic writing in context: Implications and applications. Papers in honor of Tony Dudley-Evans* (pp.215–226). Birmingham: University of Birmingham Press.

Swales, J.M. and Feak, C.B. (2009). *Abstracts and the writing of abstracts.* Ann Arbor: University of Michigan Press.

Tardy, C.M. (2009). *Building genre knowledge.* West Lafayette: Parlor Press.

Tomlinson, B. (2003). Materials evaluation. In B. Tomlinson (Ed.), *Developing materials for language teaching* (pp.15–36). London: Continuum.

Wardle, E.A. (2004). Can cross-disciplinary links help us teach 'academic discourse' in FYC? *Across the Disciplines: Interdisciplinary Perspectives on Language, Learning, and Academic Writing, 1.* Retrieved from http://wac.colostate.edu/atd/articles/wardle2004/.

Wi, S. and Frydman, L. (2001). Heteronuclear recoupling in solid-state magic-angle-spinning NMR via overtone irradiation. *Journal of the American Chemical Society*, 123, 10354–10361.

10
Tensions between the Old and the New in EAP Textbook Revision: A Tale of Two Projects

Christine B. Feak and John M. Swales

Summary

At first sight, revising an English for Academic Purposes (EAP) writing textbook seems a simple matter. All that appears to be needed is to update example texts, incorporate recent research findings, and fine-tune the tasks and explanations in the light of practitioner experience. However, it soon becomes clear that little is simple, given multiple stakeholders in the revision process. Instructors who regularly use the textbook have their favorite tasks and topics (with different instructors having different preferences), and so they want these to be retained. Then there are instructors who have become tired, as the years pass, of 'the same old stuff'. Publishers, who are, of course, profit-oriented, want a product that is a marketable new edition of a successful previous edition, rather than a completely new or new-looking book. Finally, the author has expectations since, as most materials writers know, the impetus of revising often turns into an impetus for rethinking, often quite dramatically. In this chapter we discuss these tensions between the old and the new via two case histories: the radical transformation of English in Today's Research World (Swales and Feak, 2000) into a series of small, narrowly focused volumes; and the more conservative preparation of a third edition of Academic Writing for Graduate Students (Swales and Feak, 2012). We explore, in particular, the issues related to addressing the concerns of stakeholders, who may have competing interests. The two projects reveal that at times in the publisher–author– end-user relationships critical asymmetries can arise, which may redirect an author's desired plans. At other times, when the publisher, the author, and the end-user embrace a similar vision for a textbook revision, the relationship may be more flexible, resulting in greater author autonomy in designating the content and matters of style.

Introduction

English for Specific Purposes (ESP) textbooks are many-faceted objects. Authors may describe them as a labor of love or, once completed, as an albatross no longer around the neck. Instructors may consider them to be the foundation of good teaching or a necessary evil (Sheldon, 1988) consisting of 'skillfully marketed rubbish' (Brumfit, 1980: 30, as cited in Sheldon, 1988). For students they may be a vital resource for information or the source of some financial hardship due to their high cost.[1] For publishers they are products that must meet the needs of a market and hopefully turn a profit. Further, some textbook authors are more interested in the royalty income they hope to receive, while others are more interested in positive reviews from reviewers and adopters, while most, we imagine, would hope for both. From a broader academic perspective, textbooks are often viewed as unscholarly endeavors not worthy of much recognition (see Alred and Thelen, 1993), especially by research universities, presumably because, to borrow a term from Clifford Geertz, they are a 'blurred genre' (1983: 20); they are, in fact, 'a miscegenation of scholarly fish and commercial fowl' (Swales, 1995: 5). In an academic environment where faculty value is measured in grants and publications in top-tier journals, textbooks are a result of an activity frequently done on the sidelines. Given their questionable place in academia, they have for some time been the focus of considerable debate.

As early as the 1980s, the value of textbooks in English language teaching (ELT) was being vigorously discussed, most notably by Allwright (1981), who posed the challenging question 'What do we want teaching materials for?', and Swales (1980), who highlighted 'the textbook problem', arguing, *inter alia*, that published and unpublished materials were in competition. Still others described the textbook situation as 'highly disturbing' and 'particularly regrettable' (Ewer and Boys, 1981), specifically because of a mismatch between the language covered and the actual language needed. By the early-1990s the situation had begun to change. Although some, such as Lockett (1999), maintained that published materials were still failing to meet the needs of students, the status and professionalism of ELT/ESP materials writers had improved. This is partly attributable to the establishment of TESOL Special Interest Group (SIG) for Materials Writers (http://www.tesol.org/connect/interest-sections/materials-writers), the publication of *Material*

Writer's Guide, edited by Patricia Byrd (1995), and the burgeoning research on high-priority genres (e.g., research papers). Indeed, today many in the field would argue that over the last 20 years EAP has emerged as a major industry that has, to quote Hyland, 'done extremely well in meeting the challenge involved in helping massive numbers of students to gain control of the peculiar conventions of academic English' (Hyland, 2012: 30).

Despite advances in materials development, reports of disaffection with textbooks continue (see Harwood, 2005, for a more complete review of anti-textbook sentiments), placing an even greater burden on the relatively small number of ESP textbook writers who still manage to find the time, energy, and intellectual commitment to refashion their piles of home-produced materials into specialized ELT textbooks (Hewitt and Regoli, 2010). Within this group an even smaller number will have the opportunity to undertake revisions for a subsequent edition of one of their textbooks.

We are fortunate to be in the position of having revised not one but two EAP textbooks: *Academic Writing for Graduate Students*, originally published in 1994, and *English in Today's Research World* (2000). We have also been fortunate in that reviews of these books have tended to be more positive than negative, although we have not been without a few strong critics. It is also clear from hits on Google Scholar and citations collected by the Web of Science that these books have achieved some resonance in the scholarly literatures devoted to discussions of academic discourses and the acculturation of students to those discourses. While the reasons for our comparative success are rather complex, we believe that in large part it has been due to our efforts to incorporate relevant research findings and to calibrate the input of the many different stakeholders who have a vested interest in the textbooks. These efforts, which cannot always be discerned in the final product, have in some cases entailed a considerable amount of compromise and conciliation and in others much less. No doubt, compromise and conciliation are common elements of all textbook production, yet it is rather uncommon for them to be brought to light so that end-users may have a better understanding of the influences that shape the final product. Therefore our aim here is to offer some of our own insights into the textbook publication process, beginning with a brief overview of some of the behind-the-scenes players involved and concluding with discussion of critical decisions made during the revision of *Academic Writing for Graduate Students (AWG)* and the transformation of *English in Today's Research World (ETRW)*.

The textbook revision process

Revising a textbook is a much more complicated activity than one might imagine. The process varies somewhat from publisher to publisher and author to author; even so, a number of players are involved. The dramatis personae most directly involved include the reviewers, various editors, designers, and, of course, the authors, while lurking in the background is the influence of senior managers, who may well have 'agendas' of various kinds. Of these possible editors, those concerned with our book revision 'team' have been the acquisitions editor (AE), the developmental editor (DE), and the copy editor (CE). These editors are hidden from view, their work perhaps somewhat of a mystery, but together they 'work in very practical ways' (Shipton, 2012: 44) to try and make sure that a high-quality textbook will be produced, and in doing so they bring authors and users together. To achieve their goals, these editors generally are active participants in the creation of a textbook, each with a unique role to play.

The AE assesses the existing or potential market and determines whether a textbook should be revised, an obligation that the authors agree to fulfill upon signing the contract for the first or prior edition. The role of the AE is an interesting one in that he or she is not necessarily the author's advocate. Rather, he or she is more the advocate for the users of the textbook and, even more importantly for a new edition, for the book itself (Hewitt and Regoli, 2010): after all, he or she may be a public advocate of the book at conference book exhibitions. This is not to say that the AE is not supportive of authors, but that the aim of producing a quality product is central and the AE is publication-driven (Shipton, 2012). A strong AE typically knows the scholarship, attends academic conferences, and gathers feedback on the current edition of the textbook from users (typically instructors), both solicited and unsolicited.[2] An even stronger AE can also envision an innovative textbook designed to create demand when previously none had existed or had been identified.

The AE is especially concerned about the timelines, deadlines, and launch dates, prompting authors to stay on schedule. The timeline is critical for a textbook, since it needs to become available in time for major users to adopt it at the beginning of an academic year, which in turn means that review copies need to be available for instructors several months in advance of a term and early copies need to be available for instructors to begin their course planning. If a text appears after book adoptions have been made, a major portion of first-year sales may be lost.

While perhaps less concerned than the AE about sales, the DE has a stake in authors meeting their deadlines because of the level of his or her involvement in a textbook project. Not all textbook projects have a DE, but in the case of the third edition of *AWG* a DE was an influential member of the editorial group,[3] and, as an aside, initially we really did not know what the role of this editor would be. In general, the DE is responsible for a close reading of the textbook to ensure that it has consistency and coherence. For some projects the DE may also engage in major structuring of the overall organization of the book or argue for major restructuring of the writing style. Another task of the DE is to suggest how the content could be improved, typically offering insights from a typical user of the book – either her own, if the DE is also an instructor, or from instructors known to the DE. Given that textbook materials target a broad audience, the evaluative input from others such as a DE can reveal whether the materials are appropriate for 'a range of student groups, teachers, and possibly other stakeholders, including publishers' (Stoller, Horn, Grabe, and Robinson, 2006: 176).[4] Our DE, for instance, suggested topic changes for sample texts that were deemed as potentially problematic for users, a topic that will be taken up later in this chapter. For now, suffice it to say that in our experience the DE, whose input is expected to shape the final product, functions more as an advocate of the publisher and end-user.

The CE is primarily responsible for proofreading the final manuscript to catch problems ranging from missing words to unclear sentences to awkward transitions. It is particularly important in the case of a textbook for the CE to read from the perspective of the end-users/readers – instructors and students, although it is clear that the instructors are the more important target audience. This is reasonable since it is instructors, not students, who make the decisions about which textbooks, if any, will be adopted for their classes (Alred and Thelen, 1993; Swales, 1995). Unlike the DE, the CE, at least from the author's perspective, should avoid making any unnecessary suggestions for change and most of all should resist encroaching on the author's writing style. Even so, the CE has been described as the most contentious member of a textbook project (Hewitt and Regoli, 2010), particularly when authors and the CE have conflicting views regarding the appropriate writing style for the intended audience, an illustration of which will be provided later.

Apart from the editorial staff, the feedback from 'outsiders' must also be recognized as a significant component in the textbook development cycle. As a part of the market research process, this important input can take many forms (e.g., surveys, complete manuscript reviews, focus groups, expert panels, or informal discussion); the means of obtaining feedback will differ among publishers and is tailored to the unique needs of a project as well as the publisher. Although elaborate piloting of materials was once a significant part of the feedback process that involved entire manuscripts, multiple trial locations, and many teachers (Amrani, 2011), today it is typical for a considerable amount of feedback to come from a small number of reviewers who evaluate only a portion of the proposed textbook material and do so based on their indirect experience with it, 'indirect' here meaning that reviewers read and evaluate the material but do not necessarily use it in a class.

Whatever the form, feedback is generally an invaluable contribution to the textbook production process. For the AE, feedback provides insights into the wants and needs of potential users as well as the viability of the book, given the existing market. This same feedback can also be used to settle disagreements between the AE and the authors about content, task sequence, and even layout. Because this input is so valuable, significant efforts are made to find and cultivate relationships with good reviewers, a process that has become somewhat challenging, as will be discussed later.

Having briefly described the importance of feedback and the editorial forces behind the production of a textbook, we now turn to the revision process. Although it may seem unlikely, in fact the first steps in the potential revision process for the third edition of *AWG* began as soon as the second edition was published in 2004, when we started getting feedback about what worked well and what worked less well. Further, we are aware that new research on academic discourse emerges each year, student populations change, new technologies have considerable impact, teachers' needs and desires are always in flux – in short, knowledge and markets change, which means a textbook has an inevitable and built-in obsolescence. Despite our awareness of these compelling reasons to begin looking ahead seriously to the third edition, there was an eight-year lag between the second and third editions. Two major factors were Chris's involvement in an academic speaking book, *Academic Interactions: Communicating on Campus*, and our commitment to revising the less adopted *English in Today's Research World*. Even though successful textbooks in all fields from the major commercial publishers tend to follow a shorter revision cycle – four years seems to be very common, but some publishers insist on shorter cycles (Amrani, 2011) – decisions were made to refocus our energies elsewhere until 2010.

English in Today's Research World: A writing guide (ETRW) and beyond

If *AWG* grew out of the first-year and second-year writing courses developed at Michigan's English Language Institute (ELI) in the late 1980s,[5] *ETRW* was developed from the dissertation writing/writing for publication classes that we began to offer in the early 1990s. Another important input came from the workshops on various aspects of academic and research writing that we were starting to run for the university's graduate school and for various other institutions both nationally and internationally. *ETRW* is a large-format book of 290 pages (excluding the front matter and the index). The volume has eight units, as follows:

Unit 1   Positioning of the research writer
Unit 2   The conference abstract
Unit 3   The conference poster
Unit 4   The literature review
Unit 5   More complex literature reviews
Unit 6   Further steps and stops on the dissertation road
         (Dissertation abstract, acknowledgments, extensive
         methods, unexpected results, the problematic final
         chapter)
Unit 7   Academic communications in support of the research
         process
         (Requests, reminders, apologies, submission letters,
         correspondence with editors)
Unit 8   Academic communications in support of a research
         career
         (CVs, applications, letters of recommendation)

The end of each unit offers various kinds of material under the titles of 'Notes and Comments'; this material comprises sources and references, answers to the less open tasks, reactions from our classroom and workshop participants (graduate students and visiting scholars at our own university as well as at other universities in the US and elsewhere), and the occasional teaching suggestion.

The book was published in 2000, received good reviews, and has had steady, if not substantial, sales for several years – far fewer than *AWG* but comparable to another relatively successful volume in the University of Michigan Press English for Academic and Professional Purposes series, Susan Reinhart's *Giving Academic Presentations* (2002). The lower level of sales compared with *AWG* was fully anticipated, as fewer institutions were in a position to offer such advanced courses and fewer students were likely to feel the need to take them. What we did not anticipate was the feedback from adopters collected by the AE after the book had been out for several years. Essentially this was that the book was 'indigestible' and 'contained too many different elements', such as the juxtaposition of conference posters and literature reviews (LRs). In response, after considering input from us and other *ETRW* users, the AE concluded that the solution to these problems would lie in breaking the volume up into a series of mini-volumes. This possibility met with favorable responses from trusted EAP colleagues elsewhere from whom we and the AE had solicited input and without whose support we might have abandoned any thoughts of a revision. With nothing more than this verbal support we were committed to this exciting and innovative idea, signed a contract, and began immediately to start thinking of ways and means of getting this done.

Our process here certainly did not align with the industry norm of conducting market research that often involves triangulation – multiple approaches to assessing the materials – such as piloting, reviews, focus groups, questionnaires, or expert panels (for a more complete discussion of industry norms, see Amrani, 2011). Instead, we relied on three forms of feedback. The first was discussions with our own small circle of trusted colleagues who have extensive EAP teaching experience and who also, in some cases, make scholarly contributions to the EAP literature. The second form was direct discussion with the AE, who has a postgraduate degree in Teaching English as a Second Language, extensive knowledge of the field, and a demonstrated track record of supporting textbook innovation. The third source of input was our AE's compilation of ideas from *her* trusted circle of EAP instructors at universities throughout the US. This latter group was directly asked by the AE (either in person at conferences or via e-mail) to comment on the proposed changes to *ETRW*. To date we have been quite satisfied with this process, particularly with regard to the input we receive via the AE, who serves as the intermediary and can better encourage candid responses. Whether or not we would be equally satisfied with a more rigorous approach to feedback is, of course, unclear. But we can say that so far the process has been effective for the *ETRW* project.

When we started work on this project in 2007, we had much more class and workshop material than in 1999, and the amount of published research on academic genres had dramatically increased in the new century. The content of *ETRW* (as given above) immediately suggested two possibilities: a mini-volume on abstracts, expanding Unit 2 and the first part of Unit 6, and a mini-volume on literature reviews, developing out of Units 4 and 5. John became the lead author of the first and Chris of the second. We also recruited Vera Irwin, a doctoral student in linguistics, as a part-time research assistant, using some money that John had left over in a research account. Meanwhile, the AE had made it clear that the way forward would be to have the suggested task responses and teaching suggestions placed in an online commentary,[6] and so we entrusted Vera to work through our draft activities and provide her own set of preferred answers, even if at times they were at odds with our own. In this way John, in particular, thought that adding a third voice, and particularly that of a graduate student, would achieve a more interesting three-way commentary, the benefits of which, we thought, would be clear to experienced instructors, even if it meant that a definitive answer could not always be given. Since these were essentially brand new textbooks, at the onset of the reconfiguration of *ETRW* the project team (the AE, the DE, and us) had few preconceived notions of what the volumes would look like, other than that they would be narrowly focused and short. This meant that we had a considerable amount of influence over the final product.

Abstracts and the writing of abstracts (2009) and Telling a Research Story: Writing a literature review (2009)

The first of the mini-volumes had four main sections: research article abstracts, abstracts for short communications, conference abstracts, and dissertation abstracts. For the second of these sections we found space for a short article (which had long been a favorite of ours and reflected the need to have a bit of fun in class) from the Christmas issue of the *British Medical Journal* entitled 'Why Do Old Men Have Big Ears?' In 90 pages we managed to cram in almost 40 tasks, as well as retaining a couple of the cartoons about academic writing originally in *ETRW*, yet another attempt at revealing some of the oddities and absurdities of the academic world. A discussion of the details of our materials development procedures can be found in Feak and Swales (2010).

Early in the creation of the mini-volumes we recognized that the focus on a closely related set of genres needed some wider contextualization. After all, abstracts are always the abstracts of something else, and literature reviews are typically embedded in some wider textual context. So this volume introduced one of the few consistent elements in the volumes, namely a figure depicting an Academic Genre Network that includes the academic written genres that are open or accessed with minimal effort (research papers, for instance) and those that are somewhat hidden or less easily accessed (for example, manuscript reviews).

The literature review volume is a little longer, at just under 100 pages. Again the main sections in turn dealt with some general orientations, getting started on a LR, drafting and redrafting, taking a stance toward the literature, and using your own words. Chris came up with the clever *Telling a Research Story* participial main title, and we have used the same syntactic structure in the further volumes that have so far appeared. For the drafting and redrafting section we constructed a complicated case study of an imaginary student called Joyce (although at least some users think the story of Joyce is true), the rationale for which is discussed in Swales (2009). The volume closes with a set of criteria for evaluating a LR derived from a paper by Boote and Beile (2005), plus a checklist, as suggested by Dr Jane Freeman of the University of Toronto, who was a frequent user of *ETRW*.

From our perspective the whole process of moving from origination to publication of these two volumes went smoothly; indeed, the DE seemed to have come on board rather late, either as one of the anonymous reviewers or channeling his or her comments through the AE. The CE had little to say about style, instead focusing on the customary careful proofreading to save us from any embarrassment.

Navigating Academia and *Creating Contexts*

When, some time later, we began to work on the next two volumes, the AE provided us with some unexpected feedback. She said that her main adopters – and prime sources of feedback – had little interest in Vera's input. As she stated, 'they aren't interested in what a graduate student might think; they only want to know what Swales and Feak have to say.' Because of this dissatisfaction, we felt compelled to diminish the role of Vera, who had in any case obtained her PhD by this time and was ready to move on in other directions; however, her last contribution was to come up with the title to the third volume. John had been working with titles such as 'Writing Academic Correspondence', which the AE questioned and which did not resonate with Chris. Vera's excellent solution was 'Navigating Academia', which furthermore retained the catchy participial structure that Chris had pioneered.

Despite the major change that eliminated Vera's voice, the content of the next two volumes, *Creating Contexts* and *Navigating Academia*, remained largely in our hands. From our perspective the primary input from the AE consisted of nudging us to meet submission deadlines, sharing feedback solicited from trusted EAP instructors, and ensuring that the texts were carefully designed. We again felt no pressure to adjust content. The previous two volumes had been favorably received, indicating that we were providing much-needed materials consistent with our approach to the better-known *AWG*. We also had the freedom to produce volumes that differed from each other in small but important ways. The first two volumes, for instance, have cartoons, while the others do not. One volume has a photograph; no two volumes have the same number of tasks or page numbers. Although small, these differences would not have been possible with a major textbook publisher, which would have likely insisted on identical layouts[7] and, even more importantly, with an editorial team that had an established product to safeguard.

Academic writing for graduate students

Fast forward now to early 2011. Although sales were still strong, the Director of University of Michigan Press was insisting that the AE produce a third edition of *AWG*[8] since he believed that successful textbooks should have new editions every five years at the outside. Pressure was also coming from users of the second edition, who were ready for change. In turn, we were feeling quite obligated to finish since the deadline for submitting the *AWG* manuscript had come and gone. Discussions focused on the *AWG* revision were intermittent from 2004 to 2010, and throughout the AE stressed that we would not be free to revise as extensively as we might wish. The primary reason given was that users ('users' here meaning instructors and not students) expect some change, but not drastic change, even if we (as authors) could have envisioned a rather different type of book. It was pointed out to us that a dramatically revised book might alienate instructors who had grown comfortable with the previous edition, which, in turn, would negatively impact sales. This concern, however, seemed antithetical to the other expressed need for fresh material. Thus at the onset of the revision project important challenges we faced included: creating new material while maintaining the essence of the old; finding a balance between creativity and familiarity; and working within three non-negotiable aspects of the previous editions, namely the number, order, and focus of each chapter (for instance, we might have wished to combine Unit 5, on summary writing, with Unit 6, on critiques, thus leaving space for some new chapter).

Given our more recent experience with the *ETRW* revision, we had become accustomed to shaping our texts 'our way', and so we had to come to terms with the fact this would not be possible with *AWG* since it was no longer 'ours', a phenomenon that our AE informs us is inevitable with a successful textbook. To clarify how this affected the final manuscript, in this next section we describe some important areas of contention.

Length of text

One matter of debate turned out to be the length of the new edition. Readers may recall that the first edition was roughly 250 pages and the second came in at around 330. John, in particular, did not want to see more than 10–15 per cent growth in the amount of material, despite the need for substantial updating and revision. He felt the book should show a fairly clear and fairly fast trajectory through the eight units. Any greater increase due to added texts and tasks, he believed, would cause the book to look rather more like a loose anthology. Nor did he want to be put in the position of having to produce a lot of extra material and then be told that the manuscript was seriously over the page budget. Such extensive revising would also potentially result in a text with more than the typical 25–33 per cent undergoing revision, a target proposed by Gundersen (1995). On this particular issue Chris was not so concerned, thinking that giving instructors and independent student users more, and in some cases better, choices could be accommodated. She was more focused on reviewing the second-edition tasks and texts that had been highlighted as instructor favorites (for example, the airbag text revision in Unit 2 and the test score discrepancy task in Unit 4) and those that were typically ignored. In some cases elements that one user liked and another disliked were one and the same (for example, the Turkish earthquake text and related tasks in Unit 1).

The AE's position, however, was very different from John's. Given her communications with instructors from large and from small EAP programs, her preference was for a larger volume that would cater to an increasingly diverse audience that now included both undergraduates and graduates, both native and non-native English speakers, a wider range of disciplinary specialties, and more customers outside the US and Canada. Further, she stressed on several occasions that we authors should not worry about length, but just get the job done as soon as possible. The DE only indirectly revealed her perspective on length to us, in the sense that she offered no suggestions for deleting material in order to shorten the manuscript. Despite differences in perspective,

as we proceeded to revise the units, the inexorable expansionist ten-
dencies of textbook revision took hold, and more material was added
than deleted. When we were finished and the AE had done her calculations about page length, it did turn out that we were somewhat over
the maximum length after all. In order to lose a few pages, we reduced
the length of the appendix on article usage, a fairly easy decision that
we had proposed at the start of the revision process (we understood that
this section was not much used). Another section proposed for deletion
was the index. This came as a surprise, since the AE had requested a more
extensive index than in the second edition because she and others found
that certain features in the main text had not been indexed. Given the
challenges of producing an index as well as everything else in a short
period of time, we had earlier decided that we could not really hope
to do a decent index ourselves, so a former doctoral student of John's,
Margaret Luebs-Goedeke (as she now is), who had in fact compiled the
index to the first edition in 1994, was contracted to produce a comprehensive version. This decision, as well as our own frequent use of the
index in the earlier edition, led us to argue for retaining the index and to
counter-propose that we revise or delete sections from other chapters, a
proposal in which the AE was not particularly interested and which thus
was left unaddressed until the final formatting had been done. In the
end, fortunately, when the final page-accounting had been completed,
the index was retained – albeit in a less desirable four highly packed
pages. When printed, our compromises resulted in a third edition consisting of 418 pages, considerably longer than John wanted, but to the
satisfaction of the editors and, we hope, end-users.

Disciplinary variety: The case of specific-general texts

Contrary to our expectations, we were surprised to learn from our AE
that major adopters had reported the desire for more material directed
at students of engineering, who often constituted large proportions
of course enrollees. For similar reasons, other instructors were more
interested in other areas such as biomedicine. Despite our reluctance
to comply, the AE was quite committed to this change since sales
were at stake. Further, we were able to balance the addition of some
more discipline-specific material by including some material focused
on two non-science areas. John, in particular, wanted to offer at least
something, on occasion, for students and scholars in the humanities.
An important influence on our thinking about this was the work being
done in Italy on history discourse, particularly by Marina Bondi (see,
for example, Bondi, 2007; Silver and Bondi, 2004). Their analyses of the

openings to a large number of history articles offered a reversed scenario to the standard top-down structure as exemplified by the Create A Research Space (CARS) model (Swales and Feak, 2004). Instead, scholarly historians often started out with a historical phenomenon (such as a single event or individual pronouncement), which they then would gradually place in increasingly wide-ranging and interpretive contexts. Further, John had been noticing a similar rhetorical strategy in art history essays. As Bondi (2007) suggests, these types of opening offer the reader 'immediate contact with the object of study' (p. 71). So we decided to add a humanities-focused section at the end of Unit 2, dealing with specific-to-general (S-G) texts, even if we recognized that S-G structures could be found in other genres and disciplines, including medical case reports and legal notes, and in those scientific papers that began with some striking statistics.

Eventually, we finished with seven pages devoted to the topic: a two-page introduction including a schematic diagram, followed by a textual illustration. Following this there were three S-G tasks, the first being a treatment of a statuette, the second a history piece about Germany after World War II, and the third a secret meeting that was a key element in the attempts to unify Italy in the second half of the 19th century. The final task, Task 23, ends the unit by offering users the choice of writing either a general-specific (G-S) or an S-G text describing how some line of research in their field came to be abandoned (an example would be cold fusion). In this way we hoped to place the S-G work within the wider and more widely adopted G-S framework.

John was the primary author of the first and third task in this section, and Chris created the other two. John had inherited the c. 1920 bronze and ivory statuette by Preiss from his grandmother, so he had a professional photographer take a photograph to serve as an illustration and wrote a four-paragraph description, starting with the details of the statue, then dealing with its creator, following with a summary of what is known about these Art Deco figures, and finally discussing what the statue tells us about middle-class European women of its period. Chris's text starts with 'The short story for the year 1949 in Günter Grass's "My Century" relates an encounter at a conference between [...]'. It then tells the story of the woman the narrator met at the conference and in the second paragraph generalizes from this. The third text in paragraph one describes the secret meeting between Cavour and Emperor Napoleon III; the second is left blank for the user to construct from the easily available Internet resources; the third summarizes Cavour's place in modern Italian history.

At the first proof stage (that is, rather late in the publication timeline), the DE expressed some serious doubts about this section. She offered some useful textual emendations to the first text, which we largely accepted, but then argued that the description of the statuettes stating that they were 'sometimes nude' should be deleted because it could be embarrassing to women from 'traditional cultures'. We did not, however, accept this suggested deletion; first, it is true that most of them are nude or largely unclothed; second, the illustrated figure was not provocative or offensive in any way (she is wearing clothes); and third, we did not think that graduate students were likely to be offended by this comment. As for the German text, she objected to its opening sentence as being too long and hard to process, but we did not agree with this criticism and so kept it, although we did accept some of the other clarifications she offered. Her comments on the third text opened as follows:

> Task 22-The Meeting at Plombières. This is my 'no' vote. You have three European cultural texts in a row. It's too much. This one is so specific and dull that it can't sustain interest.

Even if we could see the point about having three European texts in a row, the European focus seemed rather trivial in comparison with other matters such as the index, not to mention that there was just not enough time to search for a suitable episode from a different culture and then shape it into an effective text and task. Further, we did not think that the Meeting at Plombières was that obscure, as can be seen from the numerous web entries about it. But most crucially, we thought that constructing an appropriate middle paragraph using web resources, a task aided by some hints we provided, was a major innovation and addition to our task typology and was worth keeping for that very reason alone. And we also knew that instructors do not use every task in the book and were free to skip this. We did note for future reference, however, the DE's observation that a medical case history would also work as an S-G text, even if our experience of reading recent medical case studies suggests that today they have become much more like mini-research articles and so have an increasingly G-S orientation.

On cross-cultural issues

As intimated by the previous section, the DE was quite concerned about the cultural background of students who would be using the textbook, which we, of course, appreciated. One instance where this resulted in a significant change is in Unit 1 (An Approach to Academic Writing). In the section on organization Chris had found a problem-solution text focusing on Macao. The problem highlighted was the housing shortage caused by the tremendous growth in the number of workers needed to sustain the gambling industry. The DE stated that any mention of gambling could offend students and instructors from cultures in which this activity is taboo. Unlike our response to the comment about nudity in relation to the S-G text in Unit 2, we deferred here for two reasons. First, Chris fortunately had a suitable alternative that she had used in some of her classes and could easily be swapped in with some minor editing. Second, the new text on Ghana was in fact a better choice since no country in sub-Saharan Africa had been featured in any of our other textbooks. As demonstrated by the Macao example, sensitivities about cultural issues have to be recognized in writing a textbook for an international audience, and in the end we conceded that the perspective of the DE on this matter certainly was one that was protective of the book and more importantly of the students and instructors.

A global concern – style issues

After we had submitted a draft of the manuscript, we received a long response from the AE, probably in consultation with the DE and the CE, that came at the copy-editing stage. Most of the key opening paragraph is repeated here.

There is one place where we have made small changes from 'your voice' based on customer feedback, but tried to maintain a balance throughout the manuscript as a whole. We have had customers tell us that they don't like the 'over-use' (their word) of phrasal verbs in the student book (text and direction lines).[9] Their reasoning is that they *want* to point to *AWG* as a model for students for good writing, and many of them would not WANT their students to use many of the phrasal verbs in the book in their writing because many of them don't sound formal/academic enough. We do agree that the book might be stronger with fewer phrasal verbs. So, if you look at the book as a whole, we have tried to maintain a balance. We did not expunge *all* phrasal verbs, but we did change many, especially in the beginning of the book. We (like many educational publishers) also generally like to avoid 'write down', preferring the stronger 'write' or 'list'. So, while more phrasal verbs might make the writing more casual, we do think a strong case has been made for why the book should include fewer overall. Again, we have not deleted all of them –

just aimed for more of a balance – and you might see more changes in the first half of the manuscript than in the later half (on purpose). If you feel this approach is a problem, let's talk about this *before* you return the copyedited ms. We might add that these same customers very much enjoy the casual tone in the commentary – it makes them feel like your colleagues – so we have not edited the Commentary in this way.

(minor editing; original emphases)

As the reader can see, this is a highly articulate and well-modulated argument that well represents the publisher's viewpoint – indeed, it is almost a plea for compassionate understanding. On the other hand, from the viewpoint of genre analysts, the arguments of the 'customers' make little sense. After all, there is compelling evidence that textbooks and academic genres such as journal articles or scholarly monographs have very different communicative purposes, readerships, and writing styles. If those 'customers' really wanted a textbook that reflected formal academic style, then we would also need to see the disappearance of all the second-person pronouns and most of the (non-rhetorical) questions and imperatives, especially ones such as *notice*, which is very common in *AWG* bur very rare in journal articles (Swales, Ahmad, Chang, Chavez, Dressen, and Seymour, 1998).

So we compromised. We accepted most of the edits, but retained some of our original phrasal verbs, such as occasional uses of *look at, write up,* and *write down.* When we asked long-time ELI lecturer and frequent user of *AWG* Melinda Matice for her views on our 'casual style' in our task-directed instructions, she commented that 'I really like it; it is like having another voice in the classroom'. However, according to the AE, this would seem to be a minority view; as a result, this seemed to be a case where the views 'out there' should have priority over what we came to see might be viewed as a narrow, scholarly perspective.

Objections to some content other than culture

Here we discuss two further areas of concern and potential disagreement highlighted by the AE. The first concerned Google Scholar.

We have recommended that the Google Scholar content be de-emphasized. We think that you only need to introduce people to it once (even if the book is not used in order). We 'get' that it's a cool resource, but think it's being over-emphasized and overused; not everyone thinks this is the best place to get data.

In fact, Google Scholar is referred to on nine pages (out of over 400). We do not think that this is excessive, given that this is a resource available – and freely and easily available – to anyone with Internet access. Further, Google Scholar is by far the largest database for investigations into academic discourse. Although Google itself may not always be 'the best place' to get certain kinds of data, Google Scholar is an outstanding source for *linguistic* data. So we held our ground on this one.

The second concern was about the inclusion of positive and negative extracts from reviews of the second edition of *AWG*. We thought, in fact, that this was a pretty nifty idea, especially as we could ask users of the book whether they thought the comments were reasonable or unreasonable. The opening extract provoked particularly strong opposition: 'Students who already have a good enough command of the written language often lack the time and patience to work systematically through a textbook of this kind' (Breeze, 2005: 2). It turned out, however, that the AE and DE objected not so much to the content as to the fact that the review was taken from the online journal *TESL-EJ*, where they said that the vast majority of reviewers were 'graduate students who do not know enough about teaching or materials in general to be criticizing them'. In fact, the author of the review, Ruth Breeze, is a well-regarded and experienced EAP practitioner working in a Spanish university. So we kept this one, but compromised by adding a few more positive extracts to alleviate the editors' concerns that we did not too obviously shoot ourselves in the foot.

Lessons learned

So what are the lessons learned? It has become more apparent to us that the concept of audience is more complex than we had imagined when directed at EAP textbooks. Perhaps the concept needs to be broken into two: the immediate audience (editors and external reviewers, who together make the major decisions) and the more remote audience (the end-users, namely students and instructors). While our intended audience has always been teachers, students, and junior scholars, we have inevitably become more sensitive to editorial wishes, particularly those of the AE, who may be taking some risk when committing to a new textbook but is likely to be cautiously confident and thus more conservative in decision-making in the case of an established one. After all, the AE perhaps has much more on the line than all other stakeholders in the production of a textbook. Further, this is her full-time professional job, while the DE and the EAP authors receive their salaries for doing other things.

In the case of a new textbook, authors may choose from a range of reasonable topics that could potentially be included in the work. They are free to experiment and to shape the book as they deem appropriate. In the case of a second edition, perhaps, but definitely so in a third edition, the textbook is no longer fully within the purview of the authors. Rather, like it or not, at this point it has become a product that the authors no longer 'own' in the same way they did in the first edition. And as such, significant changes to that product must be undertaken with care. This is not to say that there is no sense of ownership, but rather that there is an additional aspect of stewardship that requires us to consider the needs and expectations of others, a responsibility that is sometimes uneasily shared by the major actors in the revision process. Coming to this conclusion has required us to have confidence that the editorial process is one in which we are all partners working toward the same goals. This can only be possible through mutual trust – trust by the editors in our professionalism and in our ability to deliver the goods, so to speak, and trust on the part of the authors in the vision, intelligence, and skill of the editors.

Acknowledgement

We would like to thank Kelly Sippell, our expert AE at the University of Michigan Press, for her many years of support. She knows all too well our vulnerabilities, shortcomings, and eccentricities, and has dealt with them with sensitivity and integrity.

Notes

1. In some fields, such as engineering, a single textbook may cost hundreds of dollars in the US.
2. Space does not permit a discussion of the range of feedback provided, but in our experience over the years it seems that, the more successful the book, the more instructors want that book to be tailored to their individual needs, an expectation that is impossible to meet.
3. While a DE was involved in all of the new *ETRW* volumes published before the third edition of *AWG*, the DE was a major factor only for the third edition of *AWG*. As was typical of the publisher's practices at the time, for the first and second editions of *AWG* there was no DE; the AE played a minor role and the most influential player was the CE, whose efforts were aimed at editing the book as a scholarly work as opposed to a textbook for students. We became aware of a DE's involvement in the *ETRW* projects only while writing this chapter!
4. The DE is generally very familiar with the market niche of the publisher and can offer input on whether a particular textbook fits with a particular line of textbooks. For instance, the University of Michigan Press series in English

for Academic and Professional Purposes would not include a textbook targeting students whose interest in learning English is neither academic nor professional.

5. For more detail see the introductions of any of the editions of *AWG*, but particularly the first.

6. The decision to have an online commentary was a cost-saving measure. According to our AE, most published teacher's guides and answer keys are unprofitable. Regardless, we found the online option attractive because we can quickly make changes or add new material as needed.

7. Consider, for instance, how the volumes in a textbook series typically have the same number of chapters, roughly the same length, and the same layout.

8. *AWG* is at present the best-selling book at the University of Michigan Press in terms of units. As such it is quite an important publication, although this is something that the Press, as a publisher of scholarly books, does not seem to publicize widely. Interestingly, our contract, like most textbook contracts, gives the publisher the right to find new authors if the original authors are unwilling or unable to revise.

9. The reference here is to our discussion of topics in the student book and the instructions for the tasks. In short, everything that we wrote except for a small number of sample texts.

References

Allwright, R.L. (1981). What do we want teaching materials for? *ELT Journal*, 36, 5–18.

Alred, G.J. and Thelen, E.A. (1993). Are textbooks contributions to scholarship? *College Composition and Communication*, 44, 466–477.

Amrani, F. (2011). The process of evaluation: A publisher's view. In B. Tomlinson (Ed.), *Materials development in language teaching* (2nd ed., pp.267–295). Cambridge: Cambridge University Press.

Bondi, M. (2007). Language and discipline perspectives on academic discourse. In K. Fløttum (Ed.), *Authority and expert voices in the discourse of history* (pp.66–88). Newcastle: Cambridge Scholars Publishing.

Boote, D.N. and Beile, P. (2005). Scholars before researchers: On the centrality of the dissertation literature review in research preparation. *Educational Researcher*, 34, 3–15.

Breeze, R. (2005). Review of *academic writing for graduate students: Essential tasks and skills, second edition*. *TESL-EJ*, 8, 1–2. Retrieved from http://www.tesl-ej.org/wordpress/issues/volume8/ej32/ej32r1/?wscr

Brumfit, C.J. (1980). Seven last slogans. *Modern English Teacher*, 7, 30–31.

Byrd, P. (1995). *Material writer's guide*. Boston: Heinle and Heinle.

Ewer, J.R. and Boys, O. (1981). The EST textbook situation: An enquiry. *The ESP Journal*, 1(2), 87–105.

Feak, C.B. and Swales, J.M. (2010). From text to task: Putting research on abstracts to work. In M.F. Ruiz-Garrido, J.C. Palmer-Silveira and I. Fortanet-Gómez (Eds.), *English for professional and academic purposes* (pp.167–180). Amsterdam: Rodopi.

Geertz, C. (1983). *Local knowledge: Further essays in interpretive anthropology*. New York: Basic Books.

Gundersen, E. (1995). Writing, editing, and publishing new editions. In P. Byrd (Ed.), *Material writer's guide* (pp.215–225). New York: Heinle and Heinle.

Harwood, N. (2005). What do we want EAP teaching materials for? *Journal of English for Academic Purposes*, 4, 149–161.

Hewitt, J.D. and Regoli, R.M. (2010). Negotiating roles and relationships. *Journal of Scholarly Publishing*, 41, 325–339.

Hyland, K. (2012). 'The past is the future with lights on': Reflections on AELFE's 20th birthday. *Ibérica*, 24, 29–42.

Lockett, A. (1999). From the general to the specific: What the EAP tutor should know about academic discourse. In H. Bool and P. Luford (Eds.), *Academic standards and expectations: The role of EAP* (pp.49–58). Nottingham: Nottingham University Press.

Reinhart, S.M. (2002). *Giving academic presentations*. Ann Arbor: University of Michigan Press.

Sheldon, L.E. (1988). Evaluating ELT textbooks and materials. *ELT Journal*, 42, 237–246.

Shipton, R. (2012). The mysterious relationship: Authors and their editors. In D. Cullen (Ed.), *Editors, scholars, and the social text* (pp.44–66). Toronto: University of Toronto Press.

Silver, M. and Bondi, M. (2004). Weaving voices: A study of article openings in historical discourse. In G.D.L. Camiciotti (Ed.), *Academic discourse: New insights into evaluation* (pp.141–160). Frankfurt am Main: Peter Lang.

Stoller, F.L., Horn, B., Grabe, W., and Robinson, M.S. (2006). Evaluative review in materials development. *Journal of English for Academic Purposes*, 5, 174–192.

Swales, J.M. (1980). ESP: The textbook problem. *The ESP Journal*, 1, 11–23.

Swales, J.M. (1995). The role of the textbook in EAP writing research. *English for Specific Purposes*, 14, 3–18.

Swales, J.M. (2009). When there is no perfect text: Approaches to the EAP practitioner's dilemma. *Journal of English for Academic Purposes*, 8, 5–13.

Swales, J.M., Ahmad, U.K., Chang, Y.-Y., Chavez, D., Dressen, D.F., and Seymour, R. (1998). Consider this: The role of imperatives in scholarly writing. *Applied Linguistics*, 19, 97–121.

Swales, J.M. and Feak, C.B. (2000). *English in today's research world*. Ann Arbor: University of Michigan Press.

Swales, J.M. and Feak, C.B. (2004). *Academic writing for graduate students: Essential tasks and skills* (2nd ed.). Ann Arbor: University of Michigan Press.

Swales, J.M. and Feak, C.B. (2012). *Academic writing for graduate students: Essential tasks and skills* (3rd ed.). Ann Arbor: University of Michigan Press.

11
Chaosmos: Spontaneity and Order in the Materials Design Process
Jill Hadfield

Summary

This chapter examines the process of writing activities for Motivating Learning (Hadfield and Dörnyei, 2013) in the Research and Resources in Language Teaching series, which aims to take new insights from research and translate them directly into practice, in the form of resource materials for teachers. It examines my materials-writing process in relation to the existing literature on materials creation – in particular, in relation to other materials writers' self-reports on their processes and the comments made on these by theorists – but it also situates the discussion within the critical landscape of debate on the creative process in general, across various disciplines.

In comparing my own and other writers' accounts of their creative processes with theorists' critiques of the process, two oppositions are defined: that between the circuitous and recursive process described by the writers and various attempts to impose a more linear, orderly progression on the design process, and that between the apparently ad hoc spontaneous and intuitive process the writers describe and the call for design to be based on principled frameworks. It concludes that textbook writing is a highly recursive and circuitous activity which cannot be reduced to a linear progression through checklists of concerns, but which demands flexibility and responsiveness to particular activities and contexts. Its spontaneity and ad hoc nature, however, does not imply a lack of principles; rather, materials writers have a 'tacit' framework of principles underlying their design decisions which can be called into play at any moment, depending on the demands of the task.

Introduction

In an earlier book Nigel Harwood (2010) identifies the need for more research on the process of materials design, citing Venezky (1992), who similarly finds that 'we have no case studies on the design of new textbook series that would allow insights into the origins of textbook innovations or the decision-making processes that lead to the retention or rejection of specific content or design' (p.444). Harwood concludes that 'What is needed initially, then, are ethnographies of materials production [...] in order to get an insight into the factors that shape the eventual form of the materials' (p.18). In this chapter I will first review two accounts that do exist of the materials creation process in the EFL field, then situate these in the landscape of critical debate on the creative process in general across other disciplines, and then, in the light of the insights and arguments from these two fields, critically examine my own process of materials creation in the writing of teachers' resource materials for *Motivating Learning*.

The writing process

Various frameworks that have been put forward to describe the process of materials creation suggest a staged and orderly process. Two relevant chapters can be found in the volume edited by Hidalgo, Hall, and Jacobs (1995). Rajan (1995), for example, suggests a five-stage procedure: assessing needs, writing objectives, deciding on course components and designing a scope and sequence, writing the design document, and writing the materials. Penaflorida's (1995) list in the same volume is very similar: analyse needs, decide on objectives, design lesson format, gather, select and grade materials, write materials, and Jolly and Bolitho (1998) outline a six-stage procedure, beginning again with needs analysis and continuing through exploration of necessary skills and language, finding ideas, finding texts and contexts, finding exercises, and physical production of materials. What these frameworks have in common, however, is that they leave an unexplained mystery at the heart of the writing process. The actual writing process in the frameworks outlined above – 'write materials', 'find ideas', or 'find exercises' – offers little guidance as to how materials are to be written or how ideas are to be found.

In contrast, accounts from writers on how they write materials offer more detail but reveal a process that is far from orderly. Two main analyses of the materials-writing process are to be found in the chapter by Philip Prowse (2011) in *Materials Development in Language Teaching*, which contains self-reports by various professional materials writers with analysis by Prowse, and in Keith Johnson's book *Designing Language Teaching Tasks* (2003), which contains a comparison of the approaches used by inexperienced and experienced materials writers in the creation of language teaching tasks. The processes described by writers in the Prowse chapter are personal and idiosyncratic, varying from very precise specifications about suitable times, conditions, and locations for writing ('materials writing mood – engendered by peace, light, etc.', p.158), to general descriptions of the process: 'My ideas and intentions boil inside me for a long time [...] then at some point I feel I can start writing. Usually after this moment everything pours out in a gulp' (p.157). The writers in this chapter tend to stress the somewhat mysterious and haphazard way ideas suddenly arrive – 'Ideas come to you at any time' (p.152), 'the best materials are written in "trances"' (p.157) – and stress the role of classroom experience and intuition about what will work well: 'I draw heavily on my own experience. I might look through what other people have done, but I basically rely on my own intuition' (p.158).

These accounts led Philip Prowse to conclude that 'most of the writers quoted here appear to rely heavily on their own intuitions' (p.158) and Tomlinson (2003), commenting on this study, to find that many writers 'describe processes which are ad hoc and spontaneous and which rely on an intuitive feel for activities which are likely to "work" [...] they say very little about any principles of learning and teaching or about any frameworks which they use to facilitate coherence and consistency' (p.107). He adds: 'This is largely true also of some of the writers talking about writing in Hidalgo et al (1995), [and] of some of the writers describing their writing processes in Tomlinson (1998)' (p.107).

Johnson's study (2003), which compares the way in which eight experienced designers and eight inexperienced designers approach the same design brief, contains some significant differences from the writers' emphasis in the Prowse study, though Tomlinson (2012) finds that, in common with Prowse's writers, there is 'no explicit reference [...] to theory-driven principles' (p.153). But the writers place less emphasis on the 'inspirational', 'intuitive', and 'creative' aspect of materials writing – that is, the initial idea creation stage – though some of them do indeed refer to this stage, 'a typical stage [...] where the light bulb goes on and you have this world-shattering idea' (p.167). However, they tend to find this stage painful rather than joyful – '[this] stage is actually quite painful – the business of floating round in a void trying to get something that'll work' (p.167) – and note that inspiration is not necessarily always to be trusted: 'there's a rather painful bit where you realise that for some perfectly simple reason it will never work' (p.167). Instead, the emphasis of the study is firmly on the patient arguing out, analysing, and rationalizing aspects of the writing process rather than sudden illumination or creative fertility. Johnson finds that among the characteristics of expert designers is a tendency to spend long periods of time analysing task demands and issues involved and exploring possibilities for task design, coming up with several different alternatives and analysing the potential of each before settling on one, often working an idea out in great detail, before perhaps abandoning it in favour of a better alternative. He calls these a tendency to 'complexify' and 'easy abandonment capacity'. Samuda (2005), summing up, finds that, though not subscribing to this view herself, materials design has often been seen, in contrast to Johnson's findings, as an 'atheoretical activity' and goes on to suggest that

> the process of task design is certainly not a matter of working through the development of a task from beginning to end in a linear fashion, nor does it entail orderly progressions through checklists of guiding principles. Task design is a complex, highly recursive and often messy process, requiring the designer to hold in mind a vast range of task variables relating to the design-in-process. (p.243)

In other words, she suggests that task design is not (cannot be?) a matter of working in orderly steps through a set of principles, guidelines, or frameworks, but entails its own procedures and processes, which require a considerable amount of expertise and knowledge.

These accounts of the materials-writing process set up a tension between the 'messy', 'recursive', 'spontaneous', 'ad hoc', 'intuitive', and possibly 'atheoretical' process that the writers describe, and a process which is linear, involving orderly progression through checklists, governed by a system of frameworks and principles, which appears to be advocated by theorists. I would suggest that these polarities in fact conflate two oppositions: the opposition between recursive and messy processes and 'orderly', 'linear' progression – in other words, *how* the process unfurls – and the opposition between spontaneous, intuitive, *ad hoc*, atheoretical design decisions and design decisions based on frameworks and principles, which ensure coherence and consistency – that is, *what* informs the process. In this chapter I propose to investigate these two tensions further, in relation, on the theoretical level, to multi-disciplinary models of creativity and, on the practical level, to my own experience of materials creation.

Two models of creativity

The accounts by writers in the Prowse and Johnson studies in fact closely resemble numerous reports of the creative process described across disciplines as varied as mathematics, design, science, art, and literature and developed into models of creativity variously by psychologists, philosophers, and literary theorists, all of whom attempt to uncover or explain the mystery of the creative process. I would argue that to better understand the materials creation process, commentary should be situated within this complex and wide-ranging debate, as well as within the narrower debate in our own discipline.

Two influential models are Wallas' four-stage model and the so-called Darwinian models of creativity, built on the theories of Campbell (1960), who saw the creative process as mirroring the process of natural selection. Wallas (1926) identifies a four-part process in creativity: preparation, a lengthy and often laborious stage when the problem is tackled from many different angles; incubation, a fallow period where not much seems to be happening – often after the preparation stage has resulted in an impasse; illumination, a sudden flash of insight or breakthrough; and finally verification, the finalization stage, where ideas arrived at in the illumination stage are more thoroughly crafted, worked out, and tested. Another model is suggested by Campbell (1960), who proposed 'blind variation and selective retention' as a model for the creative process. He proposes a three-stage model: the blind generation of large numbers of ideas – blind because it is not known in advance which ideas will be selected and finally retained – then the selection of certain of these ideas for further elaboration, and finally the retention of those most useful. Simonton (1998) elaborates on this theory, seeing creativity as beginning with chance combinations of ideas which are then subject to a selection process to determine which will finally be retained. Smith, Ward, and Finke (1995) have a similar theory in their geneplore model, which consists of a two-stage process: the generation of large numbers of ideas which are then explored to find which are most productive.

The Wallas and Campbell models are not, I feel, incompatible: the 'variation' or 'generation' stage in the latter theory seems to correspond to the 'preparation' stage in the former, while the 'exploration' or 'selection and retention' stages seem to correspond to the 'verification' stage of Wallas' theory. What is missing from the latter theory and its derivatives is the impasse-incubation-illumination stage, though it seems to me that this is one possible sequence that could happen (but may not always) within the ideas generation phase. It is also noteworthy that both models seem to combine two distinct mental processes which are often thought of as opposing one another – the generation of ideas, usually seen as the 'mysterious' essence of creativity, together with a longer, altogether more logical and analytical teasing out and elaboration of these initial ideas. Finke (1996) calls these 'chaotic thinking' and 'ordered thinking', and Deleuze and Guattari (1980), in a more poetic metaphor, contrast 'rhizomatic' thinking' with 'tree thinking'. Pope (2005) elucidates:

> Rhizomes [...] spread by underground networks, linking one 'node' to another. Deleuze and Guattari see all this as a powerful image of genuinely creative thinking: resourceful, flexible and unexpected ('springing suddenly from anywhere, everywhere'), and developing by subtle transverse networks in unseen, subterranean ways. In contradistinction to rhizomatic growth, they place 'the tree'. This they see as an image of the kind of 'aborescence' that tends to dominate mainstream, orthodox, and often authoritarian thought-patterns, as the tree is characterised by a single, central trunk with primary and secondary branches and roots that spring from a clearly defined top and bottom. The tree is organised monolithically and hierarchically on a vertical axis; rhizomes are organised as a multiplicity, horizontally, in lateral networks. (p.16).

Deleuze and Guettari thus see chaotic, rhizomatic thinking as essential to creativity, while ordered 'tree' thinking characterizes academic argument. I would argue, however, like Finke, Ward, and Smith, that creativity consists in the alternation between rhizomatic or chaotic thinking and arborescence or ordered thinking, and this is the essence underlying the idea of 'chaosmos' – a word coined by James Joyce and elucidated by Pope (2005) as 'the ways in which kinds of order (*cosmos*) emerge from kinds of apparent disorder (*chaos*), and, conversely, the tendency of kinds of apparent order to dissipate into disorder, which in turn may dissolve or resolve into yet other forms of [...] cosmos' (p.5).

My own writing experience would tend to confirm this general process, with the proviso that the stages do not necessarily happen in a fixed order – illumination may come at any time, for example, or the preparation/generation stage may yield ideas without the flash of illumination – and the whole process seems to me more circuitous than linear – what appears to be an insight, for example, may, on examination, in the verification/selection phase not prove valid and result in a return to the preparation/generation stage.

It is striking that the writers in both studies seem to follow these generalized models of the creative process, combining creative idea generation with more analytical teasing out of issues and problems in the route from initial idea to final realization. In general, while the writers in the Prowse piece place greater emphasis on the illumination and incubation stages, the writers in the Johnson study seem to me to follow more closely the geneplore or variation selection model, giving more prominence to analysis and exploration – though of course, given the constraints of the task (designers were given around two hours to design an activity and to 'think aloud' as they did so), they did not have much time for 'incubation' and subsequent 'illumination'. This difference may also be due, to some extent, to the different ways in which data were collected in the two studies: while the Johnson study employed think-aloud protocols recording designers at work on a specific activity, the Prowse study employed a written questionnaire on materials-writing processes in general.

In this chapter I would like, through examination of my own materials-writing processes, to enquire a little more closely into what the 'find ideas' and 'write materials' process might entail. I propose to do this primarily through a case study of the process of writing materials for *Motivating Learning* (Hadfield and Dörnyei, 2013). In parallel with writing these materials I kept a reflective journal on the creative process, which I then analysed for recurrent preoccupations using thematic coding and metaphor analysis. This chapter is based on that analysis.

Materials

Motivating Learning (Hadfield and Dörnyei, 2013) is one of the first books in a new series, *Research and Resources in Language Teaching*, of which I am series editor and Professor Chris Candlin is List Advisor. The books in the series are written by a partnership of authors, at least one of whom is primarily a researcher and one primarily a materials writer, with the aim of translating cutting-edge research directly into practical classroom materials. It thus aims to address the problem identified by Bouton (1996), namely that '[p]oor communication between researchers and teachers means that potentially useful findings from research often "linger in journals" instead of making it into the classroom' (p.112).

The books follow a four-part structure. Part 1, From Research to Implications, contains an account of the research with an outline of implications for practice. Part 2, From Implications to Application, contains practical classroom activities in resource book format. Part 3, From Application to Implementation, contains methodological suggestions for using the materials: for example, how to integrate them into a syllabus and how to adapt them to different contexts. And finally Part 4, Completing the Cycle Back to Research, contains ideas for using the activities from the book as a basis for further primarily classroom-based action research. The books are therefore of interest/use both to classroom teachers, as a source of practical ready-to-use activities and guidance on methodology, and to researchers or MA/PhD students, who will find a summary of the latest research and ideas for taking research further. In each book the researcher is usually primarily responsible for Parts 1 and 4 and the materials writer for Parts 2 and 3, though, of course, constant collaboration, dialogue, commentary, and feedback take place throughout the process to ensure coherence. Part 1 of *Motivating Learning* contains an account of Dörnyei's second language (L2) motivational self-system, while Part 2 contains three chapters of practical classroom activities, Part 3 contains suggestions for organizing the activities in Part 2 into a motivational programme and adapting them to different learning contexts, and Part 4 contains a range of suggestions for future research into motivation. I will focus here on Part 2, the practical classroom materials, which were my responsibility to write, though the process of dialogue and commentary referred to above took place throughout.

In this section of the book I designed a wide range of activities (for example, visualizations, role plays, discussions, jigsaw reading, creative writing) in resource book or 'recipe' format, to implement Dörnyei's L2 Motivational Self system (Dörnyei and Ushioda, 2009). This system is derived from Future Possible Selves theory in mainstream psychology (Higgins, 1998; Markus and Nurius, 1986). These theories are based on the postmodern view of identity not as single and fixed but as 'multiple', 'complex', and a 'site of struggle', as Bonny Norton Peirce puts it (Norton Peirce, 1995). These multiple Selves can exist in the present but also in the imagination as 'Future Possible Selves'.

Markus and Nurius and Higgins between them define four future possible selves:

the Ideal Self: what we would like to become;
the Ought to Self: what we feel we should become;

the Feared Self: what we are afraid of becoming; and
the Default Self: what we could become (i.e., if we did nothing to transform our Future Self into the Ideal self).

The connection between these future possible selves and motivation is outlined in what is called 'self-discrepancy theory'. Higgins finds that motivation can be defined as a desire to reduce the discrepancy between the actual self and the ideal self (Higgins, 1987, 1996). In other words, having a clear vision of a desired future self motivates you to work towards reducing the distance between your actual self and your future ideal. If motivation is a form of desire, then it is intimately connected to the power of the imagination. The more clearly you can imagine your desired future self, the stronger your motivation will be: imagination, imagery, and the ability to visualize the ideal future self vividly and in detail are therefore central to possible selves theory.

Dörnyei's application of this theory to language teaching has a tripartite structure:

Ideal L2 Self, which concerns the L2-specific facet of one's *ideal self*: if the person we would like to become speaks an L2, we can speak about an 'ideal L2 self', which is a powerful motivator to reduce the language gap between our actual and ideal selves.

Ought-to L2 Self, which concerns *L2-related* attributes that one believes one *ought to* possess to avoid possible negative outcomes (e.g., letting down parents or failing an exam), and which therefore may bear little resemblance to the person's own desires or wishes.

Of course, in an ideal case the ideal and the ought-to L2 selves – that is, what we want to do and what we think we should do – coincide! ...

L2 Learning Experience, which concerns situation-specific motives related to the immediate learning environment and experience (e.g., the positive impact of success or the enjoyable quality of a language course).

(Hadfield and Dörnyei, 2013: 3)

The Ideal Self component is described in more detail in the theory (Dörnyei and Ushioda, 2009; Hadfield and Dörnyei, 2013) than the other two components, with the process of constructing an Ideal Self seen as comprising six steps (summarized in Hadfield, 2012):

1. Creating the vision: helping the learner to visualize their L2 self;
2. Enhancing the vision: strengthening and elaborating the initial vision;
3. Substantiating the vision: subjecting the vision to a reality check to make sure it is achievable;
4. Operationalizing the vision: planning out how to actualize the vision;
5. Keeping the vision alive: maintaining enthusiasm;
6. Counterbalancing the vision: students are driven by the desire to achieve but also by the desire to avoid negative outcomes (p.6).

Part 2 of *Motivating Learning* is organized into three chapters (see Figure 11.1). *Imaging Identity* is an initial module suitable for the start of a language course containing activities designed to create a vision of the learners' future ideal L2 self, to ensure the vision is realistic and achievable, to consider what obstacles to learning might get in the way of achieving the vision and what could be done to overcome these, to consider 'ought-to' study habits and how these might help learners, and finally to enhance and elaborate the vision. It thus contains steps 1, 2, 3, and 6 above, plus a section on helpful insights from the 'ought-to self'. The other two chapters are based on steps 4 and 5 and are parallel ongoing processes to be used throughout a course. *Mapping the Journey*

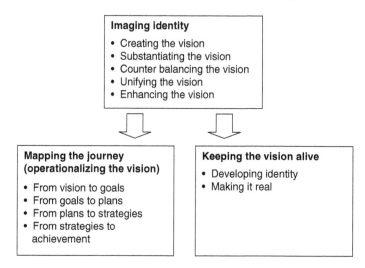

Figure 11.1   Schematic outline of contents of Part II of *Motivating Learning*

establishes a 'route map' of goals, plans, tasks, and strategies to enable realization of the Ideal L2 self, and is divided into four sections: From Vision to Goals, containing activities aimed at establishing long-term and short term goals; From Goals to Plans, aimed at breaking down short-term or weekly goals into precise plans and tasks; From Plans to Strategies, aimed at introducing useful study strategies; and From Strategies to Achievement, aimed at charting and validating progress, through activities such as study contracts, progress charts, and recognition of effort. The third chapter, *Keeping the Vision Alive,* is aimed at keeping the initial vision in the forefront of learners' minds and ensuring it does not get lost in the day-to-day realities of doing homework and learning vocabulary. It contains two sections: Developing Identity, aimed at strengthening the learners' sense of their L2 identity through activities such as targeted visualizations and interviews with role models; and Making It Real, containing real and simulated encounters with the L2 community and culture, through such activities as community placements, simulations, and cultural events. The activities are thus a balance of affective activities aimed at creating and sustaining a motivating vision and cognitive activities aimed at ensuring that the vision is realistic and achievable and that the learners can identify clear goals and a 'route map' towards achieving them.

The activities are in resource book format, designed for a range of levels, learning styles, contexts, and learner (and teacher) preferences, from which the teacher can pick and choose activities suitable for their learners and learning context. The activities are presented following the template in Figure 11.2.

The task I faced in creating materials for this book was therefore quite different from most materials-writing tasks. I was in the position of having to design materials of a type or with an aim that so far did not exist in ELT in order to actualize a theory. These materials would have a primary extra-linguistic aim (learner motivation) rather than a language learning aim, though in designing the materials I aimed to twin a language practice aim with the motivation aim.

The log

As part of the requirement for a PhD thesis by artefact and exegesis, I kept a reflective diary over the period in which I was writing *Motivating Learning,* documenting the concerns that were uppermost in my mind at different periods during the writing, in order to have data on the creative process to analyse for the exegesis. I then analysed the entries

Aim:		
Level:		
Time:		
Materials:		
Preparation:		
Language practice:		

Functions	
Skills	
Language areas	

Procedure: (i.e., list of instructions for the teacher to follow)

1

2

3. etc.

Figure 11.2   Materials presentation template

using thematic coding and a grounded theory approach, choosing to move from data to theory rather than the other way round, as I did not want to start out with preconceptions of what the writing process would entail. Coding data in this way has been called 'a central part of most research in the social sciences' (Lampert and Ervin-Tripp, 1993: 169). I used several stages of coding. The first, sometimes called open-coding (Strauss and Corbin, 1998), was a responsive approach to reading the data, to identify recurrent preoccupations. I then grouped these preoccupations into three groups, Principles, Procedures and Processes. Those to do with **principles** and beliefs I brought with me to the writing process: for example, the principle that activities should be designed to appeal to a range of different learning styles. Those to do with deliberate **procedures** or constraints I set up to facilitate writing in some way: for example, the use of checklists to ensure variety of activity types. Those less deliberate and conscious **processes** emerged during the actual writing of the activities. Finally, I broke each broad theme down into smaller categories. This chapter will focus on the last of the three groups, the preoccupations and micro-processes that emerge during the writing process.

The log contains two kinds of entries: documentation of the writing process and general reflections on the writing process. The documentary entries are immediate, describing the writing of particular activities, written as the activity unfurls or immediately afterwards. They may describe an aspect or part of writing or, more rarely, the complete process of writing one activity: in general, the entries are longer and more detailed if an activity is posing some problems, as the log is then used as a way of clarifying and teasing out those problems. In contrast, the reflective entries are more general and less immediate, not related to or analysing one particular activity but containing observations and reflections about several different activities, or about the writing process in general. I will refer to the documentary entries in the following analysis, focusing on the teasing out of specific problems, and then in the conclusion draw on some of the more general reflections.

Analysis

In the following analysis I will look at the process of writing materials by analysing the log entries for two activities. I have chosen these, first, because the writing process is recorded in some detail, since these activities presented some problems that needed teasing out. Second, the two activities are quite different, one being cognitive and analytic, the other affective and creative. Finally, although the same processes are at work in each, they unfurl in a different and sometimes opposite way in each activity.

In doing this, I will consider the two tensions we unpacked earlier: the opposition between a process which is 'messy and recursive' and a 'linear', 'orderly progression through checklists'; and the opposition between 'spontaneity', the random, the 'ad hoc' and the 'intuitive' and 'frameworks and principles which enable coherence and consistency'.

The writing process

Here we will look at log entries that detail the process of working out two different activities: *Distraction Reduction,* from the From Plans to Strategies section (see Appendix A), and *Reality Check,* from the Substantiating the Vision section (see Appendix B). These two activities presented some issues that needed teasing out: the first because of a need to match activity more closely to aim; the second because it was the first activity to be designed in a new section and involved problems of thinking out what

Stage 1	Selecting activity type
Stage 2	Aim and activity fit
Stage 3	Initial design solutions
Stage 4	Writing the student materials
Stage 5	Refining the procedure/writing the rubrics

Figure 11.3   Stages in the writing process

sort of activities might be involved in 'substantiating the vision'. The log entries catalogue the process of working through these issues and designing the activities in some detail. In the discussion below I will use the terms 'process' to refer to the entire act of writing the activity from beginning to end, and 'stage' to refer to broad sub-divisions within the process, each of which may contain a number of different 'sub-processes', which in turn contain 'micro-processes'.

The two writing processes follow roughly the same broad stages, shown in Figure 11.3.

The first stage involves getting the initial idea for an activity, the second, clarifying the aim of the activity in relation to the theory and ensuring that the initial idea for the activity fulfils the aim in the best way. The third stage contains the initial stages of design in which the activity begins to take more concrete shape. Though still in outline, the fourth stage involves the actual writing of student worksheets, role cards, etc., and the final stage involves making final adjustments to the procedure: for example, to the sequence of tasks in the activity or the different groupings, either as a prelude to or as part of writing the rubrics giving guidance to the teacher on how to conduct the activity.

Within these broad stages, however, are many sub-processes, each involving micro-processes, and whereas the broad stages follow a roughly linear, though sometimes overlapping and occasionally recursive, sequence in each activity, the sub-processes follow very different sequences in each activity and, as we shall see, are highly circuitous rather than linear: each stage may contain any or all of the sub- and micro-processes listed in Figure 11.4, not necessarily in the order in which they appear.

Selecting activity type/aim and activity fit

In *Distraction Reduction* generating the idea for the activity comes first, followed by concern with clarifying the aim (of identifying and eliminating distractions as part of the Operationalizing the Vision step in Dörnyei's (Dörnyei and Ushioda, 2009; Hadfield and Dörnyei, 2013)

Sub-processes	Micro-processes
Generating Ideas involves getting ideas for an activity, either at initial stage or as modification of original idea	brainstorming illumination
Dialoguing involves a question and answer process or justification of ideas, as if talking to an imagined reader (the teacher—and, at one remove, the student)	pose problem suggest solution offer rationale
Imagining Scenario involves visualizing how the activity would unfold in the classroom in order to determine how activity would work in practice and analyse possible flaws	imagine groupings and interactions imagine staging and sequence imagine task imagine students performing task analyse flaws
Scoping Materials involves sketching out rough outline for materials format or specifying constraints or other details to be included at the writing stage	outline format specify constraints
Trying Out involves trying out ideas on self or others to see if they work in practice	work through activity (as if a student) write example analyse flaws
Writing Materials involves the transformation of initial ideas for student materials (worksheet, role card etc.) into words on paper	draft materials finalize materials
Writing Rubrics Involves the transformation of the imagining of the classroom scenario into a set of instructions for the teacher	draft rubrics write rubrics

Figure 11.4   Sub- and micro-processes

Ideal L2 Self theory), and making sure the activity realizes that aim. In *Reality Check* the aim – to make sure the vision is realistic and achievable, as part of the Substantiating the Vision step in Dörnyei's (Dörnyei and Ushioda, 2009; Hadfield and Dörnyei, 2013) Ideal L2 Self theory – is clarified before several ideas are generated and one selected. I will consider these two stages together here.

The aim for the *Reality Check* activity, as stated in the theory, is to make sure the future self-image is achievable:

> The future self-image is perceived as *plausible*: possible selves need to be perceived as *possible*, otherwise they remain at the level of sheer fantasy [...] This substantiating process requires honest and down-to-earth reality checks [...]
>
>   (Hadfield and Dörnyei, 2013: 4–5)

In other words, while the initial section, Creating The Vision, focused on getting the learners to visualize in some detail their Ideal Future Language Speaking Self, this section is to focus on making sure that vision is achievable in reality, and the aim for Distraction Reduction is the meta-cognitive control strategy of identifying distractions that get in the way of study and taking steps to avoid them:

> *Metacognitive control strategies* refer to conscious techniques used by the learner to monitor and control concentration, and to stop procrastination [...] [e.g.,] *Identifying recurring distractions and developing defensive routines* [...] *Focusing on the first steps to take.*
>
>   (Dörnyei, 2001: 111–112)

The two paths taken towards fitting activity to aim are rather different. In *Reality Check* the process follows a fairly logical linear sequence from clarification of the aim of the section to general specification of the genre of activities that would fill this aim (cognitive, analytic), to generation of a number of ideas for activity types (discussions, ranking, etc.) that would achieve this aim, and finally to selection of one activity type (classification) to begin designing. The log entry for this stage of the process reads:

> So what does substantiating the vision entail? Analysis of the original vision to determine what is feasible/achievable. A reality check. What kind of activities? It's clear these will be cognitive and analytic in contrast to the affective visualization activities in Creating the Vision. More hard-headed. Brainstorming possible activities: discussions, ranking activities, classifying activities into unrealistic and achievable, prioritizing, lists, grids, tables and charts. Of these open-ended discussion is probably least satisfactory since activity needs outcome, e.g.: list of priorities, grid of realistic and unrealistic ambitions.

Trying out a classification activity: classify ambitions and enter into a table [...]

In contrast, the log entry for this stage in *Distraction Reduction* is far more complex, involving more micro-processes, and its trajectory is in the opposite direction – from activity to aim rather than aim to activity:

Started to look at the 'Eliminate Distractions' part of the Strategies section and suddenly, out of nowhere, had an idea for a 'Distractions Jingle', but conscious it needs more work. I know how the set up would work: students would work in small groups and each group would do verse about ways they get distracted from learning (give them the rhymes so they don't have to do most difficult part of activity – i.e., finding rhymes – also have an ABCB rhyme scheme so fewer rhymes than couplets) and make a class jingle on different distractions, e.g., my own jingle on difficulties getting down to writing might be:

I'll just wash the dishes

I'll just have some tea

I'll just read the paper

Has anyone emailed me?

Could use as an example first verse.

Rationale:

It would be more fun for ss than simply having a discussion on distraction or making a simple list of distractions. (Also, as there is a pattern to the poem, it provides more language practice: will for instant decisions.) As this is a very serious and cognitive section and the default activities would be discussion, debate, ranking etc., it's good to ring the changes and have a more affective/creative activity and always good to do class product – have concrete outcome for sense of satisfaction/achievement. Bonding to work together in groups and produce a product, also creating something and playing with language helps create sense of L2 identity.

So what is problem exactly? Something to do with getting aim clear [...]

What exactly is the aim? It's important to identify habitual distractions and what gets in the way of learning and this is a fun and engaging way of doing it – but is that enough? There needs to be more to the activity than just identifying distractions – the learner needs to go beyond identification of distractions to identification of strategies for overcoming the distractions and obstacles to learning. So, activity needs a second stage?

The Generating Ideas process in the two activities exemplifies the two models of creativity we looked at earlier. In *Reality Check* this involves brainstorming a large number of possible activity types, followed by a rationale for selection, the selection of an activity to explore, and the scoping of an outline format for the activity. In *Distraction Reduction*, however, the idea arrives 'suddenly, out of nowhere': an instance of 'illumination' rather than of 'variation'.

The process in *Distraction Reduction* involves nearly twice as many sub- and micro-processes and involves two extra sub-processes: Trying Out and Imagining Scenario, as well as Dialoguing: Imagining Scenario and Scoping Materials. Both materials and classroom procedure are specified in some detail right from the outset, whereas in the *Reality Check* process the activity is specified only at the end and only in outline, as an activity prototype rather than an actual activity.

The *Distraction Reduction* process also moves in the reverse sequence – from selection of activity to clarifying the aim (i.e., from concrete to abstract) – whereas *Reality Check* moves from clarifying the aim to selection of an activity type, or from abstract to concrete. Finally, the *Reality Check* process moves forward in a fairly linear and logical way, whereas the *Distraction Reduction* process is circuitous – by the end it has come full circle to the initial Imagining Scenario and Scoping Materials phase with the realization that both classroom procedure and material must be modified.

A summary of the process in each activity can be seen in Figure 11.5.

At the end of this stage in both activities, an activity type has been selected, but more work needs to be done on the design.

Initial design solutions

In this stage the activity begins to take more concrete shape, though it is still in outline. The *Reality Check* log reads:

> Trying out a classification activity. Students begin by reconsidering original visualizations [the visualizations of their Ideal Future Language Speaking Self which they created previously. The first section, Creating The Vision, contains several visualization activities]. First

problem – they will need to have access to the original visualizations – which means in written form. So, first thing to do: return to the activities in section 1 and add rubric to instructions specifying a writing-up component. This will be good anyway to add a writing element to a largely oral skills section.

What would activity entail – classifying the aspirations in the original visualization into achievable and unrealistic? Given what? The time frame of the course probably. So, a grid to classify ambitions. Are more categories needed for grid classification than simple binary division? As a first stage I will go back to the My Ideal Greek Self visualization I wrote for Section 1 and do the process on myself. Also get Charlie [my husband] to do it for his Ideal Maori Self vision.

The process begins with imagining the classroom scenario and immediately runs into a problem, which entails a return to and modification of an earlier activity. Thereafter the process continues with

Reality check Aim and activity fit	Distraction reduction Aim and activity fit

Dialoguing
  pose problem
  suggest solution (clarify aim)
  pose problem
  suggest solution (specify genre)
Generating Ideas (brainstorm)
Dialoguing
  offer rationale (for selecting
  activity types)
  select activity type
Scoping Material
  outline format
	Generate Idea (illumination)
	Imagine Scenario
	  imagine groupings
	  imagine task
	Scoping Materials
	  specify constraints
	Dialoguing
	  offer rationale (feasibility: ease
	  of task)
	Trying Out
	  write example
	Dialoguing
	  offer rationale (engagement,
	  variety, language practice,
	  appeal to learning styles,
	  student satisfaction, group
	  dynamics, identity-building)
	  pose problem
	  suggest solution (analyse
	  difficulty)
	  pose problem
	  suggest solution (clarify aim)
	Imagine Scenario
	  imagine task sequence

Figure 11.5 Aim and activity fit

problem-solution dialoguing to clarify the nature of the task, followed by scoping the type of material necessary: a grid. Finally there is a proposal to trial the embryo activity to see how it would work. At the end of this stage the outline of the activity is clear, though precise details, such as grouping and staging, are missing, and the nature of the materials is clear: a worksheet consisting of a grid, though precise details of the design of the grid are not yet clarified.

In contrast, the corresponding process in *Distraction Reduction* begins with a solution rather than a problem. The previous stage ended with the identification of a problem: the realization that 'there needs to be more to the activity than just identifying distractions – the learner needs to go beyond identification of distractions to identification of strategies for overcoming the distractions and obstacles to learning', and this stage begins with an answer to that problem. However, this solution necessitates rethinking and reworking material, in this case the activity itself rather than an earlier one:

> A breakthrough maybe? Combine the two strategies 'Eliminate Distractions' and 'Reward Effort', so that students identify preferred distractions and then use them as rewards for fixed period of work without letting themselves be distracted – e.g. in above verse the rewards could be tea-break or reading paper (dishes and emails are only things I do when I am desperate to avoid getting down to work!). So for Gen Y texting or going on fb [FaceBook] could be transformed from distraction to treat. So how would this work? A two stage activity: students write jingles then draw up some kind of contract – no, I think it needs more stages – a stage in between jingles and contract. Also a lead-in before the writing. The way it could work in outline is:

> SS brainstorm ways they distract themselves from working (small group or class discussion?).

> Give out a jingles worksheet (1st verse done as e.g.) SS work in small groups and each group does one verse.

> Put together as class jingle (could end up as poster – good/motivating to display creative product).

> Then discussion (class/small group?) as to which distractions are favourite and could be used as rewards.

> Then some kind of contract specifying work to be done/period of time to be worked and reward – have to have a contract buddy to witness.

In this activity, as in the previous one, the process involves constant shifting between problem-solution dialoguing, imagining the classroom scenario, scoping material, and trialling, though the Imagining Scenario and Scoping materials processes are much more detailed and concrete, with the result that by the end of this stage the activity exists in much more concrete form than the tentative outline arrived at for the *Reality Check* activity, with stages and sequencing clearly specified. A summary of the two processes in Figure 11.6 shows this intricate interplay between the different sub-processes.

Writing the student materials

Now that the activity has been designed in outline, the next two phases consist of the actual writing of the materials (student worksheets and rubrics for the teacher) – the previous mental processes now get translated into words on paper. In both activities, as in others detailed in the log, the writing of the student material (worksheets, role cards, etc.) comes before writing the rubrics for the teacher stage (see Figure 11.3).

The *Reality Check* entry for this stage is very short, containing reasons for rejecting the first design (a two-category classification of the goals

Reality check Initial design solutions	Distraction reduction Initial design solutions

Imagining Scenario
  imagine task
Dialoguing
  pose problem (no text)
  suggest solution
  (rewrite earlier activity)
  offer rationale
  pose problem (clarify aim)
  suggest solution
Scoping Material
  outline format
Dialoguing
  pose problem
  suggest solution
Trialling
  working through process
	Generating Ideas
	  illumination
	Imagining Scenario
	  clarify task
	Trialling
	  suggest examples
	Dialoguing
	  pose problems
	  suggest solution
	Imagining Scenario
	  imagine staging 1 (outline)
	Scoping Material
	  outline format
	Imagining Scenario
	  imagine staging 2 (detail)
	Dialoguing
	  offer rationale
	Imagining Scenario
	  clarify staging 2 (continued)
	Scoping Materials
	  outline format

Figure 11.6   Initial design solutions

of the original visualization into 'achievable' and 'unrealistic') plus a summary of the final worksheet design with a rationale:

> Having tried it out on myself, the first worksheet with the two category original classification of 'achievable' and 'unrealistic' is too simplistic: a 4 category classification works better, so have drawn table with four columns: Easy to achieve, Possible but more long-term, Very hard to achieve, Not really achievable (without much more time). This is much more positive than the 'focus on this, bin that' binary approach!

In contrast, the *Distraction Reduction* worksheets are more complicated than the four-column table. The activity involves two worksheets: a 'Jingles' worksheet, where students compose their jingles, and a 'Contract' worksheet, where students discuss the distractions they have written about, identify their favourites, and draw up a contract specifying how much study they have to do before they can have a distraction as a reward. The design of these worksheets needs more careful teasing out:

> Working on the jingles worksheet – first version involved getting them to make up all lines in pattern: 'I'll just . . . . . .' with a box of rhyming words so they don't have to think about rhymes. When I tried it myself, this made a rather boring jingle, so changed it so that last line is in a different pattern for variety and closure. However, this would make it more difficult for them to write than just sticking to sentence frame pattern. Also I think even with the rhyming words given, it is still a difficult activity and Ss might spend a lot of time trying to work out the rhyming lines. So have now settled on giving alternate lines in the ABCB pattern i.e., give the B lines so they have rhythm/structure as well as rhyme? – e.g.,
>
> I'll just . . . .
>
> I'll just go on Facebook
>
> I'll just . . . .
>
> And now what shall I cook?

> This would be easier for students and also mean that most of their energy is actually focused on aim of identifying distractions/obstacles instead of working out rhyme and structure.

Have done the contract worksheet. At first it just had contract specifying length of time to be worked and reward to be given but think
students need more scaffolding into the way they make these decisions – i.e. staging provided and discussion around decisions. So have
reworked so that it goes in stages from (1) identifying distractions to
(2) identifying favourite distractions to (3) the contract specifying
length of period to be worked, type and length of distraction/reward
with signature and contract buddy signature. It would then act as
a structure for discussion: groups or pairs discuss their habitual distractions and which ones are favourites, then discuss which ones
to choose as rewards and what the rewards would be awarded for,
before drawing up contract. This breaking down into stages and discussion around decisions would lead naturally into decision making
and contract specifications.

Think w/sheets look feasible in terms of task and lang difficulty and
engaging – can visualize how it would work and imagine T and Ss
having fun.

Though longer than the *Reality Check* process, it details a similar process: a preliminary design is found to be inadequate in some way (too
simplistic, boring, too difficult for the students, not focused enough on
aim, not scaffolded enough), the design is revised to eliminate these
flaws, and a rationale is offered.

The processes could be summarized as in Figure 11.7.

Both processes use trying out the task as a way of discovering inadequacies in the design, but *Distraction Reduction* also uses visualization of
the classroom scenario as a means of analysing flaws in design. Whereas
at previous stages visualization has been mainly focused on initial decisions around groupings and staging, at this later stage, when the design
is more evolved, it has a new purpose, involving imagining the students
grappling with the task and predicting their difficulties, as a means of
discovering any design flaws. Each discovery of inadequacies in design
leads to a redraft of the material. When the final version is complete,
there is a return to the Dialoguing process and a rationale offered to the
imagined reader/teacher.

Refining the procedure/Writing the rubrics

After the student materials have been finalized, the next task is to write
the rubrics: the instructions for the teacher on how to run the activity, which come under the heading *Refining the Procedure* in the activity

Reality check Writing the student materials	Distraction reduction Writing the student materials

Write Materials
  first draft
Trialling
  try out task on self
  analyse flaws
Write Materials
  final version
Dialoguing
  offer rationale
	Write Materials 1
	  first draft
	Trialling
	  try out task on self
	  analyse flaws
	Write Materials
	  second draft
	Imagine Scenario
	  students attempting task
	  analyse flaws
	Write Materials
	  final version
	Dialoguing
	  offer rationale
	Write Materials 2
	  first draft
	Imagine Scenario
	  students attempting task
	  analyse flaws
	Write Materials
	  final version
	Imagine Scenario
	  sequence and staging
	  students attempting task
	Dialoguing
	  offer rationale

Figure 11.7   Writing the student materials

template (see Figure 11.3). If the various stages in the activity and their sequence have been worked out in sufficient detail in previous stages, this stage may be a simple matter of translating notes on the activity into clear instructions for the teacher. For example, a note at initial design stage reading, 'T gives out jingles worksheet (1st one done as e.g.), ss work in groups – each group does a verse' is easily translated into the instruction:

> Give out the distraction jingles sheet and read the first verse with the students.

> Divide the students into four groups and get each group to complete a verse.

However, more often, the process of writing the rubrics is interwoven with further refinements to the procedure: staging, sequencing, and groupings. This is the case with both the processes we are considering, though *Reality Check* needs far more 'refinement' before the rubrics can be written:

> Having done the classification on my own visualization, I now think that they need some preparation before they read their own visualizations and classify them according to the worksheet. There should be an activity where they read an example (mine for instance) as a model of what to do. This would a) give them an idea of what is expected and b) get them to do the activity dispassionately, at one remove, by taking the knife to someone else's vision before pruning their own cherished aspirations. This should be separate activity though – too long to do all in one activity.

> So, back to this activity: First task is to re-read their own visualization. Then I think they need time for individual reflection before discussion. So: re-read own visualization – fill in 'reality check' worksheet, classifying their aspirations into the four columns in the table, then discuss conclusions with a partner? Visualising this, the trouble would be that they would be very familiar with their own vision and their own classification but not have thought about their partner's at all. So an extra stage needed: re-read visualization – do reality check individually – swap visualizations – do reality check on their partner's – then discuss.

> One more thought on this – couldn't it be a bit discouraging to take the axe to a motivating vision? I think this activity should end with a re-visualization in light of reality check, to end on a positive note. But as this section will offer several alternative activities for doing reality check (e.g., checklists, discussions, ranking etc.), I can't just put it as final stage in this activity: it makes more sense to put a re-visualization activity as final activity in this section. It can then follow whichever reality-check activity the teacher has chosen.

The Imagine Scenario phases of previous stages in the design of this activity have involved very little detail concerning staging and sequencing; the concern has been mostly about clarification of the aim and design of the student worksheet. Before rubrics can be written in this case, therefore, much more thought needs to be given to determining exactly what the procedure is: details of grouping, staging, and sequence of activities need to be clarified. In the course of this clarification, the need is perceived for not simply more stages but two whole new activities: a preliminary 'reality check' on the Ideal Greek Self vision to precede this *Reality Check* activity and a re-visualization activity to follow the *Reality Check* activity.

In contrast, staging and sequencing have received a lot of attention in the Imagine Scenario phases of previous stages of the design of *Distraction Reduction*, so the final sequence does not deviate much from the initial design solution and can be translated easily into rubrics. Grouping, however, has received less attention and has been left undecided at earlier stages, so needs more careful working out here:

> Started rubrics: problem is that at present the activity is all group work, so for more variety of interaction patterns and interest/pace/momentum in lesson, the sequence and staging could go like this:
>
> whole class: discussion/brainstorm on distractions
>
> small groups: write verses
>
> whole class: put verses together to make whole class jingle
>
> pair discussion: on favourite distractions, with whole class round up on what distractions could become rewards
>
> individually: contract sheets to be completed
>
> pairs: 'witnessed' by contract partner
>
> follow up in another lesson on how successfully they are keeping to contracts and if it helps
>
> This is logical – small steps, each builds on last, also has variety of group/class/ individual work for interest and pace. And activity as a whole has combination of affective and cognitive, creative and practical – flow from one into the other.

The summaries of the two processes appear in Figure 11.8.

The final process in both activities is the actual writing of the rubrics: that is, the mechanics of finding suitable wording and checking clarity. The log entries make no reference to this: I do not, in general, find rubrics difficult to write, provided the procedure has been imagined in sufficient detail beforehand, and so, given the detail in which the groupings and staging of both activities were envisaged, the actual writing of the rubrics was not a problem requiring analysis and thinking through and was not an issue for comment in the log. However, I can imagine

Reality check Refining procedure	Distraction reduction Refining procedure

Dialoguing
    pose problem (need
    preparation)
    suggest solution (write activity
    to precede)
    offer rationale (it will help them
    to be more dispassionate)
Envisage Scenario
    visualize staging and grouping
    analyse flaws
    revisualize staging
Dialoguing
    pose problem (demotivating?)
    suggest solution (end on
    positive note)
    pose problem (where to
    include)
    suggest solution (new activity
    at end of section)
	Dialoguing
	    pose problem (monotony)
	    suggest solution (variety of
	    interaction)
	Imagine Scenario
	    visualize grouping
	    visualize staging and sequence
	Dialoguing
	    offer rationale (feasibility, logical
	    progression, variety, interest,
	    pace, appeal to different
	    learning styles)

Figure 11.8   Refining the procedure

in some cases clarity of expression of instructions, for example, might be a problem, and this could give rise to further micro-processes such as re-drafting, imagining the scenario and trialling.

Some conclusions

Here I will return to the two oppositions defined earlier: between order and 'mess', an orderly linear progression vs. a recursive, apparently chaotic process; and between 'ad hoc', 'intuitive' and 'spontaneous' design decisions and design decisions based on 'principled frameworks ensuring coherence and consistency'.

Order vs. mess

The process is indeed 'messy' and certainly highly 'recursive'. Superficially it may appear somewhat chaotic: ideas can appear 'suddenly' and 'out of nowhere'; in the middle of writing an activity, for example, it can appear that, for it to work, an earlier activity must be rewritten, or an idea arriving halfway through writing can transform both the aim of the activity and its final shape. Though writing activities entails similar considerations of aim, sequence of stages, and groupings, there is no fixed order for these to be determined. In one activity the aim is clarified as a first step before writing; in another it is clarified and modified some time after the activity has been visualized in fairly concrete form.

In one activity, staging and sequencing are clarified early on, in another this happens as a last stage. One activity considers grouping early on; another finds a grouping problem at a final stage of writing which entails some redesign.

A reflection on the writing of *Distraction Reduction* highlights the complexity and circularity of this process:

> Some activities almost design themselves: it seems quite clear what the steps should be from the start – this one took a lot of arguing out and redrafting: a very circular process – having ideas/internal dialogue/dialogue with imagined teacher/seeing things from the point of view of student experience. Seems you are having to see things from several points of view simultaneously. This means you are constantly going backwards and forwards between clarifying aims of a particular piece of theory, arguing out what practical solutions would achieve the aim best, checking if resultant activity would be appealing to teachers in terms of attractiveness and feasibility, and also if activity would be engaging/relevant for students and also feasible in terms of conceptual and language difficulty.

However, I would argue that this apparent lack of order is not a fault, implying lack of systematicity; rather, it is a process that entails a high degree of flexibility and responsiveness in coping with the design requirements of very different activities. Activity design can throw up very different problems at different times, as we have seen, and a modification of the design in response to a perceived flaw is often not self-contained but can entail other necessary, previously unforeseen, modifications. A response to these problems entails a process which is circular and recursive rather than a linear progression.

Moreover, the process involves not only 'chaotic' but also 'ordered' thinking. Much of the process involves a patient teasing out of issues, often in the form of a logically ordered problem-solution-justification process, in the form of a mental dialogue with an imagined reader. I would argue that this dialogue with the imagined reader is central to the creative process in general, and at the heart of materials design. A log reflection reads:

> Seems this notion of *dialogue* is crucial. The hidden dialogue behind every book:
>
> Dialogue with yourself: principles, motivation, psychological conditions for creativity, influence of feelings, resistance/inertia

Dialogue with the task: demands of the task, types of thinking it involves, linear vs. lateral thinking, dialogue between analysis and creating, standing back and writing forward...

Dialogue between research and practice: constraints imposed by research on practice, constraints imposed by practice on theory...

Dialogue with readings, e.g.,

   research/articles

   other teaching materials

   random reading not connected with motivation – serendipity

Dialogue with commentators: different povs [points of view], external perspectives

The researcher: is interpretation in line with findings

Readers' reports: different angles: how useful for different audiences? How clear? How workable in practice? Etc.

But most of all, the dialogue with the imagined reader/user – both teacher and student: what is the aim of the activity, is this clear to Ts and Ss, will it appeal to teachers/engage students, is it feasible in terms of language level, (conceptual) ease of task, classroom management, etc.

This notion of the centrality of dialogue with the imagined audience is of the essence of creativity in other fields too, with researchers finding that, far from being the isolated and introspective activity creativity is assumed to be, it is essentially social and interactive. Csikszentmihalyi (1999) finds that 'creativity is a phenomenon that is constructed through interaction between producers and audience' (p.313). Similarly, Brophy (2009) finds that 'the writer can be the reader long before a document is put into the hands of the actual intended reader [...] In addition the writer can repeat this cycle of being writer then reader repeatedly. This creates an opportunity and an expectation' (p.146). The opportunity happens when the imagined reader responds with 'What did you mean by that?' The expectation is that 'the document will address many of the possible responses, objections and reactions going through the reader's mind' (p.147). He finds that creativity involves 'rehearsals of communication' or 'creatively imagined communication' (p.147):

If the writer is to speak to a reader, then I hold the text must bend its ear to both its own voice and the possibilities of the inner voice of the reader. (p.149)

In writing *Motivating Learning*, these imagined dialogues translated themselves into an essential part of the book's structure – the introduction to each section in Part 2 took the form of question and answer:

1. What is meant by ... (e.g., creating the vision)?
2. Why is it important to do this?
3. What does this entail?
4. What, therefore, is the aim of this section?
5. How can this best be translated into practice in terms of useable classroom activities?
6. Does this involve any issues and problems?
7. How can these issues best be dealt with?
8. How can I best use these activities in my classroom to achieve the aim of this section?

> *Which activities should I use first?*
> *Do I need to use all the activities?*
> *How much time should I allocate?*
> *How should I select activities in this section?*

The reflective log records that this formalization of the dialogue process is helpful to the design process in general:

> Phrasing headings as questions helps writing, as it makes me feel I am having dialogues with a teacher.

> The framework for the intros is still working really well. It helps me justify decisions I made in the materials writing process and refer to principles I hold – and go back into materials to modify them if I can't do this. Also makes me feel I am talking personally to a teacher, which makes the book come alive: the activities become real rather than hypothetical.

The primary audience addressed in a Teacher's Resource book is the teacher, but beyond the teacher there is a second imagined audience, the student. While dialogue with the teacher is conducted through a problem-solution-rationale process, engagement with student concerns

Forward thrust	Checks and balances
Generating Ideas	
	Dialoguing
Scoping Materials	
	Imagining Scenario
Writing Materials	
	Trying Out
Writing Rubrics	

Figure 11.9   Complementary processes

is effected through imagining the classroom scenario, playing out the various stages of the activity as they are designed and imagining student reactions, in order to discover any flaws in the design which will need reworking.

I would argue that these two processes, dialoguing and imagining the scenario, are absolutely crucial to the process of materials design, since they push the writer into seeing the materials from others' viewpoints: analysing flaws, reworking material, and justifying decisions.

The design process therefore entails ordered, logical thought as well as chaotic, messy, recursive thought, and it is the alternation between the two, with one process feeding into the other, that characterizes creativity. The processes as documented in the log can in fact be divided into two complementary processes – one creative and forward-moving, the other more logical and analytic, acting as a check on this forward momentum, as in Figure 11.9.

Any of the checks and balances can at any moment feed into the forward momentum of the creative processes, triggering a pause for analysis, reconsideration, and modification of what has just been created, with justification and rationale for change, often entailing return to an earlier stage of the forward-moving design process.

Intuitive, spontaneous, *ad hoc* decisions vs. principled frameworks: Ensuring coherence and consistency

Although the concerns (of aim, staging, grouping, etc.) brought up by the checks and balances processes may appear to be '*ad hoc*' and random, a listing of these concerns as brought up in the accounts of the two activities above reveals an underlying framework of unstated principles. The concerns surfacing in the course of the two activities could be listed as follows:

What is the aim of the theory?

How could this be translated into practice?

What should the aim of this activity be?

Does this activity fulfil the aim in the best way?

Is the activity focused on the aim, or are there distractions?

Is it engaging and appealing to both teachers and students?

Is the activity feasible – doable by students in terms of concept, ease of task and language level, and does it have the right level of challenge?

Is the staging in the best logical sequence?

Are students adequately prepared for the task?

Does the staging scaffold students by providing achievable steps?

Are the groupings appropriate to the task, and do they provide variety and balance of interaction?

Does the activity have pace and momentum to maintain interest?

Does it create positive affect?

Does it, in the context of the book, chapter or section, provide variety or is it repetitive of other activity types?

Does it, in the context of the book, chapter or section, provide appeal to different learning styles?

Will it result in student satisfaction with outcome and a feeling of achievement?

Does it promote a good group dynamic?

Does it encourage creative use of language, to encourage building of L2 identity?

This looks suspiciously like an example of one of the 'frameworks [...] to facilitate coherence and consistency' called for by Tomlinson (2003: 107) in order to impose more order and principle on the materials-writing process.

Of course, this list only concerns principles brought to bear on these two activities. Of the many other concerns brought to bear on activities in this book which resulted in modification to activities, one example is the concern of the position of English as a dominant world language with its implications of linguistic imperialism, which resulted in the inclusion of activities centring on many other languages, including endangered languages such as Maori. This was not an underlying concern in these two particular activities but does not mean that it is not part of an extensive framework of principles which may be called upon at any time to justify specific design decisions. The listing of a writer's complete checklist/framework of principles for materials design would thus entail analysis over a large number of different activities.

I would suggest that other materials writers, in common with me, have such frameworks in place, even if they have never stated them in print, and that the fact that they have not explicitly articulated these frameworks or principles does not mean that they do not exist and do not inform their writing. A careful reading of many of the Johnson writers' patient teasing out of issues will also suggest in fact that, far from making decisions in a random, unprincipled way, they base their design decisions on a system of unspoken, internalized frameworks and principles of the very kind that Tomlinson calls for (albeit in explicit form): when Designer D1, for example, considers the possibility of causing offence if classmates have to describe each other, he is drawing on some internalized framework where 'Be sensitive to learners' culture and feelings' is a principle, or when Designer D2 asks what are the 'real life applications of this [task] which would give a [...] context, a purpose, a need for the exchange of information?' (Johnson, 2003: 90), he is working within a tacit framework where 'Is the activity communicative, meaningful and natural and purposeful?' would be a checklist question.

However, the existence of what I will call 'tacit frameworks' does not mean that they can be used in the course of writing activities as a checklist or progression to be worked through in order. Rather, the framework operates as an underlying reference system which may be called upon at any moment or in any order to satisfy the particular demands of a particular activity. It is this flexibility and responsiveness, this sensitivity to the requirements of a particular activity, that is fundamental to materials design. Experienced materials writers have these internalized systems in place, ready to be drawn on at any time; however, for novice writers or students of materials writing, it could be helpful to articulate these frameworks, with the proviso that they cannot be worked through in a mechanistic way – that flexibility and responsiveness are of the essence in the materials-writing process.

Principles in materials design: A system of tacit frameworks

The fact that materials design is messy, recursive, spontaneous, and *ad hoc* does not therefore imply that it is unprincipled or lacks an underlying coherence and consistency. Further, the existence of a 'tacit framework' underpinning design decisions in a principled way does not imply that the principles in the framework need to be worked through in orderly progression – in fact, I would argue that this would be antithetical to the design process, which demands flexibility and responsiveness. Similar frameworks or lists of concerns and principles could, however, usefully form an orderly checklist at the post-creation stage of materials design, to verify that nothing has been missed. I, in fact, used several checklists at the 'after writing' stage in *Motivating Learning*: to ensure 'fit' between theory and activities, to ensure viability, to ensure variety of activity types, to ensure appeal to different learning styles, to ensure that activities promoted a good group dynamic, and to ensure that activities encouraged students to 'build' an L2 identity, though self-expression and creativity.

In conclusion, I would argue that a 'tacit framework' of principles underlies materials writing, functioning as a reference system which can be drawn on at any moment according to the demands of the activity being designed and its specific problems. Such frameworks could be made explicit and could usefully serve as a checklist after materials have been written, to make sure nothing has been missed. However, the materials-writing process does not proceed in a linear way according to 'orderly progressions through checklists' (Samuda, 2005: 243), and so such a checklist would be less useful during the actual writing process. The writing process has its own internal system of checks and balances, consisting of seeing the materials from other points of view through dialoguing and imagining the classroom scenario, and it is the alternation of these with the process of writing the materials that functions as a built-in checking system, pushing the writer to look critically at the material, analyse flaws, and provide a principled rationale for decisions.

Appendix A

Distraction reduction materials

Activity 52: Distraction Reduction

Aim:	To identify recurrent personal distractions and to identify steps to take to eliminate these or use them as rewards
Level:	Intermediate up
Time:	25 minutes
Materials:	Distraction jingles sheet
Preparation:	Make one copy of each jingles sheet for each group of three or four students; make one copy of distraction contract for each student

Language practice

Functions	making excuses, habits, intentions
Skills	writing, speaking, reading
Language areas	I'll (just) …, shall, present perfect, present simple, can, going to

Procedure

1. Introduce the idea of distractions: tell the students a few ways you distract yourself from getting down to work and ask for suggestions from the class about ways they put off working or get distracted. List some of these on the board.
2. Give out the distraction jingles sheet and read the first verse with the students.
3. Divide the students into four groups and get each group to complete a verse. Alternatively get each group to complete the whole jingle, using distraction ideas from all the members.
4. Read the whole jingle at the end with each group reading their own verse/jingle. You can make a poster for class display.
5. Then put students in pairs and ask them to identify the distractions they enjoy the most (e.g. cleaning the fridge and texting a friend may both be distractions, but you may enjoy one more than the other!).
6. Introduce the idea that distractions can become rewards: students can still do the activities that distract them, but as a reward for work done rather than a way of avoiding starting work.
7. Give out the distraction contract sheets.
8. Get students to complete this individually, then ask for ideas for the contracts and rewards. Have a discussion on what is realistic. One key is stipulating a reasonable amount of time for work and also for distractions (feedback from teenagers suggests 40–45 minutes for work then 10–15 minutes' distraction). Another key is varying indoor distractions (e.g. listening to iPod) with outdoor activity and exercise. Students can then amend their contracts if necessary.
9. Finally, put them in pairs to share their contracts and witness each other's.
10. Ask them to try to carry it out that evening and get feedback the next day.

Worksheet 1 Distraction jingles

I'll just check my cellphone
I'll just look and see
I'll listen to my iPod
And then I'll watch TV

I'll just_____
I'll just have some tea
I'll just_____
Has anyone emailed me?
I'll just_____
I'll just send a text
I'll just_____
And clean the fridge out next.
I'll just_____
I'll just go on Facebook
I'll just_____
I've nothing left to cook.
I'll just_____
I'll just wash my hair
I'll just_____
And now what shall I wear?

Worksheet 2 Distraction contracts

The main ways I distract myself are:

- _____
- _____
- _____
- _____

The distractions I most enjoy are:

- _____
- _____
- _____

From now on I am going to use these distractions as rewards:
After _____ minutes' work I can _____ for _____ minutes
After _____ minutes' work I can _____ for _____ minutes

After _____ minutes' work I can _____ for _____ minutes
After _____ minutes' work I can _____ for _____ minutes

Signed _____

Witnessed _____

Appendix A, Distraction Reduction, from *Motivating learning*, Hadfield, J. and Dörnyei, Z. (2013), Pearson Education Limited, ©2013.

Appendix B

Reality check materials

Activity 10: Reality Check 2

Aim:	To get students to substantiate their vision of the future L2 self
Level:	Intermediate up
Time:	40 minutes
Materials:	Worksheet, students' own descriptions of their ideal L2 selves
Preparation:	Make two copies of the 'Reality check' worksheet for each student in your class

---

Language practice

Functions	giving opinions, predicting
Skills	writing, speaking
Language areas	I think that..., will, will/won't be able to

Procedure

1. Get students to reread their own descriptions of their ideal selves.
2. Give out the 'Reality check' worksheet and get them to fill it in for themselves.
3. Then get students to exchange their descriptions with a partner and give out the second copy of the 'Reality check'.
4. Get them to carry out the 'Reality check' on their partner's ideal L2 self description.
5. Put them in pairs to compare ideas.

Worksheet 1 – My ideal future self: reality check

Look back at what you wrote about your Ideal self. Which situations and aims do you think are:

- easily achievable
- possible but more long-term goals
- very hard to achieve
- not really achievable (without much more time than you've got)?

Fill in the table:

Easy to achieve	Possible, but more long-term	Very hard to achieve	Not really achievable

Appendix B, Reality Check, from *Motivating learning*, Hadfield, J. and Dörnyei, Z. (2013), Pearson Education Limited, ©2013.

References

Bouton, L.F. (1996). Pragmatics and language learning. In L.F. Bouton (Ed.), *Pragmatics and language learning vol. 7* (pp.1–20). Urbana-Champaign: University of Illinois, Division of English as a Foreign Language.

Brophy, K. (2009). *Patterns of creativity: Investigations into the sources and methods of creativity*. New York: Rodopi.

Campbell, D.T. (1960). Blind variation and selective retention in creative thought as in other knowledge processes. *Psychological Review*, 67, 380–400.

Csikszentmihalyi, M. (1999). Implications of a systems perspective for the study of creativity. In R.J. Sternberg (Ed.), *Handbook of creativity* (pp.313–335). Cambridge: Cambridge University Press.

Deleuze, G. and Guattari, F. (1980). *A thousand plateaus*, trans. B Massumi. London: Athlone.

Dörnyei, Z. (2001). *Motivational strategies in the language classroom.* Cambridge: Cambridge University Press.

Dörnyei, Z. and Ushioda, E. (2009). *Motivation, language identity and the L2 self.* Bristol: Multilingual Matters.

Finke, R.A. (1996). Imagery, creativity and emergent structure. *Consciousness and Cognition,* 5, 381–393.

Hadfield, J. (2012). A second self: Motivation, imagination and L2 identity. *English Teaching Professional,* 78, 4–6.

Hadfield, J. and Dörnyei, Z. (2013). *Motivating learning.* Harlow: Pearson.

Harwood, N. (2010). Issues in materials development and design. In N. Harwood (Ed.), *English language teaching materials: Theory and practice* (pp.3–30). New York: Cambridge University Press.

Hidalgo, A.C., Hall, D., and Jacobs, G.M. (1995). *Getting started: Materials writers on materials writing.* Singapore: SEAMEO Regional English Centre.

Higgins, E.T. (1987). Self-discrepancy: A theory relating self and affect. *Psychological Review,* 94, 319–340.

Higgins, E.T. (1996). The 'self-digest': Self knowledge serving self-regulatory functions. *Journal of Personality and Social Psychology,* 71, 1062–1083.

Higgins, E.T. (1998). Promotion and prevention: Regulatory focus as a motivating principle. *Advances in Experimental Social Psychology,* 30, 1–46.

Johnson, K. (2003). *Designing language teaching tasks.* Basingstoke: Palgrave Macmillan.

Jolly, D. and Bolitho, R. (1998). A framework for materials writing. In B. Tomlinson (Ed.), *Materials Development in Language Teaching* (pp. 90–115). Cambridge: Cambridge University Press.

Lampert, M.D. and Ervin-Tripp, S. (1993). Structured coding for the study of language and social interaction. In J.A. Edwards and M.D. Lampert (Eds.), *Talking data: Transcription and coding in discourse research* (pp.169–206). Hillsdale: Lawrence Erlbaum.

Markus, H. and Nurius P. (1986). Possible selves. *American Psychologist,* 41, 954–969.

Norton Peirce, B. (1995). Social identity, investment, and language learning. *TESOL Quarterly* 29, 9–31.

Penaflorida, A.H. (1995). The process of materials development: A personal experience. In A.C. Hidalgo, D. Hall, and G.M. Jacobs (Eds.), *Getting started: Materials writers on materials writing* (pp.172–186). Singapore: SEAMEO Regional English Centre.

Pope, R. (2005). *Creativity: Theory, history, practice.* Abingdon: Routledge.

Prowse, P. (2011). How writers write: Testimony from authors. In B. Tomlinson (Ed.), *Materials development in language teaching* (2nd ed., pp.151–173). Cambridge: Cambridge University Press.

Rajan, B.R.S. (1995). Developing instructional materials for adult workers. In A.C. Hidalgo, D. Hall, and G.M. Jacobs (Eds.), *Getting started: Materials writers on materials writing* (pp.187–208). Singapore: SEAMEO Regional English Centre.

Samuda, V. (2005). Expertise in pedagogic task design. In K. Johnson (Ed.), *Expertise in second language learning and teaching* (pp.230–254). Basingstoke: Palgrave Macmillan.

Simonton, D.K. (1988). Creativity, leadership and chance. In R.J. Sternberg (Ed.), *The nature of creativity: Contemporary psychological perspectives* (pp.386–426). Cambridge: Cambridge University Press.

Smith, S.M., Ward, T.B., and Finke, R.A. (1995). *The creative cognition approach.* Cambridge: MIT Press.

Strauss, A. and Corbin, J. (1998). *Basics of qualitative research: Techniques and procedures for developing grounded theory* (2nd ed.). Thousand Oaks: Sage.

Tomlinson, B. (1998). *Materials development in language teaching* (1st ed.). Cambridge: Cambridge University Press.

Tomlinson, B. (2003). Developing principled frameworks for materials development. In B. Tomlinson (Ed.), *Developing materials for language teaching* (pp.107–129). London: Continuum.

Tomlinson, B. (2012). Materials development for language learning and teaching. *Language Teaching*, 45, 143–179.

Venezky, R.L. (1992). Textbooks in school and society. In P.W. Jackson (Ed.), *Handbook of research on curriculum* (pp. 436–461). New York: Macmillan.

Wallas, G. (1926). *The art of thought.* London: Cape.

Author Index

Subject Index

Note: Entries in *italics* refer to textbook titles.

Printed and bound by CPI Group (UK) Ltd, Croydon, CR0 4YY